Social Protection and the Market in Latin America
The Transformation of Social Security Institutions

Social security institutions have been among the most stable post-war social programs around the world. Increasingly, however, these institutions have undergone profound transformation from public risk-pooling systems to individual market-based designs. Why has this "privatization" occurred? Why, moreover, do some governments enact more radical pension privatizations than others? This book provides a theoretical and empirical account of when and to what degree governments privatize national old age pension systems. Quantitative cross-national analysis simulates the degree of pension privatization around the world and tests competing hypotheses to explain reform outcomes. In addition, a comparative analysis of pension reforms in Argentina, Brazil, Mexico, and Uruguay evaluates a causal theory of institutional change. The central argument is that pension privatization emerges from political conflict rather than from exogenous pressures. The argument is developed around three dimensions: the double bind of globalization, contingent path-dependent processes, and the legislative politics of loss imposition.

Sarah M. Brooks is an Assistant Professor in the Political Science Department at Ohio State University. She has also been a postdoctoral Fellow at the Kellogg Institute at Notre Dame. She has published articles in the *American Journal of Political Science, Journal of Politics, World Politics, International Studies Quarterly, Comparative Political Studies,* and *Latin American Politics and Society,* and she has written chapters in several edited volumes, including *Learning from Foreign Models in Latin American Policy Reform* (2004), *New Ideas about Old Age Security* (2001), and *Pension Reform: Issues and Prospects for Non-Financial Defined Contribution (NDC) Schemes* (2006).

Social Protection and the Market in Latin America

The Transformation of Social Security Institutions

SARAH M. BROOKS
Ohio State University

CAMBRIDGE
UNIVERSITY PRESS

CAMBRIDGE UNIVERSITY PRESS
Cambridge, New York, Melbourne, Madrid, Cape Town, Singapore, São Paulo, Delhi

Cambridge University Press
32 Avenue of the Americas, New York, NY 10013-2473, USA

www.cambridge.org
Information on this title: www.cambridge.org/9780521701495

First published 2009

Printed in the United States of America

A catalog record for this publication is available from the British Library.

Library of Congress Cataloging in Publication Data

Brooks, Sarah Marie.
Social protection and the market in Latin America : the transformation
of social security institutions / Sarah M. Brooks.
    p.   cm.
Includes bibliographical references and index.
ISBN 978-0-521-87767-1 (hardback) – ISBN 978-0-521-70149-5 (pbk.)
1. Social security – Latin America.   2. Pensions – Latin America.   I. Title.
HD7130.5.B76   2008
361.98–dc22   2008008313

ISBN   978-0-521-87767-1 hardback
ISBN   978-0-521-70149-5 paperback

Contents

Acknowledgments

This book began as a dissertation that was motivated by the question of when governments in capital-scarce nations would resist the seemingly inexorable pressure to enact free-market reforms. Even though the study was fundamentally rewritten at Ohio State University, I owe a tremendous debt of gratitude to my teachers and mentors at Duke University, including Robert Keohane, Herbert Kitschelt, and Peter Lange, whose guidance during and after my graduate studies made this book possible. My field research was funded by the Social Science Research Council's International Dissertation Research Fellowship and by a seed grant from Ohio State University. I must also thank Estelle James and the World Bank, who hired me to help investigate the political economy of pension reform. This association provided me with crucial insights into the economics of pensions and gave me access to people and information that otherwise would have been far out of my reach. Similarly, my thanks go to Kent Weaver, who invited me to collaborate on a study of notional defined-contribution pension reforms, opening my eyes to a new dimension of risk redistribution in pension reform. Over the years of travel back and forth to Latin America, I accumulated enormous debts of gratitude to many people. In addition to the subjects of this study, who generously shared their time, knowledge and insights, I am deeply indebted to the many researchers and friends that I met in Latin America who made this book possible, or who simply made life for this researcher more enjoyable along the way. They include José Roberto de Andrade Filho, Arturo Borja, Daniel Camacho, Daniel Chasquetti, Fabio Coppola-di-Canzano, Vinícius Carvalho Pinheiro, Júlia Conter, Jessica Scott Jerome, Thomas Lamson, Marie Claire Leger, Jorge San Martino, Vera Schattan Pereira Coelho, Helmut Schwarzer, and Vanessa Thornton. I am also very grateful to the many colleagues and scholars with whom I had the opportunity to talk about the project, or who generously read and commented on portions of the book. This list, though surely incomplete, includes Daniel Béland, Janet Box-Steffensmeier, Mark Blyth, Mary Cooper, Michelle Dion, Timothy Frye, Richard Gunther, Stephan Haggard, Martin Hering, Evelyne Huber, Torben

Iversen, Robert Kaufman, Stephen Kay, Enrique Mendoza, Scott Morgenstern, Layna Mosley, Victoria Murillo, Joan Nelson, Edward Palmer, Nita Rudra, John Stephens, Christina van Wijnbergen, Kent Weaver, and Kurt Weyland. I am also grateful for the research assistance of Miryam Farrar, Kara Heitz, Justin Lance, David Mather, David Miran, Rachel Ramirez-Hammond, Aisha Shafique, Sarah Sokhey, Michael Turco, and Abdulkadir Yildirim. I would also like to acknowledge and thank William C. Smith, who published portions of Chapters 3 and 5 in the Winter 2007 issue of *Latin American Politics and Society*. I have benefited immensely from the support and encouragement of Lewis Bateman and Eric Crahan at Cambridge University Press, and from the comments of two anonymous reviewers. For their patience and willingness to take this bet I am so very grateful.

The line between my professional and personal notes of thanks is blurred by my great fortune to have in one person an intellectual partner, spouse, and friend. Thus I owe Marcus Kurtz so much more than the customary "thanks to my long-suffering spouse." For he not only read and commented extensively on multiple versions of the manuscript, but he also provided great encouragement and unremitting support throughout the process. Indeed, it is because of Marcus, and our daughter Chloë, that it was possible to complete this book. Finally, I am grateful to my parents, who at some point convinced me that I could achieve whatever goal I wished to pursue in life. To Joan and George Brooks, therefore, I dedicate this book with my love and deepest gratitude.

Social Protection and the Market in Latin America

The Transformation of Social Security Institutions

PART I

RECASTING THE DEBATE OVER PENSION PRIVATIZATION

I

Welfare State Transformation

From Social Protection to the Market

It is not possible to get the government out of the pension business.
— Nicholas Barr (2002) "The Pensions Puzzle"

The "revolution" began quietly and without ceremony on the fourth of November 1980 in the unassuming South American capital of Santiago, Chile. On that day the military dictatorship led by General Augusto Pinochet published Decree Law 3500, abolishing the nation's state-run pension system and replacing it with a private system based on individual retirement accounts. Under the new "privatized" pension system, Chilean workers would no longer contribute to a national social insurance program for retirement, nor were pension benefits defined as a percentage of working income and guaranteed by the state. Instead, workers are required to contribute a fixed share of each paycheck to individual retirement accounts managed by private firms. At retirement, the average wage earner in Chile will lay claim to a pension based on his or her accumulated savings, and the return – be it positive or negative – to those invested funds.[1]

For the architect of this reform, José Piñera, Chile's pension privatization issued the opening salvo in a "world pension revolution."[2] Indeed, this upheaval has proved to be neither a merely local phenomenon nor inconsequential in its transformative ambitions and implications.[3] Not only did the fires of pension privatization ignite throughout Latin America in the 1990s, but the movement fanned across Europe as well, from Scandinavia to Central Asia. By 2006, pension privatizations of varying degrees had been implemented in twenty-six nations on five continents. Although reforms as drastic as Chile's

---

[1] For workers who have contributed for at least twenty years but have failed to save enough to finance a minimal retirement pension – approximately a quarter of the average wage – the Chilean government provides a means-tested guarantee to top-up the balance of qualified workers' accounts.

[2] Piñera 2001.

[3] See Piñera 1996; also see, Borzutzky 2002; Castiglioni 2001; Kurtz 1999.

have been exceptional even in Latin America, it is no less remarkable that workers in as dissimilar countries as Sweden and Kazakhstan would apportion *any* share of their state-mandated old age savings – much less all of it as in Kazakhstan – to competing private pension fund managers. In Latin America alone, by the end of 2006 more than 73 million people were enrolled in the region's private pension fund industry with more than US$136 billion in retirement assets under private management.

How did such radical transformations of old age pension systems come about? Why have some countries privatized, but not others? And why, among privatizing countries, did some adopt deeper institutional changes than others? These questions guide this book. The goal of the analysis is not only to understand shifts in retirement income programs, which are important, but also to use pension privatization as a window through which to explore the theoretical puzzle of institutional change. Specifically, I am concerned with institutional change of a specific type: where transformation entails a departure from the long-established and stable "path" of institutional development. In the case of old age pensions, such "path departure"[4] involves a shift from programs that pool risk, bind fates, and join disparate citizens in a common social project of insuring against poverty in old age, toward institutions through which individuals by themselves bear increasing responsibility for protection against the risk of old age poverty. The premise of this study is that the changing structure of risk protection inhering in old age pension privatization marks a sea change in the organizing logic of the welfare state, and thus of the very ends of state action in the social policy realm. This institutional change has been attended, moreover, by a fundamental shift in the paradigm governing pension institutions, from one based on the ideals and objectives of social protection to one based on the principles and instruments of the market. Thus it is a change that is as much political as it is economic in its implications. And the societal and distributional consequences cannot but be profound.

The transformations brought by pension privatization thus are meaningful in political, social and economic terms. For scholars of political economy and institutions, the number, location and diversity of private pension reforms present critical theoretical puzzles. Long considered the archetype of stable path-dependent institutions, pension systems are known to be subject to powerful stabilizing forces that make significant structural change ever more unlikely over time.[5] Understanding how a self-reinforcing institution such as this becomes subject to fundamental change through processes that are not solely exogenous has long eluded scholarship on the welfare state. Such an inquiry may lend critical insight into enduring theoretical puzzles about how institutions change, while addressing a recurrent dilemma of modern capitalism: how basic social contracts are revised and thus the dividing line moved between individual and collective responsibility for well-being.

---

[4] Hering 2003.
[5] Myles and Pierson 2001; Pierson 2000a.

RECASTING THE QUESTION OF PENSION REFORM

An ineluctable feature of social insurance pension systems is that they must be periodically revised.[6] Indeed, the inexorable shifts of demographic and economic tides dictate that this is so. The question of pension reform thus is not *whether* existing institutions will change but rather *how* such change will be effected. When faced with the challenge of demographic and economic shifts, governments thus have a choice: either make incremental revisions within the extant paradigm of social insurance or undertake more fundamental reform in the instruments and ends of the institution, such as through privatization. Both options can realign pension system revenue and liabilities so as to accommodate demographic and economic change.[7] Whereas parametric revisions to the existing program typically entail an increase in contributions or cuts to old age benefits, privatization involves the shift from a defined-benefit (DB) formula to a defined-contribution (DC) regime, where each worker saves for his or her own retirement in a (typically) privately managed and fully funded pension account. In DC systems, only the rate of contribution to individual pension accounts is fixed by law; the value of old age pensions is determined by the accumulation of funds during working life, and the return on invested funds. Uncertainties over retirement income thus are transferred from the state to individuals.

Why do governments privatize? Pension privatization has been touted as a policy that is good for the state, the economy, and the individual. Advocates of this reform point to the close link between individual contributions and benefits as a way to transfer the rising costs and risks of pension provision from states to individuals, and thus to correct financial imbalances and reduce state pension liabilities in the long term.[8] These were among the arguments advanced by the World Bank in the 1990s as it endorsed privatization as a way not only to cope with demographic change but also to achieve desirable macroeconomic ends.[9] Individual retirement accounts thus came to be viewed not simply as a social policy concern but also as a tool to enhance labor market flexibility, deepen capital markets, raise domestic savings, and spur macroeconomic growth. For their part, workers were enticed with ownership and control of retirement funds, and the opportunity to achieve higher rates of return on pension contributions. Although each of these claims is fiercely contested, vocal advocates of privatization and market-oriented reform have

[6] Most social insurance pension systems are organized as defined benefit (DB) schemes, wherein a worker's retirement pension is set typically as a percentage of working income. By their design, DB pensions must be adjusted periodically in response to changes in the program's liabilities and revenue from payroll contributions and taxation. Whereas gains in longevity raise state liabilities, slowing growth and declining fertility curtail program revenue, necessitating periodic adjustment of these parameters to restore actuarial balance.

[7] Diamond 1999.

[8] Feldstein 1995; James 1996; Palacios and Whitehouse 1998.

[9] World Bank 1994.

emerged in nearly every corner of the globe, inserting privatization into the center of political debate. The possibility of pension privatization reaching the political agenda thus extends as far as the market itself. As such, the fundamental political question of pension privatization is not why governments seek to privatize but rather why and how, given the dramatic implications and fierce contestation to which such reforms are subject, some privatization efforts prevail?

WHAT PRIVATIZATION IS AND IS NOT

While the shift to private management of old age pension funds in such disparate and unlikely countries as Sweden, Kazakhstan, and Bolivia is striking, it is not the "privateness" per se that makes this reform a fundamental institutional departure. For social protection and private provision are not antinomies. Indeed, social protection was at its very origin a private sector issue. The notion that social protection can or should be provided by non-state actors thus dates to the very earliest pension systems, which were organized by guilds and fraternal orders. But these primordial forms of social insurance – based in mutual aid and friendly societies – obeyed a markedly different logic than contemporary privatized pension systems do: They represented a *collective* means of countervailing insecurity, of pooling risk, and of tying fates. They rested upon the principles of mutuality and shared burden rather than on individualization or the logic of the market.[10] The privateness of social protection thus has been a defining feature of this category of institutions for most of its history.

Social protection only came under the purview of the state following the industrial revolution, when large-scale urban migration tore workers away from the safety nets of family and social relations in the countryside, making risks such as old age poverty into a *social* problem, rather than an individual one.[11] The state's assumption of substantial responsibilities in pension provision did not significantly alter the instruments or principles of risk-pooling, however; it merely applied these to an ever-larger community.[12] Nor did the state usurp altogether the function of risk-pooling from the private realm. Rather, the public and private forms of social protection long existed as compliments.[13] Privateness – the reliance on nonstate actors to administer old age income – thus is *not* the feature of this institutional change that necessarily transforms its essential logic, nor is it what makes pension privatization so revolutionary.

Nor is the real story of privatization found in the ostensible retreat of the state from the pension business.[14] Far from being consigned to redundancy,

---

[10] Ball 2000, p. 12; Gilbert 1983, p. 6.
[11] Frieden 2006.
[12] Baldwin 1990; Rubinow 1913.
[13] Gilbert 1983, p. 8; Hacker 2002.
[14] This claim contrasts, for instance, with Madrid's premise in *Retiring the State* (2003).

privatization demands that the state remain intimately involved in the creation and sustenance of the private pension market, for which it becomes the ultimate guarantor. In this sense, there is no respite for the state following privatization, as government regulations necessarily extend into almost every aspect of the private pension business. The state must establish and enforce fiduciary standards, guard against excessive risk-taking, provide citizens with information, and ensure the transparency of pension market transactions. State institutions often participate in these markets as well, providing collection and record-keeping services, and in some cases even establish pension funds that compete alongside private firms to manage individual retirement accounts.[15] Thus while the quotation from Barr at the opening of this chapter may seem paradoxical for a study of the politics of pension privatization, the inextricability of the state from the pension business may quite possibly be the closest thing to an iron truth of pension reform. Pension privatization thus is not about the *retreat* of the state from social protection; it is about the state's transformation.

Instead, the critical upheaval occurring through pension privatization is the transformation in the structure of risk protection: from a system that pools risk to one that individualizes it through self-insurance. Along with this shift is a change in the institution's broader organizing principles, from that of social protection to the ideals of the market. The concepts and underlying logics of social protection and the market could not be more different.[16] Under systems of social protection, risks are pooled, and coverage is offered irrespective of actuarial status. Risk-pooling, at its base, is thus a form of redistribution. As Baldwin has observed, it is a system of reapportioning mischance from those who are less risk-prone and advantaged by markets to those who are less fortunate and unable to bear alone the array of risks inhering in market-based society.[17] Whereas social protections *redistribute* the cost and risk of protecting against poverty, market-based systems *individualize* them, returning the cost and risk of income loss to the shoulders of each worker, who must bear these, increasingly, alone. The operating rule of the market is thus much simpler than that of social protection: You get out according to what you put in; each quid is returned with a quo.[18] Market-governed forms of income protection thus link the value of an individual's lifetime contributions tightly to his or her old age income. Risk protection in markets is apportioned by purchasing power, such that your security in old age is determined by the amount of coverage you buy for yourself with lifetime savings, regardless of differences in the ability to save.

Social protection and the market also represent starkly opposing ways of organizing human relations. Whereas market systems take the individual as their basic unit, social protection embraces an organic view of society, seeing

---

[15] Kay 1999.
[16] Polanyi 1957.
[17] Baldwin 1990.
[18] Lindblom 2001, p. 111.

its members as part of a connected whole. In markets, relationships are, at least in principle, based on unfettered, voluntary exchange; by contrast, state authority and normative order connect people in social protection schemes. Markets organize risk and preclude any guarantee of outcome; they secure for all participants, regardless of heritage or status, the chance to compete in the arena of exchange. To some takers of risk, the market lavishes rewards of great profit, but to others it issues massive loss. Social protection, by contrast, treats individuals differently in the service of shared ends. Through risk-pooling, social protection strives to countervail the vicissitudes of the market system, allaying these forces with measures to dissipate risk and share reward.

Like the organizational yin and yang of capitalist society, the principles of social protection and the market express at once a fundamental opposition, but also reciprocal dependence. Social protection offers the hope of rest from the toil and insecurity of wage dependence, limiting to some degree the precariousness of income and consumption in market economies. Where markets apportion risk protection, disparities in income and chance are largely reproduced and extend into old age. Despite such diametric opposition, social protection *needs* the market. Not only does it derive its existence from the centrifugal market forces, but the affluence generated by economic exchange provides vital sustenance for social protection – making significant forms of redistribution possible in the first place.[19] Social insurance, in turn, enhances the functioning of markets by broadening the range of tolerable economic activities in which an individual may engage, from innovating to acquiring new skill.[20] Thus while representing fundamentally conflicting logics and institutional forms, social protection and the market would become essentially lifeless without each other.

FROM SOCIAL PROTECTION TO THE MARKET: DEFINING STRUCTURAL CHANGE

The significance of the shift from social protection to the market in old age pension systems rests upon a view that risk protection, and specifically risk-pooling, is a central goal of the welfare state.[21] Of course, the objectives and instruments of social provision are diverse and have varied markedly over time, from the development of human capital through education and health care, the assurance of social peace and response to claims for justice and equality through cash transfers.[22] For Esping-Andersen, however, many other welfare state goals, such as equalization, in fact derive from "what is and always was

---

[19] Carroll 1987.
[20] Economic theory thus provides firm grounds to justify mandatory social protections. See Creedy and Disney 1985, pp. 16–18; Feldstein 1998.
[21] Baldwin 1990; Esping-Andersen 1999; Mares 2003; Taylor-Gooby et al. 2004.
[22] Moon 1988, pp. 44–5; Offe 1984, p. 195; Wilensky 1975, p. 15.

the foremost objective behind social policy, namely insuring the population against social risks."[23] Indeed, various forms of social insurance respond to one of the most pressing and ineluctable features of modern industrial – and postindustrial – society, namely, the aspiration for security against the risk that one's standard of living may be eroded by income loss due to sickness, accident, old age, or death of the family breadwinner. Of course, welfare states manage risk differently in every national circumstance and across different social policy areas according to the nature and incidence of the risk. They all, however, rest upon some objective of reapportioning social risks broadly across society. For Esping-Andersen, therefore, differences across welfare regimes reside not in *whether* there is pooling but rather in the *way* that risks are pooled.[24]

The view that risk-pooling is a central element of the welfare state provides the theoretical premise of this study: that the changing structure of risk-pooling that occurs in pension privatization constitutes a shift in the *ends*, and thus in the nature of the welfare state itself.[25] Some risk-pooling is inherent, of course, in any pension system that is sponsored by the state. Thus the shift from social protection to the market should be understood in terms of degree of structural shift along a continuum between the dominance of risk-pooling instruments and those of market governance.

RETRENCHMENT VERSUS RESTRUCTURING

The preceding claim that privatization is not so much a retreat of the state as it is its transformation suggests that as an empirical strategy, the commonplace search for evidence of state contraction through declines in social spending may fail to capture the pivotal structural transformations at issue in pension privatization. Other data are needed. For it is entirely possible that welfare state spending may remain constant or even increase while the underlying risk-pooling functions are eviscerated by privatization. The result would be the arrival at misleading conclusions of program stasis when fundamental change has occurred. Examining the overall size of the welfare state thus may fail to capture the essential structural transformation in risk protection: as Schwartz put it, "It is not the welfare state that has been killed but rather social protection."[26]

Most critically, the view of pension privatization as a withering of the state fails to capture the *creative* dimension of this project, which revolves around the establishment of new forms of market relations and property rights. Pension privatization is more than simply a process of taking away benefit

---

[23] Esping-Andersen 1999, p. 32. Other precepts such as equal social citizenship also may be subsumed within the concept of risk-pooling. See Baldwin 1990; Marshall 1964.

[24] Esping-Andersen 1999, p. 33.

[25] Green-Pedersen 2002; Hinrichs and Kangas 2003.

[26] Schwartz 2001.

guarantees and risk-pooling; it is an extension of state authority and of concepts of private ownership. Viewing pension privatization as an extreme form of retrenchment, or strictly as a *loss* of property rights, thus will invariably fail to capture the broader story and political possibilities embedded in the *transformation* from one form of socially constructed rights to another. Whereas the loss of benefit rights – to the extent that they are observable – is always unpopular, acknowledging the additional fact that privatization creates *new* areas of market operation permits a broader range of theoretical insights. For instance, the view of privatization as a multidimensional project thus allows scrutiny of the opportunities for politicians to seek, and sometimes even to win, political credit for expanding distributive benefits such as greater private investment options, choice and (putative) control of retirement income through privatization.[27] When politicians do this effectively, they can obscure the extent of losses that are simultaneously imposed by the curtailment of risk-pooling structures through privatization.

My analysis thus emphasizes two politically relevant dimensions of pension privatization: The first is *retrenchment*, involving cutbacks in state benefit guarantees and risk-pooling, and the second is *distributive*, encompassing the creative elements of privatization and the possibilities for individual gain. The existence of the second, creative, dimension sets the politics of pension privatization apart from that of retrenchment alone. For the creative elements of this reform are typically advanced under the mantle of expanding ownership, control, choice, and freedom and of increasing rates of return to old age pension contributions. These concepts are more than merely political slogans; they constitute real possibilities for reward and distributive advantage for those who can benefit from "going it alone" rather than from sharing broadly the risk of mischance and poverty in a market economy.

Although privatization upends the usual set of winners and losers in social protection, distributional advantage under privatized pension systems is often not apparent ex ante. Most citizens are unfamiliar with the stochastic properties of private capital markets or the relationship of interest rates and bond prices, the principles of annuitization, or their ideal position on the risk and reward frontier. Such uncertainty opens vast possibilities for strategic political actors to reconstitute political alliances in ways that cross-cut traditional income and power resource lines. The manipulation of perceptions of distributive advantage thus opens up vast new possibilities for reform-seeking governments to win – although not necessarily to sustain – public support for pension privatization. Whether political conflicts are organized around the distributive or loss-imposing dimension of pension privatization is therefore likely to have a critical bearing on the nature and outcome of contests over this reform. Which aspect will dominate political debate is not given ex ante; rather, it is an outcome of political conflict.

---

[27] Bonoli 2000; Esping-Andersen 1990; Kitschelt 2001; Pierson 1994, 2001; Schwartz 2001; Starr 1989, pp. 28–9.

THE ARGUMENT

This study seeks to explain the transformation of social protection institutions by analyzing three analytically distinct but interrelated arenas through which any reform must progress. The first examines the effect of economic integration on pension reform in the technocratic decision-making process. For it is in this realm that macroeconomic objectives and constraints are most directly weighed in the institutional design. Research on social welfare reform has widely viewed globalization as a source of inexorable downward pressures on state social insurance programs, especially in the developing world. I challenge this view by arguing that it is *not* the most economically open, capital-scarce countries that are more likely to privatize old age pensions. Nor should globalization be viewed as a source of strictly downward pressure on social protection. Rather, I argue that globalization has generated both incentives *and* constraints for governments seeking to restructure old age pension systems. Globalization's effect, in this sense, is to place reform-seeking governments in a double bind, with the consequence of impeding or constraining movements toward more market-oriented pension designs in the most capital-scarce nations. This is because even though global financial integration has heightened the attraction to privatization as a means to achieve long-term macroeconomic goals, it has also raised the risk of punishment – via capital flight – for governments that overstep their financial means in the short term, even if they do so in the service of long-term market-oriented reform. Government policy makers in open, capital-importing nations thus may respond to these short-term market risks by advocating that their governments curtail, if not forego altogether, the decision to privatize.

My second argument examines the process through which government leaders seek public consent to structural pension reform; that is, how they "sell" reform to society. Pension reform has long been viewed as a politically lethal endeavor for career-minded politicians. Indeed, the willingness of program beneficiaries to punish politicians for imposing losses has long been seen as providing an essential political feedback to social welfare programs that prevents radical shifts from the existing institutional path.[28] As pension systems grow in generosity and coverage, this view suggests, the prospects for radical change become ever more remote. But increasing evidence of public acquiescence, if not support, for pension privatization in democratic settings demands a reconsideration of this conventional wisdom. The approach to explaining fundamental institutional change in research on path dependence has generally been to examine how exogenous factors such as war, depression, or crisis overwhelm one set of self-reinforcing institutional feedbacks and reconstitute a wholly new path of development.

My argument takes a different approach, which is to look *within* the forces of institutional stability to understand how and when these may permit, or

[28] See, e.g., Pierson 2001.

even promote, fundamental institutional change. I argue that although the normative beliefs and performance expectations about an institution – its political legacy – may long underpin public support for the institution, these attitudes and expectations may also become levers of public support for path-departing institutional reform. This is possible where institutional performance falls short of expectations or where its products come to be seen as unfair. Political legacies also may place important bounds on the claims that may be effective in unlocking public attachments to an institution. Allegations of unfairness or institutional failure thus may ring hollow where contravened by citizens' everyday knowledge of the institution. Even where political legacies are positive, however, and institutions enjoy broad support and effective functioning, politicians may gather support for radical change by shifting political debate beyond the scope of issues about which citizens have tightly held beliefs. This may entail the introduction of new information about the program's ostensible future viability or challenges to its core principles and performance standards. Such claims require citizens to delegate their judgment on the issue to political actors; therefore, politicians who enjoy substantial credibility on social welfare issues – such as those on the left and with labor backing – are likely more likely to be persuasive in gathering support for reform on such terms. Predicting when consent to institutional change may be won thus directs attention not only to the performance of old age pension institutions but also to the credibility of the politician on social welfare issues.

Finally, in democratic contexts, formal institutional changes of any type require the sanction of elected legislatures. In this realm, the electoral hazard of imposing losses on organized beneficiaries of the welfare state has long been shown to prevent its major reform.[29] Scholars disagree, however, over whether greater dispersion or concentration of legislative authority offers the most hospitable context for enacting retrenchment; that is, whether the politics of social security reform are better explained by the number of "veto players" or the possibilities for "blame avoidance" delimited by the structure of legislative institutions. I take a different approach to understanding the legislative politics of reform. For I begin with the observation that privatization entails not only loss-imposing elements implied by cuts to risk-pooling, but it also has an important *creative* dimension that centers on the possibility for distributive gains in private savings systems. The multiple dimensions of institutional restructuring thus imply that multiple political equilibria are possible: A credit-claiming (distributive) logic, a veto dynamic, or both logics may obtain in legislative conflicts over pension reform. Neither outcome is assured, however, by the structure of legislative authority nor by the objective features of the reform itself. Although reforming governments may be expected to seek insofar as possible to enhance the perception (if not reality) of privatization as a distributive measure, success is not assured. Rather, the possibilities for building majorities behind loss imposition may depend heavily on the way in which the partisan structure of

---

[29] Pierson 1994; 1996; 2001; Pierson and Weaver 1993; Weaver 1986; 1988; 1998.

the political conflict shapes the exercise of political power. Governing parties of the left that claim the support of credible defenders of the welfare state (such as labor unions and retirees) may be better able to organize political conflicts around the distributive dimension of structural reform, downplaying the salience of losses, and thus building large, if not oversized majorities behind structural reform. Where such efforts fail and a veto dynamic obtains, privatization is not always foreclosed; however, it does become more costly to build legislative majorities in a veto context, as the salience of the loss-imposing dimension raises the political cost of voting for this reform. In this event, I argue, the likelihood and degree of institutional change depend on the extent of bargaining required to construct a majority and on the availability of institutional authority and compensation resources to cement voting coalitions behind loss-imposing reform.

In each of the arenas, my argument suggests that the possibilities for reform are not given strictly by the objective features of the proposed measure or by the nation's economic or political landscape. Rather, institutional changes are contingent and subject to contestation and strategic behavior. But agency in such conflicts is far from unbounded; everything is not up for renegotiation when structural reform is in play. Political actors are constrained powerfully by the economic, social, and political context in which such conflicts are fought. And even though the outcome of contests over structural pension reform is subject to strategic behavior and therefore is contingent, it remains very much a structured contingency.

WHY STUDY THE TRANSFORMATION OF OLD AGE PENSIONS?

In addition to the economic size and importance of old age pensions – typically the largest component of social welfare systems – the transformation of risk structures is deeply consequential in social and political terms. The importance of changes in the way that social risks are shared has been heightened and reinforced most powerfully by the vast and simultaneous transformation in the nature and magnitude of risks confronting modern society. Just as longevity has expanded the array of "old" risks against which individuals must insure, such as poverty in superannuation, privatization transfers to individuals a greater share of these rising costs. And even though workers are asked to shoulder a larger portion of this increasingly heavy responsibility, their capacity to bear such costs alone is ever more strained by the emergence of "new" risks attendant upon the opening of economies and liberalization of labor markets.[30] Workers thus are faced with the perfect risk storm: Just as the cost of retirement income protection is rising, the liability of saving for old age is falling increasingly upon their shoulders, precisely as increasing volatility of earnings and employment wear away at the capacity to go it alone in a market economy.

[30] Esping-Andersen 1999; Taylor-Gooby et al. 2004.

Individualization of risk is also important in distributional terms because earnings and employment risks do not incide equally upon all members of the workforce. Low-skilled, low-wage workers, and women – whose labor is often interrupted, poorly compensated, or not remunerated at all – are buffeted most forcefully by such risks, and thus are most disadvantaged by the shift toward individualization of risk protection.[31] For these workers, thrift alone may simply be insufficient to hedge against destitution. Where earnings are extremely low and precarious, as in many parts of the developing world, the reduction in earnings required to purchase insurance may force individuals into a dire tradeoff between deprivation during their youth and security in old age, when earning capacity is gone. Moreover, if privatization reproduces among the elderly the often-severe disparities in income and chance that characterize working life, then it may exacerbate potentially explosive political cleavages that lurk in highly unequal societies. In this way, access to risk-pooling – and with it freedom from fear – entails much more than the reallocation of financial resources. It reaches deeply into distributions of symbolic and social resources, to questions of *effective,* as opposed to merely formal, membership in a community, and thus into the very basic concepts of citizenship and prospects for social cohesion.[32]

The study of pension privatization also addresses certain longstanding theoretical puzzles in research on institutional change. The most central of these is the question of how major institutional transformation emerges from a once-stable and path-dependent process of institutional development. A path departure is understood to entail changes that are not merely adaptations of an institution to new contexts, or incremental adjustments of the instruments or levels of institutional products, but rather a fundamental revision of its ends and design.[33] It is thus an instance in which the basic social bargain in an institution is revised. Such transformations are comparatively rare and typically explained as a product of exogenous shocks such as depression or war, or of overwhelming pressures such as demographic and economic change that render a given institutional path no longer viable. Even though a rich stream of research has developed around the study of the *consequence* of such critical junctures, less is known about the causes and processes through which major institutional change emerges from within formerly stable and even self-reinforcing institutional processes.[34] But whether the forces that typically promote institutional stability also permit, or even promote, fundamental change, remains to be explored. This is precisely the theoretical puzzle in pension privatization. Although fundamental path departures have clearly taken place, they

[31] See, Diamond, ed. 1999, p.19; also see, James, Edwards, and Wong 2003; Orloff 1993, pp. 11–12; Rubinow 1913, p. 6.

[32] See Marshall 1964. For questions of social resources and effective citizenship, see Hall 2005; Moon 1988, pp. 42–3; Starr 1989, p. 44.

[33] Hering 2003. Also see Hall 1993.

[34] Collier and Collier 1991; Mahoney 2000; Pierson 2000a, 2004. See, however, Greif and Laitin 2004; Thelen 2004.

have few obvious or systematic links to exogenous pressure or shock. Nor do these reforms track neatly the structure of legislative authority, or the scope and magnitude of benefit promises in the old pension system. In other words, they are not consequences of the fiscal pressure facing existing institutions, or of the simple distribution of legislative power.

There is also an array of empirical puzzles that have not yet been resolved by existing research on pension reform. For instance, if financial pressures are important motives for privatization, then why was this measure embraced in Mexico, where the old pension system was in surplus at the time of reform, but not in Brazil, where the state pension system recorded massive financial deficits by the late 1990s? If political institutions are decisive, then why in Brazil could President Lula da Silva prevail in reforming the public sector pension system and his predecessor, President Cardoso, could not? Further, if partisan identity matters, then why could one centrist president in Uruguay win rapid sanction of a pension privatization, when the preceding centrist government failed repeatedly to win even minor revision of the state pension system? If command of a disciplined majority is essential, then why in Mexico was President Salinas's bid to privatize old age pensions stymied, while President Zedillo, of the same dominant and highly disciplined Institutional Revolutionary Party (Partido Revolucionario Institucional, or PRI) succeeded, despite Zedillo's considerably weaker position vis-à-vis the PRI and its labor base? Lastly, why did the Argentine government intervene in the *privatized* pension system in 2002, and then later enact a partial renationalization of the pension system without obvious political cost? These are among the critical empirical puzzles that are addressed in this book.

METHOD AND PLAN OF THE BOOK

This study takes a multimethod, multilevel approach to answering these theoretical and empirical questions. The next chapter begins this task with a quantitative analysis of pension privatization on a global scale. The dependent variable of this analysis is defined by the structural features of pension reforms – specifically, whether and how much transformation from social protection to the logic of the market has taken place. The empirical focus of the analysis thus centers on conflicts over the enactment of formal changes of law rather than on the ultimate political, social, or macroeconomic outcomes that these may yield in the long term. In part, this focus is justified by the very long temporal horizons over which the effects of pension reform are realized. At the same time, these texts – the formal juridical institutional changes – are suffused with evidence of the conflicts defining contemporary society.[35] For the technical minutiae of old age pension provision apportion vast distributive advantages and disadvantages – in material and political terms – and thus political conflicts over such terms are often protracted and bitterly fought. Analysis of the change

---

[35] Baldwin 1990.

of law itself lends only the first glimpse at the reach and implications of change in the structure of social and economic relations in a society that are implied by this reform; nevertheless, it remains a critical one.

Comparative Analysis and Case Selection

I further evaluate my arguments and the causal processes they imply in qualitative evidence from pension reform experiences of four countries: Argentina, Brazil, Mexico and Uruguay. The task of identifying cases for the qualitative analysis that are representative of a broader population, and from which generalizable inferences may thus be drawn, is a daunting one at best. The choice for this study begins with recognition that the unit of analysis is the reform law, rather than the country. Even though the two factors often coincide, the existence of multiple reform efforts within some countries, where the constellations of political and economic forces also shift over time, has expanded the number of cases observed within the four countries examined in Part III of the book. Within the four countries, I examine six cases of pension reform: *Law 24,241* (passed in 1993 in Argentina), the Social Insurance Law (1995, Mexico),[36] *Law 16,713* (1995, Uruguay), Constitutional Amendment 20 (1998, Brazil), *Law 9,876* (1999, Brazil), and Constitutional Amendment 40 (2003, Brazil). Of those laws, the first three (in Argentina, Mexico, and Uruguay) involve some degree of pension privatization, but the last three (in Brazil) do not. The three privatization cases, moreover, offer wide variation in the depth of structural shift from social protection to market-based designs. Whereas Mexico's reform created an approximately 90 percent private pension system, Uruguay enacted a more modest shift toward market-based provision, where the average-wage worker choosing to participate in the private pension market could receive a pension that is approximately 37 percent private.[37] Argentina's 1993 reform lies between those cases, as workers participating in the private pension market would claim a pension that was 54 percent private. In addition, four reform failures in Uruguay prior to the 1995 privatization law offer shadow cases that not only expand the number of observations of political conflicts but also include control observations of no institutional change. The cases thus provide maximum variation on the type and degree of institutional outcomes observed: from reform failure in Uruguay, to reform without privatization in Brazil, to modest privatization in Argentina and Uruguay, and finally to radical privatization in Mexico. Comparisons of the varied outcome of reform conflicts over time in Mexico, Uruguay, and Brazil also offer the advantage of longitudinal variation on the dependent variable and control for unmeasured country-specific factors that could affect reform outcomes.

---

[36] A second law, the *Ley de los Sistemas de Ahorro para el Retiro*, was enacted in April 1996 establishing the legal and regulatory structures for the implementation of the private pension system. This is treated as the same case as the 1995 *Ley del Seguro Social* for analytical purposes.
[37] Author calculations; see Chapter 2 for methodology.

The privatization cases also represent the three categories that have been identified by Carmelo Mesa-Lago.[38] The first of these archetypes is the *substitutive* model, which essentially replaces the state social insurance system with a privately funded scheme based on individual, defined-contribution accounts. Mexico provides an instance of this model. The second is the *parallel* design, which creates a private funded pension system alongside the public social insurance program; workers in these systems may choose between participation in the private and public regimes. The third category is *mixed* reform, which adds a privately funded component to a mandatory public social insurance system. In practice, the distinction between the parallel and mixed pension reforms is not clearly drawn. Both Argentina and Uruguay are categorized as mixed pension reform models; however, in both cases the option of remaining with the fully public social security program remains available to most (Uruguayan) or all (Argentine) workers. The Argentine pension reform thus lies closer to the parallel model than to the mixed regime, as it represents a case in which all citizens may opt to remain within the fully public defined-benefit scheme that competes with the private system (as of 2002, 20 percent of workers opted for the public regime).[39] In Uruguay, the highest earners *must* place a portion of their statutory payroll contributions in the private scheme, but most workers' incomes fall below that threshold, giving them a choice of splitting their payroll contributions between the two regimes. Just 51 percent of covered workers in Uruguay participate in the private system, which has a participation rate that is closer to that of Colombia – one of the archetypal "parallel" reforms – where 45 percent of the covered workers participate in the private system.[40] Thus in practical terms, Mexico represents a substitutive structural reform, Argentina provides an example of a parallel system, and Uruguay corresponds to the mixed reform design.

If there is an Achilles's heel to qualitative research, it is the problem of avoiding selection bias in the choice of cases for analysis. I attempt to mitigate the problem of sample selection bias in the analysis in two ways. The first is statistical. Chapter 2 takes a global set of countries with national social insurance systems, which constitute roughly the population of potential privatizers, and tests my main theoretical contentions in these data. Doing so subjects my hypotheses to the test of external validity, assuring that my arguments are not moored solely to the Latin American reality or to specific features of my chosen cases. The Heckman selection estimator used in Chapter 2 estimates cross-national variations in the degree of privatization while controlling for the factors that shape the decision to privatize in the first place. The selection estimator helps to correct for this initial privatization decision and thus mitigates the potential bias that would arise from analysis solely of privatizing nations. I also seek to avoid the bias arising solely from analysis of privatizers

[38] Mesa-Lago 1997.
[39] Mesa-Lago 2005, p. 49.
[40] Mesa-Lago 2005, p. 49.

by including Brazil, which enacted pension reform but did not privatize, in the structured comparative analysis of Part III.

The four countries also vary widely on the main dimensions of theoretical interest. The first relates to financial and macroeconomic factors associated with pension reform. Whereas the implicit pension debt (IPD), the cost of the existing system, in Mexico is one of the lowest in the global sample at 48 percent of the gross domestic product (GDP), Uruguay's IPD is closer to those of advanced industrial nations at 214 percent of GDP. With regard to global market constraints, Argentina reformed its pension system at a time of high international liquidity in the early 1990s, when financing constraints were slack, while Brazil did so during a time of intense credit-rationing late in the decade. And whereas Mexico's pension system was in financial surplus at the time of reform, Uruguay's recorded a wide deficit when privatization was enacted.

The four countries also vary on the partisan makeup of reforming governments and distributions of legislative authority. Argentina and Mexico represent cases of labor-based parties taking the lead in the adoption of pension privatization, whereas in Brazil (under Cardoso) and Uruguay, reforming governments faced a left-labor opposition. In Brazil, moreover, the comparison of reforms under Cardoso (1998, 1999) and Lula da Silva (2003) permits me to hold constant the political institutions surrounding pension reform while varying the partisan identity of the government. In addition, whereas reform efforts in Argentina and Mexico were led by a government holding a disciplined majority in the legislature, in Brazil and Uruguay governing parties undertook reform without control of a majority, and with relatively fragmented legislative authority.

With regard to institutional legacies, Mexico's pension system was, by local standards, functioning at the time of reform, having recently experienced a sharp rise in pension values and recording a financial surplus. By contrast, the performance of the Argentine pension system was widely viewed as a failure because it had suspended payments in the years prior to reform and accumulated vast debts to pensioners who protested regularly to demand payment of these arrears. Although perceived performance failures dampened resistance to privatization in Argentina, they did not do so in Brazil, where benefits in the old pension system were highly unequal and regressive, but where citizens would not countenance the privatization of social security. In Uruguay, pension benefits in the old system were relatively equal and had risen sharply in value prior to the reform. Still, the perception of inequities opened the door to structural reform that was billed as making the institution more "solidary, effective and just."

The coverage of the old pension systems also varies widely, as more than 70 percent of the labor force were regular contributors prior to reform in Uruguay, whereas in Mexico this rate was just 37 percent.[41] Finally, the choice of Argentina, Brazil, Mexico, and Uruguay allows me to hold constant as

---

[41] Mesa-Lago 2005, p. 51.

many relevant background features shared by these countries as possible. All four are classified as "upper middle income" countries by the World Bank; they have similar levels of per capita income and geopolitical standing and share an Iberian colonial heritage.[42] The international financial pressures and constraints emerging from the reliance on foreign savings are also comparable, as are factors such as industrialization, political mobilization, and the strength of state institutions. Lastly, all were democracies of some sort at the time of reform, where competing political parties in representative assemblies contested and sanctioned the institutional reforms that I examine.

Plan of the Book

The study begins with a broad analysis of structural change in old age income protection systems in the last quarter of a century. The general patterns of variation that emerge from the global cross-national analysis are used to sharpen the theoretical focus of the longitudinal and cross-national qualitative comparative analysis that follows. Rather than focusing on social spending, this statistical analysis uses a more sophisticated and conceptually better-grounded measure of structural change. That measure captures shifts in the structure of risk protection on two dimensions, which I use to test rival hypotheses surrounding the reform of pension institutions. The quantitative analysis helps greatly to disentangle the systematic from the idiosyncratic factors shaping structural pension reform, and especially to address the selection problems that inhere in this task, and that are more difficult to mitigate through qualitative analysis alone. The statistical analysis discloses less information, however, about the causal processes through which these outcomes emerge; thus it constitutes only the beginning of the hypothesis-testing effort. Nevertheless, systematic patterns that are evident in the variable-driven analysis provide a vital roadmap for theoretical inquiry into the causal forces of institutional change in the second part of the study.

Part II develops my theoretical arguments. Chapter 3 breaks down the process of institutional path departure into three main causal dimensions: how privatization reaches the political agenda through technocratic processes; how and when reformers can win broad public consent to path-departing change; and the legislative dynamics of structural reform. In each part of the chapter, I provide my own explanation for institutional change in old age pensions that builds upon existing research on the welfare state while addressing the broader literature in comparative and international political economy. The effort is integrative, and thus seeks a theoretical apparatus that can account for both institutional stability and change.

Part III of the study, Chapters 4 through 7, provides evidence from four Latin American countries to evaluate my theoretical claims. Since the main objectives

[42] In 1991, GDP per capita in Argentina was US$2,160, in Brazil US$2,540, in Mexico US$2,010, and in Uruguay US$2,620. World Bank 2002.

of this study are analytical and theoretical – to predict and explain institutional change – the comparative cases of pension reform in Argentina, Brazil, Mexico, and Uruguay are organized around the main explanatory dimensions rather than country or case-specific chapters. This organizing structure necessarily trades off the flow and completeness of the reform narrative for the goal of bringing relevant evidence from structured comparisons to bear on causal explanatory claims. Fortunately, there are many valuable studies of pension privatization in Latin America that provide narrative accounts of these reforms, their contexts, and their history.[43] Data for these chapters draw upon more than 120 interviews with government technocrats, politicians, academics, consultants, and social actors carried out between 1998 and 2003 in Argentina, Brazil, Mexico, Uruguay, and Washington, D.C., as well as an array of primary and secondary archival, legislative, media, and governmental data. Comparisons are made both across nations and over time, therein combining the snapshots of each reform with a moving portrait of distinct reform experiences within countries over time. By stopping and returning to each country as I move from one explanatory dimension to the other, the objective is to examine each case through a different optic in such a way that will produce a richer causal portrait of the processes and mechanisms of institutional change.

---

[43] See, for example, Borzutzky 2002; Cruz-Saco and Mesa-Lago 1998; Dion 2008; Kay 1998, 1999; Madrid 2003; Melo 2002; Mesa-Lago 1997; Mesa-Lago and Müller 2002; Müller 1999, 2003; Pinheiro 1998; Queisser 1998; Sinha 2000; Weyland 2004, 2005a, 2005b.

2

Explaining Structural Pension Reform

Theoretical Debate and Empirical Evidence

This chapter begins the analysis of institutional change by examining what we do and do not yet know about the transformation of old age pension institutions. Such an effort requires first that I examine prevailing theories of social welfare and pension reform and test them against rival hypotheses in global data. Doing so accomplishes several objectives. First, it establishes what hypotheses do and do not survive the "hard" test of external validity, and thus diminishes as much as possible the bias involved in generalization of my conclusions from a small (four-country) sample or regional setting (Latin America) to the global population. Second, cross-national quantitative analysis indicates the direction in which theoretical development of causal mechanisms should productively move. Finally, the quantitative analysis lays a foundation for the qualitative cross-national comparisons through which I assess the causal arguments developed in Part II of the book.

As part of the empirical analysis, I introduce in this chapter a measure of institutional change that captures the extent of transformation in the structure of risk-pooling in old age pensions. This measure represents the structural shift from institutional designs based fundamentally on social protection (i.e., risk-pooling) toward reliance on market mechanisms and individual self-insurance. This methodology differs in two ways from the more common approach to comparing welfare states either through analysis of spending data or through system-wide institutional variables. First, it captures institutional change as it is experienced at the micro, or individual level. Second, it allows us to examine structural change along two dimensions, capturing both the *distributive* or creative aspect of privatization through a simulation of the size of private retirement benefits that are at stake for individuals, and the *loss-imposing* elements of this reform, through which risk is transferred from society as a whole to individuals through the shift from defined-benefit to defined-contribution schemes.[1]

[1] See Mares 2003.

The analysis of the global set of pension privatizations between 1980 and 2002 suggests that critical revisions are warranted in certain theories that dominate contemporary research on the welfare state, while others are confirmed. These results set the stage for the theoretical development and empirical analysis of institutional change in Parts II and III of the book. Specifically, the analysis not only reveals the powerful effects of demographic change in bringing pension privatization to the reform agenda, but it also suggests an important qualification of the prevailing hypotheses of path-dependent change. The effect of institutional legacies on pension reform outcomes, I find, is conditional and nonlinear, rather than being a strict function of rising pension costs. And even though the statistical result confirms that globalization, domestic finances, and political dynamics shape whether and how much governments privatize their old age pension systems, the model reveals that they do so in ways that depart from conventional understandings. Far from being pressed to privatize by budgetary strains and capital scarcity, the most cash-strapped governments are *least* likely to privatize national pension systems. Also contrary to previous research, the analysis shows that executive command of a legislative majority alone cannot predict changes in pension structures; rather, the partisan structure of political conflict is a critical factor mediating the effect of institutional authority.

THEORETICAL DEBATE

Existing theories of welfare state reform offer starkly competing accounts of why, how, and to what extent national welfare systems have been transformed in the final decades of the twentieth century. Scholars point variously to the disparate pressures from global economic change, domestic postindustrial and demographic shifts, and the ascent of liberal economic ideas that have contributed directly or indirectly to such reforms. Yet there is also broad recognition that welfare state institutions are "sticky," and that powerful political and financial legacies have made institutional change far from frictionless. Scholars divide moreover on the question of how conflicts over welfare state reform are mediated by the specific political contexts in which they emerge, and over how formal political institutions shape the outcome of these reforms.

PRESSURE-INDUCED CHANGE

A central premise of research on welfare state reform is that the nature and magnitude of institutional change has corresponded in some way to the degree of financial strain and demographic pressure on social protection systems. Two hypotheses dominate this research. The first emphasizes financial pressures issuing from globalization, specifically, from trade and financial integration on the one hand and international financial institutions on the other. The second hypothesis emphasizes the effects of domestic demographic and financial pressures on national welfare states as a critical catalyst for reform.

A commonly cited argument in this stream of research holds that global efficiency pressures arising from trade competition and capital mobility have strained the ability of governments to sustain generous, state-funded social protections.[2] This hypothesis takes as a reference the expansion of state social welfare functions in the postwar era when strong controls on the movement of capital allowed both progressive taxation and domestic social policy autonomy to underpin the expansion of pension and unemployment insurance systems without the threat of capital flight. With the collapse of Bretton Woods and the resurgence of international capital mobility, scholars feared that the enhanced "exit" option of capital would place inescapable pressure on governments to reduce state social welfare spending, even detonating a "race to the bottom" in social policy provision.[3]

Evidence of persistent, and even expanding, social protection commitments in the advanced industrial world have largely allayed the most pessimistic of these fears, but many scholars continue to take seriously the notion that openness to trade and capital movement restricts the ability of governments either to implement market-correcting policies, to run large fiscal deficits, or to independently control national monetary policy and exchange rates.[4] Indeed, there is evidence that enhanced capital mobility and trade competition have coincided with shifts in tax burdens from mobile to immobile factors across rich and poor countries alike.[5] Yet, the effects of globalization on the welfare state remain deeply contested.[6] For some scholars, globalization has increased demands for social protection by exacerbating economic insecurity and spurring demands for compensation.[7] Others point to evidence of globalization's continuing relevance in the developing world, where countries pursuing the greatest trade and capital account liberalizations have made more extensive cuts in social spending, and where social outlays also have become more procyclical.[8] However, partisan politics, institutional legacies, and labor mobilization appear to mediate these outcomes even in the developing world.[9] And since manufacturers in developing countries compete on the basis of low wage costs, the lowering of trade barriers placed many of the traditional means through which governments promoted the competitiveness of domestic products out of reach, while

---

[2] Garrett 1998; 2000, pp. 941–91; Huber and Stephens 2000; Kaufman and Segura-Ubiergo 2001, pp. 553–87; Swank 2001, pp. 197–8.

[3] See, for example, Kay 2001, p. 6; Tanzi 2002, pp. 123–6. For discussion, see Scharpf 2002; Sigg and Behrendt 2002, p. 89.

[4] Andrews 1994; Guillén and Álvarez 2002, p. 67; Kurzer 1993; Rodrik 1997; Strange 1996. However, see Allan and Scruggs 2004; Esping-Andersen 1996; Garrett 1998; Garrett and Lange 1995; Gough 2002, p. 49; Hall and Soskice 2001; Kitschelt et al. 1998; Pontusson and Kwon 2003; Pierson 2001.

[5] Garrett and Mitchell 2001; Guillén and Álvarez 2002, p. 67; Schwartz 2001; Swank 2001.

[6] See, for example, Hicks and Zorn 2005.

[7] Cameron 1978; Garrett 1998.

[8] Kaufman and Segura-Ubiergo 2001; Rudra 2002; Wibbels 2006.

[9] Garrett 1998; Haggard and Kaufman 2008; Hicks 1999; Hicks and Swank 1992; Lipsmeyer 2002.

pressures from domestic businesses to reduce payroll charges increased.[10] Critically, these findings comport with a broader stream of research showing that market constraints are both stronger and broader in the developing nations compared to the advanced industrial countries; thus it is not surprising that globalization has retained a more central role in the study of social welfare reform in capital-importing nations.[11]

Scholars emphasizing the effects of globalization on old age pension reform in developing nations have drawn attention to the role of international financial institutions in this process.[12] The themes of eroding national policy autonomy and imbalances in bargaining power loom large in this research, as the power of international financial institutions (IFIs) to provide or withhold financial resources is identified as a central instrument through which IFIs influence government policy choices in capital-scarce nations. This coercive power need not be exercised explicitly. For some scholars, government actors simply *anticipate* that the adoption of a free-market policy model is a necessary condition for gaining access to development loans from IFIs.[13] The financial resource power brought to bear by IFIs, moreover, is said to afford them a privileged position in domestic policy debates where competing claims about a specific policy will be resolved in favor of the "more powerful actor" (i.e., the one in possession of the greatest financial resources).[14] In this view, the outcome of domestic reform decisions is tied closely to the resource scarcity in developing countries and to the magnitude of financial power wielded by international actors in those nations.

A second major stream of research emphasizing financial pressures for welfare state reform centers on the financial strains arising from shifting demographic landscapes and domestic economic changes. Indeed, since World War II, global life expectancy at birth has risen from approximately 45 to 65 years, and from 65 to between 75 and 80 years in the advanced industrial world.[15] Even though few social insurance programs throughout the world have escaped the strain of large financial and actuarial imbalances associated with shifting demographic trends, scholars are divided over the causal priority to attribute to aging in the process of social welfare reform. Policy makers commonly depict pension privatization as a means to avoid an "old age crisis," but scholars have generally viewed the demographic pressures more cautiously.[16]

---

[10] Dion 2006; Elliott Armijo 1999; Euzéby 2002, p. 33; Guillén and Álvarez 2002, p. 67; Kay 1999; 2000; 2001, p. 6; Ramírez and Córdova 1999; Sigg and Behrendt 2002.

[11] Maxfield 1997; Mosley 2000; 2003; Scharpf 2002, p. 89.

[12] Cruz-Saco and Mesa-Lago, 1998; Huber and Stephens 2000, p. 19; Kay 1999; 2000; Madrid 2005, pp. 23–50; Mesa-Lago and Müller 2002, p. 710; Müller 2001, p. 69.

[13] Cruz-Saco and Mesa-Lago 1998; Huber and Stephens 2000, p. 19; Kay 1999; 2000; Laurell 2000; Madrid 2003; 2005, pp. 23–50.

[14] Madrid 2005, p. 29.

[15] United Nations 2004.

[16] World Bank 1994.

In research on the advanced industrial welfare state, population aging is but one facet of postindustrial transformations brought about by the erosion of postwar social and economic structures.[17] Declining growth and rising unemployment attendant upon the shift from manufacturing to service-based economies also have strained welfare state finances and exacerbated tensions between the goals of budgetary restraint, income equality, and employment growth.[18] For Pierson, the result has been to usher in an era of "permanent austerity," where social policy debates have been reoriented around the defense of entitlements rather than around their expansion.[19] Huber and Stephens, moreover, argue that pressures associated with rising unemployment far outpace demographic change as the source of pressure bringing the advanced welfare states to the brink of crisis, leaving governments with few options but retrenchment.[20] Indeed, they argue that, "As long as unemployment crises dictated an agenda of curtailment of welfare state expenditures, the range of political choices was extremely limited."[21]

For scholars focusing on the developing world, where population aging is typically less advanced, fiscal pressures on state pension systems are linked more closely to broader macroeconomic crises and/or structural imbalances in the design and management of state pension systems. In many Latin American countries, "bankrupt" social insurance programs placed significant strains on government budgets in the 1990s, just as state social budgets and payroll charges came under rationalizing pressure from international market forces.[22] In many cases, the financial collapse of state pension funds followed the debt crisis of the 1980s, as rising unemployment, informalization, and falling wages increased demands for social assistance while diminishing the revenue base on which social security programs were financed.[23] By the end of the 1980s, pension systems throughout Latin America suffered yawning financial and actuarial deficits, while delays in indexation and other ad hoc measures to lower state pension costs eroded public confidence in these institutions.[24] These financial strains are said to constitute an important impetus for pension privatization, pressing governments to privatize in order to reduce the burden of rising state pension costs.[25]

Finally, financial pressures to privatize have been associated with capital scarcity in the developing world. In the late 1980s, technocrats in Latin America began to argue that higher levels of domestic savings would help to

---

[17] Castles 1998; Hicks and Zorn 2005; Huber and Stephens 2001b; Iversen 2001; Iversen and Cusack 2001; Pierson 1996; 1998; 2001; Sigg and Behrendt 2002; Swank 2001, pp. 197–8.
[18] Iversen and Wren 1998.
[19] Pierson 2001.
[20] Huber and Stephens 2001a, p. 136.
[21] Huber and Stephens 2001a, p. 144.
[22] Kay 1998, 1999; Mesa-Lago 1989; 1997.
[23] Mesa-Lago 1997, p. 499.
[24] Mesa-Lago 1989; Mesa-Lago and Müller 2002; Uthoff 1994, p. 218.
[25] Madrid 2003, p. 30.

achieve the elusive goal of sustained macroeconomic growth.[26] When pension
privatization came to be seen as an effective tool for raising domestic savings,
technocrats throughout the recession-plagued region took notice.[27] Indeed,
to the extent that pension privatization promised to raise domestic savings,
it held the possibility to diminish the exposure of developing economies to
increasingly volatile international capital markets in the 1990s. Although
there has been considerable debate over the strength or even the existence
of a link between privatization and domestic savings, policy makers in Latin
America are said to have largely overlooked this dispute, embracing privatization on the basis of its presumed macroeconomic effects on domestic savings
and growth.[28]

Although the literature on pressure-induced change offers diverse claims
regarding the nature of financial strains buffeting welfare states in recent years,
research in this vein shares the premise that welfare state retrenchment may be
traced to the intense financial pressures on these systems. The principal empirical predictions arising from this perspective thus hold that structural pension
reform becomes more likely as populations age, capital becomes more scarce,
and countries become more deeply exposed to the pressures of globalization
and capital mobility. In addition, this research predicts that financial pressures
associated with unfunded pension costs and capital scarcity should make privatization more likely, just as nations receiving extensive support from the World
Bank should be more prone to enact deep structural pension reform.

INSTITUTIONAL LEGACIES AND PATH-DEPENDENT CHANGE

A hallmark of research on the welfare state is the view that institutional change
is heavily path-dependent.[29] In its most basic formulation, path dependence
holds that events and policy choices made in the past systematically shape later
options and goals of institutional development. However, the precise nature
and effects of institutional legacies on subsequent developments vary markedly
in this literature. A prominent approach centers on the concept of "policy
legacies" in technocratic processes, through which, "policy inevitably builds
on policy, either in moving forward what has been inherited, or amending it,
or repudiating it."[30] Other scholars emphasize the transformative effects of

---

[26] Calvo and Mendoza 2000; Guitián 1997, pp. 17–32; Solís Soberón and Villagomez 1997,
pp. 107–26; Williamson 1990, pp. 13–16.
[27] Brooks 2002; Madrid 2003; Mesa-Lago and Müller 2002.
[28] Madrid 2002, pp. 163–5; 2005, pp. 26–9; Mesa-Lago and Müller 2002, p. 709. For the savings-
privatization debate, see Arrau 1990; Arrau and Schmidt-Hebbel 1993; Auerbach and Kotlikoff
1987; Corsetti and Schmidt-Hebbel 1997; Orszag and Stiglitz 1999; Singh 1996; Smetters 2005;
Valdes-Prieto and Cifuentes 1993.
[29] Esping-Andersen 1990; 1996; Hacker 2002; Heclo 1974; Huber and Stephens 2001b; Orloff
1993; Pierson 1994; 1996; 2001; Skocpol 1995; Weaver 2000; Weir 1992.
[30] Hall 1993; Skocpol 1985; Skocpol and Amenta 1986. Also see Orloff and Skocpol 1984;
Quadagno, 1987, p. 118.

existing institutions on the broader social and political landscape in which they are embedded, including the organization of party systems and the existence of constituencies and interest groups organized around welfare state issues.[31] For Pierson, such "policy feedback" ensures that social security institutions, once in place, become a central part of the political landscape, delimiting social rights and benefits that give program beneficiaries something for which to fight.[32] And since the clientele of the welfare state is loathe to accept losses in their current entitlements, Pierson concludes that the politics of welfare state retrenchment obey a markedly different logic from the politics of institutional development: The latter is characterized by a credit-claiming logic, and the "new politics" of retrenchment is governed by the logic of blame avoidance.[33] Path dependence thus holds that powerful and reinforcing feedback mechanisms that inhere in social welfare institutions tend to lock in existing structures over time, making frontal assaults on the welfare state politically infeasible as institutions expand and mature.[34]

Scholars taking this approach also argue that radical shifts in the structure of old age pensions are foreclosed by a powerful financial legacy, namely governments' financial commitments to the beneficiaries of those institutions. This policy feedback mechanism has been particularly important for the study of pension privatization, which entails a transition from what is typically a pay-as-you-go, defined-benefit system to a prefunded defined-contribution scheme managed by the private sector. As workers divert payroll contributions to private pension fund managers, governments must relinquish financial resources that often constituted a principal source of revenue from which they could finance ongoing pension obligations. Privatization thus imposes a gap in the finances of state pension systems during the transition to a fully – or even partially – private pension system. Where pension benefits are generous and elderly populations are large, this financing gap may be enormous, amounting in some countries to upwards of 1 to 2 percent of GDP per year. The task of financing the transitional cost of pension privatization is thus a major financial obstacle to deep structural change of those institutions. This is particularly the case where the option of either obliging the working generation to pay "twice" into the old age pension system – once for the prior generation and then again for their own pension – or cutting budgetary expenses in other areas to cover this cost is politically difficult. Where old age pension systems are generous and mature, therefore, the sheer cost of privatization – both in political and financial terms – should make deep movements toward privatization increasingly difficult.[35]

[31] Immergut 1998; Orloff 1993; Pierson 1994; 1996; Skocpol 1992; Steinmo et al. 1992.

[32] Pierson 1994; 1996; 2001.

[33] Hall and Soskice 2001, pp. 57–8; Myles and Pierson 2001, p. 327; Pierson 2000a, p. 264; Scharpf 2002; Sigg and Behrendt 2002.

[34] Myles and Pierson 2001; Pierson 1994; 1996; 2001, p. 413; Pierson and Weaver 1993; Weaver 1986.

[35] James and Brooks 2001; Myles and Pierson 2001, pp. 312–13; Pierson 1996, p. 286.

LEGISLATIVE POLITICS

A pivotal hurdle in the process of welfare state reform is the formation of a majority of elected legislators to sanction loss-imposing reform. This task is complicated by the electoral incentives to avoid blame for imposing losses on welfare state beneficiaries. For some scholars, such considerations oblige politicians either to obfuscate loss-imposing reforms through less-visible benefit cuts such as indexation changes or to negotiate retrenchment across broad coalitions that offer "political cover" to legislators against a potential electoral backlash.[36] Scholars emphasizing the centrality of blame avoidance in the politics of pension reform thus argue that programmatic retrenchment is facilitated where political institutions spread authority more broadly across participants in the reform process, therein diffusing accountability for benefit cuts across multiple political actors.[37] Broad multiparty negotiations, however, are acknowledged at the same time to militate against radical shifts from the policy status quo. Institutional change thus is more likely, but more moderate where multiple political actors are represented in the political process.

The blame avoidance perspective is countered, however, by research emphasizing the role of "veto players" in the reform process. These are actors whose agreement is necessary to sanction change from the status quo policy.[38] The veto hypothesis holds that as the range of distinct political interests represented in the policy process increases, the opportunities for reform opponents to "veto" policy change rises as well, diminishing in turn the likelihood of significant policy reform.[39] Politicians thus may be more likely to win support for institutional change where political authority is concentrated and potential opponents enjoy few opportunities to articulate their voice in the political process. For Kay, institutional veto points extend from the structure of legislative authority to broader arrangements such as the plebiscite, which became a key obstacle to radical reform in Uruguay.[40] For Madrid, it is not necessarily the broader structure of political institutions that matters, but rather the extent to which the executive controls a legislative majority that shapes the possibility for pension reform.[41] In the latter view, the extent of voting power in the legislature translates directly into authority to sanction radical reform independently of partisan ideological or institutional conditions.

Like the blame avoidance hypothesis, the concept of veto points brings attention to the ways in which the structure of political authority influences both the style and outcome of policy reform efforts. The two theories rest on starkly opposing premises, however, and offer divergent empirical predictions

[36] Myles and Pierson 2001, p. 306; Pal and Weaver 2003; Pierson 1996, p. 154; 2001a, p. 418; Pierson and Weaver 1993; Weaver 1986; 1988; 2005.
[37] Myles and Pierson 2001, p. 306; Pierson 2001, p. 418; Weaver 1986; 2003.
[38] Bonoli 2000; 2001; Brooks 2002; Immergut 1992; Kay 1998; Tsebelis 1995; 1999; 2002, p. 2.
[39] Bonoli 2000; 2001; Immergut 1992a; 1992b; Kay 1998; 1999; Tsebelis 1999.
[40] Kay 1998; 1999.
[41] Madrid 2003, pp. 54–8.

about the effect of political institutions on policy change. Whereas the veto points hypothesis anticipates that fragmented legislative authority will serve as an impediment to policy change, the blame avoidance hypothesis expects reform to be more likely within that institutional milieu. If it is the executive's majority control of the legislature that matters, moreover, then deep structural pension reform should be more likely as the size of the executive party representation in the legislature increases.

ASSESSING THE RECEIVED WISDOM AND ITS ALTERNATIVES

Extant research provides important insights into the puzzle of old age pension privatization, bringing attention to the array of actors, motives, and mechanisms through which conflicts over the apportionment of risk and benefit in society are negotiated. As important as this research has been, there is reason to remain unsatisfied with the status of our knowledge regarding the political foundations of structural pension reform. For one thing, while rising financial pressures may be linked to the decisions by governments to curtail old age pension entitlements, it is difficult to connect the intensity of financial strains on state budgets to the enactment of old age pension privatization. This is because far from alleviating short-term budgetary pressure, the immense transitional cost of pension privatization *exacerbates* such financial strains in the near to medium term. Privatization also expands the administrative and regulatory functions of the state, permitting scant relief for weak or overburdened government institutions.[42] The view of privatization as an expedient or remedy to address immediate financial pressures on deficitary or ineffective state social protection institutions thus is cast in doubt by the tremendous institutional and financial burdens entailed by the creation of private retirement accounts.

Globalization

Although financial strains are unlikely to constitute a source of pressure for pension privatization, budgetary concerns are still likely to matter for reform outcomes. Given the high costs of the transition to a private pension system and the financial strictures imposed by international market actors on open economies, however, government budgetary strains should *limit* the ability of cash-strapped governments to privatize rather than catalyze such reform as previous research asserts. Most privatizing governments have financed the transitional cost of this reform by issuing new government debt. Yet, few governments enjoy an unlimited ability to borrow (i.e., issue sovereign bonds) on international capital markets. Instead, capital mobility raises the risk of market punishment for governments that overstep the limits of prudent sovereign borrowing, even if additional indebtedness occurs in the pursuit of long-term market-friendly goals.

[42] Kay 2003.

Rather than conducing strictly toward privatization, globalization may instead create a *double bind* for governments in capital-importing nations: On the one hand, economic integration generates real incentives to privatize old age pensions as a way to attract investment and build long-term sources of private savings. On the other hand, financial integration also delimits forceful punishments for governments that overstep the limits of what owners of financial capital deem acceptable vis-à-vis the risk of default or inflation. Accordingly, governments in a more dire financial position (i.e., those with more limited borrowing capacity and tighter domestic financial constraints) may be systematically *less* likely to privatize without risking capital flight in response to rising government indebtedness following the reform. This expectation contrasts sharply with the claims of previous research that privatization is impelled by domestic financial scarcity and budgetary pressures arising from deficitary pension systems. Given the high transitional cost of privatization and the tendency for owners of mobile capital to punish capital-scarce governments that present high default risks through excessive borrowing, the most cash-strapped governments should find it more difficult to privatize in the context of financial openness, all else being equal.

Institutional Legacies

Even though the remarkable stability of old age pension systems over the course of the twentieth century provides ample evidence of the reinforcing properties of old age pension institutions, research on path dependence has difficulty explaining the striking number and location of old age pension privatizations around the world in the last quarter century. Indeed, if pension systems tend to become more stable as pension liabilities grow, then we should not see privatization in countries with such old and generous pension systems as Sweden, Denmark, or Argentina. This research also tends to rely on exogenous shocks to explain structural pension reforms. Where path-departing change occurs, this literature suggests, it results from the emergence of such great pressures that overwhelm one path-dependent process and initiate a wholly new path. Theories of path dependence thus do not accommodate the possibility that the mechanisms that long reinforced an institutional configuration may later permit, or even promote, a significant departure from this design.

An alternative to this view regards the mechanisms of path dependence as contingent rather than inherently stabilizing in their effects. Why is it that features of the institutional legacy that long sustained a given path of development could not, under certain conditions, convert into forces that undermine the status quo? Indeed, if we permit that support for the existing pension institution may erode, for example, where a pension institution comes to be perceived as unfair, corrupt, or not likely to fulfill benefit promises, then a critical positive institutional feedback and obstacle to change (i.e., the risk of electoral punishment for reformers) may be removed, making way for the emergence of public support for structural reform. Rather than expecting privatization to be ever less likely over time, we may instead look for indications of declining support for the existing institutions that narrow the political constituency that is likely to fight to retain the status quo design. Where support for the existing pension institution declines, politicians may be more likely to gather broad public support for path-departing institutional change such as pension privatization.

Legislative Politics

Finally, the literature on political institutions and pension reform encounters important theoretical and empirical problems when it comes to explaining global trends in structural pension reform. Although empirical research has amassed considerable evidence to support both hypotheses, little progress has been made toward resolving the underlying theoretical tensions between these approaches.[43] Neither the veto points nor the blame avoidance theory, moreover, has adequately explained how significant policy change may emerge after long periods of stability where the structure of legislative authority remains constant.

At the same time, scholars have challenged the universal unpopularity of social policy reform. For Scarbrough, the risk of public mobilization against welfare reforms has been overstated, since the beneficiaries of redistribution may not always be the prime candidates for collective action.[44] Castles goes further, arguing that pressure group resistance has played "no discernible part" in the restructuring of the welfare state in Europe.[45] In some cases, the putative opponents to reform, such as labor unions, have not only failed to mobilize against social policy restructuring, but they have even *lent support* to such reforms.[46] For Ross, politicians may even claim credit for social policy reforms that entail some private savings component.[47] The conditions under which political gains may be reaped from such reform are shaped powerfully, however, by the partisan structure of political conflicts, as Kitschelt has shown.[48] In particular, left or labor-based parties enjoy considerable electoral advantages in initiating welfare state reform due to the left's traditional issue-association as defender of the welfare state.[49] This effect is all the more pronounced where the left is opposed by a viable conservative rival.

The notion that left parties enjoy advantages in the adoption of structural reform has been more broadly termed the "Nixon-goes-to-China" logic, which

[43] Brooks 2002; 2005; Crepaz 2001; Immergut 1992a; 1992b; Kay 1998; 1999; Swank 2001; Tsebelis 1999.
[44] Scarbrough 2000. See also Berinsky 2004; Kurtz 2004; Shadlen 2004; Teichman 2001, pp. 5–6.
[45] Castles 1998.
[46] Anderson 2001; Hering 2003, p. 34; Kay 1999, p. 413; Vail 2003. For the partisan debate, see Allan and Scruggs 2004; Hicks and Swank 1992; Manow 2001, pp. 148–9; Myles and Pierson 2001, p. 323; Pierson 1996; Pontusson and Kwon 2003.
[47] Ross 2000b; 1997. Also see Hering 2003, p. 30.
[48] Kitschelt, 2001, p. 265.
[49] Green-Pedersen 2001, p. 966; Hering 2003; Ross 2000b.

suggests that partisan actors may more easily enact measures that play against type. In regard to the welfare state, this claim rests on the view that orthodox policy reforms adopted by left governments may be acceptable because they are considered to be motivated by objective problems, rather than ideological goals; reform by the left also would be viewed as a "lesser evil" compared to one enacted by a rival conservative party.[50] As a result, left governments can more easily overcome the usual political obstacles to reform, and even escape electoral retribution for imposing losses. The partisan structure of legislative conflict thus may substantially influence the possibilities for a market-oriented pension reform net of the institutional landscape.

We thus have reason to expect the possibilities for institutional path departure to be conditional, rather than absolute, and mediated powerfully by the way in which political conflict over reform is played out in the legislative arena. Moreover, the left's advantage in winning support for structural reform suggests that the ways in which reform is presented or "sold" to the broader public should matter critically in dampening the putative electoral costs of loss imposition. Although all governments may be expected to try to present structural pension reform as a necessary measure and a gain for the population, these claims should be more likely to be persuasive where left governments are in power. The depth of reform enacted by governments of the left and right should also vary, both on account of ideological commitments and political compromises with core constituents. In the case of the left, winning the support of organized labor is often a critical condition for enacting structural reform. Labor backing is more likely to be won, however, at the cost of compromises in the degree of market-oriented reform. Thus pension privatizations enacted by left governments should be less radical in scope than reform passed by the right.

The partisan hypothesis also has implications for the contingent view of the path-dependent institutional legacies sketched out earlier. For a premise of the Nixon-goes-to-China theory is that where citizens remain supportive of the institution in question, they will trust the left to carry out reform in such a way that will preserve and strengthen the institution, rather than eviscerate it. Where public beliefs about the institution remain generally positive, therefore, citizens may empower a government of the left to undertake pension reform, whereas reform by centrist or conservative governments may result from the erosion of confidence in the state-run social insurance model and emergence of a mandate for fundamental change.

THE DEPENDENT VARIABLE: STRUCTURAL REFORM

The task of measuring structural pension reform is beset with an array of conceptual and methodological challenges that must be addressed before undertaking the quantitative analysis. The first of these is how to measure structural

---

[50] Cukierman and Tommasi 1998; Kitschelt 2001; Ross 2000b.

change in risk protection. The second is the question of measuring reform along two theoretically relevant dimensions: the loss-imposing and creative. I address these dilemmas by combining two indices of pension privatization that capture the underlying shift in the structure of risk-sharing from designs based on the principle of social protection (i.e., risk-pooling and redistribution) to that of the market, or individual savings. The first index measures the loss-imposing dimension, or degree of structural shift from risk-pooling to individualization, while the second index captures the creative, or distributive dimension, measured as the magnitude of private benefits at stake for a worker earning the average wage in each country. These measures, which are not perfect, offer important methodological, theoretical, and empirical advantages relative to spending data and macro-level indices that dominate empirical research on pension reform.

The Dependent Variable Problem

Scholars of the welfare state increasingly recognize that progress toward the accumulation of theory about reform is hindered by the lack of agreement on precisely what outcomes are to be explained. This dissensus has led to starkly contradictory observations: Whereas some scholars argue that the welfare state is in crisis and point to evidence of significant retrenchment, others maintain that the welfare state as a whole remains intact, although subject to erosion at the margins. Others still have argued that the welfare state is expanding under demands for protection against deepening insecurity – a trend that presages further enlargement of the welfare state in the twenty-first century.[51] The accumulation of evidence around these distinct claims has varied markedly across scholarship on the advanced industrial and developing nations, as well as across distinct policy areas of the welfare state such as health care, housing, and pensions.[52] Analysis of such varied outcomes, moreover, has yielded competing and largely incompatible theoretical claims about the nature and causes of institutional transformation. What we need in order to produce cumulative knowledge on the welfare state, therefore, is a convergence of scholarly research around the concepts and measures of the basic dependent variable of institutional change.

   This "dependent variable problem" is more than simply an empirical dilemma, or a failure of coordination around a common domain of analysis; rather, it is the product of differences in theoretical conceptions of the welfare state that ground disparate streams of research, and of the vastly differing meanings that citizens attach to different elements of social policy – and to the welfare state itself – across nations.[53] Such disparities are often difficult

---

[51] See, for example, Allan and Scruggs 2004, p. 497; Huber and Stephens 2001a; Kitschelt 2001, p. 299; Myles and Pierson 2001; Pierson 2001; Scarbrough 2000, p. 225; Schwartz 2001.

[52] E.g., Pierson 1996.

[53] Green-Pedersen 2002; Kitschelt 2001; Pierson 2001, pp. 417–20.

to avoid, as broad cross-national research on welfare state transformation is beset by the dearth of comparable data on a wide range of program designs across disparate countries and regions. Even where scholarship centers on a single policy domain such as pensions, disagreement persists as to what kind and how much change constitutes a meaningful structural shift.[54]

What Constitutes a Structural Change?

In seeking to move beyond this dilemma, I begin with the premise that risk-pooling is an essential feature of the welfare state. Where the structure of risk-pooling instruments changes, the logic of social protection thus is transformed, and a meaningful structural shift in the institution may be said to have occurred.[55] In other words, social protection is fundamentally transformed where market mechanisms are incorporated into the means and ends of income protection through the individualization of risk protection. The critical task that remains is to operationalize this concept of structural change in social protection.

As a starting point, shifts in the structure and organizing logic of the welfare state may be conceptualized as movements along a continuum where the pooling of risks across a universal (society-wide) risk group defines one endpoint, and individualization, or self-insurance, the antipode. In this view, structural reform of social protection systems is not confined to movement across discrete or exclusive categories of wholesale self-insurance (radical privatization) or the status quo of collective insurance provision.[56] Even in radically private pension reform such as that in Chile, risk-pooling persists, albeit mainly in instruments consigned to the margins of the program (e.g., the residual, means-tested minimum pension guarantee). State guarantees of minimum pension fund returns and regulations of private pension markets also represent important means through which risk-pooling occurs in market-based pension systems. Market forces also influence the allocation of income protection in risk-pooling social insurance pension systems such as where benefits are linked closely to individual contributions, and hence to each worker's success in the labor market. The dividing line between systems based on risk-pooling and those governed by the market logic thus is vague, rather than clearly drawn, and differences across nations in the structure of risk-pooling institutions are better conceptualized as continuous rather than discrete categories.[57]

Nevertheless, for analytical and practical purposes, a clear dividing line may be established between institutions that have undergone structural change and

---

[54] Hinrichs and Kangas 2003.

[55] Green-Pedersen 2002.

[56] Just as the state remains intimately bound to the pension business despite privatization, so too does risk-pooling persist within any national, legally enforced and upheld private pension regime. See Mares 2003.

[57] Bodie et al. 1988; Brooks and Weaver 2006; Diamond 1997; Palmer and Góra 2004.

those that have not. Whereas risk-pooling mechanisms are typically organized around defined benefit (DB) rules, defined contribution (DC) systems are closer to the concept of self-insurance because they link old age benefits closely to the value of each worker's lifetime pension contributions. Accordingly, institutional path departure may be said to occur in old age pension systems where individual, defined-contribution accounts are established within the statutory, or legally mandated, instruments of retirement income provision, thus displacing to some degree the risk-pooling (DB) component of the pension system.[58] Empirically, the dividing line between the logic of social protection and that of the market thus may correspond, albeit roughly, to the presence and size of individual defined-contribution savings accounts within statutory old age income programs.

The shift from DB to DC provision (i.e., structural pension reform) need not involve a shift from public to private management or from a pay-as-you-go financing system to advanced or full funding. Although these changes are typically bundled together in pension privatization, a growing number of governments have altered the structure of risk-pooling in old age pension systems *without* privatization. Such changes have been effected through reforms that create virtual, or "notional" individual pension accounts. Notional DC pension systems closely link contributions and benefits, as in privatization, but maintain state management and pay-as-you-go financing of pension benefits. Like their private analogue, notional defined contribution (NDC) reforms transfer a greater portion of the risk and cost of old age income provision to individuals, and thus constitute a meaningful structural shift in the underlying logic of social protection and risk pooling.[59] Pension reforms based upon notional individual accounts have been adopted in Brazil (1999), Italy (1995), and Germany (2001), and NDC components have been combined with funded-DC pension reform, or privatization, in Latvia (1996), Poland (1997), and Sweden (1998). NDC reforms thus extend the reach of individualization in social insurance reform far beyond the visible scope of the market in old age pension provision.[60] In this analysis, however, the empirical focus remains primarily on pension privatization, for which the task of identifying the boundary between social protection and market governance is considerably more straightforward and thus reliable for a set of countries as diverse as those examined here, which span from South America to Central Asia. The case of Brazil in Part III examines a notional account pension reform adopted in that country

---

[58] The "main" components of an institution here refer to those funded with statutory payroll contributions and that cover the average wage worker. Marginal social programs, by contrast, either provide benefits on qualified terms such as means-testing or are supplementary to the mandatory pension system, as in tax-advantaged voluntary retirement savings programs.

[59] NDC reforms do not transfer investment risk to individuals, however. The difference between NDC reforms and DB pensions with a tight contribution-benefit link is subtle. Brooks and Weaver 2006; Palmer and Góra 2004.

[60] Börsch-Supan and Wilke 2003; Ferrera and Jessoula 2005.

in 1999, which moved toward more individualized risk protection without the privatization of old age pensions.

Measurement Issues

By far, the most common means of operationalizing welfare state transformation in cross-national research is through the use of government spending data. But spending data suffer a number of disadvantages for the purpose of capturing structural reform.[61] The most critical of these, as Esping-Andersen observed, is that "[e]xpenditures are epiphenomenal to the theoretical substance of welfare states."[62] Not only do spending data fail to capture the way in which risks and benefits are apportioned through social programs, but aggregate data also eclipse the underlying structural shifts in the way that such programs are organized. This is particularly a problem for the study of old age pensions, where outlays may remain stable – or even rise – during privatization, and where substantial declines in state pension spending that result from the reform may become apparent only after considerable delays, such as the thirty- to forty-year transition period.[63] Reliance on spending data alone to identify and measure structural change thus may complicate the task of developing a causal theory of institutional change.

Perhaps the most influential theoretical and methodological advance in the measurement of variations in welfare state structure was provided by Esping-Andersen, whose analysis of program characteristics in core social welfare policies yielded indices of variations across national welfare state regimes along three dimensions: decommodification, the public–private mix of responsibilities, and stratification. His 1990 study broke important theoretical and methodological ground and precipitated fruitful debate over theories of institutional development and classification as well as fundamental questions of what constitutes the welfare state.[64] As important as this research program has been, it has left unexplored two critical frontiers. The first is the political economy of welfare state reform in the vast proportion of the world's population residing outside of the advanced industrial nations, namely in middle income and developing countries. The second is the challenge of measuring the transformation of the welfare state as it is experienced at the micro, or individual, level.[65]

The first challenge has been taken up most prominently by Carmelo Mesa-Lago's research on social security in Latin America.[66] Addressing the question

---

[61] For the pitfalls of spending data, see Allan and Scruggs 2004; Clayton and Pontusson 1998; Esping-Andersen 1990, p. 19; Palier 2001; Pierson 1994, p. 14; Schludi 2005, p. 43; Taylor-Gooby 2002.

[62] Esping-Andersen 1990, p. 19.

[63] Brooks 2002; Castles 2002, p. 623; Hinrichs and Kangas 2003, p. 574.

[64] Esping-Andersen 1990. See also Allan and Scruggs 2004; Bonoli 1997; Castles 2002; Clayton and Pontusson 1998.

[65] For the benefits of measuring change at the micro level, see Kitschelt 2001, p. 299.

[66] Mesa-Lago 1989; 1994; 1997; Mesa-Lago and Müller 2002.

of structural reform, Mesa-Lago identified three distinct institutional equilibria emerging from Latin America's pension reforms. In the first, governments have adopted private pension regimes that function alongside, or *parallel* to existing public social insurance systems, and most workers can opt to participate in either the public or the private scheme. In the second category, or *substitutive* reforms, private pension schemes supplant traditional social insurance systems. In this model, the average worker receives a pension solely from the private pension system, and risk-pooling is provided through means-tested minimum pension guarantees. Lastly, in *mixed* pension systems, the bulk of the labor force may (or must) participate in a combined public and private pension system through which the typical worker's pension will derive from some combination of social insurance and individual savings mechanisms. Analysis based on these diverse paths of institutional change has brought much-needed attention to the broader political and economic contexts in which old age pension reform has occurred, while revealing striking parallels in macroeconomic liberalization and the adoption of structural pension reform in Latin America.[67] Yet, the categories remain discrete, offering less insight into how reforms may differ *within* these categories, or how significant the differences across the categories may be.

System-level reform indices also do not capture how pension reforms are experienced on the individual level, and thus offer less insight into the micro logic of this reform. Research by James and Brooks sought to address this gap by measuring the public–private mix of old age benefits that the average wage worker receives in privatized pension systems.[68] That measure covered the global set of pension privatizers between 1980 and 2000, offering two advantages over alternative measures of structural change. First, it provided a parsimonious metric of privatization at the individual level that is comparable across nations, regions, and levels of development and captured the degree of policy change from one point in time to another.[69] Second, as a continuous variable, the public–private mix in pension benefits captures the full range of institutional equilibria that lie between the endpoints of fully public systems (institutional stability) and fully private benefit provision (radical restructuring). The measure also encompasses subtle but meaningful structural variations within the broad categories of pension privatization, such as the mixed, parallel, and substitutive. For example, although Argentina and Costa Rica both

---

[67] See Mesa-Lago 1997; 2003; Mesa-Lago and Müller 2002; Müller 1999.

[68] James and Brooks 2001. Also see Brooks 2002. Other indices that capture individual replacement rates for pension systems in the OECD have been developed (Allan and Scruggs 2004), as have structural pension reform indices for Latin America (Madrid 2003). The latter combines policy outputs (the share of payroll contributions to the private system) and macro-level outcomes (the share of the labor force participating in the private pension system).

[69] Where a worker's pension benefit is fully public in t_0, the public–private benefit mix in t_2 represents the extent of structural change in risk-pooling. It may reach 100 percent in systems where the average worker will receive a pension from his or her statutory payroll contributions that is based fully on his or her own savings over working life.

adopted mixed structural pension reforms, the average wage worker retiring under the new pension system in Argentina will receive a benefit that is more than half (54 percent) private, whereas in Costa Rica just 20 percent of the average wage earner's pension will derive from his or her private retirement account. Continuous variables thus have the advantage of capturing a broader range of outcomes than categorical variables do, and thus endow even modest institutional shifts with as much theoretical and empirical significance as the endpoints of stasis and radical reform. A continuous measure also broadens the range of theoretical claims that may be tested, strengthening the causal inferences that may be derived from empirical analysis of pension reform.

Despite its advantages, the public–private mix has important shortcomings as well. Principally, by abstracting away from the absolute level of income replaced, this measure fails to capture the *substantive* magnitude of benefit change that is at stake for individuals in pension privatization. While the changing balance between public and private responsibilities remains important, so too is the tangible impact of that institutional shift for the average worker – who is a voter and critical player in the political process as well.[70] Indeed, Esping-Andersen observed that "It is difficult to imagine that anyone struggled for spending *per se*."[71] Similarly, it is hard to envision political conflicts unfolding strictly around the *share* of pension benefits to be derived from private accounts, rather than around the projected benefits at stake. Indeed, it is plausible that proponents would seek to organize public debate around projections of the size of the private "nest egg" that may be accumulated in private accounts, just as opponents might emphasize the value of an individual's retirement income that would be subject to market risks.

The size of private benefits at stake in pension privatization brings attention to the *creative* dimension of structural pension reform, where new institutional forms are developed and private savings options expanded. This dimension highlights the possibilities that reformers may find to gather public support for privatization around the potential gains to be won through private savings instruments. Lastly, the substantive magnitude of the private benefits reveals new information that the more abstract public–private mix fails to capture. For instance, although the proportion of retirement benefits that were privatized in the Dominican Republic is considerably higher than in Argentina (100 percent compared to 54 percent), the size of the private benefit is *larger* in Argentina (at 35 percent of the average wage) than in the Dominican Republic (at 30 percent). Even though the Argentine reform is less private as a share of total income, there is a larger private benefit at stake in Argentina compared to the Dominican Republic. Thus it may be important to capture not just the shift in risk embodied by the changing balance between DB and DC elements of the pension system but also the substantive magnitude of private savings that may be captured at the individual level. Ideally, therefore, a measure of structural

---

[70] I thank Herbert Kitschelt for this insight.
[71] Esping-Andersen 1990, p. 21.

pension reform would capture both the structural change in risk-pooling – the share of pension benefits deriving from DC accounts – and the distributive benefits that may be claimed through the private pension system. Together, these two indices provide a more complete representation of the substance and magnitude of this multidimensional concept of pension privatization.

AN INDEX OF STRUCTURAL CHANGE ALONG TWO DIMENSIONS

I thus measure structural reform on two politically relevant dimensions. In the first, losses are imposed through the transfer of risks to individuals through self-insurance, whereas the second dimension captures the creative elements of privatization, where private savings options offer possibilities for (or at least the perception of) distributive reward.[72] These dimensions are closely linked, for much of the fanfare surrounding pension privatization revolves around the possibility for increasing the rates of return to pension contributions for individuals. Privatizers thus tout the shift to defined-contribution pension systems as one that offers the rewards of greater wealth and ownership on private capital markets, compared to the typically modest returns from defined-benefit social insurance contributions. But essential to this shift from DB to DC systems is the transfer of an array of risks, which imposes losses on the winners of redistribution in traditional social insurance systems. The latter are often those workers with low, interrupted, and unstable earnings and who therefore are less able to face alone the array of macroeconomic and demographic risks that are socialized in defined-benefit plans. Among the risks that are transferred to individuals through privatization are those of longevity (outliving one's accumulated savings and unexpected increases in life expectancy over one's working life), investment risk (the possibility of loss of savings on financial markets), and macroeconomic risks that shape the price of an annuity in retirement. Whereas these risks are shared broadly within and across generations through defined-benefit systems, they are in large measure passed on to individuals through privately managed, defined-contribution pension reforms. For proponents of privatization, these risks trade off against the so-called political risk of unexpected changes in the rules of defined-benefit pension systems that rest in the hands of elected politicians.

The Risk Transfer (Loss-Imposing) Dimension

Any measure of structural pension reform must capture the degree to which workers come to rely on self-insurance instruments for old age income protection (i.e., the extent of this risk transfer). I measure that shift from risk-pooling to individual savings through the share of the average wage worker's pension that derives from his or her privately managed DC pension account (*Percent Private*). This measure is based on a simulation of the replacement rate that an

---

[72] See Bonoli 1997, pp. 359–61.

TABLE 2.1. *Investment Volatility*

Years	Stocks: Real Total Return	Standard Deviation	15-year U.S. Bonds: Real Return	Standard Deviation	Commercial Bonds: Real Return	Standard Deviation
1871–1895	6.84	0.143	6.89	0.311	7.69	0.029
1896–1920	3.78	0.1982	−0.2	0.064	1.79	0.0568
1921–1945	9.24	0.2451	4.92	0.0904	2.86	0.0722
1946–1970	8.01	0.1759	−1.25	0.0658	0.45	0.0417
1971–1995	6.55	0.1666	3.93	0.1328	2.9	0.03.5
Overall	6.87	0.1871	2.81	0.0883	3.11	0.0539

Source: Vittas and Alier 1999, p. 37.

average-wage earner would receive from his or her private pension account, and a projection of any defined-benefit pension for which he or she may qualify according to the laws of the country.

The simulation uses the statutory payroll contributions, net of commissions and life insurance premia, that each worker must contribute to his or her private pension account according to the text of the pension reform laws in each country. A critical consideration in simulating this replacement rate is how to account for the financial risks that inhere in privately managed DC pension accounts. These financial risks entail the possibility of investment loss, which increases with the volatility of returns to private capital markets. Indeed, with the possibility of high investment reward comes the risk of loss, and thus the higher average real return to investments on equity markets. The so-called equity premium reflects the greater variability of that investment compared to safer assets such as bonds, which return a lower average yield but are much less risky. Simulations of the likely rate of return to private pension contributions thus would be incorrect to rely on approximations based on historical yields for private capital markets without adjusting those returns to reflect the risk borne by individuals.

In measuring the risk associated with different financial market investments, scholars often examine the volatility of yields for that investment – the standard deviation of annual returns. Such volatility differs markedly across each country with the depth and size of the capital market, industry concentration, and even the level of education of investors.[73] The variability of investment returns also varies across investment instruments, and over time, as Table 2.1 illustrates. This means that the real level of risk to which workers are exposed differs markedly across cohorts, even when they own similar investment portfolios in the same market. Gardner and Orszag found, for instance, that a worker in the United States who invested her retirement income completely in stocks and retired in December 1999 would have received a retirement

[73] Xing 2004, p. 84.

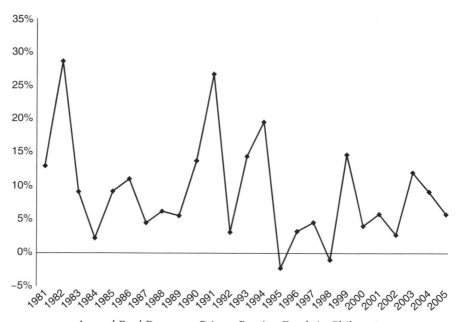

FIGURE 2.1. Annual Real Return to Private Pension Funds in Chile 1981–2005.

income twice the level she would have if she had retired in 1996. Had the same worker remained in the stock market until 2002, however, she would have been 54 percent worse off than if she had retired in 1999.[74] Statistical analysis bears out these anecdotes; Cardinale found that the equity premium is time-dependent, rather than stationary and is non-normally distributed.[75] Thus we cannot simply rely on historical trends to estimate the magnitude of investment risk to which workers are exposed through their private pension accounts. On average, moreover, developing countries experience much greater volatility in investment returns than advanced industrial countries, which is reflected in the higher real returns to investments in those markets. Xing, for instance, found that stock market volatility in the developing world was 5.4 percent (from the late 1980s to 2000) compared to 2.9 percent for the developed nations (from the early 1970s to 2000).[76] As Figure 2.1 illustrates, the volatility of returns in Latin American private pension fund investments has been much greater. Chilean pension funds have returned on average a real investment yield of 8.94 percent between 1981 and 2005; the volatility of these returns, however, has been high, at 7.6 percent.[77] Given the visible change in volatility patterns over time, such data still may not provide a reliable estimate of the long-term, risk-adjusted return to private pension funds in Latin America, let alone

[74] Gardner and Orszag 2007.
[75] Cardinale 2002.
[76] Xing 2004, p. 85.
[77] FIAP 2006.

the global sample. Investment returns thus are considerably higher and more volatile in the developing world but lower and more stable in the advanced industrial nations.

Given these dilemmas and historical variations in investment yields within and across countries, I rely on a risk-adjusted rate of return for the simulations of retirement income from private pension accounts that is considerably lower than historical averages in real investment yields on capital markets in the poor countries, and closer to those of the advanced industrial nations. In doing so, I follow previous research that takes a standard rate of return assumption for a stylized portfolio (such as 30–60–10 equities, government bonds, and corporate bonds for the developing countries, and 60–30–10 for the advanced industrial nations). Whereas Vittas and Alier assume a real rate of return of 5.66 percent for these stylized portfolios, Munnell and Sundén take a risk-adjusted rate of return of 4.6 percent for a portfolio of 50 percent stocks and 50 percent government bonds in the United States.[78] The latter rate is also used by the Office of the Actuary of the Social Security Administration in its simulation of the likely impact of privatization in the United States. I use an even lower risk-adjusted rate of return to contributions to the private pension accounts – 4.5 percent – to simulate the hypothetical return to individual pension contributions in privatizing countries. This conservative assumption, which more closely approximates the risk-adjusted returns to private pensions in advanced industrial nations, is justified by the higher volatility, and hence risk, associated with yields on investment funds in the developing world, which brings the risk-adjusted return for developing countries closer to that in the developed world. The Appendix provides the equations and further discussion of the method and assumptions for this simulation.

The Creative (Distributive) Dimension

The second measure of the dependent variable captures the distributive or creative dimension of privatization. This is operationalized using the replacement rate, or percent of the average-wage earner's income that will be replaced by the private component of his or her old age pension (*Private Benefit*). The measure uses the simulation discussed previously, taking only the private replacement rate rather than its share of the entire benefit.

The two measures are estimated for the twenty-three nations around the world that implemented structural pension reforms between 1980 and 2002 and listed in Table 2.2. The measures are also closely correlated: Where countries enact deeper privatization, the size of the private pension benefit also tends to be larger. Some countries allowed workers to choose between fully public and at least partially private schemes within their structural pension reforms, including Argentina, Colombia, Peru and Uruguay. For these countries, the pension for workers opting to participate in the fully or partially private

[78] Munnell and Sundén 2004; Vittas and Alier 1999.

TABLE 2.2. *Structural Pension Reform Outcomes*

Country	Year of Implementation	Private Benefit (% Income Replaced)	Percent Private (% Total Pension from Pension from Private Account)	Total Replacement Rate (% Average Wage)
Argentina	1994	35	54	65
Australia	1992	32	56	57
Bolivia	1997	42	92	46
Bulgaria	2002	20	37	55
Chile	1981	43	100	43
Colombia	1994	44	100	44
Costa Rica	2001	15	20	75
Croatia	2002	17	34	51
Denmark	1992	34	55	62
Dominican Republic	2003	30	100	30
El Salvador	1998	42	100	42
Estonia	2002	30	42	73
Hungary	1998	27	39	70
Kazakhstan	1998	38	100	38
Latvia	2001	34	45	76
Mexico	1997	27	91	30
Netherlands	1992	35	50	70
Peru	1993	33	100	33
Poland	1999	25	49	51
Sweden	2000	10	17	57
Switzerland	1985	30	50	60
United Kingdom	1988	18	52	35
Uruguay	1996	22	37	59

component is simulated. This is because the simulation seeks to capture the steady-state or long-term equilibrium of the reformed pension system. In most of these cases, the reforms created strong incentives for workers to migrate to the private system, which reformers hoped would eventually become the principal if not only component of the institution. In Chile and Peru, for instance, reformers used the law to effect a one-time raise in the gross pay of workers who switched to the private pension system, and additional disincentives to remaining within the public pension system were created in Peru. As a result, approximately 96 percent of covered workers in Peru have opted for the private scheme.[79] In Uruguay, most of the workforce faced the option of participating in the private pension market for part of their retirement income, which the government subsidized with a more generous DB payout for workers who took that option. In Argentina, until 2007, workers who failed to designate a choice

[79] Mesa-Lago 2005, p. 48.

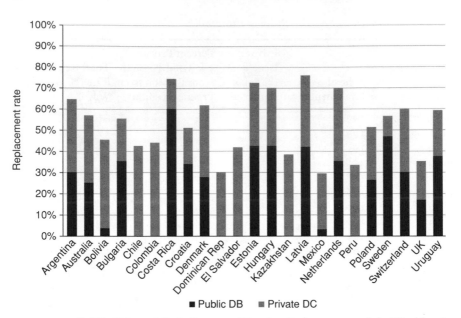

FIGURE 2.2. Public–Private Mix in Structural Pension Reforms around the World 1980–2003.

between the public and private pension systems were automatically assigned to the private pension regime for their second tier benefit. In each of these cases, the principal political battles over pension reform were fought over the terms of the private pension regime; parametric retrenchment of the public tier proved relatively less contentious. Simulations of the portion of the reformed pension system that contains the private-DC system thus offers a reasonable, albeit imperfect, portrait of the political and fiscal transformation entailed by the structural reform.

Figure 2.2 arrays the simulated public–private mix in the reformed pension systems. Figure 2.3B arrays countries according to the percentage private and total replacement rate (public and private combined), and Figure 2.3A isolates cross-national variations along the two dimensions of structural pension reform. Inspection of these dimensions of structural pension reform reveals two perceptible trends. The first is the tendency for change along the distributive and the loss-imposing elements of privatization to be positively correlated: Where the shift from risk-pooling to individualization (measured by the share of private benefits) is greater, the size of private pension benefits as a percentage of working income (the private benefit) tends to be larger as well. The second observable trend is the negative correlation between the overall size of pension benefits (total income replacement) and the degree of shift from social protection to the market (measured in the percentage private). On its face, this relationship reveals the weight of institutional legacies and the difficulty of enacting radical institutional change.

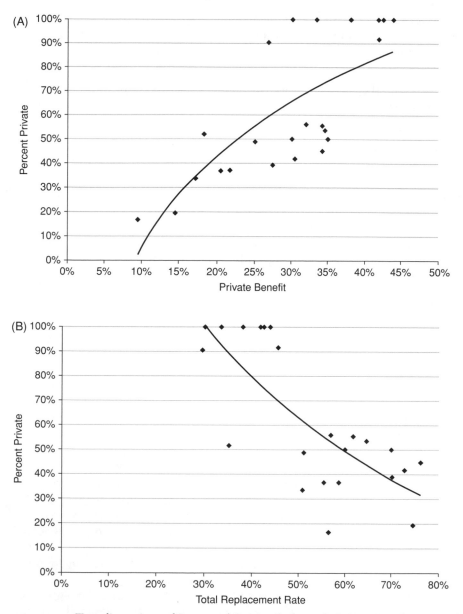

FIGURE 2.3. Two dimensions of Structural Pension Reform: A. Private Benefit; B. Total Replacement Rate.

What remains unclear, however, is precisely *how* these shifts came about and to what extent these trends are linked. In order to establish and explain these connections, and to control for potentially confounding causal influences on reform outcomes, I test the hypotheses sketched out earlier through statistical analysis of trends in structural pension reform. Such an analysis will assess how well extant theories of welfare state reform, and my alternative expectations, can account for institutional change in these two dimensions.

EMPIRICAL ANALYSIS OF STRUCTURAL PENSION REFORM 1980–2002

Explaining why some governments adopt more extensive structural pension reforms than others demands first an examination of the factors that set privatizing countries apart from other nations that do not privatize. In other words, to properly explain variations among the set of privatizing countries, we first must ask, *Who privatizes?* There are several reasons for this. The first draws from the risk that political and economic factors shaping *whether* a country privatizes also influence decisions about *how much* structural change is adopted. If that is true, then overlooking the selection process, or prior decision to privatize, would bias the analysis of variation within the set of privatizing nations in quantitative and qualitative ways. Such bias may lead us to give more importance to observed variables linked to the degree of reform and to overlook the implicit weight of those and other variables that brought the country to the point of enacting a privatization in the first place. Bias will be greater to the extent that structural reformers differ from nonstructural reformers, leading either to the discovery of differences that do not exist or to the failure to find differences that do exist.[80]

To avoid this risk of sample selection bias, I employ the Heckman selection model to estimate variations in the degree of structural pension reform adopted across privatizing countries. After identifying the explanatory variables linked to the decision to privatize, the Heckman model controls for this likelihood while evaluating the factors systematically related to variations in the reform outcome, or degree of structural pension reform. This estimator has the additional advantage of accounting for the problem of censoring, wherein our observation of the "full" set of privatizers may be limited by the scope of the time frame over which the analysis is made. Indeed, we do not know whether countries that have not privatized by the end of the observation period (2002) are likely to privatize at a later date or whether they are unlikely to privatize at all. The Heckman model accounts for such ambiguity by treating countries that have not privatized by the end of the observation period as "censored," or of unknown type, rather than assuming that they are strictly nonprivatizers.[81] Failure to account for censoring – such as in normal maximum likelihood functions – may lead to underestimation of the likelihood of privatization over the entire set of countries in the analysis, and thus would bias the analysis of critical causal variables that may be present in "late" privatizers.[82] For the

---

[80] For discussion, see Achen 1986; Brehm 1993, p. 96; Heckman 1979.

[81] See the Appendix for further discussion of this statistical model.

[82] Madrid 2003, for instance, uses maximum likelihood estimators without accounting for censoring.

TABLE 2.3. *Summary Statistics*

Variable	Observations	Average	Standard Deviation	Minimum	Maximum
Structural Reform	23	20.30	13.58	1.70	44.00
Left Party	66	0.34	0.37	0.00	1.00
Majority	63	0.60	0.15	0.27	1.00
Opposition Fragment	61	0.48	0.23	0.03	1.00
IPD	66	139.47	89.13	8.70	401.00
Age65	66	9.68	4.51	2.98	17.46
Capital Flows	63	14.38	12.29	2.09	83.43
Compliance	66	55.69	23.03	9.00	96.80
Unemployment	63	8.35	5.17	0.35	27.95
Parliamentary	66	0.93	0.97	0.00	2.00
World Bank	66	0.96	1.48	0.00	7.46
Democracy	66	2.48	1.70	1.00	7.00
Debt:GDP	58	53.14	46.05	0.44	316.71
Ln (GDP)	66	25.06	1.60	22.71	29.52

study of pension privatization, the problem of censoring is particularly important, as today's nonreformers may decide tomorrow to initiate a structural pension reform.[83] Given that scholarship must necessarily rely upon snapshots made within a finite period of time, the risk of mislabeling potential reformers as nonreformers is always present. Thus for quantitative analysis, the use of an estimator that accounts for this ambiguity – which otherwise can be discerned only through close qualitative analysis of each case – becomes essential.

DATA

Analysis of any process over a wide range of countries and significant periods of time is bound to be complicated by the dearth of high-quality data on central explanatory variables. Given the breadth and diversity of nations that are encompassed in this analysis – all member nations of the Organization for Economic Co-operation and Development (OECD), Latin America and the Caribbean, Eastern Europe, and Central Asia (see the Appendix for a list of countries and Table 2.3 for summary statistics) – the task of finding acceptable measures of key explanatory variables is a daunting one. For some variables, therefore, I must rely on rough proxies for the political, economic, and social characteristics that are expected to predict the likelihood and degree of structural pension reform across nations. The coarseness of certain measures, however, introduces a risk of measurement error that may sway the empirical analysis against the finding of significant cross-national patterns that were posited earlier. To the extent that significant relationships are found, therefore, these should be interpreted with caution, but as encouraging

[83] Hinrichs and Kangas 2003, p. 574.

signs of a connection between the underlying concept and the observed reform outcome.

Dependent Variable: Structural Pension Reform

The task of measuring structural reform along two dimensions presents a considerable challenge for empirical analysis. How, for instance, should the two dimensions be weighed? Without a theoretical basis for privileging one dimension over the other, I take the product of the two dimensions. The outcome dependent variable, *Structural Reform*, thus is calculated as the private income replacement multiplied by the percent of the average-wage earner's pension that derives from her private pension account. Such a measure, in effect, weighs the private replacement rate by its share of the total pension benefit for the average wage worker in the reformed pension system. In doing so, this measure captures both the distributive possibilities in the reform, and the extent of loss-imposing structural change.

Independent Variables

Prominent theories of welfare state reform predict that the likelihood of deep structural change is shaped variously by population aging, globalization, IFI financial leverage, the size of existing pension liabilities, and the institutional structure of legislative authority. These hypotheses are tested using the following variables.

1. **Pressure-Induced Change.** Population aging is said to increase the likelihood of structural pension reform. I measure this demographic pressure as the share of the population age 65 or older. Exposure to the forces of globalization also has been positively correlated with market-oriented pension reform. Global economic pressures are proxied first in trade exposure, or imports plus exports as a share of GDP, and through a nation's exposure to foreign capital flows, which include direct, portfolio, and other investment inflows and outflows from each country. Lastly, the pressure-induced change perspective anticipates a positive correlation between financial leverage wielded by the World Bank through its lending power and the likelihood of privatization. This source of financial pressure is operationalized as the value of World Bank and International Development Association loans and credits as a percentage of GDP for each country.

2. **Path Dependence.** Conventional views of path dependence anticipate that as the size and generosity of state pension systems increase, the likelihood of privatization declines. This institutional legacy is operationalized as the implicit pension debt, or net present value of state pension liabilities to existing workers and pensioners.[84] The IPD also approximates the

---

[84] See Van den Noord and Herd 1993; Kane and Palacios 1996; Holzmann et al. 2004. This instrument is generated using the methodology in James and Brooks 2001.

potential cost of transition from a public pay-as-you-go pension system to a fully funded private pension scheme. As the transition cost increases, the likelihood of privatization should diminish.
3. **Political Institutions.** The veto points and blame avoidance theories offer competing predictions of the effect of legislative power on the likelihood of structural reform. Whereas the blame avoidance hypothesis predicts that a greater dispersion of authority should facilitate structural change, the veto points hypothesis holds that such arrangements should inhibit the formation of majorities behind loss-imposing reforms such as old age pension privatization. I test these predictions with a variable measuring the share of seats held by the governing party or coalition, and the fragmentation of opposition parties. The former measure has the advantage also of testing the hypothesis that the executive's control of a legislative majority predicts the likelihood of privatization.

Along with the expectations from existing research, I test several alternative hypotheses of my own using the following proxy variables. To the extent that support is found for an alternative causal model of structural pension reform, I proceed in the next part of the study to develop a theory of institutional change that builds upon these expectations.

1. **Globalization's Double Bind.** I expect globalization to inhibit the adoption of pension privatization where government financing constraints are the greatest. The leeway that governments enjoy to finance the transition to a private pension system is measured in the government debt-to-GDP ratio. As this ratio increases, the financial leeway that governments enjoy to assume the transitional costs of pension privatization diminishes, and thus privatization should be less likely.
2. **Contingent Path Dependence.** To the extent that public support for a pension system declines, critical policy feedbacks that lock in a given institutional design should weaken, permitting institutional path departure. The scope of the population with a stake in the existing pension system – and thus that would be willing to fight to maintain the status quo – is proxied in the rate of active compliance with the institution. Citizens who make regular contributions are those who can expect a benefit from the existing institution. Compliance rates may also stand in for the level of public support for the basic social bargain underlying the institution.[85] As active contributors decline as a share of the working age population, the political obstacles to change that long maintained the status quo should also fall, thus making privatization more likely. Observations on this compliance variable range from 9 percent of the economically active population in the Dominican Republic to 98 percent in Switzerland.
3. **Partisan Politics.** The partisan identity of the government is expected to shape the possibilities for enacting structural pension reform. Critical in

this dimension is whether a party of the left is in a position of leadership in the legislature. Where the left is in power, pension privatization should be more likely, although the depth of such reform may be more limited than under a conservative government. To test whether such partisanship effects are mediated by the broader structure of legislative competition, I also include an index of opposition party divisions. Where opponents are more fragmented, the governing party should more easily dominate the political conflict over reform, making pension privatization more likely.

Control Variables

I control for the size of the economy, which may attenuate global economic pressures, using the natural log of gross domestic product. I also include the unemployment level in order to control for the effect of broader labor market trends on the level of compliance with the old age pension system. Controls for the broader political regime and institutional landscape take two forms. The first is a measure of whether the chief executive is a directly elected president, indirectly elected president, or leader of a parliamentary government. The second is the level of democratic freedom, which is measured as the Freedom House index of political rights.

EMPIRICAL RESULTS

The results of the empirical analysis are reported in Table 2.4. The selection model reveals that the factors shaping the likelihood of pension privatization are systematically linked to the degree of structural reform that governments adopt, confirming that joint analysis of these choices is vital to avoiding selection bias.[86]

Legislative Authority

The first two specifications examine whether the size of the governing majority independently affects the likelihood and degree of pension privatization. The lack of significance of the majority variable in the output and selection equations indicates that the capacity of a government to win support for structural pension reform is *not* given by the size of a government's legislative power. Contrary to Madrid's claim, therefore, the breadth of the governing majority not only fails to explain who privatizes but also the scope of legislative authority cannot account for differences in the extent of structural reform adopted

---

[86] The presence of such a relationship is evidenced in the coefficient on the Inverse Mills Ratio (IMR), or rho, at the bottom of Table 2.4. The magnitude, sign, and significance of the coefficient of rho indicate that there is a positive correlation between the likelihood and degree of pension privatization.

TABLE 2.4. *Predicting the Likelihood and Degree of Structural Pension Reform*

Heckman Selection Model	Specification 1	S.E.	Specification 2	S.E.	Specification 3	S.E.
Output: DV = Structural Reform						
IPD	−0.06	0.03*	−0.08	0.03***	−0.09	0.03***
Capital Flows	−0.46	0.19**	−0.39	0.17**	−0.38	0.15***
Majority	12.99	16.09	2.84	12.74	−4.56	11.75
Left Party	−8.45	5.29	−9.95	4.11**	−8.60	4.12**
Opposition Fragment	–		−34.43	9.25***	−39.36	8.29***
Const.	24.76	8.98***	49.31	9.50***	57.03	8.41***
Selection: DV = Likelihood of Privatization						
Left Party	0.12	0.48	0.31	0.52	−7.28	2.89***
Majority	−0.42	1.69	−1.17	1.81	−7.83	2.97***
Left*Majority	–		–		13.99	5.26***
Opposition Fragment	–		−2.43	1.16**	−1.84	1.29
IPD	0.03	0.01***	0.02	0.01***	0.03	0.001***
IPD*IPD	−0.0001	0.00***	−0.0001	0.00***	−0.0001	0.00***
Age65	0.27	0.09***	0.29	0.12**	0.41	0.13***
Capital Flows	0.01	0.02	0.01	0.02	0.03	0.02
Compliance	−0.04	0.02**	−0.02	0.03	−0.06	0.03*
Unemployment	−0.01	0.06	0.00	0.07	0.01	0.07
Parliamentary	−0.90	0.22***	−1.16	0.38***	−1.56	0.35***
World Bank	0.32	0.14**	0.43	0.15***	0.37	0.20*
Democracy	−0.68	0.16***	−0.57	0.17***	−0.60	0.25**
Debt:GDP	−0.01	0.00***	−0.01	0.00**	−0.01	0.00***
Ln (GDP)	0.01	0.10	−0.18	0.13	−0.09	0.20
Const.	0.004	2.60	4.88	3.07	6.50	3.69*
rho	1	0	1	0	1	0
LR test (rho = 0) Chi²	23.67		27.48		26.58	
Prob> Chi²	0		0		0	
Number of Observations	54		54		54	
Censored	33		33		33	
Uncensored	21		21		21	
Log Likelihood	−89.22		−82.99		−79.93	
Wald Chi	26.81		53.73		63.86	
Prob> Chi²	0		0		0	

*p < .1, **p < .05, ***p < .01

by privatizing governments.[87] This result is consistent with recent studies of economic liberalization in Latin America, which suggest that majority governments face stark differences in their capacities to effect structural economic reforms.[88] Without knowing *who* governs – that is, the partisan identity of officeholders – majority control of the legislature tells us little about the possibilities for meaningful institutional change.

The third specification in the selection equation tests the expectation that the partisan stripe of the governing party mediates the impact of formal legislative power on the ability to enact structural pension reform. As the first two specifications indicated, partisanship alone cannot predict whether or to what extent social insurance restructuring occurs. However, when controlling for divisions among the opposition (in specification 2), left party government becomes significant at 5 percent in the outcome equation predicting variation in the degree of privatization across reforming countries. In that equation, the negative coefficient on the left party variable confirms the hypothesis that among privatizing governments, left parties adopt somewhat less extensive institutional changes than other types of governments, all else being equal. Thus while the left has joined – and in many cases led – the movement toward pension privatization, significant partisan differences remain in the design and extent of structural change that they enact, with left governments overseeing institutional changes that rely less heavily on market-oriented designs.[89]

In specification 3, where partisanship is interacted with the size of the governing majority, the analysis confirms the joint hypothesis that it is majority power and left government that provides more favorable conditions for enacting structural pension reform. Partisanship, in other words, mediates the effect of legislative authority on the likelihood of structural pension reform. Where the largest governing party is non-left, an increase in the size of the governing majority *diminishes* the likelihood of privatization; however, increasing the size of a left-wing governing party majority *raises* the likelihood of privatization. Figure 2.4 illustrates this predicted effect. This result confirms that the governing left party must at least claim a legislative majority in order to pass legislation, as the predicted likelihood of enacting structural pension reform turns positive only when the governing party holds between 50 and 60 percent of the seats in the lower chamber. But it is only for left parties that the probability of structural pension reform rises with the size of the majority.

This result lends support to the Nixon-goes-to-China logic, suggesting that left parties may be more successful in organizing legislative conflict around the distributive dimensions of this reform – a credit-claiming logic – such as by emphasizing the potential gains to be won through privatization for which they may even claim credit. By contrast, non-left parties may be more vulnerable to an electoral backlash and accusations of loss imposition due to their lack of credibility on social welfare issues, triggering concerns for blame avoidance.

---

[87] Madrid 2003.
[88] See for example, Corrales 2002; Eaton 2002.
[89] Also see, for example, Murillo 2002.

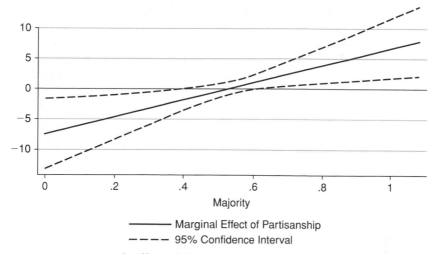

FIGURE 2.4. Marginal Effect of Partisanship on Privatization as Majority Changes Dependent Variable: Likelihood of Privatization.

This hypothesis is developed further in the next chapter and evaluated in the comparative case studies of Part III.

The variable capturing opposition divisions is negative and statistically significant in specifications 2 and 3 of the output equation, but it is significant only in specification 2 of the selection equation. Since a higher score on this index represents a more unified opposition, the result indicates that as opponents are more fragmented, the degree of structural change increases. Weak and highly fragmented opponents thus may be less able to act collectively to prevent extensive policy change. Governing parties also may be more able to draw smaller opposition parties into support for structural pension reform than they would be to negotiate with a single rival party. While this variable does not consistently predict whether reform is enacted, the significant effect in the outcome equation suggests that further inquiry into the process of legislative negotiation and bargaining over structural pension reform is warranted.

Path Dependence

The role of path-dependent forces in the privatization of old age pensions is measured first through the implicit pension debt. In order to capture any potential nonlinearity in this effect, I include the square of the IPD in the likelihood estimations. The coefficient on IPD is positive and statistically significant, while the coefficient on IPD squared is negative and statistically significant as a predictor of the likelihood of privatization across specifications. Together, these results suggest that at low or moderate levels, an increase in implicit state pension liabilities raises the likelihood of privatization, but that this effect is not linear. Rather, at very high IPD levels – where pension systems are broad

and generous – an increase in the implicit pension debt *reduces* the likelihood
of pension privatization. The effect of rising pension costs on the likelihood
of privatization thus depends on the value of those implicit pension liabilities: Policy "lock-in" does not occur until pension liabilities are very large; at
modest levels, by contrast, rising pension costs promote, rather than prohibit,
structural pension reform.

The substantive effect of this variable is also significant. Holding all variables
to their mean (except the categorical variables, where Parliamentary and Left
Party are set at 1), an increase in the implicit pension debt from 40 to 55 percent of GDP, which would be from approximately the IPD of the Dominican
Republic to that of Albania, increases the likelihood of privatization by 7 percentage points, from 11 to 18 percent. The inflection point – where policy
lock-in obtains and rising pension costs reinforce the status quo – is at 150 percent of GDP, or approximately the implicit pension debt of Switzerland. At
IPD values higher than this, "increasing returns" to the existing pension system
appear to set in as the probability of adopting pension privatization diminishes
as implicit pension liabilities rise.[90] Specifically, an increase in the IPD from 200
to 250 percent of GDP, approximately from that of Latvia to that of Slovenia,
reduces the likelihood of privatization by 27 points, from 43 to 16 percent.
Figure 2.5 illustrates this predicted effect over the full range of IPD values.

The results on the IPD variable suggest that path dependence is far from
a monotonic or linear process. Rather, the effect of an institutional legacy on
path-departing reform is highly conditional: Where pension systems are small
and less generous, rising pension costs make privatization more likely; it is only
among the more generous pension systems that the likelihood of privatization
becomes ever more remote with rising pension costs. This result provides a
bridge between the opposing findings of scholars studying the welfare state
in the advanced industrial and the developing worlds. Whereas the latter –
typically examining nations at the lower end of the IPD continuum – emphasizes
the pressures for privatization emanating from rising pension costs, the former
highlights the tremendous financial and political obstacles to privatization in
mature welfare states.[91] Both arguments thus are correct within their limited
empirical domain, even though neither holds strictly in the global analysis. Path
dependence thus may be better conceived as contingent, rather than absolute
in its effect.

The analysis also reveals a significant and negative effect of the IPD on the
degree of privatization. The negative coefficient on the IPD variable in the
output equation indicates that as the scope and generosity of the existing
pension system rise, the magnitude of institutional change that privatizing
governments adopt declines. In other words, once the decision to privatize has

---

[90] For the theory of increasing returns, see Myles and Pierson 2001; Pierson 2000a; 2001.
[91] James and Brooks 2001; Myles and Pierson 2001.

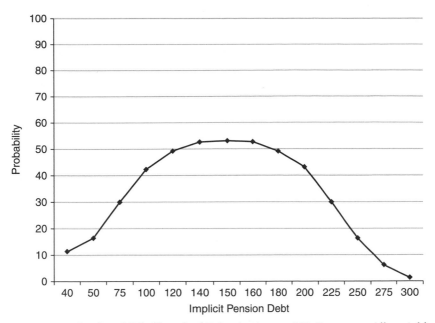

FIGURE 2.5. Predicted Likelihood of Privatization as IPD Increases. All variables are held to their mean except Left Party and Parliamentary, which are set at 1.

been made, the weight of inherited financial commitments attenuates the magnitude of institutional change toward market-based pension designs.[92] High transition costs and extensive political attachments associated with large pension systems are likely to lay behind this correlation. Thus it is reasonable to inquire further into the nature and impact of institutional legacies – both financial and political – on structural pension reform processes and outcomes.

A second approach to path dependence is captured in the compliance variable. The ratio of covered workers that actively contribute to the pension system proxies for the magnitude of stakeholders in the existing system, and thus the likely breadth of public support for the status quo design. Ideally, the analysis could capture the latter directly through attitudinal measures of confidence in the pension system. In many developing countries, however, poor enforcement capacity effectively makes compliance with social security systems quasi-voluntary, and thus to some extent compliance may predict citizens' confidence in and perceived legitimacy of the institution. Yet, for many workers, compliance is not a choice, as they either do not have access to a formal labor contract (as in the developing world) or cannot easily hide income from the tax authorities (as in most developed nations). Thus this variable most clearly

---

[92] This is consistent with a significant stream of earlier research, including Esping-Andersen 1996, p. 10; Müller 1999, p. 16; Pierson 1994, p. 54; 1996; 2001.

captures the share of the labor force that, by virtue of their contribution history, is likely to have a material stake in preserving the existing pension system. The coefficient on the compliance variable is negative and statistically significant at 5 percent in specification 1 and at 10 percent in specification 3. It thus offers qualified support for the hypothesis that as the scope of the population with a stake in the existing pension system declines, the possibility for gaining public and legislative support for deep, path-departing reform increases. The question of how shifts in public support for a pension system can work to transform this once-reinforcing political legacy of social protection is examined further in the next chapter. I consider in particular how changing perceptions of the institution's performance and fairness affect (and are influenced in turn by) efforts by strategic politicians to gather public backing for pension privatization. The credibility of a government is expected to powerfully influence the ability of reformers to redefine perceptions of the institution's effectiveness, fairness, and viability, opening the door to path-departing change.

Demographic Change

The final set of explanatory variables tests the hypotheses that pressures from globalization and demographic change impel governments to adopt market-oriented pension reform. The likelihood equations suggest that population aging has indeed brought the issue of pension privatization onto the political agenda around the world, making privatization more likely. Holding all variables to their mean (except the categorical variables, which are set to equal 1), an increase in the share of the population older than age 65 from 9 to 12 percent (approximately from the age profile of Argentina to that of Uruguay), predicts an increase in the likelihood of privatization from 4 to 30 percent. This result suggests that demographic change may generate a powerful countervailing force to the inertial mechanisms of institutional reinforcement. It does not, however, imply that privatization is a necessary or inevitable response to demographic change. As populations age, the parameters of any defined-benefit pension system must be recalibrated to account for the ever-changing balance between contributors and beneficiaries. Although aging-induced actuarial imbalances may be, and most frequently are, remedied through incremental revisions to the parameters of state pension systems, projections of financial shortfall provide reform-seeking leaders with a powerful rhetorical weapon in political conflicts over structural reform. In the face of uncertainties about the viability of state pension systems, claims of "bankruptcy" or a looming demographic "time bomb" may help to dislodge public attachments to the existing social security institution in aging nations. Where assertions of crisis gain political traction, the broader context of demographic change thus may nourish greater public tolerance for shifts toward market orientation in social protection. Given the steep aging of the world's population, we may therefore expect that the issue of pension privatization is here to stay.

Globalization

The statistical analysis provides little evidence of a globalization-induced "race to the bottom" in old age pension provision, as exposure to foreign capital flows fails to predict the likelihood of pension privatization. Among privatizing governments, however, those nations exposed to a lower volume of international capital flows on average adopt deeper movements toward private pension reform than more capital-abundant nations. This result suggests that there may be powerful incentives to adopt more private pension systems in capital-scarce nations, although exposure to global capital does not predict whether a government will privatize.

The debt-to-GDP variable tests the double-bind hypothesis that rather than simply inducing privatization, globalization may also put limits on the ability of cash-strapped governments to privatize. The debt variable proxies for the financial leeway that government actors possess to finance a structural pension reform through borrowing, which is the most common practice, without inducing international market punishment. The negative and significant coefficient on government debt supports the hypothesis of globalization's double bind. As sovereign debt burdens rise, the likelihood of adopting structural pension reform declines, all else being equal. By contrast to the view that capital scarcity raises the bargaining power of international market actors to impose or induce cash-poor governments to privatize, greater indebtedness instead makes structural pension reform *less* likely. This result reveals a critical difference in the effect of indebtedness on pension privatization as opposed to other macroeconomic reforms such as the divestiture of state-owned enterprises (SOEs). Whereas heavily indebted governments move more aggressively toward SOE divestiture, they are *less* likely to adopt pension privatization due to the latter's heavy medium-term financial cost, which typically causes government debt to rise rather than fall.[93] Globalization may help to bring pension privatization onto the agenda in capital-scarce nations by raising the salience of long-term macroeconomic goals such as increasing savings, but in the short to medium term, capital mobility raises the risk of market *punishment* for heavily indebted governments that overstep their financing constraints as a result of this reform.

The pressure-induced change hypothesis is also tested in the effect of World Bank loans on privatization decisions. The coefficient on World Bank loans is positive and significant across model specifications, suggesting that governments receiving more extensive loans from the World Bank are more likely to privatize. Even though this result suggests that countries that receive greater loans from the World Bank are systematically more likely to privatize, it is

---

[93] This rests on the assumption that the privatization is financed in some part, as it normally is, through the issuance of new public debt. See Kay 1998; Mesa-Lago 1989, p. 17.

unclear whether those financial resources represent coercion or are endogenous to a prior decision by the government to adopt structural pension reform. Moreover, it is impossible to discern through the financial resource flows alone whether the influence of the World Bank is most powerfully exercised through "hard power" coercive means – the threat of withholding financial resources – or whether the "soft power" of an attractive and well-packaged policy model that has been disseminated to middle-income countries lies behind the higher incidence of privatization among countries that receive World Bank loans.[94] The precise nature of this relationship and its causal processes represent a fecund agenda for future research.

Control Variables

Each model specification in the selection equation includes controls for the system of electing the chief executive and for the level of democratic freedoms. The coefficient on the parliamentary variable indicates that direct presidential systems are significantly more likely to adopt pension privatization than parliamentary governments are. The democracy variable is based on the Freedom House indicator of political rights, in which lower scores indicate higher degrees of democratic freedom. The negative and statistically significant coefficient on this variable across model specifications indicates that pension privatization becomes more likely as democratic freedoms increase, all else being equal. The model also controls for the size of the economy. The coefficient on the natural log of gross domestic product is negative, but in most model specifications it is not statistically significant, indicating that pension privatization is not simply a small-economy phenomenon.

THE ROAD AHEAD

The remarkable stability of old age pension systems over the course of the twentieth century provides ample evidence of the reinforcing properties of these institutions; however, the astonishing number and often-unlikely locations of pension privatization at century's end suggest that we may no longer overlook the systematic causes of path-departing change of this institution. In particular, two important questions remain open. First, how can the processes that long stabilized an institution later give way to, or become part of, processes of fundamental change? Second, what is the *political* logic of such processes when they are intentional, visible, contentious, and costly rather than automatic, unintended, or exogenously determined? How, in other words, do intrepid politicians survive such efforts with their political lives, as recent research suggests that they sometimes do?[95] To understand the privatization

---

[94] See, Brooks 2002; 2005; Madrid 2002; Weyland 2004.
[95] Castles 1998, p. 33; Hering 2003, pp. 7–10; Kitschelt 2001, p. 267; Kumlin 2002, p. 44; Ross 2000a, p. 161; Schmidt 2002, pp. 169–72.

of old age pension institutions, therefore, what we need is a political theory of institutional stability *and* change.

The empirical results of the quantitative analysis provide an important roadmap for the chapters ahead. First, the analysis identified key explanatory dimensions through which decisions about the nature and design of pension reforms are shaped, including through the partisan configuration of legislative competition, the cost and performance of existing pension institutions, and the array of demographic and economic pressures and constraints facing governments. The statistical analysis has an important place in this study of path-departing institutional change. For one, the empirical model isolates the independent effects of potential variables while holding constant the effects of other potentially confounding features of a nation's political and economic landscape. It also helps to overcome the problems of sample selection bias that may emerge from nonrandom narrowing of the set of countries under analysis either geographically or temporally, such as must necessarily occur in "small-N" comparisons, or if I had sought to understand the dynamics of pension privatization only by examining those countries that had adopted this reform. Quantitative methods also help to disentangle the systematic from random patterns of covariation in the effort to explain cross-national variations in institutional reform outcomes.

Despite these advantages and insights provided by the statistical analysis, many questions remain. Most importantly, the quantitative analysis in this chapter cannot fully specify the causal processes through which these empirical regularities emerge. Nor, given the available data, can it capture the nature or effect of strategic behavior and skillful political bargaining. The task of theory building and the development and testing of more conjunctural causal hypotheses thus still lie ahead in this study. Although we finish this chapter with a better portrait of who privatizes, and of which countries adopt more private pension reforms than others, we do not yet have answers to the fundamental questions of why and how such privatization comes about, and what causal forces lie behind the observed correlations. The next chapter takes up the task of delineating causal processes through which institutions that were long subject to self-reinforcement may be subject to path-departing change through processes that are not fully exogenous. The expectations developed there are then tested in qualitative data from structured comparisons of pension reform in Argentina, Brazil, Mexico and Uruguay.

APPENDIX

Simulation Discussion

For each country, the simulated degree of privatization utilizes the legislated contribution rate to the mandatory pension systems that can be allocated to the private component of the reformed system. This method seeks to project the private savings benefit for the hypothetical average wage worker under the rules of different pension reform models. The reasons for simulating the institutional reform design at the micro-level (i.e., for the average-wage earner participating in the private pension scheme) are straightforward. First, the architects of structural pension reform typically conceive of such institutions in terms of the share of income replaced for workers, rather than strictly in terms of the overall share of the pension provision function that will be borne by the public or private sector. On the political side, conflicts over privatization are created or neutralized on the basis of the reform's projected effects on individuals, rather than on the hypothetical reach of the private pension regime in the economy.

As in any econometric model, the results rest heavily upon the nature of the model's assumptions. In simulating the expected structure of benefits in the reformed pension schemes, I employ the following standard assumptions: (1) 35 years of payroll contributions; (2) 4.5 percent annual rate of return on investments; (3) 2 percent yearly growth in wages; (4) 20 years of retirement. Varying any of these assumptions clearly can alter the projected size of the private pension benefits for workers participating in the reformed pension systems. The simulations thus represent just one possible equilibrium outcome from structural pension reforms. Importantly, by employing the same rate of return and wage growth assumptions across the cases while allowing the statutory reform parameters to vary, any over- or underestimation of the size of private pension accounts remains consistent across the cases, and thus does not bias analysis of differences among them. As with any model, the utility of a simulation lies not in its re-creation of reality but rather in its capacity to simplify a much larger and more complex phenomenon in such a way that allows a better understanding of it. The equations used in this simulation are listed in the next section.

Simulation Equations

N_1 = number of working years
N_2 = number of years of work, without contributions
M = number of years of retirement
K = contribution rate
G = growth rate of wages
R = rate of return to capital, net of administration costs
$G_N = (1 + G)^{N_1}$ = how wages will grow over years of contribution
$R_N = (1 + R)^{N_1}$ = accumulation of interest over working years
$G_M = (1 + G)^M$ = growth factor of wages over retirement years
$R_M = (1 + R)^M$ = growth factor of interest over retirement
$C = (1 + G)^{N_1-1}$ = capital growth rate
$F_1 = (G_N - R_N)/ (G - R)$ = accumulation of funds contributed at the end
    of working years
$F_2 = (1 + R)^{N_2}$ = value of return to the contributions

$F = (F_1 + F_2)$ = accumulation value of pension fund upon retirement
$A = ((1 + R)^M - 1)/R(1 + R)^M$ = annuity (M is the annuity factor)
$PA = (K*F)/(C*A)$
PA = the yearly pension annuity deriving from the individual capitalization scheme

Statistical Model and Data

Where there is a correlation between the selection process (here, the decision to privatize old age pensions) and the outcome equation (the degree of privatization), bias may be introduced into the outcome regression estimates. This bias undermines the validity of a sample's description of the population and distorts the relationship between attributes of a population and the outcome variable of interest. The Heckman selection model offers a method of testing and correcting for such bias. This model makes the analogy of the ignored selection mechanism to the problem of omitted variable bias by including as a regressor in the outcome estimation the expected value of the error term of the censored equation (the choice of a structural or parametric reform). I use the "full information" Heckman selection model to test for such bias. In this model, the selection equation is estimated with controls for all variables expected to affect the degree of privatization, as well as the variables hypothesized to influence the likelihood of structural reform.

Because privatization decisions typically follow a significant period of technical study, drafting, and negotiation, the independent variables for all privatizing countries are taken as the average of the six years prior to the reform implementation. This period is meant to capture the political and economic context in which privatization decisions were made. For all other nations, the six-year average of 1990–5 is taken for the observation of values on the explanatory variables of interest. Since pension privatization became increasingly popular in the mid-1990s, using data from the first half of the decade allows us as well as possible to avoid the problem of reverse causality, wherein macroeconomic, political, and social characteristics of a country in the second half of the decade are influenced (negatively or positively) by the decision not to privatize social security. For the first equation, the probit analysis, nonprivatizing countries are coded 0, and countries in which privatization has occurred are coded 1. Twenty-three nations are included in the uncensored sample of countries that did privatize.

Case Selection, Variables, and Data Sources

The set of countries examined in this analysis began with all Latin American and Caribbean nations, all OECD member nations, and Eastern European and Central Asian countries. Nations from Africa, East Asia, and most of Southeast Asia are excluded for two reasons. The first is that formal pension systems rarely cover more than 10 percent of the workforce and second, when they exist, national pension systems are more commonly organized around occupational schemes and defined-contribution provident funds. The original set of ninety-three nations was narrowed further when twenty-one nations that had a population of less than 1 million were dropped. Three larger nations (Cuba, Bosnia and Herzegovina, and Yugoslavia) dropped out of the analysis due to exceedingly sparse data coverage on crucial explanatory variables, leaving a set of sixty-nine countries in the statistical analysis. The empirical models presented in this chapter have significantly fewer than sixty-nine cases in most estimations, however, due to casewise deletion of countries with missing data.

Countries Included in Reported Model Specifications[a]

Albania	Italy
Argentina	Jamaica
Australia	Japan
Austria	Kazakhstan
Belarus	Latvia
Belgium	Mexico
Bolivia	Moldova
Brazil	New Zealand
Bulgaria	Nicaragua
Canada	Norway
Colombia	Panama
Costa Rica	Paraguay
Croatia	Peru
Czech Republic	Poland
Denmark	Portugal
Dominican Republic	Romania
Ecuador	Slovak Republic
El Salvador	Slovenia
Estonia	Spain
Finland	Sweden
France	Switzerland
Germany	Turkey
Greece	Ukraine
Guatemala	United Kingdom
Honduras	United States
Hungary	Uruguay
Ireland	Venezuela

[a] Armenia, Azerbaijan, Chile, Georgia, Kyrgyz Republic, Lithuania, Macedonia, Netherlands, Russian Federation, Tajikistan, Turkmenistan, and Uzbekistan were included in the data set but dropped from reported specifications for missing data.

Independent Variables, Definitions, and Sources

Variable	Definition	Source
Age65	Population ages 65 and above is the percentage of the total population that is 65 or older.	World Bank 2007
Debt:GDP	Government debt as a percentage of GDP is the entire stock of direct, government, and fixed-term contractual obligations, including domestic debt (e.g., debt held by monetary authorities, deposit money banks, nonfinancial public enterprises, and households) and foreign debt (e.g., debt to international development institutions and foreign governments) divided by gross domestic product.	World Bank 2007
Ln(GDP)	The natural log of GDP at purchasing power parity (PPP) rates is the sum of gross value added by all resident producers in the economy plus any product taxes and minus any subsidies not included in the value of the products. GDP data are in current international dollars.	World Bank 2007
Unemployment	Unemployment refers to the share of the labor force that is without work but available for and seeking employment. Definitions of labor force and unemployment differ by country.	World Bank 2007
Capital Flows	Gross private capital flows are the sum of the absolute values of direct, portfolio, and other investment inflows and outflows recorded in the balance of payments financial account, excluding changes in the assets and liabilities of monetary authorities and general government. The indicator is calculated as a ratio to GDP in current international dollars.	World Bank 2007
Opposition Fragment	Herfindahl index of opposition parties: this is the sum of the squared seat shared of all opposition parties. Higher values indicate less fragmentation.	Beck et al. 2001
World Bank	This is the net disbursements of loans and credits less repayments of principal from the International Bank for Reconstruction and Development (the World Bank). Loan data are in current U.S. dollars, divided by GDP in current international dollars.	World Bank 2007

(continued)

(continued)

Variable	Definition	Source
Left Party	Dichotomous variable coded 1 if the largest governing party is of the Left, 0 otherwise.	Beck et al. 2001
Compliance	Ratio of contributors to working age population, where contributors are defined as workers making regular contributions to the national social security pension system.	Palacios and Pallarès-Miralles 2000
Parliamentary	Indicator of whether the chief executive is a prime minister in a parliamentary system (2), indirectly elected president (1), or directly elected president in a presidential system (0).	Beck et al. 2001
Majority	The majority is the fraction of seats held by the government, calculated by dividing government seats in the legislature by total seats.	Beck et al. 2001
Democracy	This score is the Freedom House Political Rights Score.	Freedom House "Freedom in the World" Country Ratings 1972–2004
IPD	The IPD is the implicit pension debt, or net present value of government pension liabilities to current workers and retirees. It is calculated on the basis of government pension spending, where $IPD = 30.6215 + Spend * 12.3505$, where Spend is government spending on social security and welfare as a percentage of GDP.	Calculation method from James and Brooks 2001; Spending data from International Monetary Fund *Government Financial Statistics*, various years

PART II

HOW PATH-DEPENDENT INSTITUTIONS CHANGE

3

The Institutional Transformation of Social Security

How do social institutions that have long been stable and reinforcing become subject to fundamental, path-departing change? This chapter continues the theoretical inquiry into this puzzle by analyzing three questions that are central to the politics of institutional change as it occurs in the privatization of old age pensions. The first asks how the decline in barriers to the movement of capital and goods across borders, or "globalization," has influenced the decision to launch such reforms. Even though research on social welfare reform typically views globalization as a source of inexorable downward pressures on state social insurance programs – particularly in the developing world – the analysis in the last chapter casts doubt on this conventional view by showing that it is not the most capital-scarce countries, nor those that are most financially integrated, that are more likely to privatize old age pensions. By contrast to the predominant views of globalization as *either* a source of downward pressure *or* a catalyst for compensatory expansion of social protection, I argue that globalization generates *both* incentives and constraints for governments to restructure old age pension systems; in other words, globalization places governments seeking to enact costly reforms in a powerful *double bind*. These paradoxical effects are particularly influential for the most vulnerable, cash-strapped governments. For these, global financial integration has heightened the attraction to privatization as a means to achieve long-term macroeconomic goals like raising private savings and building capital markets; however, it has also threatened to punish governments in the short term for overstepping – even temporarily – their financial means. Contrary to the view of technocrats as unflinching advocates of privatization, these insulated policy makers may respond to short-term market risks by advocating for governments to curtail, if not forego altogether, pension privatization. In the first section, I draw out predictions about when such consequences of financial integration are likely to promote and when they will impede technocratic decisions to launch a pension privatization.

The second section examines the process through which government leaders seek public support for structural pension reform – where they "sell" reform to society. On this dimension, pension privatization is considered a losing proposition for career-minded politicians: The strength and willingness of program beneficiaries to punish politicians for imposing losses has long been viewed as a powerful mechanism of path dependence that "locks" social protection programs into place.[1] As pension systems grow in generosity and coverage, such forces are said to strengthen ever more. However, increasing evidence of public acquiescence to, if not support for, privatization in democratic settings has called into question this conventional wisdom. At the same time, research on path dependence has generally been limited by its reliance on exogenous factors – war, depression, or crisis – to explain how self-reinforcing processes can be disrupted or dislodged. By contrast, I look *within* the forces of institutional stability to predict how and when these may permit, or even promote, fundamental institutional change. Even though the normative beliefs and performance expectations about an institution – its political legacy – may long underpin public support for the institution, these norms and expectations may also become levers of public support for path-departing institutional reform. Such forces also put bounds on the political strategies that may be effective in dislodging public attachments to an institution, as does the credibility of the actors engaged in conflict over pension reform. In the second section, I offer a set of expectations about the types of strategies through which public consent to deep institutional change may be won, and how partisanship underpins the credibility of such efforts.

The third section examines the final hurdle in formal institutional change processes, namely, the sanction of a reform in representative assemblies. My argument addresses two central puzzles. The first draws from the traditional claim that the political costliness of loss imposition has made the welfare state nearly impregnable to radical change. How then can pension privatization, with all the losses that it entails, be sanctioned by democratic legislatures? A second question addresses the scholarly debate over whether the politics of social security reform are better explained by the number of veto players or the possibilities for blame avoidance. The analysis in the last chapter casts doubt on the predictions of both arguments by showing that the formal distribution of legislative power alone cannot explain whether *or* to what degree governments privatize old age pensions. My argument takes a different approach to explaining both dilemmas. Because privatization entails not only loss-imposing elements, but also a creative dimension, which centers on the possibility for distributive gains through private savings instruments, I argue that multiple political equilibria are possible. Where the creative or distributive dimension is dominant in political conflict, a credit-claiming (distributive) logic may prevail in legislative processes, which may yield oversized majorities in support of loss-imposing reform. Alternatively, where the loss-imposing dimension is

---

[1] See, for example, Pierson 2001.

more salient, a veto dynamic obtains, raising the cost of forming legislative majorities behind structural pension reform. Neither dynamic will emerge necessarily perforce of the reform's objective features or of the structure of political conflict. Rather, the credibility of the governing party's efforts to enhance the distributive appearance of the reform will weigh powerfully in this process. The third section of this chapter thus examines how and when reforming governments may *induce* a distributive logic in legislative processes by diminishing the salience of losses imposed by pension privatization while playing up its creative elements. I draw out predictions as to when such efforts are likely to succeed, and examine how legislative authority and compensation may be used to build coalitions behind pension privatization in the context of a veto dynamic.

I. REFORMING WITHIN GLOBALIZATION'S DOUBLE BIND

Much attention and scholarly debate in recent years has been devoted to explaining the effect of economic globalization on the welfare state. Yet there has been surprisingly little agreement as to how, or whether at all, globalization matters. Some scholars argue that globalization has brought the expansion of social protections in response to the enhanced risks and dislocations attendant upon economic integration,[2] but some others view the international economy as a source of relentless downward pressure on state-provided social protection, particularly in the developing world.[3] Still others maintain that globalization is irrelevant to understanding transformations in social protection, which instead are rooted in domestic demographic and postindustrial economic change.[4]

In addressing this debate, I challenge conventional accounts that see globalization as a strict source of pressure either for the dismantling of the welfare state or for its expansion in response to compensatory demands. Rather, even though globalization has helped bring pension privatization to the top of the policy agenda in capital-scarce countries, financial openness also has *constrained* the ability of many cash-strapped governments to enact this deep and costly market-oriented reform. Rather than strictly conducing toward the erosion *or* the expansion of social protection, globalization's effects are better understood as placing capital-scarce nations in a powerful double bind.

Reconsidering Globalization and Pension Reform

At stake in this analysis are several theoretical propositions that have been central to contemporary research on globalization and welfare state reform. The first draws upon a rich literature demonstrating the importance of economic crisis in the initiation of structural reforms. That research has generally supported the view that poor fiscal and macroeconomic conditions create powerful

---

[2] Burgoon 2001; Cameron 1978; Garrett 1998; Katzenstein 1985.
[3] Huber and Stephens 2000; Madrid 2003; Rudra 2002; Tanzi 2002.
[4] Iversen and Cusack 2001.

pressures for governments to adopt deep structural reforms.[5] A second stream
of research has proposed that financial globalization enables capital owners to
dragoon the most capital-scarce governments to enact radical pension privatization by threatening to withhold much-needed investment resources.[6] Other
research has maintained that privatization is driven overwhelmingly by the
long-term goals of raising domestic savings and building capital markets –
objectives that are said to reflect the growing influence of neoliberal technocrats in the social policy arena in developing nations.[7] The implication of
the last argument is that only when privatization proposals leave the technocratic arenas do countervailing political pressures impose a divergence from
the market-oriented archetype.

   In many cases, however, these stylized claims do not comport with the empirical record. Not only do pension reform proposals often diverge quite markedly
from the market-oriented archetype *before* they are subject to public scrutiny,
but as we saw in the last chapter, exposure to foreign capital flows fails to predict cross-national patterns of pension privatization. Nor are the most heavily
indebted countries most likely to privatize old age pensions. By contrast to
the claims of previous research,[8] greater fiscal pressure from deficitary pension
systems cannot explain when and to what degree governments privatize. To
the contrary, I argue first that such fiscal strains place pension privatization
further out of reach in the most cash-strapped governments. Second, although
financial integration has made pension privatization attractive to governments
in capital-scarce nations, the threat of short-term market punishment may
countervail this attraction by generating even more powerful constraints on
the ability of cash-strapped governments to enact deep pension privatization.
This is likely even if such measures would be desired by market actors in the
long term. Third, I argue that financial globalization sharply curtails the time
horizon over which critical decisions relating to the design of pension privatization initiatives are often made. The result is that in the most vulnerable,
capital-scarce nations, technocratic decisions come to revolve around *short-
term* concerns of maintaining the confidence of international market actors,
often to the detriment of long-term financial and structural reform objectives.
The implication is paradoxical: Maintaining investor confidence in the short
term may entail circumscribing the extent of market orientation of the pension
system in the long term.

Technocrats in an Open Economy

In order to understand how globalization has shaped the decision to initiate
pension privatization, we must examine closely the stage of the policy process

---

[5] Drazen and Grilli 1993; Haggard and Kaufman 1992; Madrid 2003; 2005; Williamson 1994.
[6] Huber and Stephens 2000, pp. 19–20; Madrid 2003, p. 26; 2005; Mesa-Lago and Müller 2002,
   p. 710.
[7] Madrid 2003, pp. 50–1; 2002, pp. 163–4.
[8] Madrid 2003.

in which such forces are most powerfully felt, namely, the technocracy. For it is most often in the hands of highly insulated policy specialists that the formulation and design of pension reform proposals rest. Technocratic processes thus serve as a critical gateway to institutional change. In these, unelected and often unseen policy specialists filter an array of competing international policy models, weighing the broader goals of state action against the macroeconomic and political costs of their proposed solutions. In focusing on this narrow but vital component of the reform process, I temporarily set aside the broader social and political processes in order to isolate the reform arena in which global financial influences are likely to be most clearly defined. In reality, global market pressures are felt and responded to by politicians both in the executive and legislative branches, whose shared concern for macroeconomic stability and growth has made them increasingly attentive to international pressures. As agents of the executive branch, however, decisions by technocrats cannot be divorced from the broader priorities and interests of the executive branch.[9] Any model of technocratic decisions thus is part of a broader understanding of the relationship between the executive branch and international audiences.

Technocrats, simply put, are bureaucrats who possess specialized knowledge.[10] In research on pension reform, technocrats in economic line ministries conventionally have been viewed as the main protagonists behind pension privatization, and free-market reforms in general.[11] This perspective reflects a broader current of research that depicts technocrats as having gained substantial autonomy from both politicians and society as a result of a broad delegation of authority over policy making in the post–debt crisis era.[12] A common assumption in this literature is that technocrats in charge of economic reforms share a common ideological disposition toward liberal, free-market economic ideas. For other scholars, however, their embrace of liberal economic reforms owes more to intense pressures from global market actors and international financial institutions.[13] By contrast to both claims, I argue that far from being straightforward champions of global economic interests, technocrats in open, capital-importing nations may be better understood as engaging in a signaling game with global economic actors whose confidence is vital to financing the nation's economic development.

Although there is little doubt that technocrats throughout Latin America became increasingly influential in the stabilization and structural reform processes of the late 1980s, scholars disagree over whether such influence has extended into the "second generation" of social policy reforms, and whether technocrats share – much less impose – a common ideological perspective

[9] Schneider 1998, p. 78.
[10] For this definition, see Centeno 1993.
[11] Huber and Stephens 2000; Laurell 2000; Madrid 2002; 2003; Mesa-Lago and Müller 2002; Müller 1999.
[12] For example, Centeno 1997; Schneider 1998; Silva 1991.
[13] Huber and Stephens 2000; Laurell 2000.

toward policy making.[14] Madrid, for instance, has argued that technocrats espousing free-market ideals rose to the top of social security bureaucracies in Latin America, allowing them to impose the neoliberal agenda on social sector reforms. However, as Centeno has shown, it is problematic to assume that technocrats share such a common ideology.[15] Rather, Centeno finds that technocrats share only a basic cognitive framework and methodology for identifying policy problems and evaluating the best means to achieve a given ends. "Thus, rather than an ideological system that offers authoritative decisions on every policy decision," he concludes, "the technocratic mentality concentrates on shaping patterns of problem recognition, option generation and agenda placement that largely determine the eventual final choice of outcomes."[16] A more sound approach to understanding the role of technocrats in pension reform decisions thus may be to view such processes as being guided by the application of instrumentally rational techniques of weighing means and ends without ascribing a specific content to those objectives or evaluative criteria ex ante.[17]

Policy Feedbacks and Technocratic Decisions

Before a proposal for institutional change may be chosen, a new policy model must come to the attention of state actors and be perceived as an attractive reform option. At this point, a given policy model's long-term objectives and implications are likely to be most relevant in evaluative decisions. Yet, the long-term desirability of a policy is not all that matters. For once a policy model comes under closer scrutiny and serious consideration, questions of viability rise immediately to the fore as the measure's near- and long-term costs are weighed against its putative benefits. Technocratic elites exert their most crucial influence in this weighing of costs and benefits of a potential reform.

When evaluating a prospective policy change, technocrats weigh more than simply the legal and financial implications of the reform; they also consider the reaction to the policy by key constituencies. Indeed, a central proposition in research on institutional change is that reform is shaped powerfully by an array of feedbacks from existing policies. In the realm of electoral politics, such policy feedbacks relate principally to the response by organized social and political interests that benefit from the status quo. Even the most ideologically committed politicians, in this view, cannot neglect altogether the imperative of pleasing constituencies and winning votes, as reelection constitutes a necessary step in the advancement of any long-term programmatic policy goal. Politicians therefore must weigh reform objectives in light of how the measure

---

[14] For the view of autonomous and ideologically motivated technocrats, see Madrid 2003; Pastor and Wise 1999. For the opposing view, see for example Putnam 1977; Willliams 2002.

[15] Centeno 1993.

[16] Centeno 1993, p. 312.

[17] For Weyland 2007, technocratic decisions associated with the embrace of policy innovations are far from rational but rather are characterized by an array of psychological biases.

will be perceived by constituents in the next election cycle.[18] In the case of pension reform, Pierson has shown that the threat of voter reproval for imposing losses defines the essential political logic of blame avoidance underpinning social policy retrenchment.[19] The possibility of voter backlash thus creates a powerful tension between politicians' longer-term programmatic objectives and the immediate imperative of winning reelection in order to achieve those ends. In the archetypal model, the (usually multiyear) electoral cycle delimits the time horizon over which the relevant costs and benefits of policy change are weighed.[20]

In a similar way, technocrats operating in an open economy must weigh the long-term goals and expected rewards of policy change against the likely short-term responses to it by a key constituency; this time, however, the relevant audience is dominated by market actors. The economic feedbacks to state policy differ markedly, however, from those in the political realm. As Hirschman famously observed, the "exit option" provides the feedback mechanism in market contexts that is analogous to a constituent's "voice" in politics.[21] In financially open economies, the exit option can entail swift and potentially devastating capital flight. Avoiding capital flight becomes an essential short-term condition for achieving a government's long-term macroeconomic (if not social and political) objectives. Financial integration thus obliges technocrats to weigh the long-term goals and putative rewards of policy change against the likelihood that economic actors will respond to state action in the short term by moving financial resources out of the economy.

For some scholars, it is not the feedback from international currency traders and bond market actors that matters most to policy makers but rather the approval of international financial institutions that holds sway in technocratic decisions. In the pension reform literature, the World Bank has emerged as the principal source of financial incentives and punishments relating to this reform.[22] There is good reason for this emphasis, as the World Bank became the preeminent source of financial, technical, and political support for pension privatization throughout the world in the 1990s.[23] However, research emphasizing the coercive effects of the bank's financial leverage – in particular the implicit or explicit threat of withdrawal of financial support if a particular, market-oriented policy model were not adopted – is likely to overstate the capacity of this institution to intervene in domestic politics. It may also understate the autonomy and strategic capacity of domestic political actors to prioritize their policy objectives.[24] For not only are World Bank loans dwarfed

---

[18] Arnold 1998, p. 215.

[19] Pierson 1994, p. 18.

[20] See, for example, Przeworski 1991.

[21] Hirschman 1970.

[22] Cruz-Saco and Mesa-Lago, 1998; Huber and Stephens, 2000, p. 19; Madrid 2005, pp. 23–50.

[23] Kay 2000; Müller 2001, p. 69.

[24] See, for example, Nelson 1996, p. 1551; 2004; Rinne 2003, p. 35; Vreeland 2003, pp. 321–43; Weyland 2007. For other sources of international financial support for pension reform, see Dowers et al. 2001; Queisser 2000, p. 31–45.

by the vastly greater size and significance of private capital flows in Latin America, but the threat of punishment by IFIs for failure to meet specific conditions attached to development loans is quite blunt. Indeed, the latter typically entail rather slow and attenuated decisions and loans have rarely (if ever) been withdrawn for failure to enact a *specific* policy model.[25] Even if IFIs were to threaten to withhold multimillion dollar loan tranches from recipient governments, the force of such punishment would pale in comparison to the devastating consequences of multi*billion* dollar disinvestment responses by private market actors. If the withdrawal or withholding of capital by global economic actors is a critical element of policy choice in open, capital-scarce nations, then we must take seriously the feedback of private investors in response to pension reform decisions. As for the World Bank, its most powerful influence may arise from the exercise of "soft power," rather than coercion, to make pension privatization attractive to reforming governments.

Market Actors and Policy Feedbacks
Globalization has dramatically transformed the process by which government actors evaluate their options for institutional reform, particularly when it comes to the anticipation of economic feedbacks. Whereas the length of an electoral cycle typically affords politicians at least a year-long "honeymoon" in which difficult reforms can be implemented with the expectation that they will produce positive benefits before the next election, economic integration has dramatically shortened, if not eliminated altogether, this grace period. Indeed, financial liberalization allows owners of highly liquid financial assets to respond to political events on a daily or even hourly basis. At the same time, rising real interest rates have narrowed the time horizon over which real investment decisions are made, resulting in what Santiso calls "a quest for short-term profitability to the detriment of long-term investment" in emerging markets.[26] Governments that seek to attract foreign investment thus are obliged to anticipate and respond quickly to market sentiments. The result, as Santiso has shown, is that markets have imposed their more narrow time horizons on state decision making in the developing world.[27]

In addition to altering the temporality of politics, globalization has transformed the informational basis of economic feedback processes. Investment decisions typically take into consideration both an asset's prospective yield and the risk associated with that return. In regard to sovereign debt, such risks include the possibility of default or the erosion of the loan value by inflation or government policy change. Indeed, investors desire some level of assurance that the government will repay its debt, and that the investment environment will not change unexpectedly.[28] Yet, where there is substantial uncertainty over the

[25] Deacon and Hulse 1997.
[26] Santiso 2003, p. 9.
[27] Santiso 2003.
[28] Leblang 1999, p. 604; Maxfield 1997, p. 36.

future stability of public policy, it is difficult for investors to form expectations about the risk, and thus to gauge the return on an investment. In such cases, investors will either demand compensation for purchasing the asset, such as a higher interest rate premium, or they may simply withhold investment altogether.[29] Moreover, where the return is perceived to be threatened by default or inflation, credit is typically offered on a very short-term basis, allowing investors to more frequently revise their commitments and respond to changes in the investment environment.[30] Market actors thus will scrutinize both the *creditworthiness* of the government – specifically the default and currency risk it creates through state action – and the *credibility* of its policy commitments, or likelihood that the government will sustain a given course of action. For governments that rely on foreign savings to finance their nation's economic development, the desire to gain access to foreign credit on better terms (i.e., at a lower cost and longer maturity) has forced questions of creditworthiness and credibility qua its commitment to maintaining sound and stable policies to the forefront of policy-making decisions.[31]

Globalization has powerfully influenced the ways in which government and market actors have evaluated and signaled credibility and creditworthiness. On the one hand, the sharp decline in the cost of transmitting information across borders has enabled market actors to draw upon a profusion of "non-stop, real time information" in making judgments about the risks associated with government policy and economic trends in a given country.[32] Globalization has also vastly expanded the options for overseas investment. To the extent that investors take advantage of these options by achieving broadly diversified portfolios, however, they become ever less able to take advantage of the abundance of information at their disposal. Indeed, it becomes irrational to gather full information about the range of investments in a portfolio that is both well-diversified and increasingly short-term in nature.[33] Thus even though globalization has allowed investors to diversify their investment portfolios with more different and distant assets, and to revise those decisions ever more frequently, the result is that such decisions come to be guided increasingly by incomplete information, rather than by deep knowledge or expectations of the long-term performance of the asset.

Scholars have found that market actors cope with the problems of incomplete and asymmetric information endemic to overseas transactions by relying on information shortcuts such as signals of creditworthiness and the credibility of public policy.[34] Even though there are few strict or formal rules for what

---

[29] Bernhard and Leblang 2006; Mosley 2003; Rodrik 1989, p. 8.
[30] Eichengreen and Mody 2000; Kaminsky and Schmuckler 2002; Mosley 2003; Rodrik and Velasco 1999; Sobel 1999.
[31] Bartolini and Drazen 1997; Cukierman and Tommasi 1998, p. 193; Drazen 1996; Drazen and Masson 1994.
[32] Santiso 2003, p. 7. Also see Armijo 1999, p. 33; Cailloux and Griffith-Jones 2003.
[33] Calvo and Mendoza 2000; Griffith-Jones 1998, pp. 2–3.
[34] Kaminsky and Schmukler 2002, p. 171; Mosley 2003; Santiso 2003.

qualifies as a benchmark of creditworthiness, the expectations of participants in emerging markets in the 1990s converged around a set of common standards and indicators of sovereign risk. These include ratios of the government's fiscal deficit and debt burdens to gross domestic product (GDP), inflation history, and current account performance.[35] Many of these indicators are condensed further into sovereign risk ratings, published by prominent Wall Street research firms such as Moody's and Standard and Poor's. By using these indicators, market actors are able to evaluate investment creditworthiness across broadly diversified portfolios while borrowers, for their part, can use certain performance thresholds to signal their "type" – or risk status – to potential creditors. Accordingly, the risk rating criteria such as inflation, fiscal deficit, and government debt-to-GDP ratios have been transformed into critical benchmarks against which government actors evaluate policy options in anticipation of those market feedbacks. In other words, whether a policy is desirable or not has come to be gauged increasingly by its effect on the government's fiscal deficit or debt ratios – and thus market perceptions of sovereign risk – rather than solely by its domestic social or political implications.

Credibility considerations, moreover, have come to revolve around more than simply the outputs of public policy; they also entail consideration of the *processes* through which policy is made. Scholars have argued, for instance, that policy-making institutions that "tie the hands" of politicians, such as through the delegation of policy authority to an independent central bank, make state action more credible because politicians are constrained from acting on short-term interests.[36] For other scholars, simply carrying out policy change through more transparent procedures and rule-driven democratic practices inspires investor confidence. Calvo and Frenkel conclude, for instance, that a reform is credible if it is enacted through a "rule-based policy framework" that will "reduce discretion and the perception of arbitrariness."[37] Such decisions are said to be less susceptible to time inconsistency problems (i.e., where there are incentives for politicians to change direction midcourse).

Other scholars emphasize that the incursion of costs lends credibility to state action.[38] One costly maneuver through which policy makers may establish such credibility is to build domestic political coalitions in support of policy reform. Governments that enact institutional change through democratic and participatory processes, in this view, are said to offer investors greater certainty about the likely constancy of policy outputs, compared to the less costly alternative of issuing executive decrees.[39] As policy credibility has come to matter more as a means to achieve market confidence, politicians thus must anticipate that market actors evaluate not only the nature of their reforms but also the

---

[35] Cantor and Packer, 1996; IMF, 1999; Maxfield, 1997; Sobel, 1999, p. 39.
[36] Maxfield 1997, pp. 84–6; Schneider 1998, p. 78.
[37] Calvo and Frenkel 1991, p. 143.
[38] Fearon 1997; Martin 1993; Schelling 1966, p. 150.
[39] Feng 2001; Haggard 2000; Jensen 2003; Rodrik 2000, p. 141; Santiso 2003, p. 31.

processes through which those decisions are made.[40] One paradoxical implication of this argument is that by enhancing the importance of policy credibility, globalization may encourage the use of democratic procedures for policy
change, even if this entails greater compromise of reform goals (including
the market orientation of public policy) in order to signal the credibility of
the reform. Notably, this expectation runs contrary to research examining the
"first generation" of policy reform in the developing world that found that the
delegation of policy-making authority to unaccountable – but putatively more
credible – technocracies improved investor confidence and policy credibility.[41]

The capacity for market actors to respond quickly to government decisions
on the basis of short-term signals also has profoundly affected the way that
governments evaluate alternative policy actions. Specifically, as market feedback becomes more immediate, the time horizon over which technocrats weigh
the costs and benefits of a policy change has narrowed, such that the longer-
term implications of reform are discounted relative to the immediate consequences (for government credibility and creditworthiness signals) to which
owners of highly liquid assets will respond most forcefully. The goal of avoiding short-term market punishment thus should dominate technocratic decisions
in nations that are most vulnerable to capital flight. These are nations that rely
heavily on short-term and liquid capital flows, such as portfolio capital and
short-term bank loans. In such nations, technocratic evaluations of pension
reform alternatives should be shaped powerfully by the immediate effect of
competing policy models on signals of a government's credibility and creditworthiness. Whether reform will send a positive or negative signal in the short
term, in turn, depends on the financial position of the government prior to
reform (i.e., its financial leeway to assume the reform costs) and the extent
of privatization that is adopted. Before laying out the factors conditioning the
near-term market response, the next section steps back to consider where and
why privatization would reach the top of the policy agenda in the first place.

Globalization's Double Bind

If globalization only threatened pension privatizers with capital flight or higher
borrowing costs, it is unlikely that many governments would be willing to take
on the high political and financial costs of this reform. Indeed, the aggressive
movements toward pension privatization in middle-income nations suggests
that despite the costs and risks attendant on this reform, government actors
have anticipated significant rewards for their efforts as well. Several trends
coincided in the 1990s to make pension privatization attractive to policy makers in the developing world, particularly in Latin America. The first is the
unprecedented volatility of capital flows that followed the liberalization of

---

[40] Eatwell 1996, p. 38.
[41] See, for example, Bates 1994; Geddes 1994. It is consistent, however, with Keefer and Stasavage
2003; North and Weingast 1989.

capital accounts in the late 1980s and early 1990s. The tremendous cost of exposure to surges, sudden stops, and swift reversals of global capital flows turned the attention of policy makers toward the reduction of their nation's dependence on foreign savings. At the same time, economic research linked the long-elusive goals of high and sustained growth to higher domestic savings. When the World Bank, among other prominent actors, touted pension privatization as a means to raise domestic savings and deepen local capital markets, governments in capital-scarce nations took notice. And as peer countries increasingly demonstrated that this measure was appropriate for a country like their own, technocrats could more confidently expect pension privatization to be a viable solution to their domestic pension reform challenges. All of these factors increase technocrats' attraction to this policy model.

Volatility and Dependence

Following the massive outflows of capital from developing regions in the 1980s, investment returned to emerging markets in the 1990s. This time, however, capital came in the form of short-term portfolio investment – bonds and equities – rather than the more stable and long-term forms of direct investment and official loans that dominated earlier periods.[42] The vertiginous flows of new investment in the early 1990s rendered large portions of developing economies subject to the vagaries of increasingly volatile global capital markets and to fragile investor sentiments. Developing country governments learned the hard way just how costly the loss of investor confidence could be, as the social and economic costs of capital flight reverberated heavily in prolonged recession and deepening poverty. Vulnerability to foreign investment outflows thus became a highly salient concern for policy makers in capital-importing nations, orienting public policy objectives toward efforts to diminish reliance on foreign capital in the long term, and to retain investor confidence in the short run.[43] Since pension and insurance funds are among the most stable value- and diversification-oriented investors, governments that were most vulnerable to capital flight became keenly interested in developing their own private pension markets as a source of long-term or "patient" capital. Pension privatization thus came to be seen as a means to buffer middle-income economies from the costs and risks of dependence on foreign savings in the long term.

The Quest for Growth

Related to the desire of developing country governments to diminish their reliance on foreign investment was the long-elusive goal of achieving strong and sustained economic growth. Low growth and capital shortages had come to be seen as constraints on domestic investment following the 1980s debt crisis. That event, which has been compared to the Great Depression as a turning point in economic policy making in Latin America, provided an all too

---

[42] Armijo 1998.
[43] Calvo et al. 1996, p. 124.

vivid symbol for Latin American governments of the perils of foreign capital reliance.[44] The result was to deepen the resolve of policy makers to avoid the recurrence of such a devastating crisis.[45]

Just as technocrats throughout Latin America were seeking remedies to the problem of unstable growth and low savings, endogenous growth theories pointed to the potential link between higher savings and growth.[46] The goals of diminishing reliance on foreign savings and raising home-grown capital accumulation came to be viewed as means to achieving high and sustained growth – and to avoiding a return to the economic calamity endured in the 1980s. Thus when pension privatization was touted as a way to raise savings and growth, technocrats came to view this reform as a powerful policy tool with which to achieve these desirable long-term macroeconomic goals.

The link between pension privatization on the one hand, and savings and growth on the other, was promoted most visibly in the 1990s by the World Bank. With the publication of its 1994 report, *Averting the Old Age Crisis: Policies to Protect the Old* and *Promote Growth,* the World Bank radically transformed the way that policy makers around the world approached the question of old age pension reform. The report contained an array of normative and political justifications for pension privatization, including the improvement of compliance incentives and claims about its macroeconomic implications – including that pension privatization would promote financial market development and economic expansion.[47] In doing so, the World Bank changed the way that the problem of pension reform was conceived; rather than being viewed solely as a social policy challenge, the issue became linked closely to macroeconomic and microeconomic goals. The report also expanded the repertoire of policy tools through which reformers began to address financial and actuarial imbalances in state pension systems; rather than simply recalibrating the parameters of existing institutions, the fundamental transformation if not replacement of state pension programs with private sector instruments became viable alternatives. By the end of the 1990s, *Averting* had become the foundational text for state actors facing the challenge of old age pension reform around the world.[48]

In this sense, the World Bank's most powerful means of promoting the adoption of pension privatization may have been through the exercise of what Keohane and Nye call soft power, or "the ability to get desired outcomes because others want what you want . . . through attraction rather than coercion."[49] Such power, they argue, can derive from the appeal of one's ideas, or from the ability to set the agenda and to shape the preferences of others. The World Bank certainly enjoyed the advantages of status and resources with

[44] Edwards 1995.
[45] Solís Soberón and Villagómez 1997, pp. 107–26.
[46] Dornbusch and Reynoso 1989, pp. 204–9; Guitián 1997, pp. 17–32; Solís Soberón and Villagomez 1997; Williamson 1990, pp. 13–16.
[47] James 1995, p. 7; Valdés-Prieto 1998, p. 10.
[48] Brooks 2004.
[49] Keohane and Nye 1998, p. 86.

which to make its ideas heard around the world. These may have given the bank an edge in disseminating its ideas over competing paradigms, such as the recalibration of social insurance models promoted by the International Labour Organization.[50] Yet, for governments that were struggling with the questions of raising savings and growth, it was likely to have been the *content* of these ideas, namely, the packaging of pension privatization as a means to achieve higher savings and growth – rather than the financial incentives that underwrote them – that made this reform so appealing. Indeed, considering that the transitional costs of pension privatization can run to multiple percentages of a nation's GDP per year and that World Bank loans to support this reform amount to a mere fraction of that, international financial institutions could provide little in the way of direct material incentives to make privatization of old age pension systems *financially* attractive to cash-strapped governments. Enacting the reform, even with IFI support, would still impose a tremendous financial burden on governments in the medium term.

Peer Diffusion

The general terms in which the World Bank report was written, however, did little to suggest the appropriateness of pension privatization for any specific nation. Rather, confidence in the suitability of a costly innovation like pension privatization was likely to have drawn more heavily from country-to-country peer diffusion.[51] In this process, policy makers observe the decisions made by similar countries and use this information to dispel uncertainty about untested policy innovations. For policy reforms that are costly, like pension privatization, information from peer governments may be particularly valuable in resolving uncertainty about the measure's viability.[52] As more peer nations enacted pension privatization, technocrats could be increasingly confident in the appropriateness and feasibility of this measure in their own country.

Pension privatization also provided an important credibility signal for governments concerned about investor confidence. Having been endorsed by the World Bank, pension privatization became associated with the "Washington Consensus," or market-oriented reform orthodoxy.[53] The high costs of pension privatization also were likely to have enhanced its appeal as a credible signal of the government's commitment to market-oriented reform.[54] Indeed, the paroxysm of acclaim lavished on early reformers such as Chile and Argentina was likely to have enhanced the perception by government actors that enactment of this reform would bring important market rewards to reforming nations.[55] The

---

[50] Brooks 2005, p. 278.
[51] Brooks 2005; Weyland 2005a; 2005b; 2007.
[52] Brooks 2007.
[53] LoVuolo 1996; Müller 1999; 2003, p. 12.
[54] Brooks 2007; Fearon 1997; Martin 1993.
[55] See, for example, Becker 1996; "Save, Amigo, Save" 1995; Edwards 1996; "World Financial Markets" 1997; Piñera 1996.

fear of "missing out" on investment or, even worse, being punished by international market actors for failing to keep up with peer nations thus may have lent further stimulus to the embrace of pension privatization among capital-importing nations.

Globalization thus created powerful incentives for capital-scarce governments to place pension privatization on the reform agenda. Privatization thus should be more attractive to technocrats in capital-importing nations than to those with higher savings and more developed domestic financial markets. It should also be more attractive to governments with open economies that rely heavily on liquid foreign capital flows, and to governments whose peer nations have enacted this reform.

Globalization's Constraints

Along with these potential rewards, globalization has generated powerful constraints on the ability of some governments to enact pension privatization. These constraints arise from the risk of losing investor confidence – and thus of incurring punishment in the form of capital flight or higher borrowing costs – following the enactment of this measure. The risk that such punishment occurs should depend on three basic factors: (1) the size of the fiscal gap imposed by privatization in the medium term (i.e., its transition cost); (2) the financial leeway, or resources available to the government to close that fiscal breach; and (3) the government's vulnerability to short-term capital flight.

Transition Costs

Recent research on structural pension reform has focused attention on the cost of the transition from a public pay-as-you-go pension system to a private, fully funded scheme.[56] Such costs arise as the current generation of workers begins to divert payroll contributions from state coffers to their privately managed individual accounts, forcing governments to relinquish this critical source of revenue with which to finance ongoing pension liabilities. The magnitude of this financing gap varies with the inherited cost of old age pensions (the implicit pension debt), as well as with the magnitude of the explicit debt and financial deficit in the old pension system.[57]

Transition costs also depend on the extent of privatization that is enacted. Where much or all of the responsibility for old age pension provision is privatized, the financing gap created by this measure can be enormous. Even in Chile, where the implicit pension debt at the time of privatization was relatively low by international standards, at 100 percent of GDP, the budgetary cost of the transition to that nation's fully private system exceeded 4 percent of GDP per year in the first decade after the reform.[58] Governments may cover this

---

[56] Brooks 2002; James 1998; Kay 1998; Madrid 2003; Müller 2003; Myles and Pierson 2001.
[57] James 1998; James and Brooks 2001.
[58] Congressional Budget Office 1999, p. 18.

financial deficit in a variety of ways (e.g., through spending cuts, tax increases, or the issuance of new sovereign debt). Since the imposition of a "double payment" burden – obliging working citizens to finance their own pensions and those of the previous generation – is often politically unpopular, the two most common means of financing the transition to a private pension system are through the use of fiscal resources and the issuance of new sovereign debt.

Financing Leeway

A government's ability to finance the transition to a private pension system through additional indebtedness or by expanding the fiscal deficit is not unlimited. Governments that carry higher sovereign debt burdens (as a share of GDP) present a greater risk of default to market actors, and a large fiscal deficit is taken as a signal of inflation risk.[59] Where governments overstep the threshold of acceptable debt and deficit ratios, access to international credit may be curtailed and, if available, will become more costly. Fear of inflation or default may also trigger capital flight. Importantly, it is not the absolute increase in government debt or deficit per se that threatens such market punishment; rather, it is the overall levels (relative to GDP) to which these risk indicators rise that matters. Indeed, a 10 percentage-point rise in government debt as a share of GDP will have very different consequences for high- and low-debt countries. For the latter, the impact of financing the transition to a private pension system is unlikely to spark market fears of default, whereas for governments already carrying a high sovereign debt, the additional burden may indeed spur such concerns. Whether or not a government risks market punishment in response to the financial toll imposed by privatization thus depends heavily on the government's financial position *prior* to the privatization. Governments with access to strong cash flows (such as those enjoying a fiscal surplus or revenue from the privatization of state-owned enterprises) and with a low debt-to-GDP ratio thus should enjoy greater leeway to finance a costly transition to a private pension system without risking market punishment in the medium term.

It is important to emphasize that the critical risk posed by privatization is not that investors will respond negatively to the policy decision per se, nor even to its cost. Indeed, the "cost" of transition is largely a relabeling of implicit pension liabilities as explicit debt, which are equivalent from an intertemporal budget perspective. Rather, at issue are the risks arising when investors do not take the long view in their evaluations of investment decisions. In such instances, investors may respond to a short-term rise in explicit government liabilities through risk-hedging behavior such as capital flight, even if such costs are assumed in the service of long-term market-oriented goals. Where investors' time horizons are short, therefore, a government carrying a high debt burden prior to reform may face an increased risk of market punishment for assuming the transitional cost of pension privatization, compared to a similar government that privatizes with a low debt-to-GDP ratio, all else being equal. The leeway

[59] Eichengreen and Mody 2000, p. 22.

that governments enjoy to finance the transitional cost of privatization thus is at least as important as the transition cost itself in determining the viability of this reform in open, capital-importing countries.

Vulnerability

The force and likelihood of market punishment varies moreover with the vulnerability of the economy to capital flight. Vulnerability in this context refers to a nation's reliance on foreign capital – both to supplement the domestic capital stock and to support ongoing economic activity. It also depends on the economy's reliance on highly liquid forms of investment to finance their current account liabilities. For such nations, the use of public policy to signal credibility becomes all the more important.[60] Indeed, capital flows respond more vertiginously to short-term changes in perceptions of creditworthiness in countries that are considered to be a high risk, such as developing nations; the range of policy areas about which market actors evaluate such nations is also broader.[61] Accordingly, policy makers in countries that are vulnerable to capital flight should weigh the short-term market responses to state action more heavily than longer-term consequences of a policy. Such short-term signaling concerns, paradoxically, may lead the countries that are most vulnerable to capital flight to curb pension privatization or to forego such a reform altogether.

This prediction may seem illogical from the long-term perspective, particularly since pension privatization is a measure that market actors typically prefer. It also runs contrary to the claim that the more financially pressed (under the strains of costly and deficitary state pension systems) and low-savings countries are those that are more likely to privatize.[62] My expectation, however, rests on the premise that market actors, and hence government actors in capital-importing nations, operate under narrowed time horizons in the context of financial openness.[63] Where investment time horizons are short, it is instrumentally rational for capital owners to exit in response to the near-term erosion of government creditworthiness indicators; and thus it may be just as reasonable for government actors to respond to near-term incentives by subordinating long-term structural reform goals in order to maintain investor confidence.[64] And as mentioned previously, maintaining such confidence in the short term is a necessary condition for achieving many developing country governments' macroeconomic goals in the long term.

Examples abound of strategies that achieve market confidence in the short term but that make little economic sense over the longer term. Rodrik has shown, for instance, that credibility problems can prompt capital-importing

---

[60] Maxfield 1997.
[61] Kaminsky and Schmukler 2002; Mosley 2003.
[62] See, for example, Madrid 2003; 2005.
[63] Santiso 2003.
[64] Indeed, scholars have shown that credibility problems are equivalent in practice to a distortion in international relative prices. Calvo and Frenkel 1991.

governments to enact even more radical market-oriented reform than may be called for in a given circumstance.[65] Efforts to win market confidence in the short term can even be quite damaging economically in the medium to long term (e.g., where governments in developing countries raise interest rates in the face of capital flight).[66]

Efforts to signal policy credibility in the short term through the use of political processes also may result in the compromise of key government policy goals in the longer term. This would be the case, for instance, where the task of winning democratic sanction of a reform obliges a government to accept extensive compromises in the measure's market orientation in order to appease opponents. For governments struggling to establish credibility in the eyes of international audiences, however, such a strategy makes sense as a means to signal the permanence, and hence credibility, of the policy course. Where governments seek to win market confidence by enacting pension privatization democratically, rather than by decree, the long-term market orientation of the institution is likely to be compromised. Once again, long-term policy goals would be traded for the short-term economic objective of securing investor confidence. Where short-term credibility concerns are dominant, therefore, globalization may have the paradoxical effect of leading governments to take steps that curtail, rather than expand, the role of markets in reformed pension systems.

Even though technocrats charged with designing old age pension reforms may care deeply about long-term "good policy" objectives, this argument suggests that globalization has confronted them with a powerful time inconsistency problem: In order to maintain the confidence of footloose capital in the short term, technocrats face strong incentives to divert from a long-term market-oriented reform strategy. As a consequence, the poorest and most vulnerable governments may be *less* able to undertake costly structural reforms such as pension privatization without the near-term risk of market punishment. This may be true even if the same countries may be most powerfully attracted to privatization on account of its putative long-term effects, and if capital owners would prefer such a reform in the long run for the same reasons.

Summary and Expectations

James Carville, adviser to U.S. President Bill Clinton, is said to have once remarked, "I used to think if there were reincarnation, I wanted to come back as the President or the Pope or a .400 baseball hitter... but now I want to come back as the bond market. You can intimidate everybody." If any government in the world should enjoy broad latitude to carry out domestic policy decisions without concern for the feedback of market actors, it should be the United States. Yet, even with the world's largest economy and the benchmark

[65] Rodrik 1989, p. 758.
[66] Krugman 1998, p. 113.

"risk-free" sovereign debt, U.S. government actors worry about market responses to domestic policy decisions. Markets are likely to be even more intimidating to capital-scarce countries whose economic stability rests on the capacity of the government to gain – and hold – investor confidence. Such intimidation has conventionally been viewed as a catalyst for more extensive market-oriented reform in capital-scarce countries. My argument, however, suggests that this link is far from straightforward. Rather, globalization has paradoxical implications for the privatization of old age pensions. On the one hand, the volatility and vulnerability that globalization has created enhances the appeal of pension privatization to capital-importing nations as a means through which to reduce their reliance on foreign savings in the long term, and to signal their credibility in the short term. Yet, because pension privatization also may compromise a government's performance on key sovereign risk indicators in the short to medium term, globalization may present the most vulnerable, cash-strapped governments with a *higher* risk of capital flight in response to the immediate financial toll imposed by this measure as debt and deficit levels rise. Avoiding short-term market punishment may oblige pension reformers to limit the extent of privatization, or avoid the enactment of this reform altogether. Even though threats of market punishment clearly do not determine the outcomes of domestic policy processes, my argument suggests that the market's reach extends far beyond the typical conceptions of competition and efficiency-oriented pressures on state policy choice. The result is that globalization's effects may be evidenced both in what governments do and in what they fail to do.

II. INSTITUTIONAL LEGACIES AND POLITICAL STRATEGIES

Path dependence means history matters.[67]

History is what you make of it in a particular situation.[68]

The remarkable stability of state social welfare institutions throughout the second half of the twentieth century has spawned a prolific body of research on the political and economic forces that explain such persistence. By identifying and explaining how institutions become "path dependent," dominant research in this vein has answered important puzzles as to how mature and generous welfare states have largely withstood the buffeting of demographic and economic change in the final decades of the twentieth century. But a critical lacuna remains: Even though theories of path dependence effectively explain institutional survival, they have great difficulty accounting for the uncommon, but highly consequential, moments in which a change in the structure and ends of an institution *does* take place, such as in the privatization of old age pensions. Most

---

[67] North 1990, p. 58.

[68] Isocrates (436–338 B.C.) was a teacher of rhetoric, and taught of the importance of oratory in power and communication. Human nature, he argued, is distinguished by the ability to speak, and that speech imparts power in politics. See Isocrates 1968.

often, such path departures are taken to be the product of exogenous shocks that disrupt one self-reinforcing process and initiate another.[69] The next step for this research, then, is to build upon existing insights to provide a theory of path-dependent stability *and* change, particularly where such transformation entails a fundamental departure from a hitherto stable and self-reinforcing path.[70]

In seeking to understand how the mechanisms of path dependence can bridge the processes of institutional stability and fundamental change, I argue that a critical source of institutional reproduction resides in the set of tightly held beliefs about what the institution can and should do (i.e., what is a fair bargain in that society) and the associated set of perceptions about whether the institution is living up to these local expectations and standards. An institutional legacy, in this sense, comprises much more than simply the scope and generosity of program benefits; it also entails the more dynamic inheritance of shared beliefs and expectations – what may be considered the *political legacy* of the social institution. Although these beliefs and expectations are relatively stable, they are also mutable. And it is in their changeability that I find a critical window onto how the forces of institutional reproduction can long uphold a given social bargain, but later permit, or even promote, path-departing change. Specifically, perceptions of institutional performance – how well it is living up to local standards – may be revised in the face of new information about the institution, even when citizens themselves cannot verify these facts in their daily lives. Beliefs about what constitutes a fair bargain or good institutional performance, moreover, also may be subject to revision as a result of new ideas and standards transmitted through the use of ideological rhetoric in political conflict. Even where such beliefs and expectations remain stable, changing perceptions of institutional performance may transform the *effect* of this political legacy from a mechanism of institutional reproduction, to one that is supportive of institutional change.

To address this question, I focus on the political process of contestation over shared beliefs and perceptions of social welfare institutions. Such contests provide significant – but bounded – opportunities for strategic, reform-seeking politicians to *induce* a critical juncture in a once stable and reinforcing process of institutional development, opening up a window for path-departing change. Where such shifts in public sentiment occur, they may swing political power in favor of advocates of change. But political strategies seeking public support for institutional reform may also fall flat, and rhetorical efforts to alter perceptions of an institution's performance or fairness may ring hollow. In this sense, whether a given political legacy is consistent with fundamental reform is highly contingent. It is, however, a *structured contingency*. I thus explore in this section the conditions under which path departure is likely to result from

---

[69] For the concept of path departure, see Ebbinghaus 2005, p. 17; Hering 2003; Mahoney 2000.
[70] See Thelen 1999; 2004.

strategies aimed at winning support for change in what long were stable and self-reinforcing institutions.

The premise that institutional legacies and the attendant possibilities for institutional path departure may not be bound strictly to the institutional design finds initial support in the quantitative analysis in Chapter 2. That analysis suggested first that the effect of the inherited cost of pension liabilities weighs differently on the likelihood of privatization at very high and very low values. It also revealed that privatization decisions covary with rates of active compliance with the old age pension system: As compliance declines, the likelihood of privatization increases. To the extent that compliance, or acquiescence to the rules of an institution, may be taken as a signal of citizens' confidence in the fairness and effectiveness of a social institution (particularly in developing countries where weak enforcement makes such compliance quasi-voluntary), we have reason to probe more deeply the possibility that such beliefs and perceptions provide critical mechanisms of both institutional stability and path-departing change.

Mechanisms of Institutional Stability

If we are to understand how once-stable institutions give way to fundamental path departure through processes that are not fully exogenous, we must begin by examining the mechanisms of institutional reproduction. Previous research has yielded tremendous insights into this process. In particular, Pierson's studies of the advanced industrial welfare states have been foundational.[71] Once created, Pierson demonstrated that the welfare state dramatically transforms its political milieu, giving rise to new expectations and beneficiaries that hold sway over welfare state politics. These forces delimit both the possibilities for institutional change and the political strategies through which such reform may be successfully pursued.[72]

One critical element in this process, according to Pierson, is the behavioral tendency toward *negativity bias*, which disposes beneficiaries of the status quo policy to mobilize more forcefully to avoid loss than to achieve commensurate gains. Accordingly, he argues, the immediacy and concentration of reform costs, along with the delay and dispersion of its benefits, privilege the mobilization of an institution's beneficiaries in political conflicts over policy change.[73] As beneficiaries of the welfare state constitute an increasing share of the electorate over time, the task of marshalling the political resources to overcome such antireform mobilization makes significant policy retrenchment ever more unlikely.[74]

[71] Pierson 1994; 1996; 2001.
[72] Pierson 1994; 1996; 2001; also see Pierson and Weaver 1993; Weaver 1986.
[73] Pierson 1994; 2001, p. 413.
[74] Myles and Pierson 2001, p. 305; Pierson 1996; 2001.

A second critical source of institutional reproduction is the tendency toward *adaptive expectations*. Where such tendencies dominate, Pierson argues, "individuals feel the need to 'pick the right horse' because options that fail to win broad acceptance will have drawbacks later on."[75] As broad public expectations converge around existing institutions, the maintenance of such programs becomes self-fulfilling and the possibilities for change ever more remote.[76] Adaptive expectations thus contribute in this view to the reinforcing characteristic of "increasing returns" to certain institutions such as old age pension systems. Programs that are subject to this dynamic also tend to have large setup costs that increase the cost of change over time. Accordingly, not only do alternatives to the status quo institution become ever less attractive as time goes by, but they also become more costly to achieve relative to the current design. Even for citizens who may be poorly served by existing institutions, Pierson argues, the opacity or *murkiness of politics* complicates the task of identifying viable alternatives to the status quo.[77] Given the complex and multidimensional nature of welfare state issues, a dense political haze is said to hinder most citizens from independently evaluating the performance of existing institutions or discerning alternatives, much less devising specific means to achieve those ends.[78]

Path-dependent processes thus make institutions quite tenacious and self-reinforcing; indeed, they are said to account for the ability of social welfare institutions to withstand the tremendous pressures of postwar demographic and economic change. But can these sources of institutional stability – negativity bias, adaptive expectations, and the murkiness of politics – be transformed from mechanisms of institutional reproduction into instruments of path-departing institutional change? I expect that they can. In particular, public satisfaction with the status quo may be transformed through the political process where strategic political actors dislodge public attachments to the institution in such a way that permits, if not promotes, deep, path-departing reform.

Rethinking Institutional Legacies

Even though institutional legacies claim a central role in theories of institutional transformation, analysis on this level has been confined largely to structural features of an institution, such as the scope and generosity of its benefit promises. But these features are unlikely to fully encompass an institutional legacy, particularly in the case of the welfare state. For along with formal rules, sanctions, and promised benefits, social policy institutions are upheld also by a system of shared beliefs.[79] Indeed, for some scholars, beliefs *are*

---

[75] Pierson 2001, p. 415.

[76] See also Arthur 1994; Pierson 2000a, p. 259; 2001, p. 415.

[77] Pierson 2000a, p. 257.

[78] Pierson 2000a, pp. 254, 260. See also Myles and Pierson 2001, p. 312; Pierson 2000b, p. 489.

[79] Baldwin 1990, pp. 5–10; Levi 1990; 1997; Rothstein 1998, pp. 134, 222; Svallfors 2002, p. 184.

institutions.[80] Research on the welfare state has highlighted two types of beliefs that serve at once as critical stanchions of the welfare state and as powerful by-products of it. The first type encompasses shared standards of fairness, moral principles and concepts of distributive justice that inform beliefs about what an institution *should* do; the second type consists of expectations about what the state *can* do, and what constitutes an acceptable institutional product.[81] Together, these normative beliefs and performance expectations make up an important dimension of an institution's inheritance that I call its *political legacy*.

Just as beliefs and expectations provide an important source of institutional reproduction, they also may become mechanisms of institutional transformation. For as recent scholarship has shown, when beliefs associated with an institution change, the institution itself may be transformed.[82] Beliefs, and thus institutions, are said to change where new information and ideas are introduced into the political arena, resulting in the change of behavior or action associated with an institution. Scholars working in this vein differ, however, over whether changes of belief and behavior are rational and endogenous, or contested and constructed.

For Levi, the belief that the basic social bargain underpinning an institution is fair, and that others are complying with it, provides the basis for "contingent consent."[83] Such consent, she argues, underpins behavior supportive of the institution, namely, compliance, whereas the erosion of consent – and thus compliance – leads to the weakening of the institution, opening up the possibilities for institutional change.[84] Consent may erode when new information makes citizens aware of circumstances of which they were previously unaware, such as the failure of others to comply with the institution or the introduction of new ideologies that alter beliefs about the acceptability of a social bargain.[85] In this view, then, the introduction of new ideas and information through the political process can transform perceptions and beliefs that once upheld the institution, leading to action that opens the door to institutional change.

The acquisition of new information also underpins belief change in Greif and Laitin's endogenous model of institutional change. For them, belief change occurs when individuals compare institutional outputs with expectations and find the former to have fallen short of the latter.[86] Institutional change thus emerges endogenously from an institution's effect on previously exogenous

---

80 Greif and Laitin 2004.
81 Bergmark et al. 2000; Grindle 2000; Myles and Pierson 2001; Pierson 1994; Rothstein 1998. For the view that social institutions rest on normative and instrumental foundations, see Keohane 2001; Levi 1990; 1997; Ostrom 1990; 1998.
82 Blyth 2002; Denzau and North 2000; Greif and Laitin 2004; Levi 1990; 1997; Myles and Pierson 2001.
83 See Levi 1990; 1997.
84 Levi 1990, pp. 409–10.
85 Levi 1990, pp. 410–11.
86 Greif and Laitin 2004, p. 639.

parameters such as knowledge and beliefs about an institution, which are revised in the face of new information. For Greif and Laitin, when belief change leads to shifts in behavior that no longer reproduce a given institution, the institution itself is transformed. In this model, new information is not transmitted through the political process but rather through individuals' direct experiences with an institution.

Belief change is also central to research on ideas and institutional change. In this literature, however, conflict over beliefs make up the principal arena of institutional change. For Blyth, institutional change requires that political actors, "argue over, diagnose, proselytize and impose on others" a particular interpretation of the problems that beset an institution.[87] Ideas in this view dispel uncertainty, defining interests and mobilizing actors around support for a new institutional design. The notion that political discourse can dramatically alter interests associated with entrenched institutions has found broad support in comparative research showing that the language, symbols, and ideas used to present political issues can influence the shifts in broad public support behind improbable institutional reforms.[88] Important questions remain, however, about the ways in which politics can influence beliefs in the process of institutional change. Most critically, the bounds within which one interpretation of a political situation may be effective in transforming beliefs over a given set of outcomes remain unclear. *When*, in other words, can politically transmitted information and ideas alter citizens' beliefs and behaviors associated with an institution in ways that give way to fundamental change?

For Greif and Laitin, belief (and hence endogenous institutional) change occurs only exceptionally because the attention that most individuals give to self-enforcing institutions is limited, and "those who observe [the divergence between expectations and outcomes] and can bring it to the attention of others may not have incentive to do so."[89] Yet, what if individuals in power *do* have motive to bring such a divergence (whether real or not) between institutional outcomes and public expectations to the attention of citizens? This is likely where the political and financial stakes in institutional change are immense, as in the case of pension privatization. Indeed, empirical research provides numerous examples of cases in which public support for reform of the welfare state has emerged from growing perceptions of the gap between institutional performance and prior expectations. Bergmark and colleagues, for instance, found that the high postwar performance of the welfare state in Sweden lay behind falling support for these policies in the 1990s when programs no longer lived up to prior expectations.[90] Support for institutional reform emerged in

---

[87] Blyth 2002, p. 9.

[88] Bates and Krueger 1993, p. 456; Béland 2005; Campbell 1998; Haggard 2000, p. 28; Hering 2003; 2004; Kitschelt 2001, p. 267; Pierson 1994; 1996, p. 162; Stokes 2001a, p. 61; 2001b.

[89] Greif and Laitin 2004, p. 638.

[90] Bergmark et al. 2000, p. 247. Also see Esping-Andersen 1978, p. 48; Kumlin 2002, p. 27; Svallfors 2002, p. 185.

that case from what the authors called a "crisis of expectations." Similar trends were observed across the industrial world in the 1980s as welfare state programs that long enjoyed wide public backing came to be viewed as "sclerotic," ineffective, and even unfair.[91]

In addition to shifts in perception of an institution's performance, beliefs about what is a fair bargain also may change, even if such "great" transformations are rare.[92] In the United States, for instance, the expansion of social insurance after the Great Depression drew upon an upsurge in belief that the state can and should step in to protect citizens' economic security. Whether such new norms become the foundation of a self-reinforcing social bargain, however, is far from assured. In many countries, the postwar consensus behind support for broader state intervention began to erode in the 1970s as economic crises provoked dissatisfaction with the performance of state institutions. At the same time, the resurgence of liberal economic ideas fueled a rebirth of confidence in markets by reorienting concepts of fairness in public debates around greater individual responsibility and limited government.[93]

Although instances of real economic crisis have been widely linked both to shifting beliefs and dramatic institutional change, politicians' claims of crisis have proved catalytic of policy reform even where such calamity remains far off.[94] Objective conditions thus may not fully circumscribe the possibilities for broad public dissatisfaction to emerge around existing institutions. All political claims proffered in the service of institutional change, however, are not likely to induce shifts in perception and belief, and with them, support for reform. Not only do opponents of reform have powerful incentives to contest reformers' assertions, but such claims also may lack credibility, and thus may ring hollow. The task that remains, then, is to discern how and when politically transmitted information and ideas are likely to provoke broad shifts in public beliefs about an institution, opening up a door to significant institutional change.

From Stability to Change

If new ideas and information provide critical mechanisms of belief and institutional change, then we must examine the ways in which politicians use such instruments to shift public support in their favor. The premise of this argument is that the political context in which institutional change occurs is not only important, but it is also changeable.[95] However, even if politicians can shape their political milieu, prevailing beliefs and expectations associated with the institution and perceptions of its performance (i.e., its political legacy) may

---

[91] Andersen and Meyer 2003; Börsch-Supan and Wilke 2003, p. 3; Ervasti 1998; Levy 1999, p. 240; Offe 1996, pp. 171–2; Roberts 2003; Ross 2000a; Rothstein 2002, p. 218; Tanzi 2002, p. 116.

[92] See, for example, Blyth 2002; Polanyi 1957.

[93] Gilbert 1983, p. 40; Kitschelt 2001, pp. 270–1.

[94] Myles and Pierson 2001.

[95] Pierson 1994, p 146; Schattschneider 1960.

place important bounds on the rhetoric that is effective in mobilizing support for reform. Credibility also matters, and thus a political actor's traditional association with social welfare issues should mediate the face value of claims that are made in regard to the institution.

The Political Legacy

As previous research has shown, shared beliefs about what is fair and expectations of institutional performance are important by-products of social institutions that in turn reproduce them over the long term. As such, they constitute an important element of the institution's political inheritance. Just as important in such a legacy, however, are citizens' attitudes toward the institution – whether they are satisfied or dissatisfied with it – that derive from a comparison of the ongoing institutional outputs (including the behavior of other participants and managers, and the institution's products) to prior expectations on these dimensions.[96] Together, these beliefs and expectations, along with the conjunctural attitudes of satisfaction or dissatisfaction, make up the institution's *political legacy*. This inheritance is more dynamic than an institution's structural legacy (i.e., the rules and benefits that make up its formal design), and it also may change over time with or without political intermediation. Nevertheless, norms of fairness and standards of performance are relatively stable; they coevolve gradually through citizens' long-term experiences with the institution and on the basis of a society's prevailing ideologies.[97] Accordingly, such beliefs may be said to establish the "bar" or standards of fairness and good performance against which ongoing institutional performance is gauged and from which the second element of the institution's political legacy, namely, citizens' attitudes toward it, are derived.

Compared to the more tightly held normative beliefs, satisfaction with the institution's performance is more inconstant, as it may be revised with new information that is acquired through day-to-day experience of the institution. Such perceptions need not rest upon a set of unassailable facts. Rather, they often derive from highly subjective sources of "ordinary" wisdom, or what Hardin calls "street-level knowledge."[98] This type of information, according to Hardin, emerges from a fusion of socially transmitted knowledge and personal experience and gives citizens a foundation on which to make judgments on salient political issues. Because these dispositions may be informed by only fragments of firsthand experience or hard fact, shifting public attitudes toward an institution may correspond only loosely to objective changes in institutional performance.[99] Indeed, public attitudes can be changed by new information that is deemed credible, even if such information has little grounding in fact or later proves false.

[96] Levi 1990.
[97] Here "long-term" refers to a half century. See Bergmark et al. 2000, p. 247.
[98] Hardin 2002, p. 216.
[99] Similarly, see Kumlin 2002, p. 21; Popkin 1991, p. 17; Soss 1999.

Beliefs about what constitutes a fair social bargain and whether an institution is living up to it are highly subjective and deeply context-dependent. Political legacies thus may have little to do with universal standards of equity or objective performance. As a result, the same institutional stimulus – for instance, the failure of a state to adequately index pension benefits – may elicit quite dissimilar public responses in different nations and contexts: Such performance may provoke mass demonstrations and accusations of injustice in one country, while citizens of another nation may view it as unextraordinary, even if they believe such an outcome to be unfair. Just the same, pensions based on a flat benefit formula may be considered equitable and a right of citizenship in one nation and an abrogation of fairness and personal responsibility in another.

An institution's political legacy thus is highly context-bound, emerging both from prevailing norms and from the institution's own functioning over time. It is comprised of relatively stable norms and expectations and more variable attitudes based on the institution's performance relative to local standards. Even though these beliefs and attitudes may support an institution for a long time, they may be transformed in ways that later open the door to institutional change. To understand how such transformations in public support may come about after having been stable and reinforcing for so long, we must look to the role of politics and political conflict over the institution.

Political Strategies and Institutional Change

Beliefs and attitudes associated with an institution provide us with an entering wedge with which to explore the mechanisms of institutional continuity and change. For as we have already seen, scholarship on institutional change has identified the introduction of new information and ideas as critical mechanisms of belief change. In many cases, such information is provided through the political process by advocates *and* opponents of change. But rather than automatically acquiescing to political rhetoric, citizens' attitudes toward an institution are often bound by the more resilient norms, expectations, and perceptions associated with an institution, which in turn limit the effectiveness of political claims in advancing the case of reform. As a result, some claims about institutional injustice or failure may ring hollow, while others may become powerful catalysts of change. The question then is *when* can purposive political action transform once-supportive beliefs and attitudes into mechanisms of path-departing institutional change?

Rhetoric and Political Conflict

Arguments and information communicated through the political process constitute important armaments in political conflicts over institutional reform. In part, the power of such claims derives from the insufficiency of knowledge brought to bear by most citizens when forming judgments about political issues. For complex policy issues such as pension privatization, most citizens lack access to the full information necessary to make an informed, independent judgment on the issue; they also lack the motive to become so informed.[100] Uncertainty, incomplete information, and even misinformation thus are pervasive in public discussions of pension reform issues. And in conflicts over such issues where the stakes are high for both sides of the dispute, information provided through the political process is likely to be selected by partisans with the goal of advancing their desired outcome rather than clarifying issues.[101] Claims about what is "true" about an institution – whether, for example, it is fair or functioning – are therefore likely to take on a political tone, or to rest on assumptions that are chosen to sway citizens toward inferences supportive of a specific political goal, rather than to draw upon neutral premises.[102] Ideological claims are also likely to be prevalent – and effective – in such conflicts since ideas and ideologies are most powerful in swaying public beliefs where uncertainty is high.[103] Where the stakes in institutional change are also high, these tools of political conflict are likely to be employed strategically by proponents and opponents of change.

For advocates of reform, challenges to prevailing beliefs that underpin support for an institution are likely to be advanced through the provision of new information and ideology. Whereas the former includes claims about the present or impending erosion of institutional performance, the latter introduces new concepts of fairness and performance standards that favor claims for reform. Although new information can induce dissatisfaction with the status quo, a new and self-reinforcing institution is only likely to be established where governing principles of fairness and good performance are challenged and replaced through new ideas and ideologies.

New Information

Behavioral research has shown that the acquisition of new information can be an important source of attitude change.[104] By providing citizens with new details about an institution (which may or may not be factual or falsifiable), reformers may *induce* dissatisfaction with it by altering perceptions of whether the institution is living up to (adapted) expectations. This information might lead to a withdrawal of consent to the existing social bargain, as Levi has argued, where it brings attention to the inadequacy of an institution's products (e.g., if pensioners are not receiving their checks or if pension values have declined, causing a rise in poverty among the elderly) or where new information reveals misbehavior among other citizens (e.g., corruption of managers or rampant evasion by other citizens).[105] Where institutional performance falls short of the prevailing standards, then information that highlights this

---

[100] See Berelson et al. 1954, p. 308; Hardin 2002, p. 217; Kuklinski et al. 2000, pp. 790–1.
[101] Jackson and Krebs 2003; Kuklinski and Quirk 2000, p. 160.
[102] See Baker and Weisbrot 1999; Edelman 1964; Hering 2003, p. 31; Kuklinski et al. 2000, p. 791; Kuklinski and Quirk 2000, p. 160; Niggle 2003, p. 54; Schram and Soss 2001, p. 50.
[103] Blyth 2002; Denzau and North 2000.
[104] Lodge et al. 1989. Also see Kumlin 2004, p. 638.
[105] Levi 1990; 1997.

divergence – again, whether real or apparent – may trigger broad public dissatisfaction with the institution, dislodging a critical source of institutional reproduction.

Such discontent may open the door to change if it triggers behavioral shifts that undermine the institution (e.g., taking to the streets in protest or simply failing to comply with the institution).[106] The perception that an old age pension system is insolvent or heading toward bankruptcy, for instance, may lead an increasing number of citizens to under-report income, further weakening the system's finances and making its collapse self-fulfilling. Or, such knowledge may simply shift political support away from defenders of the status quo. In Scandinavia, when the performance of state institutions was perceived to have fallen below expectations, citizens became much more resistant to continued expansions of state economic interventions.[107]

How might this happen if social institutions are self-reinforcing? Even where citizens may long hold positive beliefs and perceptions of an institution, new information may transform two critical sources of institutional reinforcement into levers of institutional change. The first is from adaptive expectations. Where new information brings to light a *gap* between the adapted expectations and current institutional performance, those expectations may become a trigger for dissatisfaction with the current state of the institution. Importantly, it is precisely their resilience that should lead such adapted expectations to provoke dissatisfaction when current institutional performance is seen as falling short. Citizens, in other words, are unlikely to reduce their expectations to match the current output of an institution if they have long been habituated to anticipate better. However, if it is only the performance of the institution – and not its fairness – that is in question, then dissatisfaction may only provide a mandate for reform that would *restore* the institution to expected standards, rather than fundamentally transform it. Nevertheless, the resilience of expectations that evolve over the long term may shift from being a source of institutional reproduction to a lightning rod for change where politicians bring to light real or ostensible gaps between institutional performance and citizens' adapted expectations.

Advocates of institutional reform also may use new information to transform a second element of path dependence, the tendency toward negativity bias, into a mechanism for institutional change. Negativity bias – the tendency to weigh negative information more heavily than positive – is said to fuel threats of political backlash against politicians who impose losses on beneficiaries of the status quo.[108] However, this logic might turn against the persistence of the institution where politicians can persuade citizens that the status quo, rather than the alternative of reform, will deliver losses. This may be possible for

---

[106] Greif and Laitin 2004, p. 638; Levi 1990, p. 411; 1997.

[107] Svallfors 2002, p. 185. Also see Kumlin 2002, p. 27.

[108] Pierson 1994. For this definition of negativity bias, see Nelson 1999; Skowronski and Carlston 1989.

instance where claims that the institution is (or is about to become) bankrupt
are credible and the status quo is seen as being unlikely to return a benefit for
citizens' contributions. In this case, reform that is touted as a way to avoid
such loss or to "save" the institution may be preferred to the ostensible losses
under the existing system.

Indeed, previous research has shown that political actors may win broad
support for deep and often painful institutional reforms where citizens view
the status quo as a situation of loss, leading to supportive judgments about
a prospective reform.[109] Even where citizens may perceive a reform to entail
certain costs, opposition may be dampened if the existing institution is viewed
as an even greater liability.[110] Where this strategy is successful, the provision
of new information about institutional performance – particularly that which
is not verifiable by most citizens, as in claims about a future crisis – may induce
broad dissatisfaction even in the context of good performance. The result may
be to pry open a door to reform.

Critically, new information about institutional performance does not challenge core beliefs about what is fair and what citizens should expect from the
state; thus it is unlikely to undermine the legitimacy of the institution's basic
structure, and hence purpose. This is not to say that reformers cannot gather
support for fundamental structural reform on the basis of claims that such
measures will simply restore the institution to regnant standards. Indeed, it is
possible to change a law without renegotiating its underlying social bargain.
In such cases, however, the permanence of the new institution may be cast
in doubt. For if the new social bargain is to become self-reinforcing, the core
beliefs about what citizens are due that evolved with the old institution must be
confronted and transformed into beliefs consistent with the new design. Such
principles are put into contestation when reform is advanced on ideological
grounds.

New Ideas and Standards

Reformers can lay the foundation for fundamental structural change by confronting the core standards of fairness and expectations associated with the
institution (i.e., by challenging the underlying social bargain). These principles,
as mentioned previously, establish the basic standards or bar against which
citizens judge what is fair and what they are due, and from which their day-to-
day evaluations of institutional performance are based. These beliefs become
subject to revision when reformers persuade citizens that the old bargain – and
not just institutional performance – should change. This may happen where
reformers persuade citizens that the old institution is unfair and that they
should expect something more or different from it.

---

[109] Weyland 1998, p. 648; 2000, p. 483; 2002. Also see Przeworski 2001, pp.104–5; Stokes
     2001b, pp. 13–15.
[110] An individual's perception of whether he or she is in a position of gain or loss is considered
     to be a psychological construct more than an absolute fact. See Kahneman and Tversky 1984;
     Schram and Soss, 2001.

Ideological rhetoric provides a powerful vehicle for such political challenges, for it transmits broadly consumable visions of the good life while also pointing to a means to achieve those ends.[111] Challenges made in ideological terms thus should be most likely to subject the institution's basic normative principles and performance standards to public contestation. These challenges may take the form of justifications for reform based on new ideas about what the state or individuals *should* do, such as providing only a safety net for individuals whose responsibility it is to save for their own retirement. If such normative arguments are persuasive, they may lay the foundation for the constitution of a new social bargain, transforming the basic path of institutional development.

Expectations relating to institutional performance also may be transformed where ideological rhetoric introduces new performance standards into political conflicts over reform. These claims are likely to be influential when they suggest that citizens are owed *more* than they currently receive (i.e., when proponents of change raise the bar for what individuals should expect from the institution). This strategy is in evidence in conflicts over pension privatization where reformers introduce attractive new performance standards that revolve around considerations of increasing one's "money's worth" or broadening freedom and private ownership.[112] Citizens may be told, for instance, that they should expect high rates of return, greater choice, freedom, or enhanced personal control of their retirement savings. Ideological rhetoric that introduces such new, and in particular higher, performance standards may alter *beliefs* about what citizens deserve from the state and each other, therein laying the foundation for a new social bargain, and with it a path-departing institutional change.

The introduction of new ideas into political debate also may neutralize the third important mechanism of institutional reproduction, namely, the murkiness of politics. Such opacity, as Pierson has shown, prevents most citizens, even those dissatisfied with the present institution, from identifying alternatives to the status quo or the means to achieve those ends. But ideology cuts through this haze by reducing even the most complex of political issues into clear and simple terms, dispelling citizens' uncertainty about how the issues relate to their own values.[113] Indeed, ideology reduces multidimensional issues to what is often a single dimension: left versus right, or state versus market. And with this simplification comes an enhanced possibility for broad mobilization around the issue of reform.

The Limits of Political Rhetoric

When are these strategies likely to be successful in transforming oncesupportive beliefs and attitudes into those that permit, or even promote, pathdeparting institutional change? Although the paucity of hard facts used by most citizens when forming political judgments provides important opportunities for

---

[111] Downs 1957; Keohane 1976.
[112] Ross 2000b, pp. 157–8.
[113] See Blyth 2002; Denzau and North 2000; Hinich and Munger 1994; Keohane 1976.

politicians to sway public support toward their cause, rhetoric is not unlimited in its force. Rather, two factors are likely to mediate the effectiveness of new information or ideologies in political conflict over institutional change. The first is the political legacy – the beliefs and expectations associated with an institution – and the second is the credibility of the political actor on the issue being contested.

Political Legacies

Most citizens act as "cognitive misers" when faced with a broad range of complex policy issues that are in play at any given moment; however, they do not confront them as blank slates that are subject to the influence of any politically transmitted claim. Rather, behavioral research suggests that individuals hold firmly to certain impressions and prior beliefs that, although often informed only by the smallest grain of truth, permit them to take and hold positions on a range of specific policy issues.[114] These prior beliefs – such as an institution's political legacy – may be tenacious to the point of inoculating individuals against the acquisition of contrary facts or claims.[115] Such ordinary knowledge gives citizens a powerful compass with which to navigate complex policy debates, and thus to render judgments on the basis of what Popkin calls "gut rationality," rather than complete information.[116] For instance, where politicians allege that an institution is "in crisis" or that it is "broken," citizens may check these claims against personal experience or socially transmitted knowledge, such as whether one's parents or grandparents are receiving their pension checks and whether these seem to be adequate and fair. Tightly held everyday knowledge thus can neutralize the force of political claims in changing attitudes toward an institution. New information that is advanced in the service of reform but that can be checked by street-level knowledge thus may be unlikely to mobilize broad public support if it contradicts widely held perceptions about the institution.

Critically, there is only a narrow range of issues over which citizens possess such tightly held, street-level knowledge. Political legacies, therefore, while tenacious, are not broad in scope. And this narrowness leaves reformers with important opportunities to steer debate toward issues and aspects of the institution whose veracity cannot be confirmed by most citizens. Issues falling beyond the reach of ordinary knowledge thus may be ones on which politically transmitted information may be more effective in inducing dissatisfaction with an institution, easing the way for reform.

Citizens may be more vulnerable to political suasion, for instance, when proponents of change defend reform on highly technical claims. This is because most citizens lack access to the data or expertise to evaluate assertions that rest on technical claims or on projections of an unknowable future performance of

---

[114] Börsch-Supan and Wilke 2003, p. 48; Greif and Laitin 2004; Kuklinski et al. 2000, p. 794–8; Nelson and Oxley 1999.

[115] Nelson et al. 1997.

[116] See Popkin 1991; Popkin and Dimock 2000; Ross 2000b, p. 177.

the institution. Most voters cannot respond to political claims about the under-lying actuarial balance of a pension institution or to predictions of a looming funding crisis. Nor can gut-level rationality guide most people through debates over wage versus price indexation, optimal annuity design, or their ideal posi-tion on the risk-return frontier. Such technical or unverifiable information thus may be effective in inducing dissatisfaction with an institution that otherwise enjoys broad public support. By casting justifications for reform in terms of issues that fall beyond the institution's political legacy, reformers may be more likely to induce widespread pessimism about its viability, and thus to disengage widely supportive beliefs about the institution.

Credibility

Political strategies also may fall flat because citizens do not weigh all polit-ical claims equally. For even if people are uncertain about the truth behind competing claims, they are not left rudderless in efforts to mediate between them. Rather, most people can rely on credibility cues to discern who is more trustworthy on issues about which they do not have direct knowledge. When it comes to the welfare state, partisanship offers perhaps the most powerful sig-nal of a political actor's credibility. Leftist political parties, retirees and unions enjoy substantial powers of persuasion in debates over social policy.[117] Claims that a state's social welfare institution is unfair or broken thus may ring hollow if advanced by a party that is historically associated with cuts to progressive social policies; however, a similar claim by traditional defenders of the welfare state may be powerful in generating support for reform. Accordingly, when politicians from left parties advocate for pension privatization, they may be more effective in changing tightly held beliefs and expectations associated with the pension system. Although the left's ideological commitments make such efforts relatively infrequent, when left parties do take the lead in advocating privatization, their credibility on this issue should make path-departing change more likely to succeed.

Rhetoric and Power

Political rhetoric can shift power in favor of one side of an issue by altering the scope of conflict, and thus the outcome of contests over institutional change. Scholars have shown that the terms on which an issue achieves agenda status bear a powerful influence on political conflict by mediating the range of effective combatants. And as Schattschneider observed, the question of "who can get into the fight and who is excluded" is deeply consequential for its outcome.[118] With broad public support mobilized behind reformers, even deeply entrenched institutions may be subject to meaningful revision.

As discussed previously, the range of issues governed by tightly held beliefs and expectations about an institution is limited. Accordingly, proponents of

---

[117] Grindle 2000; Kitschelt 2001; Ross 2000b, p. 174.
[118] Schattschneider 1960. Also see Brodkin and Young 1989, pp. 142–3; Cobb and Elder 1983; Oldersma 1997, p. 146; Stone, 1984.

change may alter the scope of political conflict with the goal of engaging these dispositions where they are negative, and disengaging them where positive. How does this work? First, where an institution enjoys broad public support, advocates of change are unlikely to advance their cause simply by asserting that the institution is broken or unfair, for these claims conflict with citizens' tightly held knowledge and beliefs about the institution and thus may be dismissed. Nevertheless, dissatisfaction may be induced to the extent that new information about the institution's functioning is provided that cannot be checked by street-level knowledge or gut rationality. This may occur where arguments over institutional change are cast in technical terms, which most people cannot independently check or verify, or on the basis of future projections of institutional performance that are by definition unknowable. Because citizens cannot themselves evaluate such claims, where they come from a credible source, this strategy effectively *narrows* the scope of political conflict because citizens who lack the information or expertise to participate in the debate are consigned to the sidelines.[119] Indeed, when faced with arguments over highly technical concepts or unverifiable facts, most citizens must delegate their judgment on the issue to a select few policy "experts" who possess the specialized information that allows them to participate in these conflicts.

By contrast, the use of ideological rhetoric should *broaden* the scope of political conflict. For in addition to offering a vision of the good life, ideologies provide what Nannerl Keohane calls a "shorthand guide for action" (i.e., a means to achieve those ends).[120] Ideology thus is both a simplifying *and* an activating force, incorporating a broader range of citizens into conflicts over institutional change.[121] This is because ideology enables citizens to take a side on an issue without making heroic calculations of cost and benefit. Debates cast in ideological terms thus allow more citizens to participate in discussions over complex political issues even when they lack information on the matter.[122] Ideological rhetoric thus provides combatants in political conflict with a means to mobilize more citizens to join in their side. When most citizens hold positive beliefs and attitudes about the institution, supporters of the status quo should be most effective in combating change if they cast their arguments against reform in ideological terms, bringing the broad range of satisfied citizens onto their side in the conflict.

Summary and Expectations

Inherited beliefs and attitudes associated with the existing pension institution – its political legacy – constitute a critical mechanism of institutional stability but may also be transformed into a powerful lever of institutional change. Beliefs

---

[119] Brodkin and Young 1989.
[120] Keohane 1976, p. 82.
[121] Also see Hinich and Munger 1994, p. 5.
[122] Blyth 2002; Downs 1957; Hinich and Munger 1994.

about what is fair and what the institution should do thus may underwrite institutional reproduction for long periods of time by motivating compliance with an institution and establishing limits on the claims that politicians may effectively use to shape public attitudes toward the institution. They may also be transformed, however, where new norms and higher standards are introduced by credible actors, supplanting the old principles and spurring declining support for the existing institution. Or, where street-level evidence of institutional performance falls short of established standards and expectations, dissatisfaction with the institution may emerge. When this happens, reformers can gather crucial political support for otherwise-improbable, path-departing institutional reforms. Reformers also may transform attitudes toward the institution, such as satisfaction with its performance, by introducing new information that people cannot verify through their day-to-day lives. Whether these political strategies will be effective in prompting dissatisfaction with the institution, however, depends on the interaction between reformers' claims and citizens' everyday beliefs and expectations of the institution (i.e., its political legacy), and on the credibility of the partisans in the conflict.

Of course, the most fertile soil in which challenges to an entrenched institution may be planted is where there are widespread perceptions that the institution is performing poorly or that its outputs are unfair. In these contexts, the negative perceptions culled from everyday life will substantiate political claims of institutional failure or injustice and thus provide support for advocates of reform. Even in the face of broad public approval with an institution, however, support for reform may be won. This is possible where credible advocates of change provide highly technical information that cannot be checked through street-level knowledge about the institution. Such claims narrow the scope of conflict to exclude ordinary, satisfied citizens as active participants in the debate over reform. In the same contexts, however, opponents of change may gain advantage over reformers by casting their arguments in ideological terms. Doing so broadens the scope of conflict to incorporate the mass of citizens who are supportive of the institution, therein tilting political power in favor of opponents of the reform. Left governments, because of their credibility on the issue, should be more effective in challenging the basic principles of the welfare state through the introduction of new ideas about what is fair; the left and its labor allies also may be highly effective in mobilizing opposition to structural reform when it is initiated by a right-wing government.

III. LEGISLATING INSTITUTIONAL RESTRUCTURING

The legislative arena represents the final theater of conflict in political processes of institutional change. It is often the most difficult battle to win, moreover, as reform-seeking leaders must ask elected legislators to endorse a highly visible measure that imposes losses on what is often a sizable portion of the electorate. The unpopularity of loss imposition has been shown to make the politics of retrenchment highly contentious, setting it apart from the credit-claiming logic of welfare state expansion.[123] Even though the difficulty of social policy retrenchment has been amply borne out in extant research, we cannot simply extend the logic of retrenchment to explain the politics of institutional restructuring.[124] For institutional restructuring, as in the case of pension privatization, entails more than simply retrenchment, or benefit cuts alone; instead, restructuring also has important creative elements. In the case of pension privatization, the creative dimension centers on the establishment of privately managed individual retirement accounts. This possibility for distributive gains sets the legislative politics of institutional restructuring apart from that of retrenchment alone.

Loss imposition is an ineluctable feature of pension privatization. The losers in this reform, however, vary markedly across circumstance with important political consequences. In many Latin American cases, the beneficiaries of redistribution in traditional state pension systems were urban formal sector workers – not the poorest members of society. However, low-income workers benefit considerably from the risk-pooling elements of traditional social insurance, and therefore are also potential losers in privatization. The fact that someone stands to lose, however, is what typically makes political conflict a resident feature of this reform. Yet, a massive political backlash against legislators who sign on to this reform is not inescapable. Not only may dissatisfaction with the status quo institution emerge prior to or during conflicts over reform, but the legislative processes also may not descend inevitably into a bare-knuckled power struggle to overcome mobilized opponents of reform. Rather, in some cases, it may be characterized by a distributive, credit-claiming logic more akin to that observed in the process of welfare state expansion.

This is because, for one thing, the loss-imposing elements of privatization are associated in large part with the transfer of risk to individuals; this risk shift is difficult for most citizens to calculate or quantify in terms of the cost to their future security.[125] Moreover, many of the financial costs associated with privatization are opaque, relating to fees on investment returns or account balances, and thus they often escape the notice of affected workers prior to the enactment of the reform. Because the creative elements of privatization – the establishment of individual investment accounts – are highly visible, proponents of this measure may take advantage of significant opportunities to organize political conflict around the potential distributive gains to be won by some individuals through privatization (e.g., expanded opportunities for ownership, control, and higher rates of return), while obscuring its cost for others. To the extent that advocates of pension privatization are successful in doing so, they may reduce or even neutralize altogether the threat of electoral backlash associated with losses imposed through structural pension reform.

---

[123] Pierson 1996; Pierson and Weaver 1993; Weaver 1986; 1988; 2005.
[124] See Weaver 2005, p. 230, for the analytical distinction between restructuring and retrenchment.
[125] Hacker 2004.

Credit-claiming strategies may be undermined, however, if opponents can refocus political conflict around the loss-imposing elements of the reform. In such cases, the more familiar veto dynamic emerges, and the possibilities for building a legislative majority will depend on the structure of legislative authority and the outcome of strategic bargaining. The existence of two politically relevant dimensions of pension privatization thus permits two distinct legislative dynamics to potentially unfold around this reform. The critical analytical puzzle then is to define when the distributive elements of pension privatization are likely to be salient within legislative conflicts, and when the loss-imposing dimension will be most apparent.

Legislating Losses

The legislative objective of reform-seeking governments is quite simple: to gather a majority (or super-majority) of votes to sanction the proposed institutional change. Despite the straightforwardness of this task, immense political hurdles stand in its way, particularly where institutional change imposes direct costs on significant portions of the electorate. For legislators concerned with their political futures, the decision to vote for loss-imposing reform may put them at odds with constituents whose support is necessary to achieve those career ambitions. The path to reform for large social programs like old age pensions thus is strewn with tremendous political and electoral hazards. Indeed, recognition of such perils in the United States has earned for Social Security the moniker of the "third rail" of politics: If you touch it, you risk your political life.

The legislative arena presents an additional theoretical question: Why and how can the political structures that have long supported institutional permanence later become permissive of path-departing institutional change? Scholars typically look to the structure of legislative institutions to explain where institutional change is more or less likely, but such theories cannot explain why a given set of institutions can be consistent with institutional reinforcement for long periods of time, but later can permit radical institutional change.[126] As the analysis in Chapter 2 revealed, the likelihood of enacting pension privatization is not predicted directly by the structure of legislative power. Rather, this relationship is conditioned by the partisan structure of legislative authority, such that the likelihood of pension privatization diminishes as the size of the governing majority increases, except when a left party is in power. That result lends plausibility to my claim that institutional effects are conditioned by partisanship – an argument that I develop further in this section.

The causal process through which I expect loss-imposing reform to become likely brings attention to what Weingast calls the "distributive tendency" of

[126] Kay 1999; Madrid 2003.

a law. The capacity of reform-seeking governments to raise the salience of pension privatization's creative dimension, I argue, is a critical predictor of the ability to construct large, if not oversized, majorities behind this measure. Where such efforts fail, the more familiar veto dynamic should emerge around heightened awareness of the loss-imposing elements of structural pension reform. The next question, then, is *who* can induce such a distributive logic around pension reform, and under what conditions can they do so? Here again, partisan credibility should matter; where reformers lack such credibility, the outcome of legislative battles over pension reform will depend heavily upon the availability and use of institutional authority, pork-barrel compensation, and compromise of the loss-imposing provisions of the reform. The latter, critically, often incide directly on the extent of market-oriented reform. The depth of institutional change thus will depend heavily upon the government's partisan credibility, institutional authority and/or use of pork-barrel resources to construct voting majorities behind structural reform.

Conditioning Institutions' Effects

The notion that a given set of institutions may be compatible with policy stability in one time period and with significant change in another suggests that the effect of political institutions on legislative outcomes is conditional, rather than absolute. Indeed, there is broad theoretical precedence for such a view. Tsebelis, for instance, argues that formal institutional veto points can be "absorbed" where actors in these positions share a common ideological or partisan stripe.[127] For Aldrich and Rhode, the effect of political parties on legislative behavior is conditioned by the homogeneity of legislators' preferences over a given policy.[128] In their research, political party effects may be attenuated where legislators stake out positions apart from that of the political leaders, while the convergence of preferences gives rise to significant political party behavior. Morgenstern shows, moreover, that the effect of partisan institutions on party-oriented behavior varies significantly over different phases of the electoral cycle.[129] Electoral pressures thus may condition the force of institutional structures on partisan cooperation.

For other scholars, the possibility for building a legislative majority depends on the *nature* of the policy in question.[130] Specifically, it matters whether a piece of legislation is distributive or redistributive in its substance. Distributive policies are exemplified by pork-barrel appropriation bills, which allocate resources directly to specific communities and finance these with general revenue.[131] Importantly, Schwartz has shown that there may always be incentives

---

[127] Gunther 1989, p. 845; Tsebelis, 1999.
[128] Aldrich and Rhode 1997–8, p. 546.
[129] Morgenstern 2001.
[130] Arnold 1979; Collie 1988; Ferejohn 1974; Niou and Ordeshook 1985, pp. 246–90.
[131] Lizzeri and Persico 2001.

to form at least a minimal winning majority behind distributive policies.[132] For Riker, even a *super*-majority may form behind such measures where coalition partners are unreliable.[133] Weingast goes one step further by arguing that norms of "universalism" may emerge around the passage of distributive legislation.[134] The nondivisive nature of distributive goods makes the political logic of support for such legislation quite intuitive.

But can we extend this logic to policies such as pension privatization that entail not only distributive features, but also that result in loss imposition? There are theoretical grounds to expect so. Groseclose and Snyder, for instance, found not only that oversized majorities can form behind redistributive or loss-imposing reforms such as a free-trade agreement, but that building *super*-majorities in these contexts may even be less costly than forming a minimal-winning coalition.[135] The cost of building a voting coalition behind redistributive reform may be paid in the currency of distributive resources – benefits offered to the losers either in the form of provisions within the bill, or in compromises of the loss-imposing elements. Thus a majority – or even super-majority – may be forged behind loss imposition to the extent that the putative electoral costs of voting for this measure can be compensated to some degree through the allocation of distributive rewards.

Legislators are assumed to be strategic in their decision to support or oppose a reform; that is, they, "look ahead to see the consequences of their current votes for later choices."[136] There is reason to expect that, on average, elected politicians will behave in such a career-minded way. Not only is consideration of the electoral costs of votes on salient policies an essential condition for legislators to continue in their professional roles, but it is also vital for the pursuit of any further programmatic or ideological goals that legislators may have. As McKelvey and Niemi have shown, moreover, the informational requirements of strategic decision-making on the part of legislators are not particularly burdensome.[137] Thus career-minded legislators should consider a vote for or against privatization in light of how they anticipate that voters will receive this reform rather than on account of its objective or underlying distributional implications alone.

Uncertainty and information asymmetries are likely to be pervasive, especially on issues as inherently complex as pension restructuring. As a result, citizens' evaluations of such a policy – particularly whether it is distributive or loss-imposing – may be shaped therefore less by the technical or objective

[132] Schwartz 1994.
[133] Riker 1962.
[134] Weingast 1979; 1994. Also see Axelrod 1970; Shepsle and Weingast 1981.
[135] Groseclose and Snyder 1996, p. 306.
[136] Aldrich 1995, p. 41; Arnold 1998.
[137] McKelvey and Niemi 1978. Also see Aldrich 1995, p. 41; Ferejohn et al. 1987, p. 173; Fleck 2001, p. 77.

features of the reform than by their *perceptions* of it. And those perceptions, as discussed in the previous section, in many cases may be subject to the influence of claims advanced in the political process.

Restructuring versus Retrenchment

An important distinction must be made between the political logic of pension privatization and that of retrenchment. Whereas retrenchment entails essentially one politically relevant dimension, namely, reductions in the generosity of benefits, restructuring has two dimensions: the curtailment of traditional social insurance benefits (i.e., retrenchment) *and* a creative dimension, centering on the establishment of new forms of property rights through private savings instruments. The latter constitutes the distributive dimension of pension privatization; the former is its loss-imposing dimension. Given that the creative elements of privatization cannot be obscured or hidden, there is no way to adopt pension privatization "by stealth" in the way that parametric benefit cuts may be enacted through less-visible changes in indexation rules.

However, obfuscation of the loss-imposing aspects of pension privatization is possible. It is precisely the high visibility of its creative dimension that facilitates efforts to diminish the salience of the loss-imposing elements of privatization and thus to avoid a political backlash in response to it. This is possible where reformers heighten the salience of the potential gains to be won through market-based investments or where they emphasize the new forms of private property, "choice" and "control" of one's individual savings. Where efforts to highlight the distributive elements of pension privatization are successful, the political logic that unfolds in the legislature may permit the reform to be sanctioned by large, potentially even oversized, majorities. Claiming credit for one aspect of a reform in this way instantiates, rather than contravenes, the logic of blame avoidance in welfare state reform.

Importantly, pension privatization need not be strictly welfare-improving to be perceived as a distributive measure. For some citizens with high and stable incomes, who were the losers of redistribution in traditional risk-pooling pension systems, privatization may indeed provide real opportunities for gain. For workers with low and unstable earnings who had been the beneficiaries of redistribution in social insurance systems, however, privatization imposes considerable losses. For most citizens, the skills that are essential for predicting or achieving real gains through privatization (e.g., an understanding of the stochastic features of investment returns, interest rate and annuity relationships, risk-return thresholds, and optimal portfolio theories) are out of reach. Given the complexity of pension issues and the vagueness of this measure's distributive implications, a substantial portion of the electorate is likely to be uncertain ex ante about whether they will be advantaged or disadvantaged by this reform. Accordingly, those citizens will look to the political arena for information about the reform and its material implications.[138] Where the old

---

[138] Also see Austen-Smith and Feddersen 2006.

pension institution is widely perceived to be failing or has lost the confidence of the electorate, reformers should face even less resistance to claims that privatization is a distributive measure.[139]

Even when faced with conflicting normative principles (e.g., social insurance goals and the objectives of increasing ownership), behavioral research suggests that politicians can help citizens to eliminate such "value conflicts" by encouraging them to weigh one goal more heavily than another.[140] The information provided through the legislative process thus matters critically for predicting both the popularity of this reform and the likelihood and degree of institutional change for which reformers are likely to gain legislative – and public – support.[141] Even though substantial portions of the population stand to lose distributive advantage in the shift from social protection to market-based pension systems, the unpopularity of this complex and multidimensional measure is far from assured.

Inducing a Distributive Dynamic

Many, if not most, policies entail both the allocation of significant losses and the creation of new benefits, and thus include distributive and redistributive elements.[142] For measures such as pension privatization, where both dimensions may be significant, the political cost paid by elected legislators for supporting such a reform is likely to depend on the relative salience of its distributive and loss-imposing elements.[143] Where citizens are uncertain about these relative weights, politicians can play an important role in defining these perceptions. Reform-seeking politicians thus may be expected to seek to enhance the salience of the distributive elements of pension privatization, while downplaying its loss-imposing features. Not every politician will be successful in this attempt, however. Nevertheless, two principal strategies are likely to be in evidence where pension privatization is at issue: the use of political rhetoric to redefine the measure as a distributive one and the use of compensation to dampen the costs – both material and political – associated with the reform.

Rhetoric

Given the context of incomplete and asymmetric information inhering in political conflicts over pension reform, politicians may attempt to raise the visibility of the measure's distributive dimension in the least costly way possible: through political rhetoric.[144] As Weingast has shown, politicians may alter the "distributive tendency" of a piece of legislation by generating the appearance of gain such that "controversial programs that initially fall into the regulatory

---

[139] Roberts 2003.
[140] Alvarez and Brehm 1995; Nelson 2004.
[141] Schram and Soss 2001.
[142] Weingast 1994, p. 321.
[143] For Weingast, the categories of distributive and redistributive policy are subjective and mutable rather than objective and fixed. Shepsle and Weingast 1981; Weingast 1994.
[144] Austen-Smith 1992.

or redistributive categories are *redefined* so that they become distributive, and hence less controversial."[145] By recasting a redistributive measure in such a way that it appears to offer gains, strategic politicians may temper public opposition while raising the electoral incentives for legislators to support the reform.

Reformers may do so first by "reframing," or providing an interpretation of privatization that encourages citizens to take into consideration only a subset of relevant information about the reform when evaluating it, namely its potential distributive rewards.[146] Reframing the issue of pension privatization around the putative gains of enhanced personal choice and wealth, control over one's retirement savings, and higher rates of return (improving one's "money's worth") is thus a way to orient evaluations of the reform toward the potential benefits to be gained, while downplaying the possible risks and costs associated with investment in private capital markets, and the magnitude of cuts to risk-pooling. A second rhetorical strategy to redefine a loss-imposing reform as a distributive one is to portray the measure as necessary to avoid a crisis or to sidestep putatively greater losses associated with the existing institution. This may mean claiming that privatization will "save" the existing pension system or avert a looming "crisis" or "bankruptcy" of the institution that would occur in the absence of privatization.

The opportunity to reframe pension privatization in this way is enhanced both by the high visibility of its creative dimension (the new private investment opportunities) and by the complexity and opacity of the curtailment of risk-pooling functions. Indeed, for many citizens, it is difficult to perceive and weigh the risks associated with private capital markets against the potential rewards available through them. It is also difficult, if not impossible, to verify through ordinary knowledge whether privatization will in fact resolve a potential funding problem besetting the existing state pension system, or whether such problems are remediable through incremental revisions to the existing state pension system. Such uncertainty expands the potential influence of political rhetoric where reformers enjoy substantial credibility on the issue of social security.

Compensation

Government actors may also seek to induce a distributive logic around pension privatization by *adding* material benefits to the proposed legislation.[147] This strategy may entail compensating losers through the rules of the reformed institution, such as by providing direct monetary transfers to private pension accounts or financial incentives for workers who join the new pension system. Because compensatory benefits are immediately apparent, while the potential losses imposed by privatization emerge only after considerable delay (typically, at retirement), such compensatory provisions may dampen public opposition to reform, or even generate considerable enthusiasm for it.

---

[145] Weingast 1994, p. 321. Emphasis added. See also Stockman 1975.
[146] Druckman 2001a, p. 230.
[147] Weingast 1994.

Even in authoritarian Chile, we can find a precedent for this strategy. Although Chile's 1981 privatization was enacted by decree, the reform mandated that workers joining the new private pension system be given a substantial one-time pay raise equivalent to the employers' contribution that had been eliminated. This benefit was not available to workers who did not enroll in the new system, making it a powerful selective incentive to join. Early enrollment in the new private pension system in Chile, predictably, was quite strong.[148] By creating new benefits in association with structural reform, therefore, politicians may be able to diminish the salience of losses, dampening public dissatisfaction and even inducing a credit-claiming or distributive political logic around the reform.

Who Can Induce a Distributive Logic?

All politicians surely would like to assert their interpretation of a reform and have citizens accept that view. However, it is rare that only one explanation of an issue prevails in democratic conflicts. Even where opposition voices are muted, a government's contentions may not be persuasive enough to win legislative support for a reform such as pension privatization. Other governments simply will be unable to convincingly tout the benefits of privatization. While some political parties face ideological or programmatic constraints that foreclose this strategy, others may simply lack the credibility to claim that privatization will be beneficial.[149]

Where more than one voice is heard on an issue, citizens may be uncertain about whose version of the story is accurate. Yet, as argued earlier, citizens may use partisan shortcuts to navigate these waters and thus to gauge the credibility of competing political claims. And to the extent that credibility matters, the partisan structure of political conflict may predict whether the distributive or loss-imposing elements of privatization will become more salient in political battles over this reform.[150] Where the loss-imposing dimension is brought to the center of the political conflict, a credit-claiming (distributive) dynamic may be foreclosed and a veto dynamic is likely to obtain.

The concept of credibility has been invoked as a critical tool shaping the way that people evaluate information under uncertainty.[151] The meaning and foundations of credibility, however, differ across political contexts.[152] Nevertheless, when opposing political actors offer starkly competing interpretations of an issue, credibility should weigh heavily. Such credibility will depend on two criteria: the political actor or group's traditional association with the issue and the extent of independent corroboration of a political claim. Where reform-seeking

---

[148] Castiglioni 2001.
[149] See Kitschelt 2001.
[150] Kitschelt 2001.
[151] Austen-Smith 1990; Druckman, 2001b; Ross 2000a.
[152] Druckman 2001b, p. 1054; Lupia et al. 2000.

politicians lack credibility from the first source, they may still influence citizens' evaluations of the issue if they gain external confirmation of their claims.

Research on welfare state reform points to a critical role for partisanship in delimiting the opportunities for structural reform to be won in democratic settings.[153] The way that partisanship matters in this literature, however, varies widely. Whereas some scholars find that left parties maintain higher welfare benefits and social spending levels, others have shown that left parties take the lead in adopting welfare state reform.[154] When reexamined through the optic of credibility, these divergent findings become much less inconsistent.

The left's traditional partisan association with the defense of the welfare state and promotion of working class interests affords it substantial credibility on social policy issues. Accordingly, the left can more convincingly claim to its constituents that welfare state reform is a necessary or even *beneficial* measure. This Nixon-goes–to-China logic draws from a general view that political actors enjoy broader political latitude to take positions that are "against type." Thus the left's relative advantage in the adoption of market-oriented reform draws from citizens' confidence that the party would not do so unless it were imperative. The motives for reform thus are considered to be objective, rather than ideological.[155] Claims that a reform is necessary to "save" the state pension system thus may be more plausible if they come from a party of the left; they will be much less so if they are advanced by a party that long opposed such policies on ideological grounds. If the left takes the lead on pension privatization, therefore, claims about the measure's distributive benefits are more likely to succeed in inducing a distributive logic around the reform.

The effectiveness of the left's distributive claims is likely to be enhanced also by the fact that right parties have programmatic reasons to support such reforms; their opposition thus may seem disingenuous. And because right parties are not a likely ally for labor, unions may be less likely to oppose the reform when it is led by left parties with a viable right-wing opponent.[156] However, where left parties, labor, or retirees do mobilize against pension privatization, its loss-imposing dimension is likely to become a central issue in the political conflict. In this context, the unpopularity of losses should raise the political costs for legislators voting for the reform, activating a veto dynamic in the legislature. Accordingly, it may be more difficult for a right party to claim credit for enacting pension privatization – especially where it governs with a large legislative majority. For in such contexts the right party would stand to receive sole blame for imposing losses through the reform.

Whether labor is on the side of the reformers or opposition thus should be a critical factor predicting the likelihood that a credit-claiming dynamic emerges around structural pension reform. This is particularly likely in Latin America,

[153] Allan and Scruggs 2004; Anderson 2001; Béland 2001; Iversen and Wren 1998; Korpi and Palme 2003; Pontusson and Kwon 2003; Scharpf and Schmidt 2000.
[154] Kitschelt 2001; Remmer 2002; Ross 200b; Weyland, 1999.
[155] Cukierman and Tommasi 1998; Kitschelt 2001, p. 275.
[156] Hering 2003; Kitschelt 2001.

where labor unions have historically been a significant actor in social welfare politics.[157] Labor thus can play a pivotal role in reinforcing or undermining the claims advanced by reform-seeking governments.[158] Although labor's mobilization capacity has declined considerably in most Latin American countries since the 1980s, unions retain much greater collective action potential than do many of the beneficiaries of public social insurance programs. By lending support to structural pension reforms, labor unions thus may greatly enhance the plausibility of reformers' distributive claims.[159] And in threatening opposition to them, labor can extract significant concessions in the pension reform in exchange for their support. The negotiation of such compromises is particularly likely where privatization is led by a left-wing government. Thus even though privatization initiatives may be more likely to succeed when enacted by left parties, the degree of structural change should be attenuated in these circumstances by concessions made to win labor support.

Exogenous Corroboration

Although political claims may be powerful in the context of high uncertainty, such claims are also quite fragile, as they may be subject to counterframing by more credible opponents of reform. Indeed, reform-seeking governments will not be able to redefine pension privatization as a distributive measure where they lack credibility on this issue. Even where a reform-seeking government lacks credibility, it may still acquire such authority through independent corroboration of its claims. Such validation may be provided either by an actor that is not subject to government influence, such as a nonpartisan organization, or by objective street-level evidence, such as an overt performance failure of the institution. This does not suggest a straightforward link between economic crisis and legislative support for market-oriented reform, however.[160] Rather than simply imposing "discipline" on legislators to cooperate with reform-seeking governments, economic performance instead may simply *mediate* the plausibility of the government's claims about market-oriented reform.

Reform within a Veto Dynamic

Where the government fails to organize legislative conflict around privatization's distributive elements, the loss-imposing features become salient and a veto dynamic is likely to emerge. In this context, the unpopularity of losses will raise considerably the political costs for legislators supporting the reform. The emergence of a veto dynamic does not condemn pension privatization to failure; however, it can raise the cost of building a legislative majority behind it.

---

[157] Bergquist 1986; Collier and Collier 1991; Mesa-Lago 1978; 1989; 1994; Middlebrook 1991.
[158] Alonso 1998, p. 22; Murillo 2000; 2001; 2002.
[159] Béland 2001, p. 154.
[160] Indeed, as Haggard and Kaufman (2008) show, governments respond very differently to financial strains on the welfare state.

When faced with an unpopular agenda item, legislators have strong incentives to oppose such a measure. Where the reform is not exceedingly unpopular, legislators may exchange their vote for political resources that advance their career. The task for government leaders in this context is to use the resources available to them to align rank-and-file legislators' career interests with their leaders' goal of passing the reform. Two resources in particular are relevant: *authority* and *exchange*. Authority refers to career rewards and punishments that leaders may use to induce cooperation on unpopular legislation. Where such authority is insufficient to constitute a voting majority, however, reformers must negotiate legislation within and/or across party lines, offering distributive resources in exchange for the cooperation of reluctant legislators. Where cooperation remains elusive – such as when the piece of legislation is exceedingly unpopular – reformers may have little choice but to compromise the terms of the legislation, and hence the extent of institutional change achieved through the reform.

Institutional Authority

If authority relations played no part in legislative politics, then each and every elected legislator whose vote is necessary to enact a law would be a potential "veto player." But legislative processes are rarely so atomistic. Rather, they are organized along partisan lines, and parties are governed by authority relations. Legislative and partisan authority is delimited by electoral rules, which offer party leaders an array of instruments through which to bring legislators' career incentives in line with party leaders' goals.[161] To the extent that party leaders wield institutional authority over the careers of a majority of elected legislators, they may induce cooperation behind an unpopular reform without significant compromise of the text. Sources of this institutional authority include control over which names appear on party ballots, the order of the names on party lists, access to party resources, committee assignments, and appointments to positions of authority within the party or government.[162] Using these resources, leaders may reward partisans for cooperation by making it more likely that they win reelection or advance within the party hierarchy. Where these instruments of party discipline are limited both vertically and horizontally (the former being where party leaders are weak and the latter where their party controls a narrow share of seats in the assembly), the task of building majorities behind unpopular reforms is likely to require exchange and/or compromise.

Exchange

Where government leaders lack sufficient institutional authority to bring together a legislative majority, they must negotiate with legislators within and across party lines. Such bargains may entail the offer of distributive resources

---

[161] Ames 1995b, p. 412; Carey and Shugart 1995; Kay 1998; Morgenstern, 2002.
[162] Aldrich 1995; Ames 1994; 1995a; 1995b; Carey and Shugart 1995; Cox and McCubbins, 1993; Haggard and Kaufman 1992; 1995; Morgenstern 2002; Sartori 1976, p. 93.

(e.g., pork-barrel appropriations or subsidies within the legislation) or career rewards (e.g., appointments to positions within the government bureaucracy) in exchange for support on the legislation. Where such distributive exchange provides the glue for building majorities behind unpopular reforms, the outcome of such negotiations may correspond closely to that where a distributive logic prevails (i.e., extensive institutional change may be possible). Reform will come at a far higher price, however, when it emerges within a veto dynamic.

Where the reform is extremely unpopular, the promise of infrastructure or other pork-barrel spending for legislators' home districts may be insufficient to dampen the political cost of voting for reform. In such cases, legislative negotiations may require compromise of the reform agenda, curtailing the extent of institutional change for which majority support can be won. Attenuation of reformers' privatizing ambitions thus is likely where a veto dynamic emerges around a highly unpopular reform and where the government's institutional and financial resources are limited. As the range of bargains needed to enact privatization increases, the degree of institutional change that is likely to be achieved through the reform should therefore decline.[163]

Summary and Expectations

Just as Lipset and Rokkan showed that political cleavages within societies are not fixed or predetermined, the lines of distributional advantage also may not be a permanent feature of the political landscape determining whether old age pension privatization may succeed in a given setting.[164] Rather, the outcome of political conflicts over multidimensional reforms such as pension privatization may depend at any time on the relative salience of the reform's potential losses and its rewards – features that may not be apparent ex ante but are subject to influence and contestation in the course of legislative conflict over reform.

Politicians who advance loss-imposing legislation such as pension privatization should seek to dampen the political costs of this reform for cooperating legislators. They may do so most cheaply with rhetoric – by enhancing the salience of the potential gains to be won through private retirement accounts and by downplaying the attendant losses associated with the retrenchment of risk-pooling structures. Rhetorical strategies are more likely to succeed where parties of the left govern, or where reformers' claims are corroborated independently. Labor union support also may help to induce a distributive logic; however, this support may come at the price of compromise in the scope of market orientation of the reform. Where a credit-claiming dynamic obtains, nevertheless, loss-imposing reform may win passage by a large, if not oversized, legislative majority.

A veto dynamic is likely to emerge, by contrast, where the potential losses imposed by reform are brought to the forefront of legislative conflict. In such

---

[163] Tsebelis 1999.
[164] Lipset and Rokkan 1967. Also see Dalton et al. 1984, p. 455.

instances, the structure of institutional authority becomes important for predicting the range of bargains that are required to gather majority support for the reform. The instruments of political authority – including career rewards and punishments – and the exchange of pork-barrel appropriations may facilitate the approval of unpopular reforms. Where a reform is extremely unpopular and authority and exchange fail to bring together a majority supportive of the legislation, government leaders may be forced to compromise the extent of institutional change in order to sanction the structural reform.

CONCLUSION

This chapter has laid out three theoretical arguments to address a longstanding conundrum of institutional change, namely, when and how can institutions that have long been stable become subject to fundamental path-departing reform? The first section examined the role of globalization in the initiation of pension privatization efforts. I argued that even though financial integration has heightened incentives for governments to embrace privatization, globalization has not been a straightforward catalyst of this reform. Rather, it has placed capital-importing governments in a powerful double bind as shortened time horizons and information scarcity raise the near-term threat of market punishment for some privatizing governments. Those countries that are most vulnerable to capital flight and whose governments enjoy little financial leeway to assume the transitional cost of privatization without compromising their sovereign risk performance may be compelled by the short-term risk of market sanction to curtail the move toward market orientation of old age pensions in the long term.

The second argument examined the role of institutional legacies in the process of path-departing change. I argued that the beliefs and attitudes that long upheld and reinforced an institution – its political legacy – may be transformed through political conflict into mechanisms that permit or promote institutional change. Changes in beliefs or attitudes may result from the introduction of new ideologies and new information into political debates over an institution. This may involve claims that the institution is no longer functioning or that it is unfair, and that people deserve more than they are getting. The effectiveness of these strategies is mediated, however, by the nature of the institutional legacy itself, and by the credibility of the author of such claims. Left parties should be more credible in employing these rhetorical strategies, due to their long association with support of the welfare state.

The third argument in this chapter examined the process by which majority support can be won in democratic legislatures for loss-imposing measures like pension privatization. I argued that institutional restructuring is distinguished from policy retrenchment, or benefit cuts alone, by the possibilities for distributive gain through individual savings instruments. The latter constitutes privatization's creative dimension. The legislative politics of this reform depend on whether the creative or loss-imposing dimension becomes more salient in political conflicts over the measure. When left parties take the lead on pension privatization, they are more likely to succeed in highlighting the distributive elements of the reform while downplaying the attendant losses; in such cases, a credit-claiming logic may emerge, facilitating the formation of a majority or super-majority behind the reform. By contrast, when credible opponents highlight the loss-imposing elements of this measure, a veto logic will dominate, obliging reformers to use authority or exchange to build legislative coalitions in support of the reform. Where these resources are insufficient to gain cooperation, compromise in the extent of structural change will be necessary to win majority support within a veto dynamic.

The next part of this book takes these arguments and tests them in data from four Latin American countries: Argentina, Brazil, Mexico and Uruguay. The next chapter begins that analysis by evaluating the empirical landscape of pension reform in Latin America. Chapter 5 brings evidence from the cases to evaluate the argument about globalization's double bind, while Chapter 6 examines the role of institutional legacies in the efforts to "sell" pension reform to society. Chapter 7 then examines the legislative conflicts over pension reform in the four Latin American countries, evaluating the ways in which partisanship, external corroboration and exchange variously shaped efforts to build legislative majorities – or supermajorities in the Brazilian case – behind the approval of old age pension reforms.

PART III

THE TRANSFORMATION OF SOCIAL PROTECTION IN LATIN AMERICA

4

Pension Reform in Latin America

Overview and Scope of Institutional Transformation

This chapter begins the structured comparative analysis with an overview of the pension reforms in Argentina, Brazil, Mexico, and Uruguay. The cases will show the complex and contingent mechanisms of institutional change and highlight how reform outcomes are mediated by the political, economic, and institutional landscape of each country, as well as by the partisan structure of political conflict. Before delving into the question of the causal mechanisms of change, however, we must ask: How much change has actually occurred? As the discussion of the measurement problem in Chapter 2 revealed, this question lacks a straightforward answer. For the output of institutional change – the *formal* contours of the new pension institutions – differ markedly from the *effective* reach of the new private pension institutions. Indeed, the latter – measured by active contribution rate within the working-age population – reveals an institutional scope that is considerably narrower than the formal rules of these programs would indicate. Governments also retain a significant financial and regulatory presence in reformed pension markets, and in some cases even compete with private pension fund managers to invest individuals' retirement funds. The ultimate reach of private pension markets in Latin America, moreover, is cast in doubt by the emergence of political challenges to private pension systems in some cases, and by revisions to such programs in countries like Argentina that have curtailed the size of the private pension system. Whether new private pension institutions will endure is unlikely to be known with certainty for some time. Nevertheless, we may gather initial evidence of their solidity from the patterns of compliance with the rules of reformed pension systems. This chapter will analyze these data for the Latin American region and outline the context and reform outputs in the four countries examined in this study.

TABLE 4.1. *Simulations of Structural Pension Reform*

	Share of Average Wage Earner's Income Replaced by:		Percentage Private
	Public DB (%)	Private DC (%)	
Argentina	30	35	54
Bolivia	4	42	92
Chile	0	43	100
Colombia	0	44	100
Costa Rica	60	15	20
Dominican Republic	0	30	100
El Salvador	0	42	100
Mexico	3	27	91
Peru	0	33	100
Uruguay	38	22	37

Source: Author's calculations.

WHAT HAS HAPPENED IN LATIN AMERICAN PENSION REFORM?

Beginning with the 1981 pension privatization in Chile, governments throughout Latin America have replaced state-run social insurance programs in various degrees with private pension institutions. In the quarter century after Chile, nine other Latin American countries implemented some type of pension privatization: Peru (1993), Argentina and Columbia (1994), Uruguay (1996), Bolivia and Mexico (1997), El Salvador (1998), Costa Rica (2001) and the Dominican Republic (2003). At the end of 2006, more than 73 million people in Latin America were affiliated with a private pension system, and pension fund administrators invested more than US$225 billion in retirement savings.[1] The degree of privatization has varied dramatically across these cases, as evidenced in Table 4.1. In Chile, Colombia, El Salvador, and Peru, the rules of the reformed pension system dictate that the average wage earner participating in the private pension regime should receive 100 percent of his or her retirement income from his or her privately managed individual pension account. In Mexico and Bolivia, the reformed pension system also brought an extensive transfer of responsibility to private savings systems, with more than 90 percent of the average wage earner's retirement income expected to derive from his or her private savings accumulated during working life. At the opposite end, Costa Rica's modest 2001 reform anticipates that the average wage earner will derive just 20 percent of his or her retirement income from private savings. In Uruguay, the average wage earner can choose to split his or her retirement contributions between the public and private pension systems (receiving a subsidy in the public benefit if he or she does) that would result in a pension that is approximately 37 percent private.[2] On average, private defined-contribution

[1] AIOS 2006.
[2] These simulations are described in Chapter 2.

TABLE 4.2. *Distribution of Workers in Public or Private/Mixed Pension Systems, 2002*

Country	Percentage of Total Labor Force Enrolled	
	Public Only	Private or Mixed
Argentina	20	80
Bolivia	0	100
Chile	2	98
Colombia	55	45
Costa Rica	0	100
El Salvador	9	91
Mexico	0	100
Peru	4	96
Uruguay	49	51

Source: Mesa-Lago 2005.

pension schemes in Latin America will replace 80 percent of workers' retirement income; this represents an institutional transformation far greater than any witnessed in other parts of the world.[3]

The structural pension reforms in Latin America have undoubtedly brought a significant shift in the dividing line between the private and public responsibilities for old age income protection. Yet, the region also displays marked variation in the depth of these transformations. In Peru, Argentina, Uruguay, and Colombia, participation in the private pension market is optional. In most of these cases, as discussed in Chapter 2, however, governments provided considerable financial incentives for workers to join the private pension systems (such as lower contribution rates for workers in the private pension regime, as in Peru, or a bonus in the public pension tier as in Uruguay) and restricted their ability to return to the public pension regime.[4] Even where private pension regimes were formally optional, enrollment in these programs has been quite strong. Consequently, on average, 85 percent of the labor force in Latin America is enrolled in the private pension market for some or all of their retirement savings (see Table 4.2).

EVOLUTION OF PRIVATE PENSION SYSTEMS

The formal contours of the private pension reforms in Latin America suggest a dramatic institutional transformation in social protection through which the public sector has been relegated to a marginal role. But the formal rules and legal coverage of these institutions tell only one part of the story; states in fact continue to play a significant role in the allocation of risk and old

---

[3] Mesa-Lago 2005; Mesa-Lago and Müller 2002.
[4] Colombia, however, permits workers to return to the public pension system, as does Argentina since 2007.

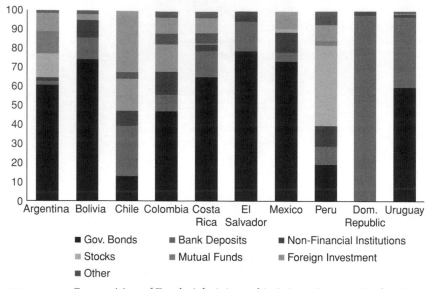

FIGURE 4.1. Composition of Funds Administered in Private Pension Market, December 2006. *Source:* AIOS 2006.

age income in Latin America. For one thing, in reformed pension systems, governments provide significant regulatory functions that curtail the scope of market forces. In some cases, these regulations were meant to limit risk-taking behavior by the pension fund managers, while other rules aimed simply at capturing the invested funds in the domestic market, and in particular in the purchase of government debt. The effect of these regulations has gone beyond the reduction in market risk borne by individuals; they also have reduced the diversification of investment portfolios, induced high correlations in the investment behavior of the private pension fund managers ("herding"), and vitiated much of individuals' effective choice among private pension funds.[5] By the mid-1990s, the vast majority of investments in the private pension funds in countries like Mexico and Argentina were held in government bonds. In recent years, governments have gradually relaxed investment regulations so that by 2006 just 42 percent of assets was held in government debt – down from 48 percent in 1999.[6] Figure 4.1 illustrates the average composition of pension fund portfolios in the reformed systems. Although a significant share of old age income will be provided by private sector firms in Latin America, the effective role of market forces in this sphere continues to be abridged by the fact that as the ultimate guarantor of the system, governments will necessarily impose stringent regulations on these systems.

In addition to this regulatory function, governments also play a significant financial role in private pension systems. In most cases, reforming governments

[5] Srinivas and Yermo 1999.
[6] AIOS 2006.

TABLE 4.3. *Compliance with Private Pension Systems in Latin America*

	Reference Year	Percentage of Labor Force Contributing	
		Before Reform	After Reform (2002)
Chile	1980	64	58
Bolivia	1996	12	11
Mexico	1997	37	30
El Salvador	1996	26	19
Dominican Republic	2000	30	16*
Peru	1993	31	11
Colombia	1994	32	24
Argentina	1997	50	24
Uruguay	2000	73	60
Costa Rica	2002	53	48

* Contribution rate for Dominican Republic taken in 2004 (Crabbe 2005, p. 36).
Source: Mesa-Lago 2005, p. 51.

have underwritten minimum-pension guarantees, which provide a publicly-funded minimal pension for workers whose investment savings will not be sufficient to finance even a modest pension. Minimum pension guarantees range from 50% of the average wage in Colombia, to 7% in Bolivia. Although reformers viewed such minimum pension guarantees as a safety net for only a small portion of the workforce, recent analyses in Chile and Mexico suggest that state guarantees are likely to capture a significantly greater portion of the population than reformers anticipated at their creation. The promise of private pensions to transfer old age income responsibilities from the state to individuals, in this sense, is unlikely to be fulfilled.[7]

The scope of private market governance in old age pension systems is also considerably narrower than the formal contours of the system suggest if the institutions' effective coverage – measured by active compliance rates – is taken into account. In every case, the number of workers actively contributing to private pension funds is considerably lower than the legal reach of the private pension systems as measured by the number of workers enrolled in the systems. Indeed, of the 73 million affiliates in private pension markets in Latin America, just over 30 million workers were actively contributing to their pension fund in 2006 – that is on average just 26 percent of the labor force of the privatizing countries.[8] As Table 4.3 reveals, only in Chile is more than half of the economically active population regularly contributing to the private pension regime. In Peru, just 11 percent of the labor force is effectively covered by the reformed pension system. And even though the data from 2002 to 2005

[7] Gill et al. 2005.
[8] AIOS 2006.

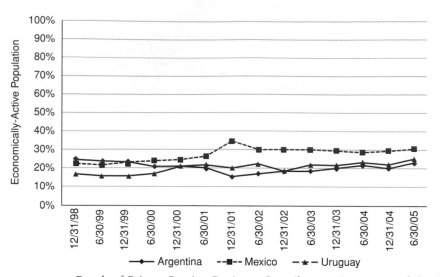

FIGURE 4.2. Reach of Private Pension Regimes: Contributors (Percentage of the Economically Active Population). *Source:* AIOS 2006.

indicate a gradual expansion of coverage in many countries, this has not been a universal or stable trend. In many cases, the recent increase only represents a modest recovery from the sharp decline in contribution rates during the economic recession at the beginning of the decade. Looking more closely at the three pension privatizations examined in this study, for instance, although Figure 4.2 reveals stable or increasing enrollment, Figure 4.3 shows that active compliance rates remain considerably lower in each case in 2005 than they were at the system's initiation, despite the economic recovery in recent years. And as Table 4.3 reveals, this trend toward declining coverage following structural pension reform is pervasive in Latin America, though varied in extent.

For all its effective limitations, pension privatization remains a significant transformation of the formal jurisdiction of public and private responsibilities for social protection. Indeed, privatization has apportioned a significant financial responsibility to the shoulders of individual workers who, under the rules of the reformed pension systems, must save increasingly for their own retirements – even where low wages and unstable labor markets make this task quite difficult. Whether those savings will be sufficient to finance the old age pensions for the next generation without significant state support remains to be seen. Without a doubt, the new institutional designs mark a significant departure in the form and function of old age income protection. And even though the future of these institutions cannot yet be foretold, the varied outputs of institutional reform processes offer a critical opportunity to evaluate the sources and mechanisms of institutional change. The reform experiences of four countries thus provide rich comparative data in which I evaluate my

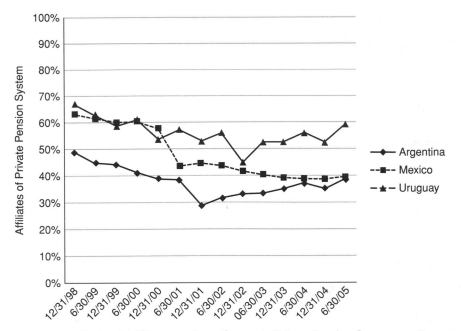

FIGURE 4.3. Ratio of Affiliates to Contributors in Private Pension System, 1998–2005.
Source: FIAP 2006.

causal hypotheses in the next chapters. The circumstance and output of those reforms are sketched in the remainder of this chapter.

ARGENTINA

Argentina was among Latin America's pioneers in the creation of a national old age pension system and the nation's Sistema Integrado de Jubilaciones y Pensiones (SIJP) had achieved near universal legal coverage by the 1990s. Argentina's President Carlos Saúl Menem also broke new ground by legislating the partial privatization the SIJP in 1993, making Law 24,241 the first democratically sanctioned pension privatization. That law created a multi-pillar pension regime in which workers may choose between a reformed public defined-benefit pension system and a "mixed" regime that combines a basic state pension with a privately managed defined-contribution retirement benefit.[9] By 2007, 11.6 million workers in a labor force of 15.3 million were enrolled in the private pension regime, and 2.4 million workers were affiliated with the public defined-benefit system.[10]

[9] The SIJP has been absorbing the regional pension funds since the 1990s. In 2000, of the approximately 13 million active workers in the labor market, approximately 6.8 million workers did not contribute to any pension system. Rofman 2000, p. 1.
[10] SAFJP 2007, p. 3.

The 1993 structural pension reform dramatically restructured the institutional landscape of old age pension provision in Argentina. Yet, of the nearly 12 million workers enrolled in the system in 2007, just 4.8 million workers made contributions to their private pension accounts in the month of May, and 1.4 million workers contributed to the public system.[11] These patterns betray a far less dramatic movement toward self-insurance than the formal profile of Argentina's partially privatized social security institution would suggest. Since its implementation, moreover, the private pension system has been subject to substantial revisions and interventions that have weakened the performance of, and public confidence in, the private component of the system, while gradually broadening the role of the state in social protection. The long-term balance of state and market functions in Argentina's old age pension system thus is far from clear, as the nation's private pension system has proved highly unstable since its inception.

The 1993 Reform

Law 24,241 was approved by the Argentine National Congress in September 1993 and implemented in July 1994. The reformed system permits all workers to choose between two regimes. Each includes a basic universal benefit (Prestación Básica Universal, PBU) administered by the state and financed with employer contributions. The PBU is a flat benefit of approximately 28 percent of the average wage in 1994; it was originally calculated on the basis of a reference unit, the average mandatory pension contribution (Aporte Medio Provisional Obligatorio, AMPO), which tracked changes in real wages in the absence of a formal indexation mechanism.[12] Eligibility conditions for receiving this benefit were tightened from a minimum of 20 to 30 years of contributions, while the retirement age was increased by five years, to 65 for men and 60 for women. In addition, the replacement rate for the defined-benefit component of the pension system was reduced from approximately 70 to 82 percent of the final three years' wages, to approximately 60 percent of the last ten years' wages.[13]

For their "second pillar" benefit, Argentine workers may choose between a public DB and private DC pension scheme. For workers choosing the private scheme, 11 percent of wages (initially) were transferred to one of the newly created private pension fund administrators (Administradoras de Fondos de Jubilaciones y Pensiones, or AFJPs). The ordinary retirement (Jubilación Ordinaria, JO) pension in this defined-contribution system is based solely on the investment of workers' contributions. Net of an insurance premium and AFJP commissions, 7.5 percent of covered wages were invested in workers' individual accounts and expected to yield a JO benefit equivalent to approximately

---

[11] SAFJP 2007, p .3.
[12] The PBU was 2.5 AMPO plus 1 percent for every year of contribution between 30 and 45 years.
[13] Rofman 2004, p. 3.

35 percent of the average wage. The JO could be taken as an annuity, purchased at market prices from an insurance company, or by scheduled withdrawals. For all workers in the transitional generation with contributions in the old public system, a compensatory benefit (Prestación Compensatoria, PC) provides rights-holders with a benefit of 1.5 percent of covered wages for each year of contributions in the old pension system.‾

Workers who opted to participate in the reformed, state-run pension system for their second tier benefit would receive the additional permanence benefit (Prestación Adicional por Permanencia, PAP) in addition to the PBU. The PAP is a defined-benefit pension with an accrual rate of 0.85 percent (of the average final ten years of income) for each year of contributions in the new pension system. For an average-wage earner contributing for 35 years, therefore, the PAP would provide a replacement rate of 30 percent of wages. Along with the PBU of 28 percent of wages, workers staying in the fully public pension regime could anticipate a total replacement rate of 58 percent under the rules of the reform.

The 1993 law held that workers who failed to specify a choice between the public and private schemes would be automatically transferred to the private regime for their second-pillar benefit. This rule would subsequently account for the overwhelming majority of new enrollments in that scheme in the 1990s. Indeed, of the 5.8 million workers that joined the private pension scheme after the reform, 4 million were assigned to it by default for failing to choose between the public and private regimes.[14] Finally, a social assistance pension (the PEA, Prestación por Edad Avanzada) provides benefits for workers older than age 70 who lack sufficient contributions to qualify for the PBU.

Institutional Outcomes

The immediate fiscal impact of Argentina's pension reform was sharply negative for the government. Although parametric revisions to the public pay-as-you-go (PAYG) system brought significant cost savings, the state retained significant pension liabilities just as pension revenue began to fall.[15] Indeed, as workers began to divert payroll contributions to private pension fund managers and employer contributions were nearly halved – from 16 to an average of 8 percent of covered wages – pension system revenue fell by 45 percent between 1994 and 2001.[16] Tightening eligibility requirements brought important cost savings, but the data reveal that these were outweighed by the loss of employee and employer contributions following the reform. Higher-than-anticipated pension costs resulted in part from compromises made by the Menem government in the political process in order to overcome opposition to the reform. For

---

[14] These workers were randomly assigned to an AFJP upon being enrolled in the private regime. Rofman 2004, p. 4.

[15] Isuani et al. 1996.

[16] Crabbe and Giral 2004, p. 17; Mesa-Lago 2002, p. 8.

instance, the original proposal did not include a compensatory benefit to recognize workers' contributions to the old pension system; this provision was
added during negotiations over the reform. The generosity of the second-tier
public pension (the PAP) also increased from the proposed accrual rate of
0.5 percent of wages per year of contributions to 0.85 percent per year – a
change that was conceded in order to win labor support for the reform. By
the end of the 1990s, the higher-than-expected costs and sharp fall in revenue
meant that Argentina's pension system required funding from general revenue
to cover approximately 70 percent of its expenditures.[17]

Argentine technocrats saw these imbalances coming and moved to revise
the terms of the reformed pension system shortly after its implementation.
In 1995, President Menem decreed the Pension Solidarity Law (DL 24,463),
which restricted payment of the basic universal pension to the limits of pension system revenue. The basic pension value was changed again in 1997 when
Menem issued Decree 833/97 replacing the AMPO with the MOPRE (Módulo
Previsional), which further enhanced the discretionary power of the government in the payment of the basic pension (PBU).[18] These changes were of
more than simply budgetary consequence; they also increased workers' sense
of uncertainty about benefit values, undermining confidence in the reformed
pension system.[19]

Compliance with the reformed pension system, moreover, which was
expected to increase with the tightening link between contributions and benefits, fell far short of reformers' expectations. Although enrollment increased
sharply in the 1990s, the number of actual contributors in Argentina's private
pension system remained fairly constant, resulting in a sharp decline in the
ratio of affiliates to active contributors from 70 percent in 1994 to just 31
percent in June 2002 (Figure 4.3).[20] Given the tightening rules for eligibility to
receive a state pension, the result of declining compliance rates is likely to be a
50 percent drop in the share of citizens older than age 65 with rights to a pension
benefit in the next quarter century.[21] This is because in addition to requiring
thirty years of contributions to qualify for the PBU, the Argentine pension
system requires that workers be "regular contributors" in order to claim state
pension benefits. Even if a worker has contributed regularly for several years
but has failed to do so in the eighteen months prior to retirement, he or she
would not be eligible for survivor or retirement benefits.[22] As a result of such
rules, the share of Argentina's population older than age 65 without a pension
rose from 23 percent in 1993, to 37.3 percent by 2003, while the proportion

---

[17] Bertranou et al. 2003, p. 106.
[18] Kata 2001, p. 20; SAFJP 1998, p. 25.
[19] Rofman 2000, p. 18.
[20] SAFJP 2003a, p. 13.
[21] Rofman 2000, pp. 14–15.
[22] Such workers may claim a benefit financed with the funds they have accumulated in their
individual accounts. Rofman 2000.

of the elderly population without access even to a spouse's pension rose from 12.5 percent in 1993 to 26.5 percent a decade later.[23] Much of the declining contribution rates has been attributed to the expansion of informal employment in Argentina; nevertheless, data reveal that contribution rates were in fact more irregular in the private system than they were for workers who remained within the public defined-benefit regime. This suggests that confidence in the private pension market in particular has been low, although both regimes have suffered sharp declines in compliance in the decade after structural reform.

The private pension market in Argentina has been characterized by relatively high operating costs and commissions, which consumed approximately 35 percent of contributions in 2007; the market also has been highly concentrated in a subset of the competing funds.[24] Despite fierce competition, the top three AFJPs received 56 percent of contributions in 2007, and the top six held 92 percent of invested pension funds.[25] The portfolio investment structure across the competing funds is very similar, moreover, revealing a strong herd effect and poor diversification.[26]

Without a doubt, the profound economic crisis that gripped Argentina at the turn of the century placed the most significant strain on the nation's reformed pension institution. Not only did unemployment rise during the crisis, but investment returns in the private pension market also fell sharply, as illustrated in Figure 4.4. Making matters worse, the Argentine government made a series of ad hoc changes to the pension institution that weakened its structure, compromised its finances, and undermined public confidence in the midst of the economic downturn. The first of these was a cost-saving measure in 2001, through which the government temporarily slashed the basic pension benefit by 13 percent. Although this benefit cut was repealed the following year, state-financed pensions were not adjusted for inflation between December 2001 and September 2004 – a period in which inflation reached 50 percent.[27] In late 2001, with the goal of stimulating consumption, the Argentine government lowered employee contributions to the pension system from 11 to 5 percent of wages – more than halving the retirement benefits that would be provided through the private pension system.[28] Since a portion of commissions and management costs charged by the private pension fund administrators were either flat or relatively rigid, this change resulted in administrative costs consuming more than 65 percent of contributions to the individual accounts.[29] Although employee contributions were subsequently raised to 7 percent, the private tier

[23] Rofman 2004, p. 5.
[24] Rofman 2000 notes that these charges are high by regional standards. Also see SAFJP 2007, p. 5.
[25] SAFJP 2007, p. 5.
[26] SAFJP 2003b; Srinivas and Yermo 1999.
[27] Rofman 2004.
[28] Rofman 2000, p. 14; SAFJP 2002, p. 88.
[29] UAFJP 2002.

FIGURE 4.4. Annual Rates of Return to Argentina's Pension Funds, 1996–2000. *Source:* Rofman 2000, Figure 5; SAFJP 2002.

of Argentina's new pension institution had been fundamentally weakened – both institutionally and in terms of public perceptions of its efficacy.[30]

As budgetary constraints tightened in 2001, the government of Fernando de la Rúa looked to the private pension industry to obtain foreign exchange needed to meet its external debt obligations. At first, the government strongly "encouraged" the private pension fund industry to make a "patriotic investment" of its dollar-denominated assets in domestic banks in government bonds (at below-market interest rates).[31] However, this mega swap of US$30 billion in government debt only provided the Argentine government with temporary breathing room. By late 2001, the government once again faced a shortage of foreign currency and *seized* US$42 billion in dollar-denominated assets in domestic banks, much of which was held by the private pension fund industry. These deposits were replaced with government bonds that had even worse terms than were previously offered: They carried a lower interest rate and had no secondary market. Then, in early 2002, as government bonds constituted nearly 80 percent of pension fund assets, the Argentine government announced the largest sovereign debt default in history. It subsequently converted all of its dollar-denominated bonds to pesos at the rate of 1.4 pesos to the dollar,

[30] Rofman 2003.

[31] In November 2001, the government lifted the cap on public debt investments in pension fund portfolios, which had been set at 50 percent in the original reform law (24,241).

immediately slashing the dollar value of pension fund holdings by more than 40 percent.[32] In the process, Argentine citizens lost more than US$12 billion in the dollar value of pension fund savings, or what pension industry sources estimated to be dollar-value losses of 60–70 percent.[33] By the end of May 2002, the majority of the bonds held by private pension funds were trading at 20 percent of their nominal value, while the "guaranteed loans" had no identifiable market value.[34] Strikingly, these interventions failed to generate a broad outcry among Argentine citizens; instead, they were greeted largely with apathy outside the financial community.[35]

In part, such a tepid reaction may owe to the fact that coverage of the pension system had fallen dramatically by the end of 2002, narrowing the share of the population with a meaningful stake in the new pension system. Indeed, just 18 percent of the economically active population in Argentina was covered by the pension system at that time and only a third of the citizens older than age 65 could claim rights to a pension.[36] Citizens' stakes in the private system also were diminished by the reduction in payroll contributions to the system, which diminished the capital invested in each worker's fund. Even after restoring employee contributions to 7 percent of covered wages, the deduction of insurance and commissions resulted in a net transfer of just 4.46 percent of covered wages to individuals' private retirement accounts.[37] Within a decade of its reform, an institution that had once been among the broadest-reaching, most generous, and most effective pension systems in Latin America had ceased to function as an effective means through which most workers could insure against the risk of poverty in old age.

Public confidence in Argentina's private pension system failed to recover even after the economic crisis abated. As a result, President Néstor Kirchner took advantage of this sentiment to revise once again the terms of old age pension provision in Argentina – this time reinforcing and expanding the role of the state.[38] Law 26,222, promulgated in March 2007, increased the generosity of the universal basic pension and raised the accrual rate for the public second-pillar benefit, the PAP, from .85 percent per year to 1.5 percent. The measure also removed what had been the principal source of new enrollments in the private pension market: the automatic enrollment of undecided workers. Workers who fail to specify a choice between the public and private regimes for their second-pillar benefit now are assigned to the *public* pension system. And by contrast to the original terms of the reform, workers enrolled in the private pension market are permitted to return to the public social insurance pension system. In the first six months after the law's implementation, 10 percent of

[32] This resulted in a 30 percent *profit* in peso terms. Bertranou et al. 2003, p. 110; FIAP 2003.
[33] Bertranou et al. 2003, p. 109; Nielsen 2003.
[34] Organización Internacional del Trabajo 2002, p. 14.
[35] Organización Internacional del Trabajo 2002, p. 10.
[36] Bertranou and Rofman 2002, pp. 77–8; Rofman 2003, p. 19.
[37] AIOS 2007.
[38] Sociedad de Estudios Laborales 2000.

affiliates – 80 percent of whom were regular contributors – had moved back to the state DB pension regime.[39] The 2007 law also increased the taxable wage ceiling (from 60 to 75 MOPRES or from US$1,560 to US$1,920) and raised the maximum pension ceiling (from US$992 to US$1,244, approximately 65 percent of the maximum taxable income). Finally, the 2007 reform imposed new restrictions on the private pension market, including a cap on AFJP commissions equal to 1 percent of taxable income. This measure represented a significant expansion of the role of the state in pension provision, and a firm public rebuke of the private regime that President Kirchner called "perverse" upon signing the law.[40]

Although a complete analysis of the cause and consequence of the dramatic shifts in Argentina's pension institution since its privatization is beyond the scope of this study, the analysis in the next chapters offers several insights into the roots of that institution's instability. First, the technocratic origin of the structural reform shows that decisions regarding the design of Argentina's privatization were governed by extremely short time horizons. As the country's vulnerability to capital flight grew in the early 1990s, government actors attached ever-greater urgency to the goal of sending credibility signals to international market actors as a way to ensure continued short-term inflows of capital. As the enactment of some kind of pension privatization came to be viewed as a vital credibility signal, reformers made significant compromises in the legislative process in order to rapidly sanction the reform. Even though these compromises lowered political obstacles, they raised the financial cost of the reform far beyond the level that the government anticipated. And even though the cost of these compromises appeared to be affordable in the midst of the fiscal bonanza of the early 1990s, tightening budgetary constraints later in the decade would reveal the short-sightedness of these calculations and the unsustainability of the reform's costs.

Recent government interventions in and revisions to the Argentine pension system also betray the Menem government's view of the private pension system as a means to achieve short-term macroeconomic goals rather than as an ends in itself. The roots of this posture may be traced to the political conflict over the pension reform and in particular to the terms on which President Menem won political support for the privatization. Menem did not build support for market-oriented reform within his own political party or in society on principled or programmatic grounds. Rather, he won consent to reform largely on instrumental foundations. In the legislature, Menem drew upon his institutional authority as president and party leader to gain partisan cooperation on his reform. Rather than engaging reluctant party members or redefining the Peronist Party ideology, Menem circumvented these, using raw power to discipline reluctant partisans.[41] Because Menem could form a majority

---

[39] "ING: Higher contributions to compensate affiliate flight – Argentina," 2007.
[40] "Empezaron los traspasos a la jubilación estatal," 2007.
[41] Levitsky 2003, p. 149.

without the support of the opposition Radical Party, moreover, he did not make concessions to his partisan rivals to broaden the base of political support for the private pension system. Menem's departure from office in 1998 thus left the incipient pension system in the hands of a governing party – led by former Radical Party President Fernando de la Rúa – that possessed little in the way of political commitment to the private pension system.

Similarly, President Menem made the case for pension privatization to society largely on material grounds – promising wealth, growth, and stability through the market-based system. He also pledged a firm break with the past economic chaos of the state-centered development model. But there was little in the way of normative claims that the reformed pension system was fair or appropriate for Argentina. By many accounts, Menem himself lacked a firm normative commitment to the principles of the market.[42] Support for the private pension system thus rested heavily on citizens' (if not also politicians') instrumental expectations – specifically, that of material reward – rather than on persuasion that the new system was fair. Thus when falling wages and rising unemployment at the end of the 1990s undercut the institution's potential material rewards (e.g., by undermining citizens' ability to save for their own retirement and slashing rates of return to pension investments), what had been the principal grounds for the system's support eroded as well. Indeed, the street violence that erupted in late 2001 laid bare the depth of disillusionment not only with the depth of market-oriented reform in Argentina, but also with politicians who had promised much more than they could deliver to the population.

Argentina's 1993 structural pension reform thus effected a significant and dramatic departure from the long-established path of welfare state development by creating a mixed public and private pension regime. The new institution, which began operating in July 1994, transformed the role of the state from the dominant provider of social insurance pensions, to a secondary and subsidiary role in the provision of old age income. In the years since its implementation, the new institution has been highly unstable, having undergone significant revisions that weakened the structure and function of the private pension system, and that increased again the role of the state in pension provision. A full return to the state-run pension design is unlikely; nevertheless, the prospect for a dominant market-based pension system to endure in Argentina is rather dim.

MEXICO

The privatization of the Mexican pension system was sanctioned by the Mexican National Congress in December 1995 and took effect on July 1, 1997. The reform replaced the nation's public pay-as-you-go pension system with a private pension system based on individual pension accounts. The rules of the new system suggested that the average wage earner should earn approximately

---

[42] See, for example, Levitsky 2003, pp. 148–9; Palermo and Novaro 1996, pp. 24–5.

90 percent of old age income from his or her contributions to a private pension account. The state, by means of the Mexican Social Security Institute (Instituto Mexicano del Seguro Social, IMSS) continues to play an important financial role in the pension system by providing a minimum pension guarantee and by making a financial contribution to each worker's individual pension account. The state also plays important oversight and enforcement functions in the private pension market, while also competing in it through a state-sponsored pension fund. Although Mexico's pension reform is one of the deepest privatizations in Latin America and the world, the role of the private sector in old age pension provision is considerably more limited in practice than the rules of the new institution would suggest.

The 1995/1996 Pension Reform

In December 1995 the Mexican National Congress approved the Social Insurance Law (Ley del Seguro Social), which transformed the IMSS social insurance pension system into a defined-contribution scheme based on a system of privately managed individual savings accounts. A second law, the Ley de los Sistemas de Ahorro para el Retiro, establishing the legal and regulatory structures for the implementation of the private pension system, was enacted in April 1996. These laws transformed the largest component of the IMSS system, namely the disability, old age, severance and life insurance system (Invalidez, Vejez, Cesantía en Edad Avanzada y Muerte, or IVCM) into two systems: an old age and severance pension system (Seguro de Retiro, Cesantía en Edad Avanzada y Vejez, RCV) and disability and life insurance (Seguro de Invalidez y Vida, IV). The life insurance system continues to be administered by IMSS and to function on risk-pooling principles. It is financed by a contribution of 2.5 percent of wages, divided between employers, employees, and the state. A voluntary pension system also was created for supplemental contributions to workers' retirement accounts.

Mexico's private pension regime came into effect in July 1997 for voluntary contributions, and in September 1997 for mandatory contributions. In the new scheme, 6.5 percent of covered wages, plus a state-funded 'social quota' (equal to 2.2 percent of the average wage, or 5.5 percent of the 1997 minimum wage, indexed to prices) is transferred to individual accounts managed by private sector firms called Administradoras de Fondos de Ahorro para el Retiro (AFORE). In addition, contributions of 5 percent of each worker's salary continue to the individual retirement accounts in the national housing insurance fund (Instituto del Fondo Nacional Para La Vivienda de Los Trabajadores, INFONAVIT). Workers can use this money for retirement only if they do not draw upon it as part of a mortgage to buy a house. The 1995 reform provided for the integration of workers' Sistema de Ahorro para el Retiro (SAR) savings into new pension accounts. Contributions to the new individual retirement accounts are invested in retirement investment funds (Sociedades de Inversión Especializadas en Fondos para el Retiro, SIEFORES), which are managed by the AFOREs. As in Argentina, the Mexican pension reform allows labor unions and the state (specifically, IMSS) to manage a private pension fund. Unlike in Argentina, however, the IMSS AFORE competes on the same terms as the private sector pension fund managers.

Although the role of the state in Mexico's pension institution was fundamentally transformed, it was not relegated altogether to the sidelines of the institution. Rather, the Mexican government continues to play significant financial and regulatory roles in the reformed pension system while also retaining the contingent liability for the pensions of current retirees and workers with acquired rights in the old pension system. Most significantly, the 1995 law obliges the Mexican government to provide a minimum pension guarantee for workers whose savings after twenty-five years of contributions are insufficient to finance a minimal pension equal to the nominal value of the 1997 minimum wage, indexed to prices. The 1997 minimum pension was equal to approximately 38 percent of the average wage. The value of this benefit relative to the average wage is expected to fall over time, however, on account of the price indexation rule since the average wage tends to rise more rapidly than prices. The reform also tightened eligibility conditions for claiming the minimum pension guarantee from ten to twenty-five years of contributions.

Institutional Outcomes

Estimates of the number of workers covered by the IMSS pension system at the time of the reform range from 10 million to 10.9 million out of a labor force of 33.5 million.[43] Since its inception, the private pension system in Mexico has enrolled more than 21 million workers and accumulated assets of more than 700 billion pesos by March 2007 (US$68.9 billion), or 13.75 percent of GDP.[44] Despite strong enrollment in the AFORE market, active contribution rates have fallen steadily as a share of affiliates in the new system over the last decade.[45] This decline is much sharper and steadier than in neighboring countries, but it has occurred at a time of strong economic growth and declining rates of self-employment.[46] One study found, for instance, that just 6.3 million workers, or 31 percent of registered affiliates, were contributing actively to their individual accounts in 2003.[47] The evasion rate may be deceiving, however, for it may be at least partially an artifact of high affiliation rates that have been inflated by multiple enrollments. Indeed, the number of workers assigned to a fund in the private pension system by the oversight institution (Comisión Nacional del Sistema de Ahorro para el Retiro, CONSAR) because they failed to specify

[43] Edmonds 1996; Grandolini and Cerda 1997.
[44] CONSAR 2007, p. 17.
[45] AIOS 2004.
[46] The share of self-employed workers in the labor force fell from 17.4 percent of the labor force in 1996 to 15.9 percent in 2000. Alarcón and Zepeda 2004, p. 77.
[47] Crabbe and Giral 2004, p. 14.

a preferred pension fund has risen more rapidly than the number of workers who actively register and express a choice of fund. In 2005, moreover, the number of AFORE members was 2.7 times greater than the number of workers affiliated with the IMSS institution for other social insurance functions.[48] These data suggest that Mexico's new pension system may suffer the problem of duplicate accounts that plagued the earlier, failed SAR reform. Such administrative problems complicate not only the task of gauging system performance, but they also will make it more difficult for workers with multiple accounts to receive an adequate pension based on the contributions they have made to the system.

Also casting doubt on the ultimate effectiveness of the pension system is evidence that many workers are contributing infrequently to private pension accounts. Because low-income workers typically have more unstable incomes and thus more uneven contribution history, analysts have projected a sharp decline in pension coverage as a result of the lengthening of the required contribution time (from ten to twenty-five years) in order to qualify for the minimum pension guarantee. According to one study, 61 percent of women will lack coverage by the pension system as a result of insufficient contribution time, but only 40.6 percent of men in the system will be denied the minimum pension for this reason.[49]

The accumulation in private pension accounts has been reduced further by high commissions and fees charged by the pension fund managers. Before 2007, private pension fund managers in Mexico were permitted broad leeway to charge management fees on pension accounts. The result was a wide range of fees and charges that consumed 36 percent of the total contributions transferred to private pension accounts and 56 percent of net funds capitalized for retirement in 2003.[50] Although the gross rate of return to the pension fund investments has averaged 7.65 percent between 1997 and 2005, the net return to workers after the margin claimed by the AFOREs was only 2.09 percent.[51] In other words, the margin claimed by the pension fund management companies (5.56 percent) was 2.7 times higher than that returned to the workers.

Poverty and low wages present important constraints on Mexico's private pension system. Nearly 70 percent of Mexican workers earn less than three times the minimum wage. For these workers, unless investment returns are very high, the combined effect of low wages and high commissions charged on contributions are expected to make it very difficult to accumulate enough savings in their individual accounts to retire without the state's minimum pension guarantee.[52] Despite its more radical degree of privatization, the accumulation of private pension resources in Mexico thus falls far short of that in Argentina

---

[48] Valencia Armas 2005, p. 311.
[49] Valencia Armas 2005, p. 321.
[50] AIOS 2004.
[51] CONSAR 2005; Valencia Armas 2005, p. 316.
[52] Azuara 2003, p. 20; Edmonds 1996, p. 5.

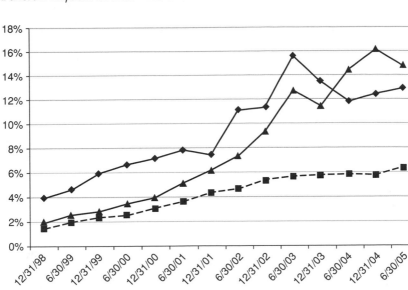

FIGURE 4.5. Private Pension Funds (Percentage of GDP). *Source:* AIOS 2006.

and Uruguay (as a share of GDP), as illustrated in Figure 4.5. The Mexican government thus retains a significant contingent liability for more than two-thirds of the participants in the private pension system who are likely to qualify for the minimum pension guarantee. For minimum wage earners, moreover, the extent of privatization is even smaller, given that the state-funded "social quota" represents more than half of the contributions to their individual accounts.[53] The combination of low wages and high AFORE fees thus may sharply curtail the "privateness" of Mexico's private pension system.

The regulatory role of the state in the private pension system is also significant, and limits on the market have broadened considerably over time in response to early performance problems. From the beginning, CONSAR established strict regulations on the investment portfolios of the private pension funds in order to avoid excessive risk-taking. Restrictions that were imposed in legislative debate also assured that most of the investments initially remained in the domestic market. The avoidance of excessive risk-taking had become an important political objective following the 1994–5 domestic banking sector crisis in Mexico, which resulted in Mexican citizens bearing an enormous cost to rescue domestic banks. Although many of the limits on investment – such as restrictions on stock and foreign currency holdings – have been gradually eased since the reform's implementation, the restrictions have had the effect of limiting the diversification of investment portfolios and encouraging

[53] Azuara 2003, p. 18.

"herd" behavior among the AFOREs.[54] Pension fund portfolios have been highly correlated and they have been heavily invested in government bonds. In 2000, varying forms of government bonds accounted for 92 percent of the investment in the AFORE system in Mexico.[55] By 2007, however, the gradual easing of regulations on investments resulted in this rate falling to just 69 percent of pension fund portfolios on average being held in Mexican government securities.[56]

In response to the early performance challenges of the privatized pension system, the Mexican National Congress in 2007 overhauled the regulation of the private pension system and imposed new restrictions on the types of commissions that private pension funds could charge. The 2007 law also established that workers who fail to make an explicit choice among the AFOREs will be assigned by CONSAR to the fund with the highest rate of return (previously, they were assigned to the fund with the lowest fees). In addition, CONSAR created a tool by which workers can easily compare the fees charged by the different pension fund administrators with the goal of improving workers' choice among pension funds.

Despite early performance problems, the Mexican government, led by the conservative National Action Party (Partido Acción Nacional, PAN), took steps to broaden the share of the labor force covered by the private pension system. In 2004, President Vicente Fox sought to incorporate employees of the Mexican Social Security Institute (IMSS) into the private pension system. However, the powerful SNTSS (Sindicato Nacional de Trabajadores de Seguridad Social) union representing IMSS employees waged a vigorous protest and won the exemption of current IMSS workers from the reform; only the new IMSS employees will be obliged to join the private defined-contribution pension system.[57] President Fox also attempted to privatize the much-larger pension system for Mexico's 3 million public sector employees, Instituto de Seguridad y Servicios Sociales de los Trabajadores del Estado (ISSSTE). Although strong opposition from public sector unions forced the Fox government to withdraw this proposal, his successor, President Felipe Calderón, also of the PAN, enacted a similar law in March 2007. According to that measure, public employees will begin to contribute to individual, defined-contribution retirement accounts in 2008. A new public and tripartite institution, PensionISSSTE, will manage the new system, which again will only be mandatory for new entrants into public sector employment. Current public employees younger than age 46, however, may choose to join the retirement savings system or remain in ISSSTE's defined-benefit pension program. Public sector workers who switch to the new program will receive a recognition bond to compensate for contributions made under the old pension system and will be eligible to transfer yearly between PensionISSSTE and a private AFORE.

[54] Srinivas and Yermo 1999.
[55] Sinha 2002, p. 31.
[56] CONSAR 2007, p. 34.
[57] Dion 2008.

The 1995 pension privatization in Mexico brought a radical break with the traditional state monopoly in old age pension insurance. Even though it replaced the traditional, defined-benefit, pay-as-you-go pension system with a privately funded, defined-contribution system, it did not remove the state from the business of pension provision. In addition to retaining critical regulatory functions in the private pension fund industry, the Mexican state has a significant financial role in the new retirement system through the minimum pension guarantee and social quota. Furthermore, the rules of the new pension system will not take full effect for a generation, as the current workforce retains the option of retiring under the benefits promised in the old pension system. Even for the next generation, the reach of the private pension system may be curtailed significantly by the effects of very low incomes, high rates of evasion, and high fees charged by the pension fund managers, which further reduce workers' private retirement savings.[58]

URUGUAY

The Uruguayan government enacted a structural pension reform in September 1995, with the new system coming into operation in April 1996. The reform created a multipillar pension system based on a public defined-benefit pension system – the "intergenerational solidarity" component – and a private defined-contribution pension scheme based on individual retirement accounts. Although all workers must participate in the basic public pension system, the private pension system is optional for most members of the labor force. Uruguay's pension reform is among the more modest structural reforms in Latin America. At maturity, the public, defined-benefit pension component remains the dominant pillar in the reformed institution and is expected to provide for roughly 75 percent of the pension benefits in Uruguay.[59] There is also a state-run pension fund that competes in the private market and claims the largest share of affiliates among the fund managers. Uruguay presents a case in which the very high implicit pension debt in the old system did not impede privatization. This was made possible by the decision to maintain the previous ceiling on public pension benefits for most workers and by reducing state pension benefits for workers that opt to participate in the new private pension system for part of their retirement income.[60]

The 1995 Reform

After a series of failed reform attempts in the early 1990s, the Uruguayan National Assembly passed Law 16,713 in September 1995, restructuring the nation's old age pension system. The law created a mixed public and private

[58] Azuara 2003.
[59] Forteza et al. 2004, p. 7.
[60] Noya and Laens 2000, p. 9.

pension system in which participation in the private scheme was optional for all but the highest income earners. Most workers were given a significant financial incentive to participate in the private pension market for part of their retirement income, which has encouraged broad enrollment in the private pension market. The pension reform also revised substantially the parameters of the pay-as-you-go state pension system, which continues to provide the majority of pension benefits in Uruguay. Employee contributions were increased from 13 to 15 percent of income, while employer contributions were reduced from 14.5 to 12.5 percent of income. Under the new pension rules, the retirement age for women was increased by five years so that the minimum retirement age for men and women would be 60, while the years of work required for retirement was increased from thirty to thirty-five years. The reform substantially reduced benefits in the state pension system. For workers retiring at age 60, the replacement rate was cut from 70 to 50 percent, with a three-point increase for every year after age 60 that workers delayed retirement.[61] The government also revised the method of calculating pensions to extend the number of years over which the base salary is determined. Whereas in the old system, pension benefits were based on the average of the last three years of wages, the new system utilizes the last ten years, or the best twenty years of income where no year may rise more than 5 percent over the previous year. Participation in the reformed system was mandatory for workers younger than age 40 who were in the labor market at the time of reform, and for new entrants into the labor market.

The new pension system in Uruguay called for all formal sector workers with income up to 5,000 pesos in 1997 (~US$800) to contribute to the public, defined-benefit pension system. For workers with income greater than 5,000 pesos, the personal contribution of 15 percent on the first 5,000 pesos would be paid to the public pension system, while 15 percent of income between 5,000 and 15,000 pesos would be contributed to a defined-contribution pension account administered by one of the newly constituted pension fund administrators (Administradoras de Fondos de Ahorro Previsional, AFAP). For income greater than 15,000 pesos, voluntary contributions to the pension system could be made to the third-pillar system of private pension savings. A unique design feature of the Uruguayan pension reform is that workers in the first income category (less than 5,000 pesos per month) – fully 87 percent of the labor force – could opt to participate in the private pension system by splitting their 15 percent contribution between the public and private pension systems. Workers who chose to do so would receive a subsidy from the state in the form of a bonus to their public pension benefit. The bonus meant simply that although a worker's contributions to the public pension system fell by 50 percent, his or her state pension benefit would be reduced by just 25 percent.[62] Employer contributions and the portion of employee contributions less than 5,000 pesos

---

[61] Mitchell 1996, p. 9.
[62] The bonus, detailed in Article 8 of the law, was also offered to workers with income between 5,000 and 7,500 pesos who chose to contribute the majority of their contributions to the private pillar. Noya and Laens 2000, p. 19.

that were not contributed to the AFAPs were expected to finance the state pension benefits.

Uruguay's pension law called for the state social insurance bank (Banco de Previsión Social, BPS) to constitute an AFAP. It also provided advantages for that fund by prohibiting the private funds from beginning to advertise or enroll affiliates before the state pension fund had been established.[63] AFAPs are responsible for investing funds and may individually determine their commissions and fees for these services. However, the Uruguayan government obliges the private funds to guarantee a real return of at least 2 percent per year. The 1995 law allowed workers to change funds twice per year; once they join the private system, however, the law initially prohibited a return to the state regime. The BPS continues to provide the state defined-benefit pension, along with the collection, transfer, and recordkeeping of payroll contributions to the public and private pension regimes.

Institutional Outcomes

The government expected significant cost savings to result from the tightening of eligibility requirements for receiving a pension, and from the reduction in benefits in the public pension system and falling rates of evasion (which were expected as a result of the closer link between contributions and benefits). Like other privatizations, however, Uruguay's pension reform brought a sharp reduction in revenue to the state as workers began transferring payroll contributions to the AFAPs. Early estimates suggested that the fiscal deficit in the Uruguayan pension system would be reduced over the long term (between 1996 and 2050) only by a margin of 0.5 and 2 percent of GDP as a result of the reform.[64] In the short to medium term, however, the reform resulted in a widening of the pension system's financial deficit as workers began to divert payroll contributions to the AFAPs, and as the government stopped collecting contributions on income above 15,000 pesos. The latter resulted in a loss of approximately 1 percent of BPS revenue.[65] The government also instituted a series of reductions in employer payroll contributions in order to reduce the cost of labor. At the same time, pension spending continued to rise, although at a slower rate than early in the 1990s. Whereas the BPS deficit (excluding the parastatal regimes) reached 3.1 percent of GDP in 1995, this financing gap widened to 4.8 percent of GDP in 2002.[66] General revenue and value-added tax (VAT) resources are used to cover the fiscal deficit in the Uruguayan pension system, resulting in a heavy burden on lower-wage earners for whom VAT taxes represent a greater portion of income.[67] The financial strain on Uruguay's pension system was exacerbated by the macroeconomic context of a deep

[63] Noya et al. 1999, p. 23.
[64] Noya and Laens 2000.
[65] Márquez Mosconi 1997, p. 17.
[66] Forteza et al. 2004, p. 33.
[67] San Martino 2007, p. 16.

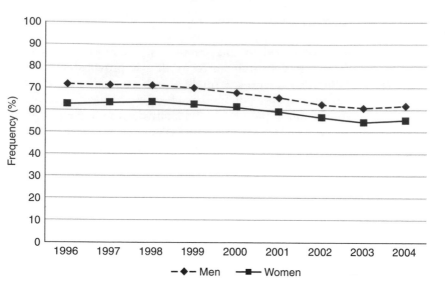

FIGURE 4.6. Average Share of Months of Contribution to Uruguay's Pension System, 1996–2004. *Source:* Bucheli et al. 2006.

recession that depressed employment and strained pension system revenue. Thus, despite the projections of a long-term reduction in the government's primary budget deficit, that gap was expected to widen by 1.6 and 1.8 percent of GDP in the short to medium term.[68]

The new pension system in Uruguay, like that in Argentina, obliges workers to contribute for thirty-five years in order to qualify for the common state pension. Unlike in the old pension system, Uruguayan workers can no longer claim years of service on the "testimony" of a third party; beginning in 1996, the BPS established a labor history registry for all affiliates. Despite the relatively high rates of compliance in Uruguay, early evidence suggests that a significant number of workers will have difficulty achieving thirty-five years of contributions by the time they reach the minimum retirement age of 60. The frequency of months in which workers record contributions (the contribution density) was initially high for men and women, but it fell steadily between 1996 and 2003, recovering only slightly in 2004. As Figure 4.6 illustrates, men have considerably more stable contribution rates than women in Uruguay. Even leaving aside the years of economic recession, the density of contributions to the pension system between 1996 and 2004 suggests that only 24 percent of affiliates are likely to achieve thirty-five years of contributions by age 60, and that only 42 percent will do so by age 65.[69] Unlike workers in Argentina, however, those who fail to meet the requirements for the ordinary pension will not be excluded from

[68] Noya and Laens 2000, p. 10.
[69] Over this period, men on average contributed 63 percent of the time, while women made contributions in 59 percent of the months observed. Bucheli et al. 2006, pp. 8, 17.

the state pension system altogether, as the Uruguayan pension system provides two additional pension programs for the elderly. The first, an "advanced age" pension, is a contributory benefit for workers who manage to record at least fifteen years of contributions (but less than thirty-five) and reach age 70. In addition, the government provides a noncontributory "old age" pension for workers without other pension benefits who reach age 70. For both programs, the age at which these benefits can be claimed was increased from 65 to 70 years by the 1995 reform.

Although the Uruguayan government expected that very few workers – approximately 80,000 – would join the private pension system, by December 1996, 360,000 individuals had done so.[70] By 2001, nearly 600,000 workers were enrolled in the private pension system in Uruguay.[71] At the outset, six AFAPs competed to invest workers' retirement funds; six years later this number dropped to 4, three of which claimed approximately 40 percent of the members and 56 percent of the funds invested in the market.[72] The state-owned AFAP ("República") initially claimed more than half of the private pension market, measured both in terms of affiliates and funds invested. This market share has declined over time to approximately 33.4 percent of affiliates and 56 percent of assets by 2007; nevertheless, it remains the largest private pension fund operator in Uruguay.[73] In 2005, the Uruguayan government instituted a change to permit some workers who were part of the private system to switch back to the government pension regime. Of the 60,000 who were eligible to do so in 2005, some 5,000 chose to return to the state pension system.[74]

Uruguay's pension reform has brought a profound change in the structure of old age pension provision through the creation of a private, defined-contribution pension system. Nevertheless, the state continues to be the principal source of old age income in terms of the coverage, financial contributions, and benefits. Employer contributions are channeled exclusively to the state to finance the pay-as-you-go pension system, and only high-income earners are obliged to participate in the private pension system for part of their retirement benefit. Low-income earners face the option to participate in the mixed pension system with a significant state subsidy; most have chosen to do so, but many are unlikely to record sufficient contributions in the system to qualify for the full retirement pension.

BRAZIL

Of the four countries examined in this study, Brazil is the only one that did not privatize its old age pension system. This does not mean that reform in

---

[70] Comité de Evaluación y Seguimiento 1998.
[71] San Martino 2007, p. 13.
[72] San Martino 2007, p. 14.
[73] Noya and Laens 2000, p. 19; República AFAP 2007.
[74] Social Security Administration 2005.

Brazil was a failure, or that the government lacked initiative to undertake institutional restructuring. Rather, the government made considerable revisions to Brazil's two principal social regimes: the Regime Geral de Previdência Social (RGPS) for private sector workers, and the Regimes Próprios de Previdência Social (RPPS) for public sector workers. In the nearly decade-long series of conflicts over pension reform in Brazil, three important pension reform laws were enacted: Two constitutional amendments and a reform of the private sector pension system passed through ordinary law.[75] Together, these three reforms brought significant changes to the first pillar – the publicly managed pay-as-you-go component – of Brazil's pension institution. They also extended the nation's third pillar of voluntary pension savings for private and public sector workers. Although the three measures did not close the immense financial gap in the old age pension system, they represent anything but an "aborted" reform that others have claimed.[76] Indeed, the net result of this decade-long reform struggle is projected to be a reduction in the state's pension liabilities borne by approximately 6 percent of GDP over thirty years.[77] Brazil's pension reforms thus took an important step toward closing the financial and actuarial imbalances in the system; they also reduced considerably the sharp and deeply entrenched inequities in the institution's benefit structure. These reforms did so, moreover, despite immense political and institutional obstacles lying in the path of institutional change.

1998 Amendment

President Fernando Henrique Cardoso launched his first pension reform effort in the form of Constitutional Amendment Project #33 shortly after his inauguration in 1995. The project had vast ambitions. It sought to remove from the 1988 Constitution the rules for calculating old age pension benefits while tightening eligibility conditions for retirement, eliminating several privileged pension regimes and equalizing the rules of the public and private sector pension systems. After nearly four years of legislative conflict, Cardoso's first pension reform was enacted in a 1998 constitutional amendment (Emenda Constitucional No. 20). The amendment strengthened the contributory nature of the pension system in Brazil while deconstitutionalizing many of the benefit calculation rules. The most significant change brought by the amendment was the replacement of the "time of service" pension with a requirement of "time of contribution" – altering the methodology of benefit calculation along with the basis of social rights to state benefits. Private sector workers continue to be able to retire on the basis of the "age pension" at age 65 (for men) or 60 (for women) if they have contributed to the pension system for at least fifteen

---

[75] For Brazil's pension reforms prior to 1998, see Weyland 1996b.
[76] See, for example, Madrid 2003.
[77] Giambiagi and Mello 2006, p. 8.

years. The length of contribution pension, however, has no minimum retirement age but requires thirty-five years of contributions (for men, or thirty years for women). The overwhelming majority of pensions conceded in the private sector pension scheme are age pensions, however, which are typically claimed by lower-income workers.[78] Pension benefits in the RGPS system are capped at approximately ten times the minimum wage, and private complementary pension funds are encouraged for workers who wish to save above that ceiling. For public sector workers, the 1998 amendment created a minimum retirement age of 53 (for men, 48 for women) for current workers, and 60 (55 for women) for new entrants into civil service. On January 28, 1999, President Cardoso also enacted Law 9783, which created a graduated tax on public sector pensions above R$600 per month.[79] This tax had been part of the 1998 amendment project, but had been defeated repeatedly in legislative voting. It was only after the country succumbed to an international financial crisis that the Congress enacted the law – and in a more ambitious form than previously proposed.

The 1999 Reform

President Cardoso did not rest following the enactment of the 1998 constitutional amendment. As Brazil recovered from the currency crisis of early 1999, the Cardoso government launched the second stage of institutional reform: the redesign of the private sector pension system. This reform project (Projeto de Lei 1527) was approved in October 1999, introducing a new benefit rule, the "social security factor" (*fator previdenciário*) for private sector workers. The measure also shifted from a system of calculating pensions on the basis of the last thirty-six monthly contributions to one that would eventually base pensions on contributions into notional individual accounts made over each worker's entire working life. Although the new system more closely links contributions and benefits, it is not a strict defined-contribution system. Rather, the new formula uses the 80 percent highest earnings over working life and applies a coefficient based on each worker's retirement age, cohort life expectancy, and time of contribution. The decision to use only the 80 percent highest earnings maintains some element of risk-pooling to buffer individuals from the cost of unstable income and of periods of unemployment – a risk that falls most heavily on lower-income workers.[80] Nevertheless, the new benefit rule transfers to workers a greater share of the cost and risk of unstable income and of rising longevity. In the absence of a minimum retirement age for private sector workers, the new benefit rule penalizes early retirement by tying old age pension values to life expectancy at the time of retirement. The new structure of risk-sharing in the private sector pension scheme is expected to slow the growth

[78] Ornélas and Vieira 1999, p. 10.
[79] Taxes are progressive up to 25 percent for pensions over R$2,500.
[80] Ornélas and Vieira 1999, p. 15.

of the pension deficit; however, it does so without privatizing. Incentives to delay retirement so far appear to be effective, as the average retirement age for the time-of-contribution pension rose from 49 in 1998 to 53 in 2005.[81] Moreover, the 1999 reform significantly curtailed the transfer of income to the mostly higher-paid workers who typically retired in their 40s or 50s under the "time-of-service" rules. Finally, by taking unisex life expectancy rates the new benefit formula, the social security factor, does not penalize women for their higher average life expectancy than men. Even though the measure will only slow the dramatic rise in the RGPS deficit to 1.2 percent of GDP over the next twenty years, the social security ministry estimates that, without these reforms, the deficit over this same period would have reached 3.6 percent of GDP.

2003 Amendment

The third Brazilian pension reform examined in this study was approved by the nation's Federal Senate on December 11, 2003. That reform, which became Constitutional Amendment 40, was launched by President Luiz Inácio Lula da Silva shortly after his inauguration in 2003 and was sanctioned by the National Congress just seven months after its initiation. The reform established more stringent retirement rules for public sector workers in active service and dramatically curtailed retirement privileges for new entrants into the civil service. It also placed a ceiling on pension benefits and increased the minimum retirement age for public sector workers. The amendment permits civil servants to retire at age 60 (for men, 55 for women – up from the previous ages of 53 and 48) and after thirty-five years of service (for men, thirty for women). Civil servants also must have at least twenty years of employment in the public sector and five in their last job to receive a full pension. After 2006, each year that a civil servant retires short of the required age (60/55) will result in a reduction of the pension by 3.5 to 5 percent. The reform also imposes an 11 percent tax on high-income pensions (as the previous law passed in January 1999 was struck down by the country's Supreme Court later that year) and reduces by 30 percent any pension amount over R$2,400 – which is the ceiling on private sector benefits. Civil service pensions were capped at the salary of the highest Supreme Court justice (although most workers will be governed by "subceilings"), and the erstwhile full inflation-adjustment parity with active workers was curtailed. Benefits for new civil servants will now be based on the (price-indexed) contributions made over the entire course of the worker's career, including those made during work in the private sector. A ceiling on the full replacement of public sector pensions was created at the level equivalent to the private sector, which was raised from R$1,869 to R$2,400 per month (approximately US$800).[82] The reform also established private, defined-contribution pension funds for workers wishing to save voluntarily above the benefit ceiling, and

[81] Giambiagi and Mello 2006, p. 15.
[82] "A Reforma e o INSS" 2003.

civil servants with acquired rights who choose to delay retirement until age 70 would receive a bonus equal to the 11 percent contribution rate.

The nearly decade-long conflict over social security reform in Brazil thus yielded tremendous shifts in the design of the nation's pension system, without privatizing it. Pension reform in Brazil thus does not represent an institutional path departure as in the other cases. Nevertheless, the parametric revisions gave a sharply new dimension to Brazil's social security model, which centers on a larger and stronger role for the state at the lower- and middle-income levels. By contrast to the Argentine case where public pension benefits cover income up to approximately US$200, the Brazilian state ensures retirement income up to a ceiling of approximately US$800. In addition to reinforcing the public nature of the pension system, the reforms marked a significant shift toward greater equity by dramatically (but gradually) curtailing the privileges of public sector workers.

The four countries examined in this study thus display striking, but highly varied outputs of political conflicts over old age pension reform. The task of the next chapters is to explain these outcomes and to disentangle the systematic causal mechanisms across the three cases from the nation-specific and idiosyncratic features of each political experience. The next chapters thus address three critical components of the institutional reform process across the four countries: the technocratic decision-making where international economic pressures and constraints are more directly felt in reform design decisions (Chapter 5); the process of "selling" reform to society, where the legacies of the old pension system weigh powerfully on the task of winning public support for the reform (Chapter 6); and the task of building legislative majorities behind loss-imposing institutional change, where the partisan structure of political conflict and institutional landscape of the political system shape the possibilities for legislating institutional reform (Chapter 7).

5

Pension Reform in an Open Economy
Negotiating Globalization's Double Bind

Although welfare states around the world were resilient in the face of social and economic change for most of the twentieth century, they had begun to undergo dramatic transformation by the century's end. In the case of old age pensions, redistributive social insurance systems that provided a bulwark against the effects of market forces were transformed into institutions that increasingly replicate and reinforce market-based allocations of risk and income. For many scholars, such transformations are inextricably linked to the integration of product and capital markets that accelerated in the last quarter of the twentieth century. Competitive pressures, this argument suggests, along with the enhanced "exit option" of capital, have imposed an agenda of reform on increasingly open economies. The pressures of globalization are said to be especially potent in the developing world, where dependence on foreign savings enhances the tremendous bargaining power of capital holders vis-à-vis domestic governments. And where authority to design and implement reform is concentrated in the hands of executive-branch technocrats, welfare state dismantling is said to be likely to advance the furthest. Such technocrats, the argument goes, are insulated from the time inconsistency problems that bedevil reform-seeking politicians, where the deleterious short-term effects of reform create incentives to depart from a long-term strategy of institutional change. Technocrats thus are freer to design reforms on the basis of long-term macroeconomic objectives and "good policy" concerns. The conventional story is thus that globalization creates pressures for long-term institutional changes in the direction of greater market orientation of social protection, and that such reforms are most likely to be realized when placed in the hands of well-insulated technocratic actors.

This study challenges these conventional accounts on both theoretical and empirical grounds. On the one hand, the quantitative analysis in Chapter 2 indicated that pension privatization is *not* more likely in countries that are more exposed to global capital flows, nor is it more probable in the most deeply indebted (and therefore dependent) nations. The argument that I proposed in Chapter 3, moreover, suggests that rather than impelling privatization under the onus of efficiency pressures or promoting the expansion of state-funded social protections as compensation for market-driven dislocations, globalization has presented government actors with a powerful double bind. Even though economic integration has increased the attractiveness of pension privatization in many cases, it also has sharpened the near-term risk of market punishment if capital-importing nations overstep the limits of market confidence. And as a reform that exacts a heavy financial toll on governments in the medium term, pension privatization threatens precisely such a loss of investor confidence before its putative benefits obtain.

When and where privatization is likely to threaten such a loss of investor confidence – and thus may be curtailed or set aside by technocratic actors themselves – depends on the strength of global market constraints and on the government's financial leeway to pay the transition cost without overstepping the limits of its sovereign risk threshold. The potential cost of privatization – proxied by the implicit pension liabilities – thus becomes endogenous to the depth of institutional reform that is feasible in an open, capital-importing economy. Market strictures are likely to be heaviest when global liquidity is low, for it is in this context that investors become more discriminating with regard to risk; they also are most powerful in high-risk nations. The latter are governments that rely heavily on foreign capital to finance their balance of payments and perform poorly on key sovereign creditworthiness indicators. Contrary to previous research, I expect the cash-strapped, high-risk governments to be *less* likely to privatize, or to do so deeply, even if such a reform may be desirable to market actors and government technocrats in the long term. Countries in the middle of the income distribution, by contrast, may be more likely to privatize old age pensions and to do so most radically; these nations may have the leeway to finance the transition, but they are not so affluent as to be inoculated altogether from the globalization-based incentives to privatize.

EVIDENCE IN THE CHAPTER

The four countries examined in this study provide marked variations both in the weight of external economic constraints, the leeway with which to finance the transition, and in the potential cost of privatization. Table 5.1 provides comparative statistics on the macroeconomic landscape in each nation in the year prior to the adoption of structural pension reform (i.e., when technocrats were formulating structural reform plans). Even though the four countries provide important variations in their domestic economic structures and links to the global economy, international market conditions mattered greatly for them all. Each country experienced significant current account deficits in the 1990s that increased the economy's vulnerability to capital flight; and all were exposed to highly volatile global capital flows, as illustrated in Figure 5.1. However, the four countries differed in the sensitivity of international investors to

TABLE 5.1. *Macroeconomic Indicators*

	Reference Year	GDP Growth (Annual %)	GDP per Capita (Constant 2000 US$)	Government Consumption (% of GDP)	Gross Private Capital Flows (% of GDP)	Market Capitalization of Listed Companies (% of GDP)	Population Ages 65 and Older (% of Total)	Short-Term Debt (% of Total External Debt)	Trade (% of GDP)
Argentina	1992	11.9	6964.9	3.0	6.4	8.1	9.1	23.7	14.7
Brazil	1998	0.1	3446.1	19.1	13.3	20.4	4.9	12.4	17.2
Mexico	1994	4.4	5314.2	11.6	7.8	30.9	4.2	28.4	38.5
Uruguay	1994	7.3	5743.7	11.9	5.0	1.0	12.2	24.3	40.1

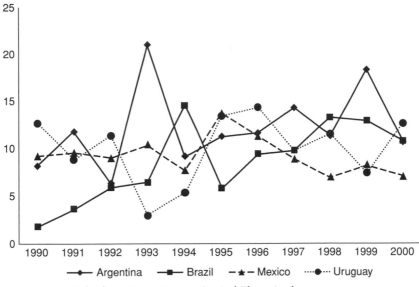

FIGURE 5.1. Volatility: Gross Private Capital Flows in the 1990s.

domestic risk conditions, as shifts in global liquidity diminished investors' appetite for emerging market risk as the decade wore on (see Figure 5.2).[1] Argentina privatized in the context of high international liquidity, and thus strong capital inflows offered the government broader scope for maneuver in terms of compromising key sovereign creditworthiness indicators. But Argentina's wide current account deficit and falling international reserves left it highly vulnerable to the reversal of these flows, which would have been devastating (see Figure 5.3). Such vulnerability lent urgency to technocrats' efforts to design a structural pension reform in order to signal the government's commitment to maintaining its macroeconomic strategy based on a strong, fixed currency.

Mexico and Uruguay faced tighter international constraints at mid-decade as diminished international liquidity increased the sensitivity of international investors to signs of sovereign risk in emerging markets.[2] In the second half of the decade, investors thus could be expected to countenance less of an erosion of sovereign risk performance before exiting an economy, compared to earlier in the decade. As Figures 5.4 and 5.5 indicate, both nations drafted structural pension reform laws in the context of significant current account deficits. In the Mexican case, however, the recovery that followed the peso crisis temporarily widened the government's financial leeway, as evidenced in the sharp rise in foreign currency reserves in 1994.

---

[1] International liquidity is proxied by U.S. interest rates: Where rates are low, liquidity is high as investors move capital abroad – often to developing countries – in search of higher yields. Calvo et al. 1993.

[2] Maxfield 1998, p. 1210.

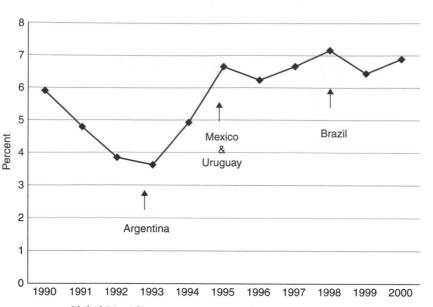

FIGURE 5.2. Global Liquidity 1990–2000.

Brazil undertook pension reform in the context of the least favorable external conditions. In the wake of the 1997 Asian financial crisis and 1998 Russian default, investors revealed very little tolerance for emerging market risk. The need to send positive risk signals thus became highly consequential for the Brazilian government at the time it was considering pension reform. Indeed, despite rising international currency reserves, the much greater deficit in Brazil's

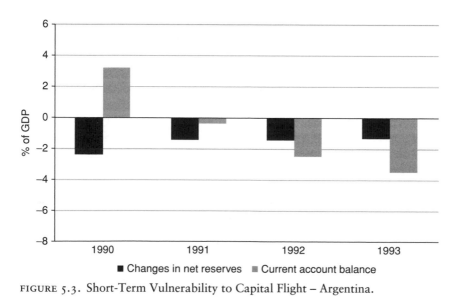

FIGURE 5.3. Short-Term Vulnerability to Capital Flight – Argentina.

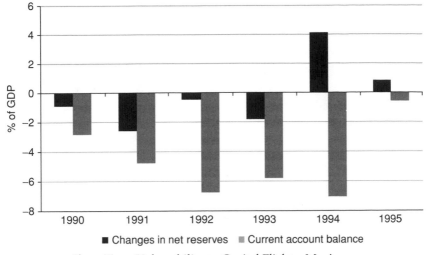

FIGURE 5.4. Short-Term Vulnerability to Capital Flight – Mexico.

current account rendered the economy highly vulnerable to capital flight, as Figure 5.6 illustrates. As a result, the government enjoyed much less scope for maneuver in terms of assuming the transitional costs of structural pension reform.

Domestic financial leeway also varied markedly across the four cases. Since the financing gap imposed by pension privatization is most commonly paid through the fiscal budget or by issuing new sovereign debt, the budget balance

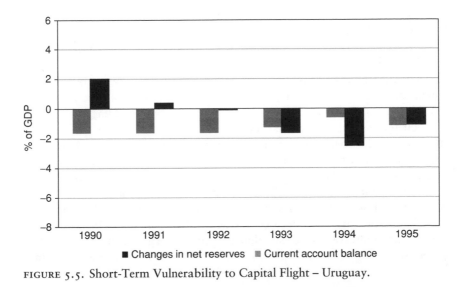

FIGURE 5.5. Short-Term Vulnerability to Capital Flight – Uruguay.

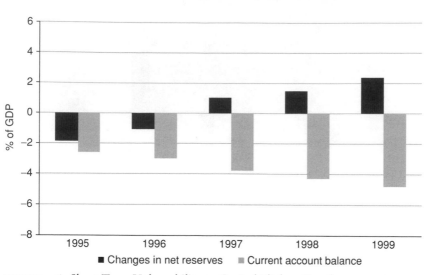

FIGURE 5.6. Short-Term Vulnerability to Capital Flight – Brazil.

and debt-to-GDP ratios proxy for the fiscal leeway that governments enjoy to finance a pension privatization. As Table 5.2 shows, Argentina enjoyed broad financial leeway with its low debt and primary fiscal surplus. Deep vulnerability, however, sharply curtailed technocrats' policy-making time horizons. Along with the slackening of global market constraints, these conditions permitted technocrats to design a costly pension privatization that, while attending to the executive's short-term credibility concerns, compromised longer-term financial and institutional goals of the reform by resulting in a privatization that was more costly and that retained a larger public role than technocrats originally desired. Indeed, the cost of pension provision increased steadily over the course of the 1990s and ultimately became unsustainable when the government's financial leeway narrowed and international market constraints tightened at the decade's end.

Mexico and Uruguay occupy intermediate positions in terms of both financial leeway and international market constraints. Mexico had a moderate debt ratio and low fiscal deficit at the time of its reform, while Uruguay had a large fiscal deficit but a modest sovereign debt ratio when technocrats designed its structural pension reform. Both countries faced tighter international liquidity conditions compared to Argentina, which heightened investors' sensitivity to sovereign risk signals; the result was a narrowing of the scope for these governments to expand their debt and deficit ratios in the transition to a private pension system. But the two cases differ markedly in the potential transitional cost of a full privatization, as proxied by the implicit pension debt. The lower potential transitional cost in Mexico thus permitted the government to adopt a deeper pension privatization than the Uruguayan government, despite the fact

TABLE 5.2. *Parameters of Globalization's Double Bind*

	Vulnerability:		External Constraint:	Financial Leeway:		Transition Cost:
	Current Account Balance (% GDP)	Domestic Savings (% GDP)	U.S. Interest Rates (%)	Debt (% GDP)	Budget Balance (% GDP)	Implicit Pension Debt (% GDP)
Argentina	−2.5	15.2	3.6	32.9**	14**	124.9±
Mexico	−7.0	17.1	6.7	35.2	−0.002	48±
Uruguay	−2.7	15.3	6.7	24.5	−2.62	214§
Brazil	−4.3	18.9	7.2	38.94*	−0.86	187§

Source: World Bank CD-ROM (2007). Except: *from Banco Central do Brasil; **from Krueger 2002; ±from James and Brooks 2001; §from Kane and Palacios 1996.
Reference years: Argentina (1992), Mexico (1994), Uruguay (1994), Brazil (1998).

that these privatizations occurred in the context of similar international market conditions. Still, Mexican technocrats took measures to avoid any short-term increase in sovereign debt by retaining considerable unfunded public pension liabilities to workers in the transitional generation. The creation of a "lifetime switch" option allowed all current workers with acquired rights in the old pension system the better of the balance in their individual pension account or their benefits owed under the old pension system at the moment of retirement. Through this design decision, technocrats traded off the medium-term goal of closing the unfunded state pension liabilities for the more pressing short-term objective of avoiding a significant increase in sovereign debt during the transition.

Uruguayan officials also responded to tightening market constraints by designing the structural pension reform in such a way that they avoided the need to issue new sovereign debt to finance the transition to a private pension system. They did so by maintaining the ceiling on public pension benefits in the reformed system at the same level as in the old state pension system. In neither case was the transitional arrangement driven entirely by global market conditions – as questions of acquired rights became important in both cases – however, Mexican and Uruguayan technocrats designed their structural pension reforms in such a way that curtailed the long-term role of market forces in the country's reformed pension system. In both cases, therefore, the role of market forces in old age pensions was constrained in the long term in order to avoid the risk of market punishment in response to the erosion of government creditworthiness signals in the short term.

Of the four cases, Brazil represents the combination of the least favorable external conditions and the narrowest domestic financial leeway. Together, these conditions led government technocrats to set aside a structural pension reform proposal in 1998 on the anticipation that external creditors would not tolerate any reform that increased the government's debt-to-GDP ratio. Instead of privatizing, the Brazilian technocrats designed a pension reform based on individual "notional" accounts, which transferred income and longevity risks to individuals without imposing a transitional cost on the government. As in the previous cases, the risk of market punishment was not deterministic of the design or outcome of the pension reform but, along with domestic financial conditions, powerfully influenced both the decision whether to enact structural pension reform and where to draw the line between state and market responsibilities. As we will see in the next chapters, the ultimate design and political fate of the pension reforms also depended heavily on the way that political conflicts over these reforms unfolded both in society and in the legislative arena.

ARGENTINA

The Argentine government reformed its national pension system in the context of high international liquidity, which spurred strong capital inflows to the nation and diminished the importance of creditworthiness signals. Nevertheless, Menem's credibility problems and the sense of vulnerability arising from Argentina's wide current account deficit led reformers to prioritize the rapid approval of pension privatization through democratic processes as a means to signal the government's commitment to fiscal probity and its fixed currency. Achieving these short-term credibility goals, however, led technocrats to compromise the longer-term reform objectives by maintaining a larger institutional and financial role for the state in the reformed pension system. As a result of compromises made to facilitate the rapid democratic approval of the reform, pension costs in Argentina rose steadily over the course of the 1990s. Although it was feasible to finance these costs in the context of high global liquidity and broad financial leeway of the early 1990s, the fiscal costs became much more burdensome when domestic and international economic conditions changed late in the decade.

Incentives to Privatize

The Argentine government's macroeconomic strategy in the early 1990s centered on the adoption of deep market-oriented structural reforms including trade and financial liberalization and on the adoption of a fixed currency regime called the Convertibility Plan. In large part, this strategy drew from a quest by Argentine president Carlos Saúl Menem to establish his credibility in the eyes of international market actors. Such credibility was considered vital to attracting investment in the wake of a profound social, economic, and political crisis that engulfed the nation in the late 1980s. During the crisis, inflation spiraled above 200 percent per month in July 1989, bringing about a collapse of public finances and prompting an early transition from outgoing President Raúl Alfonsín, of the centrist Radical Party (Unión Cívica Radical), to Menem, of the labor-backed Peronist Party (Partido Justicialista). The first and most urgent task facing the new government was to stabilize the country and restart growth. To do so, Menem sought to improve his image in the eyes of international market actors whose investment was considered vital to stimulating the country's economic recovery.

Credibility, however, was Menem's biggest challenge. As an outsider in the Peronist Party and one who had campaigned on a populist and protectionist platform, Menem enjoyed little confidence or esteem in the eyes of domestic or international market actors.[3] Upon taking office, however, Menem effected a radical volte-face of his statist and populist campaign pledges and embraced an orthodox market-oriented stabilization and structural reform plan.[4] When Menem's first stabilization plan failed, he radicalized his economic policies toward the orthodox extreme – both to quell the crisis and establish his credibility in the eyes of the international community.[5] As a way to assure investors that they could count on consistent, market-based economic policy that was free of political influence, Menem delegated authority for economic policy to an insulated economic team under the leadership of Domingo Cavallo.[6] Widely regarded as a close friend of the investment community, Cavallo was well-known in domestic and international market circles as a free-market advocate. For Cavallo, like Menem, credibility was a currency of power: Having it would attract investment and spur growth, whereas its loss could incite capital flight and a potential return to crisis.[7] Credibility thus came to be seen as a fundamental condition for achieving economic stabilization.

Cavallo brought with him to the Economic Ministry (Ministerio de Economía y Producción) a group of economists who designed and launched a series of deep, market-oriented structural reforms. The cornerstone of this agenda was the Convertibility Plan. Designed as a mechanism of self-restraint on government monetary emission, this plan centered on the creation of a new currency, the peso, which was pegged to the dollar at parity and was guaranteed by foreign currency reserves equal to 100 percent of the monetary base.[8] Immediately upon its adoption, the Convertibility Plan slashed hyperinflation from an annual rate of over 2,000 percent in 1990 to 24 percent by 1993 and single digits thereafter.[9] Cavallo also launched a deep liberalization of the economy, dismantling capital controls, liberalizing domestic financial institutions, and launching an ambitious domestic privatization effort.

---

[3] Palermo and Collins 1998, pp. 36–62.
[4] Stokes 2001a, pp. 46–7.
[5] Cortés and Marshall 1998, p. 11; Palermo and Collins 1998; Torre 1997; Torre and Gerchunoff 1998, p. 16.
[6] Gerchunoff and Machinea 1995, pp. 39–92; Palermo and Collins 1998, pp. 45–7; Torre 1997.
[7] Torre 1998.
[8] Gerchunoff and Machinea 1995, p. 43; Palermo 1998, p. 46.
[9] World Bank 2000.

The success of the Convertibility Plan was rewarded with a surge of foreign capital inflows, inducing a swift economic recovery and sharp rise in domestic consumption. As the Argentine economy rebounded in 1992, Cavallo turned his attention to attacking the structural sources of the nation's budget deficit. High on this "second-generation" reform agenda was a restructuring of the nation's ailing social security system. Cavallo began by appointing Walter Schulthess, a liberal macroeconomist, as his new secretary of social security. Schulthess assembled a team of economists and actuaries who worked in what they describe as "laboratory conditions" – insulated from the social security bureaucracy and interest groups associated with the pension system.[10] Indeed, the group answered directly to Cavallo rather than to the social security bureaucracy on which it was formally dependent.

Although the Argentine technocrats shared a commitment to market-oriented reform, their embrace of pension privatization cannot be explained simply as an outgrowth of those beliefs. Indeed, the government did not make a universal neoliberal turn in social policy reform but rather embraced market-oriented policies only selectively in the social policy realm, notably excluding labor market and health care reforms from this agenda.[11] Although both the World Bank and International Monetary Fund were active in lending to Argentina in the early 1990s, the idea to privatize the state pension system cannot be attributed to externally imposed conditions from these institutions. Rather, Argentine technocrats maintain that the decision emerged from consultation with a broad range of domestic and international actors, including domestic banks and insurance companies, international financiers, staff from the Washington-based multilaterals, and Chilean economists.[12]

One of the driving goals of the Argentine pension reform was to rein in the cost of pension provision – a concern that was heightened by economic liberalization.[13] Fiscal excess had come to be seen as the root cause of chronic inflationary problems in the 1970s and 1980s, and the pension system was viewed as a key contributor to that excess.[14] Although financial deficits in the state pension system were largely hidden by inflation in the late 1980s, price stability in the early 1990s unveiled the deep fiscal imbalances. By 1993, the financial deficit in the Argentine pension system had grown to 45 percent of its promised benefits, and the failure to adequately index pension benefits in the late 1980s spurred a series of lawsuits that also left the system with considerable debts to existing pensioners.[15]

Argentina's open economy and currency board heightened the importance of fiscal discipline; they also raised concerns about the toll of high social security costs on the competitiveness of domestic industry. Because the Convertibility

---

[10] Demarco 1998; 2004.
[11] Murillo 2005; Murillo and Schrank 2005.
[12] Demarco 1998; 2004, p. 88; Diaz 1998; Nelson 2004, p. 46; Rofman 1998; Schulthess 1998.
[13] Rofman 1998; Schulthess 1998.
[14] Gomez 1997, p. 645; Guidotti 2006, p. 73.
[15] Isuani et al. 1996, p. 95.

Plan precluded monetary creation as a means to finance the public sector, the maintenance of the country's newfound stability depended heavily on the government's ability to remove structural deficits in state spending. At the same time, the liberal capital account regime meant that the loss of investor confidence in the pegged currency could induce a swift reversal of capital flows, plunging the country into crisis. As one pension expert put it, "the mobility of capital simply does not support high public deficits."[16] By the early 1990s, therefore, a consensus had emerged among Argentine technocrats that the existing pension system was simply too expensive to maintain in the liberalized economy, and that privatization would provide a way to reduce that cost.

Reformers also expected that pension privatization would enhance the competitiveness of domestic industries, which had been hampered by the appreciation of the peso and dismantling of trade barriers.[17] Liberalization had brought a swift expansion of imported goods in Argentina in the early 1990s, raising concerns about the ability of domestic industries to compete in the open economy.[18] Reformers anticipated that privatization would allow them to reduce the high payroll charges, which reached 26 percent of salary prior to the reform – 16 percentage points of which were paid by employers.[19] Pursuant to this goal, the pension privatization was accompanied by the gradual reduction in employer contributions – a decision that further deepened the short-term financial toll imposed on the government by the reform.

The idea of pension privatization was also attractive to Argentine government actors on account of its putative effect of deepening domestic capital markets. Although the economists leading the reform claim that they were well aware that the link between pension privatization and higher domestic savings had not been firmly established, they expected that even if overall savings did not increase, privatization would at least cultivate a source of loyal, long-term investment in the country.[20] This home-grown pension market was seen as a way to reduce the nation's reliance on volatile foreign capital flows and to buffer the economy against global economic shocks.[21] Argentina's economic liberalization strategy thus enhanced considerably the attractiveness of pension privatization for government actors, who saw this measure as a way to achieve three goals made more important in the open economy: cutting pension costs, improving the competitiveness of domestic industries, and deepening local capital markets.

Globalization's Constraints

Financial integration heightened the attraction to pension privatization in Argentina, but it also constrained the options through which the government

---

[16] Facal 1998.
[17] Cetrángolo 1998; Rofman 1998; Schulthess 1998.
[18] Cetrángolo and Grushka 2004, p. 18; Cortés and Marshall 1999, p. 198.
[19] Reductions varied by sector and geographic location of the firm. Cetrángolo and Grushka 2004, p. 20.
[20] Caro Figueroa 1998; Demarco 1998; Gonzales Gaviola 1998; Rofman 1998; Schulthess 1998.
[21] Bustos 1998; Etala 1998; Facal 1998; Gonzales Gaviola 1998; Santín 1998.

could achieve this reform. Indeed, the country's liberalization of international financial transactions and cross-border capital flows brought a strong influx of investment in the early 1990s. Private capital inflows to Argentina reached US$26 billion between 1991 and 1993.[22] Even though these flows were abundant, they were overwhelmingly short-term and unstable, thus rendering the economy highly vulnerable to capital flight. Capital scarcity and dependence on foreign investment had long been problems for the nation, and the increasing vulnerability of the economy to capital flight in the early 1990s presented critical new challenges.[23] In part, this vulnerability owed to constraints imposed by the fixed currency regime, which constrained the ability of the Argentine government to respond to market shocks through countercyclical spending. Thus it became all the more important for the government to avoid a loss of market confidence in the first place. Coping with this vulnerability turned the government's attention closely toward efforts to maintain investors' confidence through the adoption of market-oriented reform and by maintaining good performance of key sovereign risk indicators.

The Argentine economy's vulnerability to capital flight was heightened further by the country's wide current account deficit in the early 1990s. As mentioned earlier, the sharp appreciation of the peso had induced a relative price distortion that strongly favored imports to the detriment of domestic traded good sectors and exports. Between 1991 and 1994, imports to Argentina surged by 417 percent, while exports grew by only 23 percent.[24] Argentina's trade surplus of US$3.7 billion in 1991 thus converted into a deficit of US$5.9 billion only three years later.[25] Given the low levels of domestic capital accumulation in Argentina, this deficit was financed almost completely through the capital account (i.e., with foreign capital flows). And with central bank reserves tied to maintaining the currency peg, the loss of financing for the external trade balance could be destabilizing for the domestic financial system as the central bank lacked the ability to intercede as lender of last resort. Capital flight and the resulting balance of payments crisis thus would be devastating for the Argentine economy.

The specter of capital flight reoriented domestic policy-making goals around the immediate objective of avoiding a loss of investor confidence. Winning such confidence, technocrats expected, would involve "playing by the market rules."[26] Input from international financial market interests thus became an important consideration for technocrats designing the structural pension reform.[27] Rapid approval of the pension reform, government actors expected, would provide a credible signal of the government's commitment to fiscal

---

[22] Rozenwurcel 1994, p. 3.
[23] Torre 1998.
[24] Bustos 1995, p. 27.
[25] Bustos 1995, p. 27.
[26] Diaz 1998; Facal 1998; Santín 1998.
[27] Caro Figueroa 1998.

discipline and thus to the stable currency regime.[28] In addition, reformers sought to maintain good performance on key indicators of sovereign risk, particularly its debt and deficit ratios. Although the Argentine government had achieved a primary (before-interest) budget surplus in 1992 (see Table 5.1), technocrats were aware that this balance was illusory, as it was driven heavily by temporary conditions such as low international interest rates, low debt service costs (due to currency appreciation) and windfall revenue from an extensive privatization effort.[29] Indeed, the positive bottom-line fiscal balance concealed heavy structural deficits that reformers hoped pension privatization could resolve by cutting state pension costs. Menem's economic team thus found itself in a race against time to design and carry out structural reforms that would signal the government's credibility and maintain the confidence of foreign creditors.[30] In doing so, however, reformers perceived the importance of minimizing the immediate impact of the reform on key indicators of sovereign risk.

Maneuvering within the Double Bind

President Menem's concern with establishing his credibility in the eyes of international market actors, along with the growing vulnerability of the economy to the loss of such credibility, reoriented government priorities in the early 1990s around the short-term implications of state action on investor confidence. As the current account deficit yawned, the overwhelming goal of the reform team thus became to pass *some* kind of pension privatization as a signal of the government's commitment to the stable currency regime. Doing so, however, would oblige the government to make important compromises that limited the market orientation of the reform and raised its medium-term cost. The ability of the Argentine government to finance these commitments was enhanced – albeit temporarily – by conjunctural economic conditions in the early 1990s.

Financial Leeway

Given the Argentine government's concern for maintaining the confidence of owners of mobile capital in the early 1990s, it may be surprising that the government could undertake such a costly reform as pension privatization. Despite the high implicit pension debt – at approximately 125 percent of GDP – the Argentine government enjoyed critical advantages in the early 1990s that broadened its financial leeway to accept the cost of privatization without risking the loss of investor confidence in the short term. These conditions included

---

[28] Etala 1998; Gerchunoff and Machinea 1995; Isuani et al. 1996, p. 94; Torre 1997; Torre and Gerchunoff 1998.

[29] Rozenwurcel 1994, p. 9.

[30] The shadow of market approval was considered by technocrats to have been "a source of acceleration of the reform." Schulthess 1998.

high international liquidity, which slackened market constraints, and strong domestic growth, which strengthened the government's financial position.

High international liquidity in the early 1990s fueled a surge of capital flows to developing countries in search of high yields. Following Argentina's successful economic stabilization in 1991, the attendant surge of capital inflows stimulated a boom in private consumption and macroeconomic growth. Rising tax revenue strengthened the government's fiscal budget balance, while the overvalued currency allowed the Argentine government to reduce its sovereign debt obligations.[31] The government's financial position was strengthened further by windfall revenue from the government's extensive privatization of state-owned enterprises, which reached 0.4 percent of GDP in 1993.[32] Argentina also enjoyed a low debt-to-GDP ratio, which allowed the government's sovereign debt to achieve "investment grade" status in 1991, further stimulating capital inflows to the country. Together, these factors offered the Argentine government broader scope to finance the costly pension privatization without pushing government debt or deficit ratios beyond the threshold of market confidence in the early 1990s.

Narrowing Time Horizons

But globalization also increased the urgency that executive-branch technocrats attached to the pension privatization, leading them to make costly tradeoffs in the process and design of the reform. The first of these tradeoffs came in the decision to submit the pension reform proposal to legislative approval. This decision was notable because the modus operandi of Menem's structural reform efforts to that point had been to issue presidential decrees of "Necessity and Urgency." This authority had long existed in Argentina as a privilege of the executive; however, its use had been infrequent. In the 136 years of democracy prior to 1990, such decrees had been used by presidents to legislate only 25 times. In his first five years in office Menem exercised this decree power 336 times.[33] When it came to the pension reform, however, Menem's advisors, who had been in close communication with market actors who would potentially participate in the private pension market, urged him not to enact that measure by decree. Investors, they warned, would have little confidence in the permanence of a pension reform that was implemented by decree.[34] As the secretary of social security explained in an interview, pension fund managers making long-term investments in the country wanted assurance that the private pension system in Argentina would be stable. Any reform that was created by executive fiat would not be credible, they explained, because it also could be changed just as quickly as it was created.[35] By contrast, democratic policy

[31] Bustos 1995, p. 25; Eaton 2001, p. 19.
[32] International Monetary Fund 2004a, p. 81.
[33] Jones 1997.
[34] Schulthess 1998.
[35] Schulthess 1998.

processes assured the broad public backing and transparent procedures that gave investors confidence in the measure's permanence.

Winning democratic sanction of a pension privatization in Argentina, however, would oblige the government to accept significant compromises in the proposal's design that would limit the market-orientation of the new pension system while raising the reform's fiscal cost for the government. The first of these design shifts emerged from a roundtable for political dialogue that the government convoked with representatives of important political and economic groups in early 1992. This dialogue was intended to gain a preview of the arguments that the reform proposal would encounter in Congress and to establish consensus on the main provisions of the pension reform. A vital insight that technocrats gained through that dialogue was that a private pension reform would not gain legitimacy in Argentina if it lacked a substantial "solidarity" – public and redistributive – component.[36] Although such a condition would mean limiting the extent of privatization that they could achieve, reformers concluded that even a private pension system that retained a modest public component would still achieve the government's principal objectives of signaling its credibility to market actors. Reformers thus designed the reform to include a basic public pension benefit for all participants, a feature that also would distinguish the Argentine pension reform from the more liberal Chilean archetype.

The executive reform team sent the first pension reform proposal to the National Congress in June 1992. The project envisioned the creation of a mixed pension system with a small public component based on a flat "universal basic pension" and a larger component based on privately managed individual retirement accounts. Participation in the new pension system would be mandatory for all workers younger than age 45. Given the importance of maintaining a balanced budget, reformers sought to limit the transitional financial impact of the reform by not including provisions to compensate workers for benefit rights earned under the old pension system. Under the proposed rules, workers would retire only with their savings accumulated in the new private pension system and the modest universal basic pension. Reformers anticipated, moreover, that basic public pension benefits would be financed solely by employer contributions (which would be gradually reduced over time).[37] Overall, technocrats anticipated that their original reform proposal would not diminish government performance on key sovereign risk indicators but would send a credible signal of the government's commitment to market-oriented reform.

This initial pension reform proposal met with a firm rebuff by legislators, prompting the executive team to withdraw the measure even before it was discussed within the legislative committees.[38] A key sticking point for legislators was the absence of any recognition of workers' acquired benefit rights from the old pension system. Rather than allowing political actors to revise the proposed

[36] Demarco 1998. The state was also constitutionally obligated to provide pension benefits.
[37] Rofman 1997; SAFJP 1998, p. 25; Schulthess and Demarco 1996.
[38] Isuani and San Martino 1995.

legislation, the executive withdrew the proposal so that the technocratic reform team could design a transitional rule to acknowledge acquired pension rights. Recognizing those acquired rights through the use of a recognition bond, as the Chilean government had done, however, would have significantly elevated the government's debt-to-GDP ratio. Even if this increase in public debt merely involved the recognition of liabilities that otherwise were hidden by the pay-as-you-go pension system, monetization of the government's pension debt would threaten a loss of investor confidence in the short term. To diminish this risk of market punishment, Argentine technocrats created a new public benefit in the reform proposal – called the compensatory pension – that would recognize workers' contributions to the old system through a defined benefit rule. The public, DB design of the compensatory pension had important implications: It kept transitional pension liabilities "off the books" and spread their recognition over the three to four decades of transition; however, it also implied a larger and more institutionalized role for the public sector in pension provision than reformers originally anticipated. By keeping the pension debts owed to workers in the transitional generation implicit, the government debt-to-GDP ratio would not be directly affected. Protecting the government's sovereign risk signals in the short term, however, meant that the financial liability that the Argentine government retained in the longer term would be significant.

The macroeconomic conditions that enabled Argentina's government to make these costly tradeoffs to advance the pension reform were transitory, however. The fiscal leeway narrowed in the late 1990s as U.S. interest rates rose and capital flows to emerging markets became more volatile. At the same time, the Argentine government's domestic financial position eroded as workers began to divert payroll contributions to private pension fund managers and employer payroll contributions were gradually reduced. The government's obligation to continue to meet ongoing pension liabilities to existing workers and pensioners required it to issue new debt to finance the fiscal deficit imposed by the reform. Much of this new debt was purchased by the pension funds, which were obliged to invest up to half their assets in government bonds. But the swelling government debt was not simply a result of declining revenue; pension spending rose as well after the reform. As Table 5.3 shows, rising pension spending coincided with a sharp increase in Argentina's debt-to-GDP ratio while economic growth stalled.

Cetrángolo and Jimenez have shown that a significant source of this rising pension cost was the compensatory pension, which in fact promised workers in the transitional generation a benefit that was better than the one promised under the old pension system. Whereas the average wage worker could expect a pension equivalent to approximately 60 percent of his or her working income prior to reform, the combination of the newly created basic universal pension and the compensatory benefit (PC) would amount to an 80 percent replacement rate for a worker having accumulated thirty-five years of service.[39] The

---

[39] Cetrángolo and Jimenez 2003, p. 40.

TABLE 5.3. *Argentina: Macroeconomic and Government Financial Performance*

	Total Revenue	Social Security Revenue	Noninterest Expenditure	Social Security Expenditure	Primary Balance	Debt-to-GDP Ratio	Real GDP Growth
1991	20.1	4.6	20.6	5.4	−0.5	38.8	10.5
1992	23.4	5.1	21.9	6	1.4	32.9	10.3
1993	24.6	5.9	23.1	5.6	1.5	32.8	5.7
1994	24.1	5.7	24.1	5.9	0.1	35.1	5.8
1995	23.2	5.3	23.7	6	−0.4	39.2	−2.8
1996	22.2	4.4	23.3	6.2	−1.1	39.8	5.5
1997	23.2	4.2	22.9	5.9	0.3	38.1	8.1
1998	23.7	4	23.2	5.8	0.5	41.3	3.8
1999	24.3	3.8	25.1	6.2	−0.8	47.7	−3.4
2000	24.7	3.7	24.2	6.1	0.4	50.8	−0.5
2001	23.5	3.6	25	6.2	−1.5	64.1	−4.5

Source: Krueger 2002.

creation of the PC removed a critical barrier to the implementation of the reform, allowing the government to achieve its short-term signaling goal of approving some form of pension privatization, but it traded off critical medium-term fiscal objectives of reducing pension costs and closing unfunded pension liabilities. Paradoxically, Isuani and colleagues have pointed out that the (albeit modest) improvements in the long-term financial and actuarial balances of the Argentine pension that resulted from the 1993 pension reform law were achieved overwhelmingly through the revisions made to the public, pay-as-you-go component of the pension system.[40]

By the end of the decade, the Argentine pension reform accounted for nearly half (48.3 percent) of the increase in government debt between 1993 and 2000.[41] This increased indebtedness came on top of a stock of debt in the beginning of the 1990s that was expanded by the government's decision to settle demands for pension arrears owed to retirees in the amount of US$7 billion.[42] The new debt issued to cancel these demands, called Bonos de Consolidación (BOCONes), accounted for a quarter of Argentina's debt stock in 1993, although it was not recorded "above the line" as new debt.[43] As the government debt burden grew and the fragility of the fiscal position became apparent, investors began to lose confidence in the ability of the Argentine government to meet external credit obligations.[44] This response was exacerbated

[40] Isuani et al. 1996, p. 95.
[41] Guidotti 2006, p. 78. Its effect on the public sector borrowing requirement was even greater, accounting for more than 70 percent of the Argentine government's borrowing needs by the end of the decade.
[42] Cetrángolo and Jimenez 2003, p. 39.
[43] Guidotti 2006, p. 82.
[44] Guidotti 2006, p. 80; Krueger 2002.

by the shift in external conditions that followed the 1997 Asian financial crisis and 1998 Russian default, which resulted in a sharp rise in risk premia for emerging markets and greater volatility of capital flows to developing countries. As external creditors reduced the level of public indebtedness that they would tolerate, foreign credit dried up, and the ability of the Argentine government to sustain the high debt burden and to continue to finance the fiscal gap imposed by the pension reform diminished markedly.[45] As we have seen, this situation became untenable in 2001 as the government intervened in the private pension system to seize foreign currency deposits in order to pay external debt obligations. The replacement of these cash deposits with peso-denominated government bonds, on which the government subsequently defaulted, resulted in a sharp cut in the dollar value of citizens' pension savings and severe weakening of the private pension institution. What had seemed a reasonable fiscal bet in the context of fulsome inflows of foreign investment and strong growth thus proved much more difficult to sustain when external conditions worsened and the government's leeway to finance the reform without triggering a loss of investor confidence diminished.

Argentina Summary

An OECD study described Argentina's pension reform as "a large fiscal bet, encouraged by the optimism that prevailed in capital markets at the beginning of the decade."[46] More than simply a case of excess hopefulness, technocratic decisions regarding Argentina's pension reform reveal a sharp and consequential narrowing of the time horizon over which technocrats weighed the costs and benefits of key design decisions relating to the reform. The result was to privilege the short-term goal of securing the confidence of international market actors while discounting longer-term fiscal and macroeconomic objectives of reform. This tradeoff was not entirely irrational. Argentina's low savings, wide current account deficit, and fiscal straightjacket imposed by the Convertibility Plan meant that a loss of investor confidence could provoke a potentially devastating balance of payments crisis. Decisions made to signal the government's credibility, however, imposed a higher transitional cost on the government than technocrats originally intended. Although it was feasible to finance this transitional cost in the context of the slackened market constraints and broad financial leeway of the early 1990s, when these conditions changed, the costs proved much more difficult to sustain, ultimately compromising the sustainability of Argentina's reformed pension institution.

MEXICO

In Mexico, as in Argentina, neoliberal technocrats were attracted to pension privatization on account of its putative long-term macroeconomic benefits.

---

[45] Guidotti 2006; Reinhart et al. 2003.
[46] Guidotti 2006, p. 71.

Also as happened in Argentina, however, the factors that ultimately shaped the design of Mexico's pension privatization were overwhelmingly short-term in nature and revolved closely around concerns for signaling credibility to market actors. For although the Mexican pension reform was much less costly than the Argentine – despite its more radical ambitions – Mexico privatized in the wake of a devastating financial crisis and in the context of diminishing international liquidity. Technocrats thus were highly sensitive to the imperative of winning and maintaining investor confidence. In order to diminish the reform's impact on government debt, the well-insulated reform team chose a transitional rule that maintained significant unfunded contingent liabilities to the generation of workers that had acquired pension rights in the existing system. Rather than "sewing up" the old pension system, as technocrats intended, they postponed the closure of state liabilities for a generation, again trading off longer-term objectives for the goal of sending positive creditworthiness signals in the short term.

Incentives to Reform

Of the four cases examined here, globalization was perhaps the least relevant to the original reformist intentions of the Mexican government. Rather, privatization emerged in Mexico as a component of a broader economic restructuring program that was driven by ideologically committed free-market advocates within the Institutional Revolutionary Party, the PRI. Indeed, well before the international spotlight fell on the issue of pension privatization – or on the Chilean experience – Mexican government officials identified Chile's 1981 reform as a key policy measure that could potentially remedy their long-term problems of capital scarcity and low, uneven growth. Mexican technocrats thus were strongly committed to the principle of free-market reform as the 1980s had witnessed an ideological sea change both within Mexico's ruling PRI and within the country's mainstream economics profession. Whereas in the postwar era, Keynesian economists defined the country's revolutionary doctrine around a central role for the state in the industrialization and regulation of the economy, the 1980s saw the ascent of U.S.-trained economists deeply devoted to neoliberal doctrine and free-market reforms.[47]

Adherents to neoliberal ideas ascended to positions of power within the Mexican government as well. In 1988, President Miguel de la Madrid Hurtado (1982–8) launched an orthodox stabilization program and a series of deep market-oriented structural reforms aimed at improving the efficiency of market mechanisms in key sectors of the economy.[48] Economic reforms were deepened under President Carlos Salinas de Gortari (1988–94), who was committed to hiring "the best and the brightest" U.S.-trained economists into key positions in his government. This coterie of economists initiated a broad structural reform

---

[47] Babb 2001; Dion 2002; O'Toole 2003, pp. 270, 273.
[48] Aspe 1993, p. 17.

agenda aimed at correcting the "excesses" of state intervention, which they saw as a critical encumbrance on growth and as a key source of the debt crisis.[49]

The 1982 debt crisis thus defined the pivotal referent for these new macro-economic policy priorities in the late 1980s, spurring a dramatic reorientation of Mexico's economic development path. In the wake of the government's sovereign debt default, the swift and massive reversal of foreign capital flows from Mexico launched the nation into a profound economic crisis. As a condition for receiving a bridge loan from the International Monetary Fund (IMF) and Western governments, President de la Madrid initiated the process of structural reform that sought to replace the import-substituting industrialization model with one based on export-oriented policies. This reorientation entailed extensive market-oriented structural reforms, including trade liberalization, financial deregulation, and privatization of state-owned enterprises, credit contraction, and deep fiscal retrenchment. President Salinas extended this reform program by advancing economic integration with the United States through the ratification of the North American Free Trade Agreement (NAFTA) and by liberalizing the domestic financial system in Mexico.

For technocrats in the Salinas government, the state's role as the driver of economic development had undermined private sector financial development and diminished both private and public savings. Scarce capital accumulation, in this view, explained both the country's excessive reliance on external financing and the state's tendency to use inflation to cover fiscal deficits.[50] The search for structural remedies for these problems began in earnest in the Salinas government by officials that were strongly committed to free-market principles.[51] For these efforts, the government received significant support – both technical and financial – from international financial institutions such as the World Bank.[52] Rather than simply being the recipients of external pressure to adopt market-oriented reform, however, the Mexican government actively sought international models for market-oriented reform, including in the social policy realm.[53]

Mexican government actors sought advice on their pension reform directly from Chilean technocrats. The ideological and intellectual affinities between Mexican technocrats and the free-market "Chicago Boys" in Chile made the latter's reform a natural referent for Mexican officials in the late 1980s. Chile's macroeconomic situation also stood in stark relief next to Mexico's. Whereas private savings in Mexico had been almost cut in half in the 1980s, Chile had both increased domestic savings and achieved positive rates of growth during this period.[54] So when those outcomes came to be linked to Chile's 1981 pension privatization, Mexican officials took notice.

---

[49] Babb 2001; Olave 1999.
[50] Aspe 1993, pp. 72–3.
[51] Bejar et al. 1993, p. 35.
[52] Dion 2002.
[53] Sales et al. 1996, p. 1.
[54] "Save Amigo Save" 1995.

In interviews, Mexican economists argue that they were aware that the link between pension privatization and growth in Chile was not firmly established.[55] Yet, they trace their decision to embrace pension privatization to a concerted effort to increase rates of growth in Mexico. Consistent with endogenous growth theories, technocrats expected that the development of private financial markets would spur economic activity by making capital investment more efficient and productive.[56] With higher savings translating into greater investment, and thus higher output, the Mexican economists discerned that the most likely growth effect of pension privatization would emerge through its effect on capital market development. Mexican government officials thus expected pension privatization to spur growth through the mechanism of financial sector development.[57]

Increasing private sector savings also was closely related to the goal of diminishing Mexico's vulnerability to foreign capital flows. For government actors did not view the 1982 debt crisis as a singular event but rather as an extreme symptom of a chronic problem: reliance on foreign investment to finance the nation's economic development. As the aftershocks of the debt crisis continued to be felt throughout the 1980s, destabilizing state financing and economic activity in Mexico, technocrats in the Salinas government became firmly committed to finding a long-term departure from the vicious cycle of volatile growth and vulnerability to foreign capital flight. Such vulnerability remained a critical problem in the early 1990s. The decline in public and private savings over the course of the 1980s, combined with the appreciation of the peso at the end of the decade, resulted in a wide current account deficit. Given the low level of private savings in Mexico, this deficit was financed largely with foreign savings. Any decline in capital inflows thus threatened to provoke a potentially devastating balance of payments crisis.

Mexican officials were concerned not only about the impact of a reversal in capital flows on the current account, but also about the government's access to foreign credit. Because the price at which the Mexican government borrowed internationally was shaped strongly by perceptions of the soundness of its fiscal and macroeconomic policies, technocrats perceived that any measures to reduce the fiscal expenditure would help to secure the state's access to low-cost foreign credit. Pension reform, insofar as it was expected to reduce fiscal spending, thus was seen as a way to improve the country's creditworthiness and thus to help maintain access to foreign capital in the short term, while advancing critical macroeconomic savings goals in the long term. As one central bank official in Mexico explained, "the government had to do what was necessary in the pension realm to make sure that government financing sources were available and affordable for other areas. The interest rate prices, set abroad, would be better if the government had diminished its commitments in the pension realm."[58]

---

[55] Noriega 1999; Reynoso 1999. See, however, Dion 2002; Madrid 2003.
[56] Reynoso 1999.
[57] Aspe 1993, pp. 37–8; Cerda 1999; Martinez 1999; Solís and Villagomez, 1997, p. 108.
[58] Interview with official in the Banco de México, quote used on condition of anonymity.

As Mexican technocrats moved ahead with pension privatization efforts, they collaborated with specialists from the World Bank, who provided technical advice on Mexico's early pension reform plans. The Bank issued a report in 1990 that endorsed a pension reform proposal that had been designed by Finance Ministry and Central Bank officials to create a multipillar pension system.[59] Although the World Bank did not impose such a model on Mexico, its endorsement was likely to have been a valuable asset for the Mexican government as it sought to persuade external creditors of the seriousness of its commitment to market-oriented reform. Pension privatization thus was attractive to Mexican technocrats on account of its long-term macroeconomic implications.[60] Important factors governing its ultimate design, as we will see next, however, were decidedly shorter-term in nature.

Reform Proposals

The privatization of the Mexican pension system was first initiated in 1989 under the presidency of Carlos Salinas de Gortari. Specialists in the Ministry of Finance (Secretaría de Hacienda y Crédito Público, or Hacienda) offered a proposal modeled closely on the Chilean pension reform that would replace Mexico's existing pension system with a fully private scheme.[61] This proposal was the culmination of numerous trips taken by Mexican technocrats to Chile in order to study that nation's pension reform. The Salinas cabinet was sharply divided on the issue, however, as representatives of the Mexican Social Insurance Institute (IMSS) and labor interests fiercely opposed the idea. As we will see in the next chapters, the allied labor movement had offered broad support for Salinas's economic liberalization process, including NAFTA, in exchange for claiming broader influence within the social security bureaucracy and a veto over social security policy.[62] When the pension reform was proposed, therefore, labor interests called in their loan of support for NAFTA by vetoing the idea to privatize IMSS in 1991.[63]

Instead of privatizing, members of Salinas' cabinet reached a compromise to create a system of individual pension accounts that complemented the existing public system, to which employers would deposit a 2 percent payroll contribution on the behalf of workers. This new Retirement Savings System (Sistema de Ahorro para el Retiro, or SAR) was approved by the government-dominated Congress in 1992 and quickly implemented. The SAR lacked a strong regulatory framework, however, and was immediately beset with administrative

---

[59] Dion 2002.

[60] Cerda 1999; Noriega 1999. Also see Solís and Villagomez 1998, p. 6.

[61] The proposal allowed certain modifications in the design of the private pension fund industry that differed from the Chilean market. Martinez 1999; Noriega 1999; Parmentiere 1999; Reynoso 1999.

[62] Trejo and Jones 1998, p. 75.

[63] Dion 2002.

difficulties.[64] After only two years of operations, the SAR was deemed a failure and government technocrats began to consider again the possibility of more fundamental restructuring of the nation's pension system.

Among the technocrats who had become attracted to the idea of pension privatization when it was originally raised was Ernesto Zedillo Ponce de León, a Harvard-trained economist and minister of planning and budget under Salinas. Zedillo had been present during cabinet-level discussions of the privatization proposal in 1991. Officials from the Mexican central bank (Banco de México) and Hacienda, including Guillermo Ortiz and Pedro Aspe, also supported the idea of a deep pension privatization. However, the political resources in which to advance a second reform waned in the final years of Salinas's *sexenio*, or six-year term in office, postponing further movements on pension reform until the next government – headed by President Ernesto Zedillo (1994–2000).

Crisis and Credibility

A radical shift in Mexico's economic circumstances – symbolized by the 1994–5 peso crisis – helped to bring pension privatization to the top of the political agenda once again. Financial integration, in this sense, provided a catalyst for the decision to re-initiate deep pension privatization, although it did not provide the original motive for the reform.

President Salinas oversaw the liberalization of Mexico's economy in the early 1990s, which brought a revival of foreign capital inflows and fueled growth. Although exports grew in this period, the appreciation of the peso following stabilization caused imports to grow much faster. As in Argentina, the success of the stabilization plan resulted in a wide current account deficit – and with it, growing vulnerability to capital flight. Between 1992 and 1994, Mexico's current account deficit averaged 7.4 percent of GDP.[65] Although the Mexican government significantly reduced its debt burden after 1990, domestic savings also declined, so the current account deficit was financed largely with short-term private capital inflows.[66] Of the US$95 billion of private capital inflows in this period, US$71 billion came in the form of highly volatile portfolio flows; more than half of these flows involved the purchase of government bonds.[67] The growing vulnerability of Mexico's economy heightened the urgency that technocrats attached to pension privatization, especially in light of the measure's anticipated effects on financial sector development.

This vulnerability of the Mexican economy was laid bare in December 1994 with the swift and massive reversal of foreign capital flows from the country. The Mexican government's financing was hard-hit by this crisis as well, as

---

[64] For discussion, see Grandolini and Cerda, 1997; Sales-Sarrapy et al. 1996.
[65] International Monetary Fund 2000.
[66] Domestic savings fell from 20 percent of GDP in the 1980s to 16 percent in 1992. Solís and Villagomez 1998, p. 7.
[67] Whitt 1996, p. 9.

it had come to rely fundamentally on short-term dollar-denominated debt. As investors sold local assets, the Mexican government drew down its foreign reserves and was forced to float the peso. As the currency plunged, the threat of economic catastrophe prompted an emergency financial rescue from the United States, the International Monetary Fund, and other international lenders.

The peso crisis coincided with a change of presidential administrations from Carlos Salinas to Ernesto Zedillo, also of the long-governing PRI. The change of government provided a critical opportunity to re-initiate the pension privatization and to send signals that would regain the confidence of market actors. For President Zedillo, pension privatization offered a remedy for the root cause of the crisis: the scarcity of domestic savings in Mexico. Zedillo thus made the goal of raising domestic savings a cornerstone of his National Development Plan (*Plan Nacional de Desarollo* 1995–2000, or PND), in which he identified pension reform as a key policy measure through which to achieve that goal.[68] Indeed, the PND stated that "personal and family savings would receive a great stimulus if all contributions for retirement and housing were individualized and accumulated in personal accounts that were paid attractive real returns."[69] Thus while the chronic problems of slow growth and capital dependence were closely linked to the privatization goals in Mexico, the two calamitous financial crises that Mexico endured in the 1980s and 1990s also provided an important stimulus for political efforts to re-initiate these plans after an earlier reform failure.

President Zedillo began his reform process by convoking a team of economists, several of whom had participated in the earlier privatization effort.[70] As in Argentina, technocrats working on Mexico's pension reform were insulated from the influence of the social security bureaucracy. In this case, the directors of the Mexican Social Security Institute created a think-tank called the Center for Strategic Development of Social Security (Centro de Desarrollo Estratégico para la Seguridad Social, CEDESS), which provided technocrats with broad latitude to elaborate an ambitious structural pension reform plan.[71]

The group began working in late 1994 and produced its first proposal called the Eagle Project (Proyecto Águila) in early 1995. This project became the foundation of a "diagnosis" of the institutional weaknesses of IMSS, which would provide the technical justifications for the fundamental reform of the institution. The study cited Mexico's rapidly changing demographic and epidemiological profile as sources of actuarial imbalance in the state pension system. Although the IMSS pension system was at that time running a financial surplus, the history of unproductive investments of pension reserves and cross-subsidization of other social insurance programs, particularly the maternity

---

[68] "Plan Nacional de Desarollo" 1995; Sales-Serrapy et al. 1996, p. 20.
[69] "Plan Nacional de Desarollo" 1995, p. 116.
[70] Zedillo likewise appointed a new head of the Mexican Institute of Social Security, who was more receptive to the notion of reforming the pension system.
[71] Dion 2002.

benefit, was highlighted as key sources of the institution's actuarial imbalance, or projected future deficits if no changes were made. The diagnosis also pointed to problems in the design of the benefit formula for old age pensions and concluded that the pension system was unsustainable in the long term and "unfair" in its present form.[72] A key assumption of the report thus was that the problems in the public defined-benefit model were irremediable through parametric revision, and that privatization was the only option for strengthening and preserving the social security institution.

Maneuvering within the Double Bind

Although the basic case for privatization in Mexico was made by technocrats in response to long-term macroeconomic problems, the specific design of this reform was shaped in important ways by short-term concerns. In particular, the worsening of external conditions following the peso crisis oriented reformers' attention toward regaining investor confidence. At the same time, however, the peso crisis had the paradoxical effect of *broadening* the financial leeway that the government enjoyed to finance the 1995 pension privatization. By inducing a short-term influx of capital in the form of a financial rescue package and by forcing the government to privatize an array of state-owned enterprises, the Mexican government was able to liquidate much of its public sector debt. The government's falling debt-to-GDP ratio expanded the financial leeway with which the government could assume the transitional costs of privatization in the wake of the crisis. By mid-1995, the Mexican government's debt-to-GDP ratio had declined to 35 percent, which was well within the threshold of market confidence.[73]

The devaluation of the peso also improved the government's access to international capital by expanding exports and moving the national trade balance into a positive position. By the end of 1995, private investment had returned to the Mexican economy, allowing the government to accumulate substantial foreign currency reserves and to exceed the public sector surplus target set by the IMF.[74] Particularly in comparison to the country's financial position the previous year, by mid-1995, finance ministry officials deemed the government to be in a "good" position to finance the costs associated with the transition to a private pension system.[75] The peso crisis thus had the unexpected effect of broadening the financial leeway with which the Mexican government could pay for the transitional costs of pension privatization.

Also favoring the adoption of a deep privatization was the fact that the potential cost of the transition to a private pension system in Mexico was

---

[72] IMSS 1995.

[73] World Bank 2006.

[74] Foreign reserves reached US$15.8 billion, which exceeded the requirements for servicing public debt for 1996. By February 1996, the Mexican government had redeemed all of its dollar-denominated Tesebonos. OECD 1996.

[75] Martinez 1999.

comparatively modest. In addition to having one of the lowest age dependency ratios in the region, the Mexican pension system was in surplus in 1995, and benefits were relatively low. Indeed, IMSS pension outlays amounted to just 3 percent of GDP, and its implicit pension debt, at 48 percent of GDP, was quite small by international standards.[76] The positive balance in the pension system also meant that the short-term financing gap created by privatization could be paid for out of general revenue rather than with extensive new public debt issues. Since a lower debt-to-GDP ratio was seen as a critical condition for retaining access to lower-cost international credit, Mexico's broadening financial leeway became an important parameter enabling the government to move ahead with the pension privatization.[77]

Mexican officials were not free from concern about international market actors' perceptions, however. Market jitters that lingered from the peso crisis obliged Mexican officials to avoid as much as possible any expansion of the government's debt ratio. Rather than replicating the Chilean decision to monetize liabilities in the old pension system through the extension of "recognition bonds" to workers in the transitional generation, Mexican officials proposed a transitional rule that allowed existing workers a "lifetime switch" option. Through this rule, all workers who had acquired rights under the old pension system could choose at the moment of retirement either their balance in the new individual pension fund, or the benefits owed under the rules of the old system. This arrangement was desirable from a technocratic perspective because it allowed the Mexican government to keep most of the pension liabilities implicit, and thus "off the books," so that it would not increase government debt ratios. Transitional costs instead would accrue gradually and over a long time horizon. While attending to concerns for short-term credibility, however, the lifetime-switch option compromised the government's longer-term objective of closing the state's unfunded pension liabilities.

Mexico Summary

Pension privatization was attractive to Mexican technocrats on account of its long-term macroeconomic implications. It also represented an important institutional signal through which the Mexican government sought the approval of international market actors. For one architect of the Mexican pension reform, this measure constituted "a signal to the international community as a whole that Mexico was doing something positive for change; that it is worth their time."[78] With a low debt burden and a pension system in surplus with low implicit liabilities, the Mexican government could advance a deep privatization with less of a risk of losing investor confidence. Yet, Mexico's pension privatization was not as radical as it could have been, or was originally intended to

---

[76] Sales-Sarrapy et al. 1996, p. 5.
[77] Interview with anonymous Banco de Mexico official.
[78] Cerda 1999.

be because technocrats altered the design of the reform in such a way that the state retained a substantial contingent liability to the transitional generation. This design decision avoided a sharp increase in sovereign debt in the short term; however, it curtailed the medium-term role for market forces in the new pension system.

BRAZIL

Brazil's effort to reform the state pension system for private sector workers offers important contrasts to the Argentine and Mexican cases in terms of its domestic financial leeway and international liquidity constraints. Although Brazilian technocrats drafted a structural pension reform proposal when external conditions were relatively favorable, by the time the proposal was ready to disseminate within the executive branch in early 1998, global capital market conditions had become inhospitable to any policy shift that would worsen the government's sovereign risk profile. That profile was strained by the Brazilian government's debt-to-GDP ratio, which was already dangerously high. The decline of international risk tolerance thus led government actors to set aside structural pension reform plans out of concern that the measure's impact on the government debt profile might invoke a negative market response. Domestic and international economic conditions thus combined to encourage the Brazilian government to forego any degree of structural pension reform that would impose a short to medium-term transitional cost on the government. Instead, the Brazilian government adopted a notional account pension reform in 1999 that individualized pension benefit allocation without privatizing.

Incentives to Reform

The closing of the wide financial and actuarial deficits in Brazil's pension system were the primary objectives of pension reform in the 1990s. These goals became especially important as the economy's vulnerability to shifts in the confidence of foreign creditors increased in the second half of the decade.[79] As in Argentina, the quelling of hyperinflation in Brazil caused a sharp appreciation of the currency, which induced a decline in export competitiveness. As Brazil's current account deficit grew from about 2 percent of GDP in 1995 to 4.7 percent by 1998, the threat of a balance of payments crisis rose substantially, since much of this deficit was financed by foreign capital.[80] Because a cessation or reversal of foreign capital flows could be economically devastating, Brazilian policy makers vigilantly tracked the impact of state action on sovereign risk indicators as a way to maintain international market confidence. As international liquidity fell in the late 1990s, such concerns only increased,

[79] Mody and Taylor 2002.
[80] Savitsky and Burki 2003, p. 19.

and narrowed the government's latitude to enact a policy change that would result even in a temporary worsening of the government's risk status.

The quelling of hyperinflation in Brazil also created new policy challenges for the government. Because the stabilization plan, called the Plano Real (Real Plan), precluded the government from running large fiscal deficits, the maintenance of the country's newfound stability depended heavily on its ability to carry out a fiscal adjustment (i.e., to eliminate the sources of the budget deficit that had long been masked by inflation). The option of simply increasing revenue, however, was foreclosed by Brazil's already very-high tax rates. At 37 percent of GDP – the highest in Latin America – Brazil had little room to increase either corporate or payroll taxes to increase pension system revenue. The government thus had few options but to engage in difficult, cost-cutting measures. As the largest source of budgetary pressure, the nation's public and private sector pension systems moved to the top of the reform agenda following economic stabilization.

In 1995, shortly after his inauguration, President Fernando Henrique Cardoso launched an ambitious set of constitutional reforms, including one focused on the pension system. The latter required the passage of a constitutional amendment because the minute details of social protection benefits had been enshrined in the text of the 1988 Constitution. Before any structural reform of the pension system could be undertaken, these rules would have to be removed from the text of the constitution. Many of these benefits had only recently been expanded in the constitution-writing process that accompanied Brazil's transition to democracy in the mid-1980s. Although additional sources of funding for these benefits were created, new revenue fell far short of the vast new pension liabilities. As a result, pension outlays more than doubled between 1988 and 1996, while receipts rose by only one-third.[81] And without the inflationary tool to finance this imbalance, Brazil's newfound economic stability would depend on the government's ability to close the fiscal gaps created by the state pension system. As pension liabilities soared, Brazilian government actors thus began to view the pension system as the "biggest threat to the fiscal stability and hence autonomy of the country."[82]

In July 1995, President Cardoso introduced a reform proposal that sought to remove the details of old age pension provision from the 1988 Constitution and to add rules that would tighten eligibility requirements and limit pension costs. The idea was that once the terms of pension benefit provision had been "deconstitutionalized," a deeper restructuring of the nation's pension system could be enacted through ordinary law, which required only a simple majority, compared to the three-fifths majority required to change the constitution. President Cardoso faced an arduous battle to approve the constitutional amendment project. In the first two years of legislative debate, critical

[81] Ministério da Previdência Social 1997, p. 5.
[82] Crusius 1999.

provisions fell to defeat at the hands of the powerful opposition. By early 1997, the constitutional amendment project bore only slight resemblance to the president's original proposal.

As the pension amendment wended its way through the legislature, President Cardoso began the second stage of pension reform – the restructuring of the private sector pension system. To do so, he created a special technocratic reform team headed by André Lara Resende, the architect of the inflation-ending Real Plan. The group answered directly to the president, and thus was tightly insulated from legislative or interest group pressures, as well as from the social security, finance, and planning ministries.[83] Reformers took advantage of this autonomy to survey a wide array of international policy models, including the Chilean reform and the World Bank's 1994 pension reform report, *Averting the Old Age Crisis*, among others.[84] Unlike the pension reform plans in neighboring countries, however, the Chilean pension privatization held little appeal to Brazilian reformers.[85] For some of these technocrats, Brazil's high level of inequality made the Chilean reform an inappropriate model.[86] Others noted that the Chilean reform had begun to lose its luster by the late 1990s on account of the system's high administrative costs and failure to broaden effective coverage.[87] Brazil's macroeconomic conditions also dampened the allure of privatization's ostensible ancillary benefits. Having established domestic capital markets in the 1960s, Brazil's financial sector was relatively well-developed (by regional standards) by the mid-1990s, although it had considerable room for improvement.[88] With over US$86 billion invested in private pension funds in 1998, moreover, the voluntary pension market in Brazil was twice the size of the Chilean industry at the time.[89] Indeed, assets in the private pension industry grew from 2.2 to 14.3 percent of GDP between 1990 and 2002.[90] Reformers also anticipated that very little in the way of additional real savings could be gained through radical privatization, since approximately 80 percent of the Brazilian labor force earned less than two times the minimum wage (less than US$200 per month).[91] Brazil's immense implicit pension debt also would have made a Chilean-style privatization exceedingly costly in the short term. Any radical shift toward a prefunded pension system thus would be financially infeasible in the context of the government's fiscal constraints. Even World Bank actors who lent financial and technical support to Brazil's pension reform throughout the 1990s advised against the adoption of such a radical

---

[83] Oliveira 1999; Weyland 1996b, p. 61.

[84] Najberg 1999.

[85] The Chilean model was considered by technocrats in the Collor de Mello government. Melo 2004b, p. 332.

[86] Bier 1999.

[87] Beltrão 1999; Oliveira 1999.

[88] Bevilaqua et al. 2001, p. 49; Loureiro and Barbosa 2003.

[89] ABRAPP 1999.

[90] Medici 2004, p. 8.

[91] Bier 1999.

model.[92] Thus although rising vulnerability to capital flight in the second half of the decade lent powerful impulse to Brazil's pension reform effort, it did not make privatization more attractive or feasible.[93] Rather, as we will see shortly, these conditions placed structural pension reform even further out of reach.

Global Pressures and Constraints

The Lara Resende group worked intensively throughout 1997 to design a structural pension reform that would restore the financial and actuarial balance to Brazil's pension system. The group developed a structural reform proposal based on a mixed public and private pension system. The plan would lower the ceiling on state pension benefits and encourage voluntary individual savings above that level. Whereas the current system covered income up to ten times the minimum wage, the Lara Resende group proposed that the ceiling on public benefits be lowered to five times the minimum wage, and that workers earning between five and ten times the minimum wage would contribute to a defined-contribution pension scheme that could be either publicly or privately managed. For all income above ten times the minimum wage, workers could contribute to a voluntary DC pension account, which would be managed within the existing occupational pension market.[94]

The proposed reform would tighten the link between old age benefits and lifetime contributions, and thus was expected to reduce unfunded pension liabilities in the long term. In the short term, however, the reform would generate a financing gap of approximately US$33.3 billion in the state pension system as higher-income workers began to divert payroll contributions to the private pension fund industry.[95] Although reformers anticipated that this deficit could be financed partially by an increase in employer contributions, the measure would nevertheless require transitional financing from the government to cover the loss of pension contributions.

The basic outline of the Lara Resende group's proposal was approved by President Cardoso and his close advisers in November 1997.[96] In early 1998, the group began to present the proposal more broadly within the executive branch, beginning with officials from the central bank (Banco Central do Brasil) and finance ministry (Ministério da Fazenda). The influence of these actors over government policy decisions had been amplified since the end of 1997, when a contagion from the Asian financial crisis heightened international market pressures on Brazil. With diminishing risk tolerance on the part of foreign creditors, state policy goals came to be oriented overwhelmingly toward

---

[92] Melo 2004b, p. 332; Weyland 1996a, p. 69.

[93] "Memorando de Política Econômica" 1998.

[94] Different versions of the proposal permitted the ceiling on the defined-benefit component to range from three to ten times the minimum wage. Beltrão 1999; Najberg 1998; Oliveira 1999. See also Oliveira et al. 1999.

[95] "Governo planeja 2a etapa da reforma" 1998.

[96] This group included Finance Minister Pedro Malan but not Social Security Minister Reinhold Stephanes.

avoiding any erosion of key indicators of sovereign risk, namely government debt and deficit ratios.[97]

But the proposed pension reform would do precisely that, by increasing the state's fiscal costs in the short term. As a result, central bank officials rejected the pension reform proposal on the argument that the government simply could not expand its debt burden without losing international market confidence.[98] Although reformers argued that the transition would only *recognize* the existing liabilities implicit in the existing pension system, the central bank and finance ministry officials explained that if they did anything in the short term that would require additional indebtedness of the public sector, including a structural pension reform, "it would look bad internationally."[99] Even if the Brazilian government could have financed the transitional cost in the long term, the near-term imperative of retaining the ever-more fragile confidence of international investors made any increase in the government debt burden untenable. Thus it was not the cost of the structural pension reform per se that precluded this measure in Brazil, but rather the rationing of international credit and the government's narrow financial leeway that placed structural pension reform out of reach.

Brazilian technocrats' concerns for international market confidence proved well-founded after the Russian government announced a massive sovereign default in August 1998. As investors moved to limit their exposure to further emerging market losses, capital fled Brazil at the rate of more than US$500 million per day. Between August and October 1998 US$25 billion flowed out of the country, approximately three times the amount of currency that the country earned in trade in that period. In order to stem capital flight and restore investor confidence, the Brazilian government signed a US$41.5 billion emergency loan package with the IMF in October 1998. In the accord, Brazil committed to eliminating its primary fiscal deficit by the end of 1999 and set up quarterly fiscal performance targets to achieve that end. These targets quickly became benchmarks used by investors to gauge expectations of the likely success of the fiscal adjustment. For policy makers, in turn, state actions came to be evaluated heavily according to their near-term impact on the fiscal targets specified in the IMF accord.

The financial leeway that the Brazilian government enjoyed to finance a structural pension reform without risking international market punishment thus diminished markedly between the time in which the first pension reform proposal was drafted and when it was disseminated within the executive branch. Remarking on this shift in external conditions following the initial drafting of the proposal, a member of the technocratic reform team explained, "the fiscal situation was different then, the public debt would not have exploded and we still could have thought about issuing public debt to make it through the transition. Now, that would be insane." He concluded, "The size of the

[97] Bier 1999.
[98] Beltrão 1999; Oliveira 1999; "Poupar com a Previdência" 1999; "Privatização adiada" 1998.
[99] Oliveira 1999. Also see Melo 2004b.

fiscal crisis required a change of plans."[100] Indeed, the government's debt burden reached 45 percent of GDP in 1998, and its nominal fiscal deficit had risen to 8.65 percent of GDP. In light of the new fiscal targets, technocrats perceived that it would be impossible at once to assume the near-term costs of structural pension reform and to maintain the confidence of international investors in an increasingly volatile international context.

The Second Reform Proposal

Reform efforts in Brazil continued despite the rejection of the first pension reform proposal. In December 1998, President Cardoso signed into law his constitutional amendment (Emenda Constitucional no. 20, EC-20/98), which removed significant details of old age pension provision from Brazil's constitution and established a minimum retirement age for public sector workers. Important provisions of the amendment were defeated in the final voting, however, including a minimum retirement age for private sector workers and a tax on high-income civil service pensions. Significant reforms thus remained necessary in order for the government to meet its fiscal deficit-reduction goals.

The sanctioning of the 1998 pension reform amendment also failed to persuade international market actors that Cardoso's fiscal adjustment would be successful.[101] Fears that Brazil would be unable to service its high public debt burden crested in January 1999 after the governor of the important state of Minas Gerais declared a moratorium on his state's debt payments to the central government. The ensuing panic and sell-off of the *real* forced the Brazilian government to float the currency, resulting in a sharp devaluation. The exchange rate crisis lent considerable impulse to Brazil's pension reform effort.[102] Following President Cardoso's inauguration to his second term in January 1999, the Lara Resende group was recomposed due to the departure of its eponymous leader and shifts in Cardoso's political coalition. At this time, technocrats from the social security ministry joined the group, which was placed under the aegis of the minister of social security.

Technocrats thus began work on a structural pension reform that would take into account not only the changes in the international economic scenario but also the new domestic political constraints resulting from the recent constitutional reform process. For one thing, since the 1998 amendment had been nearly derailed by opposition from public sector workers, the urgency of passing some sort of cost-cutting measures led the government to focus its efforts solely on the more politically feasible goal of reforming the private sector pension system. In addition, the defeat of a minimum retirement age for private sector workers in the constitutional amendment meant that the structural pension reform plan would have to produce short-term financial savings

---

[100] "Governo planeja 2a etapa da reforma" 1998.
[101] Goldfajn 2000, p. 6.
[102] Cechín 1999.

without mandating a higher retirement age (or any retirement age, for that matter). The option of raising revenue through higher payroll taxes was also foreclosed by competitive trade pressures resulting from Brazil's already-high labor costs.[103] And the continuing market pressures meant that pension reform could not increase the government's debt-to-GDP ratio without running the risk of potentially destabilizing capital flight.

Technocrats struck upon a reform model that would fulfill these requirements when two members of the reform group attended a World Bank–sponsored pension reform workshop at Harvard University in mid-1998. At the workshop, they learned about a recently adopted pension reform in Sweden based on notional defined-contribution pension accounts.[104] NDC systems incorporate key features of pension privatization such as individual retirement accounts while transferring more of the cost and risk of pension savings from the state to individuals, thereby reducing state pension liabilities. It does so, however, while maintaining pay-as-you-go financing and public management of old age pension funds. Notional account pension reform thus does not impose a transitional cost on reforming governments – a feature that was highly appealing to Brazilian technocrats. The NDC model also appealed to Brazilian reformers because it would create incentives for workers to remain in the workforce longer without mandating such outcomes. It does so by incorporating life expectancy into the calculation of old age pension benefits in such a way that workers who retire younger would receive a smaller pension in line with their longer number of years they would spend in retirement. In this way, an NDC system could transfer the cost of early retirement to individuals without requiring a formal adjustment of the retirement age.

In 1999, Brazilian reformers drafted a structural pension reform proposal that was based on the NDC model, but with certain adjustments to accommodate their political and economic constraints. For one thing, reformers could not attach an explicit interest rate to the accumulated balance of the notional accounts as is done in the classic NDC model. Whereas notional pension accounts in Sweden are credited with an interest rate based on the growth of the wage bill, Brazil's high short-term interest rates, which ranged in 1999 from 45 percent on liquid bank deposits to 21.12 percent real average return on certificates of deposit, made this option infeasible. Indeed, any effort to match these rates would be exceedingly costly for the government, while the use of a lower interest rate would be politically unacceptable.[105]

The centerpiece of the proposed pension reform in 1999 was thus a benefit formula called the *fator previdenciário*, or social security factor. This equation incorporated into the benefit formula each worker's cohort life expectancy, contributions during working life, and time of contribution. By linking contributions and benefits as closely as possible, the reform was expected to restore

---

[103] Beltrão 1999; Oliveira 1999.
[104] Najberg 1998; Pinheiro 1998.
[105] Pinheiro and Vieira 2000, p. 11.

actuarial and financial balance to the pension system – without imposing a transitional cost on the government. This reform proposal was introduced into Brazil's National Congress in mid-1999 and approved as Law 9876/99 in late November of that year. Between the revisions approved in the 1998 constitutional amendment and the 1999 private sector reform, President Cardoso's pension reforms were projected to cut in half the long-term pension system deficit.[106] Indeed, according to the social security ministry, the pension system closed the first year after the reform with a deficit of 0.9 percent of GDP. Even though this deficit is immense, it satisfied government actors because it was the first decline in the pension deficit in five years.[107] The Brazilian government thus achieved its near-term goal of reducing the cost of old age pension provision without an erosion of its sovereign risk status.

Brazil Summary

The technocratic process leading up to the 1999 pension reform in Brazil illustrates how financial globalization may impel governments toward pension reform but at the same time place costly measures such as privatization out of reach for cash-strapped governments that are vulnerable to capital flight. Even though pressures to reduce the government's fiscal deficit created strong incentives for the Brazilian government to enact a structural pension reform in the context of deepening vulnerability to capital flight, the government's narrow financial leeway and the tightening of international market constraints rendered any degree of privatization infeasible. However, by adopting a notional account system, Brazilian technocrats advanced, albeit modestly, the short-term goal of cutting pension costs without generating a significant transitional cost. Because the overwhelming source of the pension system's deficit derived from the civil service pension system, however, the more significant task of reining in the privileges of public sector workers would be left to Cardoso's successor, President Luiz Inácio Lula da Silva, whose Workers' Party had stood firmly between Cardoso and his goal of civil service pension reform. The next chapters will examine Lula's 2003 pension reform and the legislative conflicts over pension reform during the Cardoso government (1995–2002).

URUGUAY

The technocratic process of pension reform in Uruguay bears important similarities to the Brazilian case, despite the evident differences between the two countries in their relationship to the global economy. In Uruguay, as in Brazil, pension reform in the 1990s was motivated primarily by the goal of closing the financial imbalances in the state pension system, rather than by macroeconomic objectives such as raising domestic savings or developing the nation's

---

[106] World Bank 2005, p. 8.
[107] Marques et al. 2003, p. 116.

capital market. Although Washington-based IFIs lent financial and technical support to Uruguay's government, they did not – and indeed *could not* – persuade state actors to adopt a Chilean-style private pension reform. Also as in Brazil, Uruguayan technocrats looked to Europe for policy models, and even embraced a proposal for a notional defined-contribution pension reform at one point. Macroeconomic vulnerability heightened technocrats' interest in adopting structural pension reform, which they expected would help reduce the government's fiscal deficit, and thus improve access to international credit by improving the country's sovereign risk rating. In the short term, however, constraints imposed by the Uruguayan government's wide fiscal deficit and vulnerability to capital flight encouraged technocrats to design the privatization in such a way that precluded a sharp increase in government debt in the short term. The result was to keep in place a substantial public presence in pension provision in Uruguay, despite the creation of a private, funded tier in the pension system.

Incentives to Reform

The costs of Uruguay's old age pension system escalated rapidly in the early 1990s after a 1989 referendum that substantially increased the frequency of old age pension indexation. The new system of revaluing pension benefits came into effect in 1990 just as inflation reached an historic high of 130 percent.[108] Over the next four years, state pension benefits rose by 40 percent in real terms, prompting government pension outlays to swell from 10.2 percent of GDP in 1989, to 15 percent by 1997.[109] Although the Uruguayan government established new sources of revenue with which to finance rising pension costs, the rise in tax receipts was outpaced by the sharp increase in pension expenditures. By 1994, the Uruguayan pension system recorded a deficit of 4 percent of GDP while pensions accounted for half of government outlays.[110] Not surprisingly, government actors viewed the 1989 referendum as a "fiscal time bomb."[111]

Along with the steep rise in pension costs, Uruguay's sharply aging demographic profile generated ominous projections of the medium-term cost of old age pension provision. With one of the oldest populations in Latin America, Uruguay possessed a very low ratio of active to passive workers in the mid-1990s, at 1.4:1.[112] If no changes were made in the state pension system, government technocrats projected a geometric rise in state pension costs over the medium term, necessitating transfers from general revenue equivalent to 44 percent of the pension system's revenue.[113]

[108] Noya and Laens 2000, p. 16.
[109] Noya and Laens 2000, pp. 16–17.
[110] Noya et al. 1999; OPP 1996.
[111] Filgueira et al. 1999.
[112] Mila Belistri 1997. Also see Mesa-Lago and Bertranou 1998.
[113] Comité de Evaluación y Seguimiento 1998.

These projections brought the issue of pension reform to the top of the policy agenda in the early 1990s. Although Uruguayan state actors understood that the emergent deficit in the pension system would mean an even greater financing gap would follow structural reform in the near term, they saw privatization as a desirable way to reduce old age pension liabilities in the long term. By reducing the budgetary pressure created by the pension system, moreover, Uruguayan technocrats expected that privatization would improve the government's access to international credit and liberate financial resources with which to cope with exogenous economic shocks.[114] Privatization thus was perceived as a means to strengthen the government's ability to cope with economic openness in the short and long term.

The concern for assuring access to international credit was driven by Uruguay's vulnerability to external economic shocks. As a small, relatively open economy with low levels of domestic savings, Uruguay relies heavily on foreign savings to finance its economic development. Uruguay also was vulnerable to the threat of capital flight in the mid-1990s since its current account deficit was financed largely by foreign capital inflows.[115] As the government's international reserves declined, as we saw in Figure 5.5, vulnerability to exogenous shifts in market sentiment or terms of trade shocks rose, heightening the risk of a balance of payments crisis in the event of a cessation or reversal of capital flows. Uruguay's declining terms of trade for agricultural exports compounded this problem. In the postwar era – what Uruguayans call the era of the "fat cows" – agricultural exports financed much of the expansion of this nation's extensive welfare state. With the decline of the country's primary product export model, however, this source of foreign currency became much less reliable. Uruguayan politicians thus began to argue that the traditional paternalist state paradigm could not continue without strong negative macroeconomic consequences.[116]

Critically, Uruguayan technocrats did not conclude that neoliberal reform was the only or necessary means to adapt to the contemporary economic era – that of the "thin cows." Rather, "sustainability" of the nation's welfare state became the watchword of Uruguay's structural reforms in the 1990s.[117] The main objective of structural pension reform in Uruguay thus was not to dismantle the public social insurance model but rather to redesign it so that long-term fiscal liabilities could be financed and the system's redistributive foundation sustained.[118] Unlike Mexico and Argentina, where pension privatization was embraced as a means to signal the government's credibility as a market reformer, in Uruguay structural pension reform thus centered on the goal of improving the government's fiscal balance and securing its access to

---

[114] Comité de Evaluación y Seguimiento 1998.
[115] OPP 1996.
[116] Colotuzzo 1998; Quisique 1998.
[117] Michelín 1998.
[118] Calvo 1998; Davrieux 1998; de Posadas 1998; Quisique 1998; Vera 1998.

international credit.[119] The importance of creating domestic capital markets through structural pension reform was considered by technocrats to be "secondary, at best"[120] and "tangential" to fiscal objectives of the reform.[121] As long as the reform curtailed state pension costs, another official explained, "the ability of the state to finance itself looks good, and consequently the risk rating improves."[122] Medium-term goals of the structural reform thus centered on improving state solvency rather than on expanding the private sector role. As in the other countries, to the extent that Uruguayan technocrats prioritized the need to "look good" to market actors in the short term, they would have to curtail the private sector role in the pension system in the long term.

In addition to their cost-cutting objectives, Uruguayan technocrats sought to correct structural problems within the pay-as-you-go pension system. Chief among these was the problem of evasion. Many technocrats and citizens alike believed that the benefit formula, which utilized only the last three years' salary as a base for determining pension rates, diminished incentives for compliance over most of working life. Economists also argued that the high replacement rate distorted private savings decisions. Rather than citing these problems as justification for dismantling the pension system, however, Uruguayan technocrats sought to adjust the parameters of the defined-benefit model while creating a small private scheme on top of it. Without a doubt, proposed revisions of the pay-as-you-go component were substantial: They were projected to enhance compliance and slow the rise in benefit costs and thus to improve the pension system's finances in the medium term.[123]

Constraints on Structural Pension Reform

Uruguayan technocrats worked within powerful financial and political constraints when designing the 1995 pension reform. In large measure, the financial constraints resulted from the five unsuccessful pension reform attempts between 1990 and 1994, which left a yawning financial gap in Uruguay's pension system.

Shortly after taking office in 1990, President Luis Alberto Lacalle de Herrera (1990–5) introduced a pension reform bill aimed at revising the parameters of the Uruguayan pension system to control the rise in costs that were projected to result from the 1989 referendum. Although most parties in government agreed on the need for *some* type of reform, there was little consensus over the specific terms of such a revision. Lacalle's proposal thus faltered upon its arrival in the General Assembly, the nation's legislature. Undaunted, Lacalle assembled a technocratic reform team to develop new pension reform

[119] Davrieux 1998; Comité de Evaluación y Seguimiento 1998; Vera 1998.
[120] Berchese 1998.
[121] Parmigiani 1998.
[122] Davrieux 1998.
[123] Salazar and Sanchez 1997.

proposals. Technocrats worked with a team of pension experts commissioned by the Inter-American Development Bank (IDB) to study both the economic and political landscape as they affected Uruguay's pension system.[124] After ten months of work, the Uruguayan team offered three structural pension reform proposals; each had the principal goal of controlling pension costs and tightening the link between contributions and benefits.[125]

Of the policy models proposed by the IDB team, Uruguayan technocrats chose one based on a notional defined-contribution pension system. The NDC proposal took as its reference an earlier Italian proposal, which had not yet been implemented and which used a notional interest rate based on GDP growth (rather than on growth in the wage bill as in Sweden).[126] President Lacalle designated the NDC proposal an "emergency law" and sent it to the General Assembly without prior discussion or agreement among his coalition partners – let alone opponents.[127] The proposal met with firm opposition in the legislature and was rejected before reaching the floor of the General Assembly. By the end of 1992, President Lacalle's already-weak legislative coalition began to crumble, leaving him with a very narrow political base with which to advance a pension reform.[128] Nevertheless, Lacalle sent three more pension reform proposals to the General Assembly, all of which ultimately failed.

As state pension outlays swelled, government technocrats began to look more broadly for reform models that would reduce state pension costs. Radical privatization, as in Chile, was financially infeasible in Uruguay given the high implicit pension debt – at more than 200 percent of GDP. Indeed, as one of the oldest and most comprehensive social welfare systems in Latin America, Uruguay's Social Insurance Bank provides benefits for more than 80 percent of the population ranging from housing to maternity, retirement, and social assistance. With nearly 18 percent of the population older than age 60 in the 1990s, the financing gap that would be created by a deep privatization would have been untenable for the government facing increasingly volatile foreign capital flows. Adding to this cost was the deep financial deficit in Uruguay's pension system, illustrated in Figure 5.7, which made radical privatization less, rather than more, attainable for the Uruguayan government.

Nevertheless, reformers expected that a modest structural reform would be financially viable. This is because reformers expected such a reform to increase pension system revenue and reduce pension liabilities. On the one hand, private individual retirement accounts were expected to increase compliance as individuals perceived stronger incentives to contribute during working life; at the same time, reformers counted on parametric revisions to the public

---

[124] Beltrão 1994. This IDB team included two Brazilian economists who later became members of Brazil's Lara Resende group.

[125] Labadie 1998.

[126] Transcript of roundtable comments by Saldaín 1996, p. 6.

[127] Filgueira et al. 1999.

[128] Filgueira et al. 1999, p. 7.

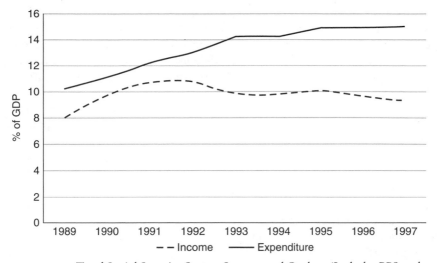

FIGURE 5.7. Total Social Security System Income and Outlays (Includes BPS and special regimes) – Uruguay.

defined-benefit system resulting in substantial cost reductions.[129] The government also proposed to increase the number of years of contribution required to claim a pension. All of these changes were expected to increase pension revenue in Uruguay by 3 percent of GDP in the first five years of the reform's operation, and by 7 percent of GDP by 2035.[130]

Although the Uruguayan government's debt-to-GDP ratio was moderate in the early 1990s, tightening budgetary constraints placed firm limits on the magnitude of interest payments that the government could finance. Using sovereign debt to finance a pension privatization thus would be difficult for the government. Nevertheless, budgetary constraints and rapidly escalating pension costs compelled Uruguayan technocrats to move ahead with structural pension reform. They were aware, however, that the greater the reduction in long-term pension liabilities through privatization, the deeper the short-term financing toll imposed on the government. This transitional cost posed an important dilemma for Uruguayan technocrats, whose wide budget deficit precluded the diversion of fiscal revenue to finance the transition. Although long-term government liabilities could be reduced more dramatically by the use of recognition bonds to acknowledge citizens' acquired rights, Uruguayan technocrats anticipated that a significant rise in the government debt burden would compromise Uruguay's sovereign credit rating, and thus access to international credit.[131]

---

[129] These measures reduced the replacement rate from 72.9 percent to 62 percent of the average wage. Salazar and Sanchez 1997.

[130] Mitchell 1996, p. 17.

[131] Davrieux 1998; Parmigiani 1998; Vera 1998.

Although Uruguay's external debt burden was not excessive by regional standards in the mid-1990s – it had fallen from 48 percent of GDP in 1989 to 28 percent in 1995 – reformers perceived that any measure that increased this ratio would induce a loss of investor confidence.[132] And given the country's wide current account deficit, the loss of investor confidence could threaten a devastating balance of payments crisis.

To avoid the imposition of a significant transitional cost on the government – and thus the issuance of new public debt – Uruguayan technocrats opted to design a pension privatization that retained a substantial role for the state in the reformed system. To do so, they maintained the ceiling on state pension benefits at the *same* level as it was in the old pension system. This decision, as one architect of the plan explained, meant that there would be "nothing to recognize, no bonds!"[133] Most citizens also were given the option, rather than the obligation, to participate in the private pension market, and thus were not obliged to forfeit public pension rights. As we saw in Chapter 4, most workers could opt to split their pension contributions between the reformed public component and a private individual retirement account, to which the government added a significant subsidy. Because many more workers participated in the private system than they anticipated, however, pension outlays rose steadily despite the structural pension reform, as Figure 5.7 demonstrates.

If the World Bank could hold financial sway over any government, it should do so over tiny, capital-scarce Uruguay. Despite the World Bank's significant financial presence in Uruguay in the early 1990s, it is difficult to find support for the hypothesis that the bank imposed privatization on this nation. In early 1995, shortly after the inauguration of President Julio Sanguinetti, the World Bank issued a study analyzing the financial status of Uruguay's pension system and outlining options for structural reform. The report endorsed a deep market-oriented pension reform that substituted the current public system with a substantially private, multipillar system. Despite the attractiveness of the deep cost-saving implications of such a model, Uruguayan technocrats rebuffed the bank's advice.[134]

Instead, the Uruguayan government sought a loan from the Inter-American Development Bank to support the implementation of its more modest structural pension reform.[135] The World Bank responded not by punishing the Uruguayan government for its refusal to adopt the bank's preferred model; instead, it offered a US$100 million loan to support the implementation of Uruguay's modest structural reform. Along with this loan, the World Bank lent technical advice on the creation of legal and regulatory structures to support the private pension fund industry. The World Bank's role in Uruguay's pension reform was therefore mainly financial. As one technocrat put it, "The World Bank

[132] World Bank 2005.
[133] Vera 1998.
[134] Davrieux 1998; Kane 1995.
[135] IDB 1997; MacCulloch 2003.

functions for Uruguay not so much as a source of models for policy, but rather as a source of financing. For others it is a source of policy paradigms. Here, the question is how to finance the reform, once made."[136]

Uruguay Summary

Globalization created important incentives and constraints that shaped the technocratic process of pension reform in Uruguay. These conflicting imperatives generated significant tensions between long- and short-term objectives of the reform. On the one hand, rising pension costs and vulnerability to capital flight became significant concerns for Uruguayan state actors in the early 1990s, prompting them to consider structural pension reform. The principal goal of reform, however, was to cut costs and maintain access to international credit; it was not to raise domestic savings or "retire" the state from the pension business. Fiscal discipline in the short-term, however, obliged reformers to compromise the degree of privatization adopted in the long term on account of Uruguay's very narrow financial leeway to assume the transitional costs of reform without risking destabilizing capital flight. As a result, Uruguayan technocrats kept the ceiling on public pension benefits at the same place as in the old system, and allowed workers to opt for a lower public pension benefit by participating in the private system. For workers who took this option, the reduction in public benefits would not be fully compensated, therein allowing the government to cut long-term pension liabilities without issuing new sovereign debt in the transition to a partially private pension system. As in Brazil, the goal of reducing the fiscal cost of old age pensions in Uruguay clashed forcefully with the even more powerful short-term imperative of coping with increasingly unstable foreign capital flows in the 1990s. And once again, the near-term imperatives of globalization won out over the long-term macroeconomic goals of privatizing old age pensions.

CONCLUSION

In each of the four countries, market forces generated powerful and often contradictory incentives and constraints on technocratic reform processes. On the one hand, the high cost of dependence on foreign savings created significant long-term incentives for government actors in Latin America to embrace structural pension reform; in the near term, however, capital mobility imposed tremendous constraints on the extent of costly structural change that these governments could enact without risking market punishment. Even though the nature and importance of market feedbacks varied greatly in each country, a critical time inconsistency problem emerged in every case: In responding to the imperative to signal sovereign creditworthiness in the short term, technocrats took measures to diminish the market orientation of reformed pension systems

[136] Vera 1998.

in the long term. Even before domestic political conflicts unfold, therefore, government actors in open, capital-importing nations must respond to a powerful constituency empowered by financial globalization to "vote" on government policy maneuvers through cross-border capital movements. The result is that the curtailment of market-oriented reform agendas may derive not simply from the imperatives of satisfying domestic political constituents on whose vote a government's electoral fate depends; it also may owe, paradoxically, to the imperatives of pleasing the diffuse and often-myopic constituents that make up the global financial markets. Far from detonating a "race to the bottom" in social protection, therefore, globalization places tremendous obstacles in the path of the privatization of social insurance systems in open, capital-importing nations. The power of markets thus may be evident not only in movements toward privatization, but in the failure to move in that direction as well.

Of course, in any pension reform process, the technocratic arena marks only the beginning of institutional transformation. Once the design of the initial pension reform proposal has been cast, it must clear the often-significant hurdles of societal approval and legislative sanction. In these realms, political conflicts over reform may forge new social bargains altogether or they may simply revise the terms of an existing social contract. Both the political legacy of the old age pension institution, and the strategy through which consent to a revision in the terms of the bargain are sought will determine the outcome of these processes. It is to these political conflicts that we turn next.

6

Contesting Institutional Change in Society

Where Political Strategies Meet Institutional Legacies

Scholarly research has long struggled to define the nature and role of institutional legacies – the inheritance of earlier forms – in processes of institutional change. Although conceptualization of such legacies varies widely, from distributions of power and resources to institutional performance and ideologies, the avatars of an institution's past are generally considered an ineluctable feature of its present. And while legacies often enter accounts of institutional stability, how such history bears upon processes of institutional change remains far from clear. In the case of pension reform, some scholars argue that as the cost of an institution's prior financial commitments rises, so too does pressure for fundamental change; others claim precisely the opposite: that expanding political constituencies and financial liabilities make radical change increasingly unlikely. As the analysis in Chapter 2 showed, both accounts may be correct, but not universally so. The effect of prior pension commitments on the likelihood of privatization depends upon the magnitude of that commitment, such that rising pension costs generate pressure for structural reform only when these liabilities are modest; only in large and generous pension systems does policy "lock-in" obtain with rising benefit costs.

The cross-national analysis also pointed to an alternative conceptualization of institutional legacies that helps to explain how large and small welfare states can long be stable but later become subject to path-departing change. Such legacies entail citizens' beliefs about and perceptions of the institution, or what I call its political legacy. I argued in Chapter 3 that even though positive beliefs and perceptions may long uphold and stabilize an institution, these may later become mechanisms of change where the institution is seen as having fallen short of expectations, or where those standards or norms are themselves revised. If active compliance with old age pensions may be taken not solely as a worker's financial stake in the institution, but also as evidence of citizens' approval of it and confidence in its efficacy to make good on an intertemporal promise, as is often the case in the developing world where enforcement is imperfect,[1] then the statistical analysis in Chapter 2 offers preliminary support for this expectation. Controlling for the size and cost of the pension system, lower compliance rates are associated with a higher likelihood of pension privatization. This chapter evaluates this expectation further by examining how institutional legacies bear upon the political conflicts through which public consent to path-departing institutional change is sought (i.e., efforts to "sell" reform to society).

RECAPITULATION OF THE ARGUMENT

How does the political legacy of an institution shape the process of transformation? Although the basic social contract need not be explicitly renegotiated to legislate an institutional path departure – it is, after all, possible to change a law without revising the social bargain that it represents – in most democratic contexts reformers expend considerable time and energy in precisely such efforts. And quite often they are stymied by resilient beliefs about, and commitments to, the status quo institution. An institution's political legacy and the partisan structure of political conflict should create systematic opportunities and constraints on institutional change, depending upon the nature of inherited beliefs and performance expectations associated with the institution. I have argued that strategic political actors can open the door to institutional change (1) by providing new information to alter citizens' perceptions of how well the institution is performing relative to established standards of performance and fairness or (2) by challenging those standards through ideological rhetoric, introducing new norms and performance criteria (against which the existing institution putatively falls short). Where an institution comes to be seen as lacking relative to the new or existing "bar" for performance and equity, reformers may mobilize public dissatisfaction into support for reform of an institution that was previously stable and self-reinforcing.

Critically, such discontent may be induced even where performance failures or injustices are not self-evident. These strategies will not be effective, however, for all political actors. Rather, the efficacy of claims meant to win support for reform will be mediated by the credibility of the political actor and by citizens' everyday or street-level knowledge of the institution.[2] Left or labor-based parties' traditional defense of the welfare state offers them distinctive advantages in appealing for public consent to structural reform on claims of restoring or improving the existing design or that reform is necessary to save the institution. Conversely, where the left and labor oppose reform, they may effectively neutralize reformers' allegations about the necessity or fairness of the change. Reformers lacking issue-based credibility may acquire such authority, however, if their claims are corroborated by independent, credible sources. The latter may

---

[1] This draws upon the notion of "compliance as consent" from Levi 1997.
[2] For "street-level" knowledge, see Hardin 2002.

include street-level evidence of institutional failure or the endorsement of the reform by credible interests such as retirees or labor unions.

EVIDENCE IN THE CHAPTER

I evaluate the observable implications of this argument by examining the extent to which the political legacy of the pension institution and the partisan structure of political conflict predict variations in the outcome of pension reform within and across the four countries. I draw upon interviews with participants in and observers of the pension reform in each country, as well as local media accounts and scholarly analyses in order to reconstruct the political legacy and terms on which conflict over reform was fought. Evidence of the institution's political legacy is also captured through public opinion surveys about the pension system in the mid-1990s. As for the reform outcomes, since it is possible to change a law without changing the basic social bargain, the product of legislative conflicts alone cannot bear out when a new and self-reinforcing institutional path has been established. Although strong evidence for whether reform has resulted in a new and self-reinforcing institutional path will emerge only in the medium to long term, preliminary data to evaluate this possibility may be taken from two sources. The first is in public opinion surveys. I examine Latinobarometer data on beliefs about the public and private sector responsibilities for pensions to establish the status of mass beliefs before and after political conflicts over pensions were fought. These data must be interpreted with caution, however, for they do not probe the basis of support for public or private pensions and often underrepresent the voices of the poor.[3] Although we are limited in precisely what we can know about citizens' beliefs about the pension institution, we may gain further insight into this dimension through analysis of citizens' compliance patterns following privatization. For without the confidence that the institution will someday return a decent or fair pension, citizens face powerful incentives to evade contributions, particularly where incomes are low and state enforcement mechanisms are weak. Where compliance with the new private pension institutions is quasi-voluntary, as in much of the developing world, active contribution rates thus may provide a more meaningful signal of beliefs about the fairness and efficacy of the new institution.

POLITICAL INHERITANCE, BEHAVIOR, AND BELIEFS

What was the landscape of inherited beliefs and expectations onto which reformers stepped in the 1990s? And, how did this terrain change as a result of conflicts over pension reform? Data from public opinion surveys taken by Latinobarometer offer a glimpse at the pension institutions' political legacies. In 1995, the survey asked citizens whether the state or private sector should be

---

[3] Berinsky 2002.

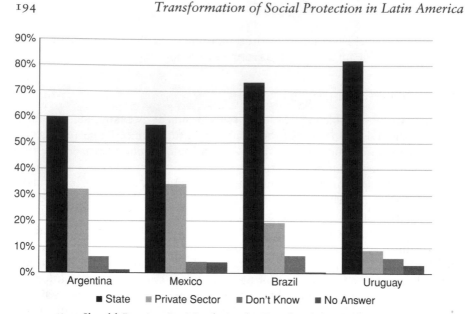

FIGURE 6.1. Should Pension Be Mostly in the Hands of the State or Private Sector? Latinobarometer 1995.

responsible for old age pensions, among other institutions. Citizens were asked, "From the list of activities that I am going to read out to you, which do you think should mostly be in the hands of the state and which should mostly be in the hands of private companies?"[4] Figure 6.1 illustrates responses for pensions from the 1995 survey. For Brazil, Mexico, and Uruguay, these data serve as a proxy for inherited beliefs about the pension system *prior* to structural reform; they capture mass beliefs for Argentina only *after* this conflict. It is impossible to distinguish for the latter, therefore, whether these perceptions resulted from the government's efforts to win support for the 1993 reform, or whether they simply reveal the prior beliefs that paved the way for that measure.

Prima facie inspection of the data reveals just how significant a path departure pension privatization was in Latin America: A substantial share of respondents said that pensions should be primarily in the hands of the *state* rather than the private sector. Privatization thus contravened deeply seated beliefs about how old age pension provision should be organized in Latin America. Even in Mexico, where the broadest support for the private sector is evident, just 34 percent of respondents thought pensions should rest primarily in the hands of private businesses. Cross-national differences in support for private pensions, moreover, correspond to the ordinal rankings in extent of privatization enacted across the three countries. Confidence in the private sector is highest in Mexico, which also enacted the deepest pension privatization of these cases, and it is lowest in Uruguay, which retained the largest state role

---

[4] In 1995, this was question P60G, and in 1998, SP12G.

among the three privatizers examined here. Argentina holds the middle ground on both the endorsement of a private sector role in pensions and the structural reform outcome.

For all the confidence expressed in the state pension system in Argentina, however, the data reveal a striking departure from the predictions of the structural institutional legacy: Despite the old, broad, and generous benefits and coverage of that country's public pension system, nearly a third of survey respondents supported the idea of a fundamentally *private* pension system. Supportive attitudes toward the status quo thus are not strictly determined by the structural profile of an institution. Rather, we have reason to believe that attitudes toward an institution can transform over time, opening the door to deep structural change. In the Argentine case, as we will see, public acceptance of pension privatization was won largely on instrumental claims – the promise of greater material benefits – rather than on efforts to change fundamental beliefs about what is fair and what the state should do. This foundation has proved highly unstable, as we have seen in Chapter 4. In Brazil, by contrast, the resilience of beliefs that pension provision should be a state responsibility firmly bridled the reform ambitions of domestic political actors, making a radical, Chilean-style privatization untenable under any political condition. Indeed, by pillorying the center-right Cardoso government's pension reform proposal as a "privatization," opponents stymied even the adoption of incremental reforms to the state pension system.

The survey data indicate that the starting point in each of these countries was a substantial endorsement of the state's responsibility for pensions. How did these attitudes change following political conflicts over pension reform? Figure 6.2 compares responses to this question in 1995 and 1998 – the only subsequent year in which the same question was asked. The data reveal several important insights, the most striking of which is that in all cases except Mexico, the share of respondents supporting a fundamentally public pension system *increased* in the 1990s; this is despite the purported privatization "revolution" that swept the region.[5] In Uruguay and Brazil, however, support for *private* pension provision also increased, albeit slightly. It is notable that whereas the adoption of a substantially private pension reform was followed by a sharp rise in support for state-run pensions in Argentina, this was not the case in Uruguay, which retained a substantial public sector role while adding only a modest private component to the state pension system. The 1995 data may represent the political inheritance of the state pension institution in Brazil, Mexico, and Uruguay; however, the change in these attitudes over time provides insight into the question of whether political conflicts – and the resulting institutional changes – could alter perceptions of approval of old age pensions. It is in the link between these attitudes pre- and post-reform, however, that we may find the critical role for the political legacy of old age pension provision. Before turning to the cases, I will sketch these reform outcomes and the case evidence

[5] Piñera 2001.

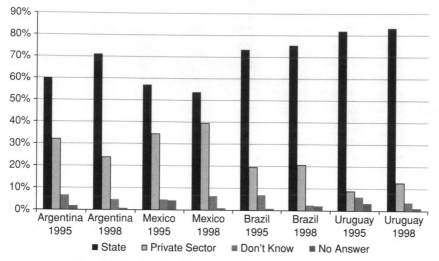

FIGURE 6.2. Should Pension Be Mostly in the Hands of the State or Private Sector? Latinobarometer 1995; 1998.

presented in this chapter. (Table 6.1 summarizes this comparative case evidence linking institutional legacies to reform outcomes.)

Argentina

In Argentina, the share of respondents endorsing a *state-run* pension system rose from 60 percent in 1995, one year after implementation of their country's privatization, to 71 percent in 1998. Active compliance rates in Argentina are consonant with this shift toward stronger endorsement of a publicly run pension system. As Figure 6.3 reveals, 58 percent of workers enrolled in the private pension system in 1994 were active contributors, but only 29 percent were contributing regularly in 2001; by 2005, amid strong growth, compliance rates had recovered only modestly to 40 percent. Compliance with the pension system is unlikely to be driven solely by the economic cycle: Although the contribution rate in Argentina reached its nadir in the midst of a severe economic crisis, compliance continued to fall steadily despite strong growth in 1996 and 1997, and turned positive again in 2002 prior to the broader economic recovery. Were this rate driven solely by macroeconomic trends, moreover, we should see comparable rates of contribution in the public and private second-pillar regimes. However, this was not the case: Active contribution rates to the private pension scheme in Argentina were *more irregular* than those to the public defined-benefit scheme.[6] Economic hard times undoubtedly force low-income citizens to explicitly trade off current for future consumption, but they also

[6] DeBiase and Grushka, 2003 pp. 22–4.

TABLE 6.1. *Institutional Legacies and Political Strategies*

Political Legacy	Government Strategy	Who Has Credibility?	Outcome
Argentina: • Support for solidaristic pension system. • 1980s performance failures.	**Menem:** • Reform presented as a way to improve material wealth, avoid chaos and uncertainties of past.	**Government** • Claims reinforced by earlier performance failures and partisan issue-association.	**Partial Privatization, 1993** Compliance falls as gains from market-oriented reform diminish.
Mexico: • State's commitment since revolution to provide solidaristic pension. • Performance improved early 1990s. • Open to private sector role.	**Salinas:** • Emphasized macroeconomic benefits. **Zedillo:** • New information: projected impending financial crisis. • Revolutionary ideology of economic nationalism.	**Opposition** • Labor representatives in cabinet vetoed privatization. **Government** • Partisan issue-association and labor support. • Projections of crisis produced by IMSS.	**Failed Privatization Proposal Deep Privatization 1995** • Steady decline in compliance with new system.
Brazil: • State can and should provide social security. • Tolerance for unequal benefits. • Benefits must be protected by the Constitution. • Financial imbalances and their consequences not apparent until 1998–9.	**Cardoso:** • Pointed to regressivities and privileges to claim the existing system is unfair. • Presented reform as necessary to avert macroeconomic crisis.	**1995–1998: Opposition** • Left-labor coalition counters technical, ideological claims. **1998–1999: Government** • Crisis corroborates claims of necessity of benefit cuts.	**Parametric (Constitutional) Reform 1998 Structural Reform (without privatization) 1999** Broad opposition reform; relatively high compliance rate.

(continued)

TABLE 6.1 *(continued)*

Political Legacy	Government Strategy	Who Has Credibility?	Outcome
	Lula: • Existing system is unfair. • Reform will benefit the nation.	**Government** • Partisan and personal issue-association.	2003 (Constitutional) Reform of Civil Service Pensions
Uruguay: • State should provide generous, solidaristic social pensions.	**Lacalle:** • Technical rhetoric.	**Opposition** • Left and retiree associations oppose reform as unfair, unnecessary.	Five failed reform Proposals 1991–1994
• Perceptions of widespread cheating permitted by old benefit rules.	**Sanguinetti:** • Ideological rhetoric: reform will enhance equity.	**Government** • Financial problems and inequities apparent. • Retirees endorse the reform.	Partial Structural Reform 1995 Relatively high, stable compliance rates.

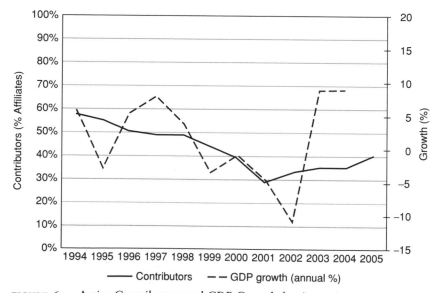

FIGURE 6.3. Active Contributors and GDP Growth for Argentina, 1994–2005.

test beliefs that today's contribution will return a decent and fair pension in the future. A decade after its creation, the mixed public-and-private pension system in Argentina failed to elicit regular contributions from most of its participants. Given that workers must achieve 30 years of contributions in order to qualify for the basic state pension, the institution's coverage rate is only likely to deteriorate in the future.

The political legacy of Argentina's pension institution, and the terms on which support for reform was won, help to explain both how such a deep structural change could have occurred in this democracy, and why the reformed institution has proved so unstable. First, long-term expectations that Argentina should have a large, effective, and "solidaristic" pension system persisted into the 1990s and placed firm limits on the government's privatizing ambitions. At the same time, however, the pension system's conspicuous performance failures in the 1980s nurtured widespread dissatisfaction with it that opened the door to institutional change. President Menem won support for partial privatization on claims that such a reform would significantly improve pension benefits and assure a firm departure from the economic uncertainty and chaos of the past. Menem's identification as leader of the Peronist Party, which was closely associated with Argentina's welfare state, lent credibility to these claims, as did the recent gains associated with market-oriented stabilization in the early 1990s. But the material rewards of market-oriented reform eroded as the decade wore on, and with them went support for the private pension system. Thus while dissatisfaction with performance failures created a mandate for reform, it did not undermine tightly held beliefs supporting a state-provided social insurance program. And without a challenge to or substantial transformation of those beliefs and standards, the reformed institution became vulnerable to a loss of support when the material rewards of the market system dissipated in the late 1990s.

Mexico

The structural legacy of pension provision in Mexico casts a profile of mean benefits and limited coverage by a relatively young institution. Unlike the other three "pioneer" cases, Mexico's pension institution was created in the 1940s, placing it in the "intermediate" category of social security institutions in Latin America.[7] Despite its modest size and relative newness, the IMSS system claimed strong political support. Indeed, that just over one-third of respondents to the Latinobarometer survey thought that pensions should rest primarily in private-sector hands was many fewer than the structural legacy should predict. After implementation of the new private pension system, however, Mexican citizens appeared even more favorable to the concept of privatization, with 39 percent of survey respondents supporting the view that pensions should rest in private-sector hands. Compliance trends tell a different story, however. As

[7] Mesa-Lago 1997.

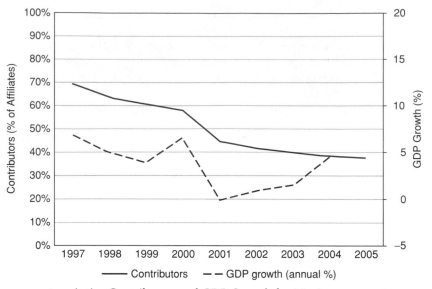

FIGURE 6.4. Active Contributors and GDP Growth for Mexico, 1997–2005.

Figure 6.4 reveals, active contribution rates in Mexico have fallen every year since the institution's creation, even in the context of economic growth. Even though conventional path dependent theories would predict a relatively frictionless institutional path departure should have been possible in Mexico, the new private pension system has failed to win the confidence of citizens enrolled in the institution. Even with commanding political majorities in the legislature, the Mexican government thus did not enjoy free rein to privatize.

The political legacy of Mexico's pension system helps to explain this paradox as it reveals obstacles to institutional change that were much greater than the system's structural legacy would predict with so few, poorly remunerated beneficiaries. Indeed, reformers confronted formidable political obstacles arising from the norms and expectations associated with the existing pension institution. In particular, citizens held tightly to the expectation (and constitutional mandate) that the state should play a financial role in old age pensions, and the belief in the inviolability of acquired pension rights. What is more, the performance of the old IMSS system had not fallen short of expectations. For although pensions were historically low in Mexico, benefits had increased significantly in the early 1990s. The IMSS pension system also was in financial surplus at the time of reform, and thus provided little evidence of a funding crisis. When President Carlos Salinas defended his 1991 pension privatization largely on macroeconomic grounds, therefore, his claims rang hollow. It was only when President Ernesto Zedillo relaunched this effort using the rhetoric of economic nationalism, which, ironically, had long endorsed the government's role in Mexico's economy, that the critical foundation of labor support was won for privatization.

Winning the endorsement of Mexico's official labor movement obliged the Zedillo government to make considerable compromises in the reform, however, which broadened the state role in the private pension system. As we saw in Chapter 5, these included the concession of a lifetime switch option that effectively delayed implementation of the reform for a generation, and an ongoing state financial contribution to each worker's individual account – the social quota. Such compromises point to the continuing importance of the pension system's political legacy. Why, then, were the contribution rates falling since the reform? For one thing, this outcome may be in part the result of the inadequate effort made by the Mexican government to sell the pension reform to the broader population. Mexican citizens also had become wary of private banks following the collapse of the domestic financial sector in 1995 and thus may have little confidence in the efficacy of the system. The moral hazard created by the lifetime switch option also cannot be dismissed: Falling contribution rates may simply be a rational response to the transitional rules that allow workers to claim a benefit that is not tied to their accumulation in private pension accounts.

Brazil

The strong support for a state-run pension system reported in the 1995 Latinobarometer survey only strengthened after the protracted conflict over pension reform in Brazil. While significant, the 1998 constitutional amendment achieved only part of its ambitions; strong support for the state pension system proved to be an immense hurdle before any reform of that institution. Although the centrist President Cardoso pointed to the pension system's stark regressivities as a way to challenge its fairness, highly unequal benefits had become part of adapted expectations and thus were not generally considered unfair. And because the institution's financial deficits were not apparent at the street level, Cardoso's claims of crisis also rang hollow. These claims were contradicted further by opponents in the Workers' Party (PT) and its labor allies, who inveighed against the government's alleged "privatizing" ambitions as a way to mobilize opposition to the reform. It was only when an international financial crisis corroborated Cardoso's claims about the necessity of reform that he could muster legislative support for modest institutional change; reform nevertheless remained deeply unpopular. Revision of the most regressive privileges in Brazil's pension system, namely, public sector benefits, was left to President Luiz Inácio Lula da Silva of the PT. Lula used much of the same rhetoric as Cardoso to advance a reform that was also similar to that of his predecessor. This time, however, the left-wing president, using the credibility that came with his partisan orientation, won broad public support for his reform of the nation's highly regressive civil service pension system. That reform has claimed broad public support, signaling perhaps that Lula's challenge to the fairness of the regressive system has begun to induce a shift in beliefs of what is fair – a renegotiation of Brazil's highly unequal social bargain.

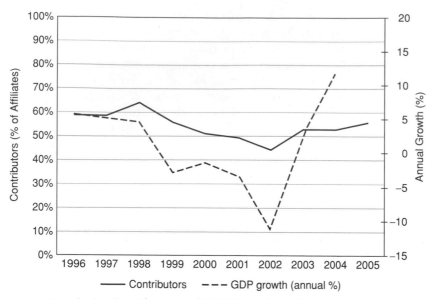

FIGURE 6.5. Active Contributors and GDP Growth for Uruguay, 1996–2005.

Uruguay

The structural legacy of Uruguay's social security system – with its broad cover-age and generous benefits – would predict privatization to be nearly impossible there. The Uruguayan pension system, however, was long reinforced by a polit-ical legacy of broad support for an expansive state-run system. This context permitted the government to gain broad support for only a modest privatiza-tion in 1995. Yet it also shows that even institutions with powerful and firmly entrenched interest groups favoring them can change if their fairness and effi-cacy are seen as divergent from established expectations. Indeed, despite the strong backing for the state pension system articulated in 1995, the share of respondents endorsing a private pension system had risen by 1998, as shown in Figure 6.2.

Nevertheless, pension reform in Uruguay was not easily won. After five unsuccessful pension reform efforts between 1990 and 1994, centrist President Sanguinetti overcame left-labor opposition by pointing to both a conspicuous financial crisis in the pension system and widespread perceptions of cheating. Sanguinetti defended his reform, moreover, by invoking common normative themes of "solidary, effective and just." He also won the endorsement of the center-left Nuevo Espacio Party, which lent partisan legitimacy to the reform. The ability of the centrist government to credibly frame reform as consistent with the political legacy of the pension system thus allowed it to win broad support for the 1995 reform. Uruguay's new pension institution, despite being the (structurally) least probable location for privatization, has been sustained

TABLE 6.2. *Structural Features of the Institutional Legacy*

	First State Pension Law	Age Older Than 65, 1990	Fertility: Births per Woman, 1990	Active Contributors to Old Age Pension System (% EAP), 1990
Mexico	1943	3.9	3.3	31
Brazil	1923	4.3	2.7	31
Argentina	1904	8.9	2.9	39
Uruguay	1829	11.5	2.5	78

by relatively stable and strong compliance rates by the large swath of the labor force that chose to participate in the partially private system, as illustrated in Figure 6.5.

Alternative Explanations

How well do conventional notions of institutional legacies predict the institutional changes observed in these four countries? Research on path dependence tends to predict the likelihood and degree of institutional change through reference to the demographic profile of a country, the maturity of the institution, and the depth of economic crisis. Table 6.2 provides data on these variables for the four Latin American cases. These variables point to a consistent ordering of the likelihood of pension privatization where Mexico presents the most hospitable context for structural change and Uruguay the least likely. With the youngest demographic profile and least mature pension system, path-dependent theories would predict that the pension institution in Mexico should have been most likely to change; indeed, it was. Yet, we will see in this chapter that the Mexican government encountered immensely greater obstacles to privatization than the size and maturity of the pension system would predict. Key features of the reform – the minimum pension guarantee, social quota, and the lifetime switch option – are difficult to explain through reference to the structural legacy alone, as is the failure of President Salinas's 1991 pension privatization proposal. The structural legacy variables fail, moreover, to predict the rank-ordering of pension reform outcomes in the other three countries. Whereas privatization should have been more likely in Brazil than in Argentina or Uruguay by the conventional account, the reverse was true, as privatization proved infeasible in the former, but not in Argentina or Uruguay.

Alternatively, economic crisis may place such great stress on an institution, exposing structural weaknesses that were hitherto obscured, that it disrupts what had long been stable and self-reinforcing processes.[8] In Latin America, severe inflation has been viewed as such a force – even equivalent to war – that could catalyze dramatic institutional restructuring of social and economic

[8] Gourevitch 1986.

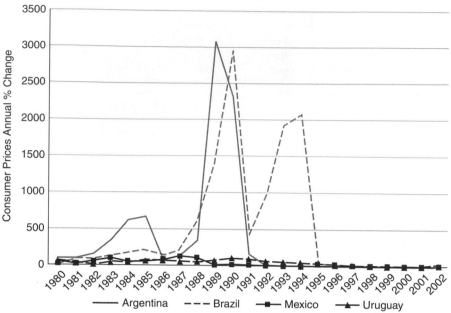

FIGURE 6.6. Inflation in Argentina, Brazil, Mexico, and Uruguay, 1980–2002.

relationships.[9] Among the cases examined here, hyperinflationary crises were most extreme in Argentina and Brazil. The consumer price index in Argentina topped 3,000 percent (annual) in 1989, while Brazil suffered two bursts of hyperinflation, with consumer prices rising over 2,000 percent annually in 1990 and 1994, as Figure 6.6 illustrates. By comparison, inflation in Uruguay and Mexico was milder – on the order of 100 percent per annum; by Latin American standards, these were far from "crisis" levels. However, we cannot explain the pension reforms in this study as "the children of high-inflation crises."[10] For despite two hyperinflationary crises, the Brazilian population remained supportive of the state-run pension system and strongly resistant to the notion of its privatization. And as we will see, it was the *defeat* of hyperinflation in Brazil that forced the government's hand toward structural reform when it could no longer use inflation to erode pension costs. The Mexican government, meanwhile, embraced deep market-oriented reform without a hyperinflationary stimulus, and Uruguay privatized, albeit modestly, without undergoing hyperinflation. Thus it was only in Argentina that hyperinflation coincided with a move toward deep structural pension reform. In Mexico, moreover, we will see that the 1995 peso crisis *complicated* negotiations with

[9] Drazen and Grilli 1993, p. 598; Hirschman 1987; Rodrik 1994, p. 81. Also see, Haggard and Kaufman 1992; Haggard and Maxfield 1996, pp. 35–68. See, however, Coralles 1997; Remmer 1991.
[10] Bruno and Easterly 1996, pp. 213–17.

labor unions over the pension privatization by raising the value that workers attached to the social insurance program and by deepening suspicion of the private financial sector. Neither the structural features of the pension institution and demographic landscape nor economic crisis thus can explain where public support can be won for structural reform of old age pension systems. These factors are neither irrelevant nor sufficiently predictive of these outcomes to account for the incidence and depth of path-departing institutional change.

Structural features must be taken into account in any analysis of institutional change, but we must also examine the beliefs and expectations that citizens have adapted over the long term, and the efforts by strategic political actors to shape perceptions of institutional fairness and viability in the short term. Whereas the hyperinflationary crisis in Argentina was interpreted in political conflicts as evidence of the failure of the state-centered economic model, inflation in Brazil was treated as a remediable "illness" that simply required measures to restore "order" to public accounts. The subsequent implications of such disparate interpretations of crisis were profound. Nor can we look to objective institutional performance to predict when public support for an institution will collapse. As an empirical matter, old age pension systems throughout Latin America were suffering deep financial imbalances and performance problems in the 1980s.[11] In many countries, rising inflation slashed the real value of old age pensions in the late 1970s and early 1980s – by as much as 31 percent in Uruguay and 66 percent in Mexico.[12] Yet, public responses to such performance varied starkly because they depend very much on what citizens came to expect from the state and public institutions. These expectations are critical factors shaping whether objective declines in institutional performance rupture the existing social bargain, or whether these simply elicit demands for repair of the existing system. Although the ranks of citizens who had fallen into poverty swelled dramatically by the end of Latin America's "lost decade," such trends also did not translate directly into the erosion of support for the state-led model of social protection. Indeed, in Uruguay and Brazil, citizens responded to declining pension values and diminishing access to social protection benefits by demanding *more* of the state, rather than its dismantling. Thus we must look to the specific long- and short-term political legacies of the institutions and the nature of political conflicts over their reform to understand how and when path-dependent institutions change, and when such revisions are likely to endure.

ARGENTINA

As one of the oldest, broadest, and most generous social security systems in Latin America, the Argentine pension system should have been among the most

---

[11] Mesa-Lago 1989; 1994.
[12] See Lustig, 1995; Mesa-Lago 1997; Thesing 1995.

politically difficult institutions in the region to privatize.[13] Rather than facing a career-threatening political backlash, however, President Carlos Menem won an overwhelming victory to earn a second term in office just one year after the launch of Argentina's new private pension system. To understand how such a backlash was avoided, it is necessary to examine how Menem drew upon negative perceptions of the performance of Argentina's pension institution to make the case for reform. Performance failures did not provide Menem with a blank check to privatize, however, as beliefs supportive of a solidaristic pension system placed firm limits on the extent of institutional transformation that could be sustained in Argentina.

Long-Term Legacy

The Argentine social security institution dates to 1904 with the creation of the first National Retirement and Pension Fund (Caja Nacional de Jubilaciones y Pensiones) – making it one of the pioneers, or early adopters of social insurance in Latin America.[14] Although the first state-sponsored pension program covered only civil servants and the military, in 1915 social insurance coverage became mandatory for workers employed in the export sectors. Other sectors of the economy were added incrementally to the Argentine pension system as they gained power and influence with the state.[15] The piecemeal expansion of the institution was reflected in its structure, which maintained separate pension funds and vastly different benefit rules for different sectors. These characteristics changed dramatically, however, with the emergence of Juan Domingo Perón and his nationalist project.

The ideological roots of the modern social insurance system are found in the collapse of the liberal trading order and a broadening perception of the risks inhering in unfettered markets. With the breakdown of the gold standard and international trading system in 1930, state intervention in social protection expanded dramatically in Argentina. The shift toward activist industrial policies and closure of international capital accounts was driven more by pragmatic concerns for meeting domestic consumption needs, than a coherent ideological paradigm. Nevertheless, state intervention was explicitly defined in opposition to the liberal, free-trade model. In the social policy realm, expanding protections in the 1930s drew upon the premise that the liberal claim of "the freedom of work" was "more apparent than real" and was apportioned unequally moreover by workers and employers.[16] Social policy legislation in this period traced its normative and institutional antecedents to international policy models and

---

[13] Isuani and San Martino 1995, p. 44; Rofman and Bertín 1996, p. 4.
[14] Mesa-Lago 1989.
[15] Many trade organizations maintained privately organized mutual aid societies that remained independent of the state system until the Peronist reforms of 1949. Antokoletz 1941, p. 430; Mesa-Lago 1978.
[16] Antokoletz 1941, p. 11.

to the mutualism and insurance principles at work in private sector social protections.[17] Even though the expansion of social insurance in Argentina defined itself in opposition to liberal principles, state-sponsored pension provision drew upon few consistent normative principles.

It was not until the 1940s that a coherent ideological framework began to take shape around Argentina's pension system. In 1943, a military coup hardened the antiliberal policy shift that had begun in the previous decade and discouraged competition as much in the political sphere as in the economic realm.[18] As part of the governing military junta, General Juan Domingo Perón began to take an active role in the organization of labor and extended social protection benefits to the working class. With his election to the presidency (1946–55), Perón began to rapidly expand the coverage and generosity of the Argentine social security system, while at the same time articulating a set of normative and ideological principles on which social benefits were extended. Perón launched a nationalist–populist program that extended deeply into the political and social organization of the country, focusing the ideological discourse and collective imagination of Argentine society around the concepts of social justice and the centrality of the state role in achieving that end. Perón's 1949 Constitution enshrined the goals of social justice, economic freedom, and political sovereignty into public policy, which Perón viewed ultimately as a means to achieve national unity.[19]

Peronism was a deeply transformative project that became embedded in Argentine national mores. More than simply rewriting the discourse of social rights and political doctrine, Perón sought to restructure the Argentine economy in a "third position," between free markets and socialism.[20] The principles of solidarity and national unity were thus enshrined in the 1949 Constitution, which elevated social security to the status of a right for every worker and charged the state with guaranteeing a "moving," or indexed, pension benefit.[21] Peronist discourse revolved closely around the principles of solidarity and unity, including for example Perón's pronouncement that "if we suffer, we suffer together, if we enjoy, we also enjoy together," which provided justification for new forms of redistribution both within and outside of the social insurance system.[22] Social security in Argentina thus became associated with a "national doctrine" founded on social justice, inclusion, and social rights, which placed the state firmly at the center of resource distribution.

These reforms created their own political backing in the emboldened and expanded labor movement. Organized labor comprised the core of the

---

[17] The antecedents of Argentine social insurance legislation trace to International Labor Organization and Latin American Labor Conference declarations and the 1936 meeting of the Labor Conference of the American States in Santiago, Chile. Antokoletz 1941.

[18] Collier and Collier 1991, p. 331.

[19] Remorino 1953, p. 11.

[20] Remorino 1953, pp. 18–19.

[21] Rodriguez 1998.

[22] Remorino 1953, p. 13.

Peronist political machine, which Perón fashioned around a top-down structure of control and co-optation inspired by Mussolini's corporatist doctrine. The expansion of social insurance and employment benefits through organized labor not only served to further Perón's goals of national unity but also broadened and consolidated Perón's control of the popular sectors, and with it, his political power.

In the first five years of social security development under Perón, pension coverage quintupled with the expansion of benefits to urban and rural workers, and even to the self-employed and domestic labor force.[23] Perón likewise brought private sector occupational pension funds under public management, consolidating the state's central, if not monopolistic, role in the provision of munificent social protection.[24] Pension benefits were generous under Perón, averaging 94.3 percent of the average salary in 1950.[25] This vast expansion of benefits was not matched with the creation of commensurate funding sources, however; by the 1950s, the Argentine pension system had begun to operate on a pay-as-you-go basis.

In addition to establishing social security as an "inalienable" right guaranteed by the state, Perón institutionalized redistributive goals of the system by transforming the tight earnings-related pension benefit formula into a progressive formula offering higher replacement rates to low-income workers.[26] Law 14,370 of 1954, which established this rule, marked a critical change in the social bargain of old age pensions by shifting from strict social insurance principles toward greater reliance on social justice principles and explicitly redistributive goals. Thus the expansion of pension coverage and increase in the value of benefits served important economic and political goals of Perón's populist and nationalist programs. These institutions also generated significant normative and political by-products, including a powerful legacy of state-centered social protection based on principles of solidarity and progressive redistribution.

In 1955, Perón was deposed in a coup and forced into exile. The military regime that took control of the government thereafter was dedicated to orthodox liberal principles, evidenced even in its motto, the "Liberating Revolution." Led by General Juan Carlos Onganía, the military regime sought to effect a dramatic shift toward a more liberal market orientation of social and economic institutions. However, the military dictatorship had difficulty reversing the path of statist institutional development. Although relatively new, Peronist ideas had become deeply embedded in public expectations and beliefs. For instance, a 1958 decree seeking to rationalize the state role in social protection merely supplanted the progressive benefit formula in the pension system with a flat, but generous replacement rate of 82 percent of the covered wages.[27]

---

[23] Isuani and San Martino 1995, p. 42; Mesa-Lago 1978, pp. 164–5.
[24] Diéguez and Petrecolla 1975, p. 17.
[25] Isuani and San Martino 1995, p. 42; Lloyd-Sherlock 1997, p. 12.
[26] Law 13, 478 established pensions as the inalienable right of workers. Diéguez and Petrecolla 1975, p. 17.
[27] Isuani and San Martino 1995, p. 42.

This was hardly a liberal reversal. Nearly a decade later, the military regime sought again to overhaul the social security system, unifying the contribution and benefit rules and consolidating the (nonmilitary) pension systems under the management of a unified secretariat of social security.[28] But the same basic structure that Perón established remained in place until the 1993 structural pension reform. Successive, brutally repressive military governments thus could not fundamentally revise the structure or redefine the normative social foundations of the Argentine pension system.

Short-Term Performance Legacy

The stability of the Argentine pension system's design was not mirrored in its performance, however, which deteriorated considerably under the military dictatorship. Beginning in the 1960s, pension values began to decline steadily from a high of 94.3 percent of the average wage in 1950 to 66.3 percent in 1969. And despite Onganía's rationalizing reforms, the financial balance of the pension system suffered as special benefits for groups such as the military were not financed by contributions.[29] Whereas the pension system recorded a surplus of 4.2 percent of GDP in 1950, this converted into a deficit of 0.9 percent of GDP by 1969.[30] Payroll contributions to the pension system, although high (at 26 percent of wages), fell far short of government obligations so that by 1990 fully one-third of pension system financing came from taxes on gas, oil, and telephone services and transfers from the national treasury.[31] It became common practice for the government to finance unfunded pension liabilities simply by delaying their indexation, the adjustment in pension values for rising living costs.

With the return to democracy in 1984 the government of Radical Party President Raúl Alfonsín attempted to fill the yawning financial deficits in the Argentine pension system by transferring funds from the state treasury, as well as by delaying indexation of benefits. Yet, with rapidly mounting inflation, the sharp erosion of pension values proved to be politically explosive, triggering more than 20,000 lawsuits by pensioners demanding full payment of pension benefits.[32] The performance failure of Argentina's social protection system was also visible in rising poverty rates in the late 1980s. Data from Buenos Aires show a surge in the ranks of individuals falling below the subsistence level of income, from 5 percent in 1970, to 25 percent in 1990.[33] For a country that

---

[28] Lloyd-Sherlock 1997, pp. 12–13; Mesa-Lago 1994, p. 149.

[29] Isuani and San Martino 1995, pp. 43, 51; Mesa-Lago 1994; Rofman and Bertín 1996; Urbiztondo 1998.

[30] Diéguez and Petrecolla 1975, pp. 17–20.

[31] Cetrángolo and Grushka 2004, p. 12.

[32] By 1993, the value of the consolidated debt owed by the Argentine government to pensioners was valued at US$12.3 billion, nearly 0.5 percent of GDP. Lloyd-Sherlock 1997, p. 15; Rofman and Bertín 1996, p. 5.

[33] Lloyd Sherlock 1997, p. 16.

had been among the wealthiest in the world at the beginning of the century, the rising poverty rates signaled a clear failure of national social institutions.

A lack of confidence in the old age pension system was evident in the declining rates of compliance that attended the collapse of pension values.[34] Despite the legal principal of universality, by the early 1990s, 25 percent of Argentines older than age 70 were not covered by social security, and less than 50 percent of the legally covered workers were actively contributing to social security.[35] A significant portion of the workers left outside the system simply lacked formal employment; however, informality cannot account fully for the decline in effective contributions since the informal market constituted just 37 percent of the labor force in 1990.[36] By the early 1990s, public perceptions of the pension system in Argentina had soured considerably, with widening discontent over disparities in benefits accorded to privileged groups (such as the military), its lack of transparency, and the perception that many citizens were getting away with not contributing to the pension program.[37] A Gallop poll commissioned by the Argentine government revealed deep dissatisfaction with the performance of the state pension system. Beliefs in the principle of solidarity, or redistribution to the poor, however, remained strong; in that survey citizens articulated deep misgivings about the transfer of pension responsibilities to the private sector.[38] Nevertheless, the government forged ahead with privatization plans.

For a nation that once enjoyed European living standards and a social welfare state, the eroding performance of the state pension system provoked broad public discontent with the existing social protection institution. Even after the government settled its pension claims, retirees continued to hold weekly demonstrations outside the National Congress. What they demanded, notably, was *improvement* of the state pension system – not its dismantling. Thus while declining performance provoked broad dissatisfaction with the existing pension system in Argentina, it did not provide the government with a carte blanche to privatize.

Political Strategy of the 1993 Reform

When President Carlos Saúl Menem took office in 1989 in the midst of a dire economic crisis, a sense of disappointment with the state-led economic model pervaded the Argentine public.[39] After more than a year and a half of failed stabilization efforts, Menem launched the orthodox Convertibility Plan in 1991. As we saw in Chapter 5, the rapid vanquishing of hyperinflation

---

[34] Mesa-Lago 1994, p. 150; Rofman 1996; Rofman and Bertín 1996, p. 5.

[35] Workers lacking coverage in the 1980s were divided across the rural sector (46 percent), urban informal sector (36 percent), and domestic workers (11 percent). Lloyd-Sherlock 1997, p. 14.

[36] Lo Vuolo 1991. See also Isuani and San Martino 1995, p. 46; Rofman 1996, p. 10.

[37] Cetrángolo and Grushka 2004, p. 13. See also Margheritis 2002.

[38] Demarco 2004, p. 90.

[39] Bustos 1998. Cetrángolo 1998; Margheritis 2002.

brought a resurgence of investment to Argentina, stimulating a sharp rise in real wages, consumption, and industrial production. The success of the Convertibility Plan armed Menem with considerable advantages as he sought support for his market-oriented reform agenda.[40] Menem's political leverage also drew from the performance failures of the state-centered economic development model and from his distinctive political strategies.

Memories of the economic calamity of the 1980s lingered heavily in the public memory as a "frightening and disorganized period" in Argentine history.[41] For many Argentine citizens, toleration of the austere structural reform was grounded in a resolve to "never again" (*nunca más*) return to the chaos of the economic crisis.[42] Menem seized upon this sentiment to portray himself in opposition to the legacy of state-centered economic policy. Although he was the leader of the Peronist Party, which had championed precisely the economic model that he was assailing, Menem was careful to distance himself from both the statist and nationalist economic project and from the segments of his party that continued to defend it. He thus attributed responsibility for the hyperinflationary crisis to the "traditional model of party action and public management" that placed the state at the center of economic management; he then presented his market-oriented reform agenda as antipode of that model.[43]

Menem thus set up a stark dichotomy between statist institutions and economic calamity on the one hand, and market-oriented reforms, growth, and wealth on the other. This strategy had deep roots in the Argentine political tradition, which had long been organized around opposing values such as liberalism versus nationalism, Peronism versus anti-Peronism. Menem interpreted the contemporary reform options as a national struggle between backwardness and modernity, and between poverty and prosperity. Market-oriented reform, he argued, represented a "change of epoch" that would bring the nation to a place of wealth and stability.[44] Menem asserted that whereas statist economic policies had caused the nation's ruin, market-oriented reform would restore the country to its place at the table of "first-world" countries.[45]

The case for privatization thus rested heavily on material and instrumental grounds: A new market-oriented policy model would provide citizens with economic stability, financial control, and wealth, whereas the status quo would bring chaos and financial loss.[46] Menem argued, for instance, that a private pension system would be "more secure, more certain and also [would] allow the person who makes the contributions direct control over their funds, to see how they accumulate and accrue interest."[47] Menem also used the memory of

[40] Bustos 1995, p. 25.
[41] Palermo and Collins 1998, p. 36; Torre and Gerchunoff 1998, p. 3.
[42] Facal 1998.
[43] Palermo and Novaro 1996, p. 25.
[44] Palermo and Novaro 1996, p. 29.
[45] Bustos 1998; Cetrángolo 1998; Diaz 1998; Rodriguez 1998; Torre 1998.
[46] Bustos 1998; Santín 1998.
[47] Lloyd-Sherlock 1997, p. 19.

hyperinflation to reinforce the belief that the existing pension system had failed irremediably. Menem argued that "if the government was running it, it would fail."[48] As the minister of labor and social security put it, "there was no room for a purely public system because of the hyperinflation."[49] A centerpiece of Menem's effort to sell the pension privatization to the Argentine public thus was to cast the experience of economic crisis – to which they would inexorably return if the status quo were maintained – into sharp relief against the gains to be won through market-oriented reform.[50]

Menem's claims were lent credibility by street-level evidence of the recent performance failures of the state-run economic institutions, including the pension system, and by the apparent success of the inflation-quelling, market-oriented Convertibility Plan. Menem also relied on claims about future institutional performance that could not be verified through ordinary knowledge. Menem reminded citizens that market-oriented reform would bring the nation to "more fertile grounds," although they would first have to "cross the desert" of structural reform.[51] Although this strategy was risky, Palermo argues that it was successful in the near term because "when the hot sand burned his followers' feet," citizens could maintain confidence in the reform strategy because hyperinflation indeed did not return. Of course, when the material gains and economic stability associated with market-oriented reform dissipated by the end of the decade, citizens proved much less willing to continue their march through the desert of the free market.

Menem's justifications for the move toward pension privatization thus rested heavily on the material gains to be won through markets. He did not challenge the principles of solidarity that had long underpinned broad public support for the Argentine social insurance system. Indeed, widely held beliefs that solidarity and state involvement should be central components of social protection proved to be "stubborn and enduring."[52] The resilience of these shared beliefs placed important limits on the extent of privatization for which Menem could win – and sustain – public support. For instance, following the initial roundtable for political dialogue, Argentine technocrats were obliged to include a public and redistributive basic universal pension in the design of their pension reform proposal. And when the material benefits of the private pension system diminished, so too did confidence in and compliance with the institution.

Political Legacy and Reform Limits

When the new private pension system came into effect in 1994, it was greeted by many Argentine workers with confusion and pessimism. Although early

---

[48] Rofman 1998.
[49] Diaz 1998.
[50] Castillo Marin 1998; Facal 1998; Roca 1998; Schulthess 1998.
[51] Palermo and Collins 1997, p. 50.
[52] Quote from Lloyd Sherlock 1997, p. 20; also see Schulthess and Demarco 1994, p. 49.

participation in the private pension market was strong, this trend was driven overwhelmingly by the government's enrollment of workers into the private system by default: Workers who failed to designate a choice between the public and private systems for their second-tier benefit were automatically enrolled in the private system.[53] The steady rise in the number of workers enrolled in the new pension system was not matched with a commensurate rise in active contribution rates, however, which lagged behind those in Uruguay and Mexico (as shown in Figure 6.3).

This trend was puzzling for Argentine technocrats precisely because a central claim of proponents of the market-oriented model was that it would improve incentives for compliance and, with it, the coverage and effectiveness of the pension system. The government thus commissioned a survey of workers' opinions about the private pension system in 2000. The poll revealed considerable doubts: only 30 percent of respondents reported having "some confidence" in the private pension industry, whereas 51 percent claimed to have "little or no" confidence in it at all. A full 82 percent of the more than 700 respondents believed that the private pension funds could go bankrupt, and two-thirds of the citizens believed that the functioning of the new pension system depended on politics. Neither the state nor the market, the survey showed, enjoyed great confidence in Argentina by the end of the 1990s. By December 2001, just 36 percent of the affiliates of the private pension regime were classified as "regular" contributors – that is, with rights to claim a benefit under the new system. By the end of 2002, only 18 percent of the economically active population in Argentina was covered by the pension system.

The fragility of the social foundations of the new institution was further laid bare in the public response to the government's interventions in the private pension system during the economic crisis. As we saw in Chapter 4, in late 2001 the Argentine government appropriated the dollar-denominated bank deposits of the private pension funds and replaced these with peso-denominated government bonds on which it later defaulted. The government also slashed employee contribution rates to the private pension system from 11 percent of wages to 5 percent, more than halving the retirement benefits that would be provided through the private component of the institution.[54] An International Labour Organization analysis of the crisis found that these incursions were greeted largely with apathy outside the financial community.[55] Even though active compliance rates began to rise again in 2002, the return to growth did not help to reconstitute political support for the private pension system in Argentina. Rather, the government of Peronist President Néstor Kirchner would further weaken the private pension system by allowing workers to switch from the

---

[53] Rapid enrollment was also an artifact of the incorporation of the provincial pension funds into the national system.

[54] Decree 1676/01 of December 19, 2001 increased contributions to 7 percent of wages. Rofman 2000, p. 14; 2003; SAFJP 2002, p. 88.

[55] Organización Internacional del Trabajo 2002, p. 10.

private to the public pension system for their second-tier benefit. Previously, workers were only allowed to transfer from the public to the private system.

Thus nearly a decade after the reform of the old age pension system in Argentina, beliefs and behaviors supportive of the market-based system had failed to consolidate. While the performance failure of the state pension system in the 1980s contributed to a loss of public confidence in the old pension system, discontent with such performance did not undermine the basic norms that long upheld the state-centered social insurance model. Indeed, by 2004, public opinion surveys found that 64 percent of Argentines disagreed with the statement, "It does not matter to me if private companies take over the country if they can solve problems."[56] The same survey found that more than three-quarters of the population had little or no confidence in private banks. Support for the market-oriented reform strategy in the early 1990s, which rested heavily on the promise of material rewards, thus proved infertile ground for a new market-oriented social bargain in Argentina.

Argentina Summary

The political legacy of the old age pension system in Argentina generated both important opportunities and constraints with respect to pension privatization. On the one hand, performance failings induced broad dissatisfaction that opened political space for reform. Menem seized upon this opportunity to make his case for pension privatization on the basis of the material gains to be won through markets, while associating the old public institution with the hyperinflationary crisis of the 1980s. But the deeply embedded norms of solidarity and expectations of state pension provision were unshaken by the economic crisis and unchallenged by Menem's political strategy. These beliefs would place important limits on the extent of privatization for which Menem could sustain political support. And with a fundamentally material foundation for public consent, the private pension system would prove to be exceedingly fragile when economic bad times returned and the gains from participation became much less apparent.

MEXICO

If the broad, generous, and mature institutional profile of the Argentine pension system made privatization unlikely there, the structural legacy of the Mexican pension system represented a "most likely" scenario for institutional path departure. The Mexican pension system was both relatively young and narrow in coverage, reaching just a third of the labor force in the mid-1990s.[57] Old age pensions also were relatively modest by international standards. Yet, approval of Mexico's pension privatization by one of the most significant veto

---

[56] Latinobarómetro 2004.
[57] Grandolini and Cerda 1997, p. 4.

players – organized labor – was far from assured. Rather, as we have seen, the Mexican government's first attempt to privatize in 1991 failed to win labor support and was abandoned in favor of an "add-on" private pension benefit, the SAR. Even in a less-than-fully-democratic context, structural change of the pension system was possible only when the government acknowledged and operated within the constraints of normative beliefs and expectations of the social protection system.

Long-Term Legacy

The Mexican pension system traces its roots to the beginning of the twentieth century when certain state governments mandated that employers offer insurance for the risks of accident or death. A national pension system could only be established after the Mexican Revolution (1910–20), which overthrew the authoritarian regime of Porfirio Díaz (the *Porfiriato*, 1876–1911). The 1917 Constitution, which grew out of the revolution, committed the national government to providing a solidaristic social protection system, including pensions and health care. The first postrevolutionary governments of Obregón and Calles took steps in this direction with the support of the main labor confederation (Confederación Regional Obrera Mexicana). These early efforts were attenuated, however, by strong opposition from employers.[58] President Calles nevertheless extended pensions to the public sector and the military, and President Lázaro Cárdenas later broadened the scope of these pensions to include private sector industries such as petroleum and railroads. The present-day Mexican Social Security Institute was created in 1943 by Cárdenas' successor, President Ávila Camacho. The latter extended pension benefits to a broader range of private sector workers, although these remained fundamentally urban and thus were limited as a portion of the workforce.[59]

The development of IMSS was closely related to the political authority claimed by Mexico's Institutional Revolutionary Party, which governed for most of the twentieth century.[60] The PRI was founded in the Mexican Revolution and drew upon the doctrine of the revolution to legitimate its strict control of social and political relationships in Mexico for more than seventy years. The ideology of the Mexican Revolution emphasized nationalism, participation, economic redistribution, and social justice.[61] The constitutional obligations of the state included the provision of universal health care and education, retirement and disability insurance, worker compensation, and child care and maternity benefits. In the area of old age pensions, the state guaranteed a dignified living standard (*nivel de vida digno*) for the insured population in retirement.

[58] Solís Soberón and Villagómez 1999, p. 103.
[59] Dion 2008; Solís Soberón and Villagomez 1999, p. 104.
[60] Dion 2002; 2008.
[61] Middlebrook 1991, p. 3.

The IMSS pension system was designed initially to be a partially capitalized system through which reserves would accumulate as the first generations contributed to the system. Returns to those invested funds, in turn, were expected to finance benefits when later generations reached retirement. Early on, however, pension contributions were diverted to finance the infrastructure requirements of the national IMSS health care system and particularly the construction of an extensive hospital network.[62] The pension contributions of later generations also were used to subsidize the IMSS health, maternity, and child care benefits. Although the system produced little in the way of financial yield, by the end of the 1990s, the IMSS health care system reached more than 80 percent of the municipalities in Mexico.[63] Support for IMSS thus often referred to the extensive health care institution, rather than to the more narrowly reaching pension system.

Short-Term Legacy

Pension benefits provided by IMSS were meager by international standards. Inadequate indexation had caused the real value of pension benefits to diminish considerably in the context of inflation in the 1970s and 1980s. This erosion was partially corrected, however, by a 1989 law that set the minimum pension equal to one real urban minimum wage (up from its previous rate of 40 percent of the minimum wage).[64] With nearly 90 percent of pensions in the early 1990s paid at the minimum value, the result was a vast improvement in the purchasing power of old age benefits for most beneficiaries of the IMSS system.[65] Thus by the early 1990s, most pensioners' benefits had been more than doubled from the previous decade, providing clear street-level evidence that the system was making good on its promises, modest though they were.

Although Mexico was not fully democratic when it privatized its old age pension system, the government was nevertheless obliged to justify, or sell, its reform to society. Doing so required winning the consent of a critical stakeholder in the pension system: organized labor. This was not an easy task, for despite the comparatively low pension benefits in Mexico, workers were deeply attached to their acquired pension rights. The Mexican government's obligation to protect these rights would become an unyielding political constraint on the government's privatization plans. The apparent effectiveness of the IMSS pension system at the time of the reform obliged the government to justify its privatization as necessary to avert a looming financial collapse of the system. The government also portrayed the reform as being consistent with the nationalist ideology of the revolution. Indeed, the Mexican government went

---

[62] Grandolini and Cerda 1997, p.7; IMSS 1995.
[63] Pension coverage was estimated in the 1990s to reach 27.5 percent of the economically active population. Grandolini and Cerda 1997; Solís Soberón and Villagómez 1999.
[64] Solís Soberón and Villagómez 1999, pp. 114, 124.
[65] Grandolini and Cerda 1997, p. 7; Solís Soberón and Villagómez 1999, pp. 114, 124.

to much greater efforts to win support for reform than we might expect from the narrow structural profile of the institution.

The political conflicts over pension reform in the early 1990s in Mexico framed the subsequent design and strategy of pension privatization in 1995. In particular, reformers drew important lessons from the defeat of a pension privatization proposal that had been developed under the government of President Carlos Salinas de Gortari. In that effort, technocrats justified their pension privatization proposal strictly in macroeconomic terms: as a way to enhance macroeconomic growth and deepen Mexico's capital markets. For representatives of labor within the Salinas cabinet, however, these were not persuasive grounds. Labor representatives responded that macroeconomic goals could and should be achieved through means other than the privatization of IMSS, which had an important social function. For government actors involved in this reform, it became clear that the macroeconomic rhetoric was "going nowhere" in the face of arguments emphasizing the social mission of the institution.[66] An early plan to replicate the radical Chilean privatization thus was abandoned in favor of a modest "add-on" pension benefit to complement the IMSS social insurance pension scheme.

Technocrats concluded from that experience that "arguments had to be made at the institutional level" if reform claims were to be effective.[67] The political strategy for the next reform thus began with an analysis of the IMSS institution (i.e., its organization and financial systems) to establish the grounds for reform as "necessary to protect the resources" of the pension system.[68] Mexican officials thus sought to *induce* negative perceptions of the institution's viability as a way to loosen workers' attachments to the status quo scheme.[69] This strategy was particularly important because the IMSS system was experiencing a financial surplus at the time of the reform, and because for most beneficiaries of the system, the institution was functioning better than it had in recent decades.

A second aspect of Zedillo's political strategy drew from the failure of a pension privatization effort in the state of Nuevo León. In 1993, central bank officials who had participated in Salinas's privatization initiative were asked to provide support for privatization of the civil servants' pension system of Nuevo León (ISSSTE–León). The technocrats who had studied the Chilean privatization for their earlier effort modeled the reform in Nuevo León closely after that system. The proposal was rapidly sanctioned by the state legislature and signed into law with little public dialogue or negotiation. Immediately upon enactment, however, the measure was met with a fierce political backlash from public sector workers. Led by the well-organized teachers' unions, state employees in Nuevo León unleashed weeks of broad and vehement protests against

---

[66] Reynoso 1999.
[67] Anonymous interview, Banco de México.
[68] Reynoso 1999.
[69] Noriega Curtis 1999.

the pension reform. As part of a vertically integrated national civil servants' labor confederation, ISSSTE–León called upon the assistance of the national confederation of civil servants (Instituto de Seguridad y Servicios Sociales de los Trabajadores del Estado, ISSSTE), which viewed the Nuevo León experience as a portent of future plans to privatize the national civil service pension system. The peak confederation lent generous assistance to that conflict, sending a clear signal to government actors of its capacity to upend privatization at the national level as well.

At the center of the civil servants' grievance was the creation of a "recognition bond" to acknowledge the benefits owed to workers who had contributed to the old pension system. The bonds would be added as initial capital to workers' individual accounts in the new private pension system. Although reformers pointed out that the recognition bonds were "fair" in actuarial terms, that is, they were equivalent to present value of past contribution rates to the old ISSSTE–León pension system, these technical claims held little sway against accusations by civil servants that they had been "betrayed" and "shortchanged" by the government. At issue was the perception that a recognition bond did not adequately represent their acquired rights in the pension system. Protests continued until the governor of Nuevo León repealed the state privatization law.

For officials in the federal government, the lessons of this reform debacle were clear: They had to "leave aside technical reality" and work within the realm of citizens' perceptions of the issue.[70] Regardless of the *actuarial* fairness of the recognition bonds, they reasoned, the perception that such a bond was *politically* unfair meant that pension privatization would only be viable if it rested on the perceptible protection of acquired rights. A "vital piece of the selling" of the 1995 IMSS pension reform thus became the protection of acquired rights such that "the [average] worker would not feel affected" in a negative way by the reform.[71] The consequence was to permit the current generation of workers with rights in the old system to effectively opt out of the privatized pension system. This was done through the concession of the "lifetime switch" option, which guaranteed workers at the moment of retirement the better of their accumulation in their private pension account or the benefit they would have received under the rules of the old pension system. Given the tremendous moral hazard implied by this provision, it was not one that technocrats would have likely conceded if it were not perceived as an indispensable condition for approval of the reform.

Political Strategy of the 1995 Pension Reform

The inauguration of President Ernesto Zedillo in 1994 offered an opportunity to re-initiate the structural pension reform project at the national level in

[70] Reynoso 1999.
[71] Solís Soberón 1999.

Mexico. President Zedillo was convinced of the macroeconomic benefits of pension privatization, as we have seen, and immediately set in motion plans for such a reform. The task of winning public support for pension privatization in Mexico was complicated, however, by the effects of the nation's recent economic crisis on citizens' confidence in the private financial sector. Unlike the situation in Argentina, where free-market reform brought swift and widespread benefits for society, economic liberalization in Mexico resulted in a deepening distrust of the private sector. Following the liberalization of the domestic financial system and the deregulation of international capital flows, Mexico suffered a massive currency crisis in December 1994 and early 1995. The peso crisis provoked a deep economic recession as interest rates were raised to stem the outflow of capital. Businesses across the economy went bankrupt, resulting in falling wages and rising unemployment. The economic contraction rapidly spilled into the financial sector, triggering a system-wide collapse as nonperforming bank loans proliferated throughout the system. Mexican citizens were obliged to bear the cost of the massive state bailout of the country's banks, which reached more than US$65 billion.[72] Bitterness over this resolution of the domestic banking crisis, along with the social and economic costs of the crisis, continued to be deeply felt throughout Mexico as the government announced its plans to privatize the pension system. The association of the pension privatization with the failed domestic financial sector fueled resistance to the plan, as many citizens had come to see the private financial sector as being not only a source of risk but corrupt and opaque as well.[73] Indeed, by 2004, the Latinobarometer found that nearly two-thirds of Mexicans had "little or no" confidence in private banks.[74]

The task of building political support for the 1995 pension reform fell to officials in the finance ministry (Secretaría de Hacienda y Crédito Público).[75] This project took shape around a two-pronged rhetorical strategy. First, government actors challenged widely held perceptions that IMSS was financially sound by providing information about a putative looming funding crisis in the system. In addition, Hacienda officials depicted the privatization as being consistent with the ideals of the revolution, invoking the reform as an instrument of economic nationalism and touting its solidaristic characteristics.

The Mexican government thus began to lay the political grounds for reform by "raising consciousness" of institutional weaknesses in the IMSS system. As we saw in Chapter 5, technocrats in the Zedillo government commissioned an actuarial analysis of the social security institution. That "diagnosis" of the IMSS system was published in early 1995. Pointing to declining fertility rates and increasing life expectancy, the study concluded that IMSS was facing "severe financial problems," which made structural reform necessary and urgent to

[72] Wilson et al. 2000, p. 298.
[73] Banco de México official on condition of anonymity.
[74] Latinbarómetro 2004.
[75] Gonzales Pier 1999.

avert a financial collapse. Officials estimated that without reform, the IMSS pension system would require large government transfers in order to meet its obligations or it would have to increase payroll contributions to 23.3 percent by 2020.[76] According to one official, the message of the diagnostic report was that without a structural overhaul of IMSS, "it all would go under in a big catastrophe."[77] The study sought especially to disseminate projections "that were not evident to many people before" so that the government could justify deep structural reform as a way to "protect" the financial resources of IMSS.[78]

By defending the privatization of IMSS on the basis of projections of its future funding status, which were unverifiable by ordinary citizens, the government sidestepped debate over such issues as the institution's current performance and whether the private sector was a legitimate provider of social protection – issues for which the institutional legacy would not be as supportive of change. The diagnosis was shared with the "interested parties" within the government and the core constituency of the PRI including the IMSS leaders and labor union representatives.[79] During interviews in 1999, members of the reform team argued that the diagnosis helped to change perceptions of the viability of the IMSS system particularly among the actors whose consent would be necessary to advance the reform – the PRI's labor base. By stating simply that "we are [financially] short, this much," reformers said, "it became clear that something had to be done" to avoid the collapse of the pension system.[80]

Government actors also defended the pension reform as consistent with the revolutionary ideology of economic nationalism and solidarity. The Mexican Revolution had defined itself partly as a response to the domination of foreign corporations controlling the railroads and extractive industries during the Porfiriato. Reformers depicted the 1995 Peso crisis as a consequence of Mexico's dependence on short-term savings and argued that private pension reform would end this dependence by cultivating long-term sources of domestic savings. This claim was expected to resonate powerfully with workers who were feeling the direct consequences of capital flight in 1995.[81] As one participant in the reform process recalled, the rhetoric of foreign capital dependence was invoked strategically: "[W]hen the crisis was at its most profound moment, the social security reform was presented as a solution that could most simply resolve the broader economic problems of the country."[82] The pension system thus was presented as a "way out" of the hardships imposed by the peso crisis.

This strategy represents an important contrast to the experience in Argentina, where Menem sought support for economic reform by distancing himself from the Peronist doctrine of economic nationalism. In Mexico, the

[76] Solís Soberón and Villagómez 1999.
[77] Interview with anonymous Banco de México official.
[78] Interview with anonymous government official who participated in the pension reform.
[79] Vaquera García 1999.
[80] Reynoso 1999.
[81] Solís Soberón 1999.
[82] Saenz Garza 1999.

PRI's revolutionary doctrine that had previously legitimated state expansion in the economy was not disavowed in the process of economic liberalization; instead, nationalism was reinterpreted as a critique of the state-led economic model. This process began in the 1980s under President de la Madrid as the PRI leadership came to be dominated by committed neoliberals. President Salinas's "Reform of the Revolution" redefined the PRI's nationalist ideology to legitimize his market-oriented reforms as a way to "modernize" the state's relationship with the economy.[83] The Zedillo government continued this practice by justifying pension privatization as being consistent with the nationalist ideology of the revolution.

Zedillo also emphasized the continuity of the principles underlying the private pension system by arguing that such a reform would "give permanence to [the] original principles" of the IMSS institution, while making it more "socially oriented and fair."[84] In addition to cloaking the measure in this ideological rhetoric, government actors designed the 1995 reform to incorporate "solidaristic" principles that were consistent with this ideology – and the constitutional obligation of the government. They did so by including a provision that committed the state to contribute one peso a day to each worker's individual pension account. This "social quota" not only expanded the responsibilities of the state in the reformed pension system beyond the original intentions, but it also provided a meaningful and progressive subsidy for the large segment of Mexican workers at the lowest end of the income distribution.

The Zedillo government also enjoyed important partisan advantages in seeking labor support for the 1995 pension reform. As the party most closely associated with the Mexican Revolution, the PRI could credibly invoke these symbols as a way to legitimate its reforms. The PRI thus drew upon its long-term ties to the labor movement to negotiate union support for its reform agenda. Labor's confidence in the PRI was not granted unconditionally, however, nor was it based strictly on the institutional ties to the government. Rather, the PRI and its labor base, the Confederación de Trabajadores de México (CTM), enjoyed a long-term relationship based on exchange – albeit unequal – through which the PRI used its control over public resources as an instrument for obtaining political support and legitimation of its revolutionary project. Labor, in turn, demanded important benefits – such as the creation and expansion of social insurance – as a condition for its collaboration with the Mexican state. In the 1990s, labor's consent to liberalization, especially the signing of the North American Free Trade Agreement, was conceded in exchange for a veto over social policy legislation – a veto that was issued over Salinas's 1991 privatization effort.[85] Nevertheless, President Zedillo benefitted greatly from the relatively strong ties with the CTM that had been cultivated under his predecessor, President Carlos Salinas de Gortari. Salinas' finance minister, Pedro Aspe,

---

[83] O'Toole 2003, p. 271.
[84] IMSS 1995, p. 5. The rhetoric of social justice would emerge once again in the 2004 reform of the ISSSTE pension system. Marier and Mayer 2007.
[85] See Dion 2002; 2006; Trejo and Jones 1998.

had won the confidence of labor leaders over the course of extensive negotiation of his economic liberalization project.[86] During Zedillo's first years in office, he drew heavily upon those reserves of confidence to gain labor support for reforms such as the pension privatization. As we will see in the next chapter, however, such backing still required meaningful concessions to labor.

Mexico Summary

The political legacy of social security in Mexico centered on the widely shared perception that the pension system was effective and that the state should play a key role in providing a solidaristic social protection system – and defending the nation against foreign capital. This legacy powerfully influenced the Mexican government's political strategy and obliged it to make critical revisions to the design of the 1995 pension reform proposal. The government's justification of pension privatization in terms of the putative looming bankruptcy of IMSS reveals that it perceived broad public support for the existing institution that it had to dislodge. The government also invoked the ideological symbols of the revolution in order to portray the privatization as consistent with those principles. For a semiauthoritarian government, these efforts bear witness to a powerful concern for legitimating the private pension system in the eyes of the workers whose consent to reform would be vital to securing the viability of the new private pension system. Such legitimation efforts, and the attendant compromises in the pension reform design, cannot be predicted or explained through reference to the structural contours of the Mexican pension system alone.

BRAZIL

The two constitutional amendment projects launched in Brazil in 1995 and 2003 met with very different political fates. Although both projects imposed losses principally on public sector workers and were defended in similar terms, President Cardoso's constitutional amendment remained widely unpopular and endured a long and arduous political battle, while President Lula da Silva's project claimed broad public support and rapid approval by the National Congress. Analysis of the political legacy of Brazil's pension system, and the credibility with which the two presidents sought to defend their measures helps to explain how the forces of institutional reproduction could be so resilient in one instance and mutable in another.

Long-Term Political Legacy

The political legacy of Brazil's pension system created a distinctive set of obstacles to structural reform compared to neighboring countries in Latin America.

---

[86] Gonzalez Pier 1999.

For one thing, Brazil's national pension institutions were bolstered by a strong and widely held belief that the state can and should be the principal provider of social insurance. What is more, the stark disparities in the benefits provided by the system were not seen as inherent failures or injustices; rather, citizens had come to expect, if not even to accept such inequalities. And although the performance of the institution suffered under the nation's military dictatorship, this experience only reinforced citizens' attachment to the constitutional status of pension benefit rules. As in Mexico, pension reform reached the top of the political agenda in Brazil at a time in which real pension values were rising, providing street-level evidence that the system was not broken.[87]

Brazil's pension institution dates to the colonial period, making the country a social security pioneer in Latin America.[88] State pension provision dates formally to the Eloy Chaves Act of 1923, which set up the first retirement and pension funds (Caixas de Aposentadorias e Pensões). These institutions rapidly expanded to cover a variety of professions with 183 different funds by 1937. Under Brazil's populist leader Getúlio Vargas (1930–45, 1951–4), the pension system was expanded and organized into sector-specific retirement and pension institutes (Institutos de Aposentadorias e Pensões, IAPs). The IAPs became an important component in Brazil's corporatist system, through which the state organized and controlled labor; the pension funds also provided important political and financial resources for Brazil's national industrialization project.[89]

Sectoral fragmentation became a defining characteristic of Brazil's social security system even as Vargas increased the central government control of these funds in the 1930s and 1940s. Like in other Latin American countries, state pension benefits in Brazil often corresponded to the political bargaining power of different occupational groups.[90] This characteristic would persist throughout the postwar era even as Brazil's bureaucratic authoritarian military regime (1964–85) centralized the institution. Although the military expanded coverage among rural and low-income workers, pension benefits remained highly unequal and regressive.[91] Indeed, pensions became a surrogate for citizenship rights under the military, providing a compensatory mechanism to legitimate the vast expansion of state action in the economic realm.[92]

Pensions thus became the "solid core of state social intervention" under the military, providing financial and political resources to support the state-led model of import substituting industrialization.[93] Economic development – and specifically, the achievements of Brazil's developmental state – justified and reinforced public confidence in the state's central role in the allocation of

---

[87] Melo 2004a, p. 195.
[88] Mesa-Lago 1978.
[89] Pinheiro 1998.
[90] Mesa-Lago 1978.
[91] Weyland 1996b.
[92] Draibe et al. 1995; Pinheiro 2004, pp. 110–38.
[93] DIAP 1998, pp. 20–1; Draibe et al. 1995, pp. 1–4.

social benefits.[94] Although Brazil provides many examples of the pitfalls of an overextended state apparatus, it also recorded considerable successes in state-led economic development, offering citizens first-hand experience of a capable state.[95] With the capacity to extract nearly 40 percent of GDP in tax revenue – far above that of most other Latin American governments – the Brazilian state channeled tremendous resources into industrial development, infrastructure, and social welfare institutions.[96] The developmental state thus achieved important advances in sectors such as aviation, mining and steel production that in turn fueled high rates of growth in the early 1970s and earned Brazil praise as an economic development "miracle." For all its difficulties, Brazil's industrialization effort provided citizens with street-level knowledge of effective public action and expectations that the state can and should play an important role in domestic allocative functions. This belief would later be expressed in the vast expansion of state social obligations that citizens demanded with the return to democracy in the late 1980s. It would also underpin a broad public distaste for privatization in the realm of social security.

Social and economic development in Brazil was highly unequal, as the gains of growth failed to reach the vast majority of citizens. Although the Brazilian government achieved marked improvements in the areas of infant mortality, basic sanitation, literacy, and infectious disease control between 1940 and 1980, critical lags remained in terms of social inclusion and the reduction of glaring inequalities that were deeply etched in Brazil's political and social landscape.[97] Critically, however, these disparities, and the state's role in reinforcing them, appealed not to citizens' shared sense of injustice but rather to their *aspirations*. As a social security expert in Brazil explains, "[i]n the culture of the Brazilian Social Security system, the trend is to consider special conditions granted by the system to certain sectors not as a privilege, but as a future possibility for those who do not yet receive them. In that sense, the culture of social movements aims at the generalization of privileges rather than [at] their elimination, for the elimination would mean closing the doors to future access."[98] For Pinheiro, this legacy finds expression in the popular quip, "It's not that *he* makes too much money, it's that *I* don't make enough."[99] Inequality thus constituted such an entrenched part of the adapted expectations in Brazil that where themes of social justice entered in public demands, these revolved closely around the aspirations of *broadening* access to state-provided benefits, rather than curbing bold regressivities or expanding redistribution from rich to poor.[100] The Brazilian public thus entered the 1990s broadly supportive of a state-provided social insurance system, even if it reinforced, rather than

[94] Melo 2004a, p. 195.
[95] Evans 1995; Weyland 1996b.
[96] "Brazil Comes of Age on the Global Stage" 2004.
[97] Draibe et al. 1995, p. 47. See also Scheper-Hughes 1992.
[98] Oliveria and Ferriera 1997, p. 67; Oliveira et al. 1997.
[99] Pinheiro 2004.
[100] For Weyland, the paucity of demands for progressive redistribution owed to the "state-engineered fragmentation" of collective identities. Weyland 1996b.

ameliorated, the sharp disparities of wealth and power that had long gripped the country.

This belief in state-run social insurance persisted despite the considerable erosion of the social security system's performance under the military regime (1964-85). This was a period characterized by falling pension values and seemingly arbitrary changes in the institutional rules. Pension values began to decline when General Castello Branco (1964–7) "without explanation" overturned a law obliging the government to regularly adjust social security benefits in line with inflation.[101] As a result, real pension values fell by more than two-thirds over the next two decades. The military government also loosened the link between contributions and benefits by expanding rewards to high earners and straining pension system finances.[102] As inflation rose in the 1980s, the government frequently delayed indexation, causing a 34 percent drop in pension values between 1980 and 1990 alone.[103] The decline in purchasing power incited broad public discontent as citizens mobilized around calls to "humanize" the social security system.[104] Notably, it was *not* the relative disparities in benefits that citizens deemed unjust; rather, only the decline in pension values provoked claims of unfairness.[105] The institutional performance under Brazil's military regime resulted in what later would become a critical element of the institution's political legacy, namely, the belief that what the state could give, it could also take away, if not constrained by constitutional rules. Subsequent efforts to remove the terms of pension provision from the 1988 Constitution thus would run sharply afoul of this legacy, as "deconstitutionalization" would come to be seen as a government request for a blank check to slash pension benefits.

The 1998 Constitution

The political legacy of Brazil's social insurance system was concretized in the constitution-writing process that followed the transition to democracy in 1985. This process offered Brazilian citizens an important opportunity to rewrite the rules of social provision; and it was one that interest groups took full advantage of to redress an array of pent-up social demands. Rather than seeking to remove or limit the government's role in social protection after the poor performance under the military, Brazilians sought to reinforce and institutionalize that responsibility. As Draibe and colleagues observed, the diverse array of social and political actors competing to influence the profile of state social policies "all share[d] a strong tendency to define demands for provision of goods and services by the state."[106] Brazilian citizens sought to bind the state to these commitments, moreover, by enshrining the minute details of pension rules and

---

[101] Nobre 1974, pp. 195–6.
[102] Ness et al. 1992.
[103] Ness et al. 1992.
[104] Weyland 1996a, pp. 59–84.
[105] Nobre 1974.
[106] Prominent slogans included "growth, income redistribution and greater social justice." Draibe et al. 1995, pp. 62–4.

benefits within the legal and procedural safeguards of the 1988 Constitution. As one political analyst explained, "After so many years of hard times, Brazilians wanted their rights and privileges etched in stone."[107] The result was the creation of an immense, 240-chapter text that detailed an array of new entitlements and benefits, including bonuses and lifetime job stability rules for public and private sector workers.

Themes of social justice entered prominently in this process. These claims revolved closely around the extension of social protection to the poor and the equalization of urban and rural pension benefits; the curtailing of privileges for the rich was not part of the equation.[108] The new constitution thus expanded access to health care and social services for citizens at the lowest end of the income distribution, but it did so at the price of even greater gains for better-off sectors as well.[109] These disparities were most apparent in the civil servants' pension system, which by 2002 would consume 42 percent of pension resources to finance benefits for the 3.2 million public sector employees representing just 13 percent of pension system beneficiaries. The civil service pension system would, moreover, be responsible for 72 percent of the deficit in the nation's pension system.[110] The 1988 Constitution thus enshrined the stark inequalities that long imprinted Brazil's economic, social, and political life within an array of legal and procedural protections.

Although new sources of revenue were created to finance these benefits, this income proved far from sufficient: Social security outlays increased by 126 percent between 1987 and 1997, while contributions grew by just 19 percent.[111] Keenly aware of the structural imbalances in the constitutional rules, social security technocrats began planning for a constitutional reform under the government of President Fernando Collor de Mello (1990–2).[112] The government proposed an amendment to remove the pension benefit rules from the text of the constitution so that deeper restructuring could be undertaken through the lower institutional hurdles of ordinary law. This endeavor was short-lived and timid, however, as it lacked support within the government and in society.[113] The task of reforming the nation's pension system thus was left until 1995 when the quelling of hyperinflation by the Real Plan (*Plano Real*) would make it impossible for the government to continue to finance structural imbalances through inflation, forcing it to enact an agenda of structural reform.

The Real Plan itself bears witness to an important element of the political legacy of state intervention in Brazil that sets it apart from other Latin American countries. A broadly shared belief that the state can and should intervene

[107] Quote from Boulivar Lamounier in "The Smile of a Real Winner" 1997.
[108] Weyland 1996b, p. 66.
[109] Draibe et al. 1995, pp. 61–6.
[110] World Bank 2005, p. 51.
[111] de Souza 1999, p. 56.
[112] The 1988 Constitution called for amendments of the text to be considered in five years from its sanction.
[113] Weyland 1996b, p. 70.

in domestic allocative processes proved highly resilient to repeated inflationary crisis and to the process of economic restructuring. The Real Plan was launched in the end of 1993 by then-finance minister Fernando Henrique Cardoso. It involved a number of measures including the creation of a new currency in July 1994, the real, which was pegged loosely to the dollar. The Real Plan slashed inflation from more than 50 percent monthly to an average of 1.5 percent monthly in 1995.[114] It did so, crucially, without allocating responsibility for the economic crisis to inherent weaknesses of the state-led economic model, as we saw in Argentina and Mexico. Rather, the Real Plan drew from the premise that the government was "sick," and that it could, and should, be cured of the hyper-inflationary illness (*doença inflacionária*).[115] The plan thus aimed to reorder the role of the state in the economy through privatization and policy reform, rather than to dismantle it. More than just sparing the state from full blame for the crisis, the Real Plan apportioned responsibility to "economic elites" as well, including large businesses and banks that reaped high profits from hyperinfla-tion.[116] Growth and economic stability in Brazil thus were not understood to be conditioned on supplanting state intervention with market forces but rather were thought to depend solely on modest reforms of state spending. Broad public confidence in the state-as-provider thus was not challenged in Brazil as it was elsewhere in the region following the hyperinflationary crisis.

Political Strategy of the 1998 Amendment

Although financial deficits in the pension system had not yet appeared when President Fernando Henrique Cardoso took office in January 1995, it was widely accepted in technocratic circles that economic stability won through the Real Plan could not be sustained without removing structural imbalances in public expenses.[117] Just two months after his inauguration, Cardoso launched a constitutional amendment project (Proposta de Emenda Constitucional #33, PEC-33) to reform Brazil's pension system. He sent this measure to the National Congress along with other constitutional reform projects including tax and administrative reforms, a proposal to allow presidential reelection, and a pri-vatization law. Like the earlier pension reform effort under Collor, PEC-33 sought to remove the terms of pension provision from the 1988 Constitution so that deeper reform could be enacted through ordinary law. It also sought to establish certain new rules to limit costs such as the creation of a minimum retirement age and a cap on public sector pensions.

President Cardoso provided both technical and normative justifications for his pension reform. In the "exposition of motives" accompanying the amend-ment, Cardoso cited the financial and actuarial imbalances in the structure of

---

[114] "Desempenho dos índices de preços."
[115] Ministério da Fazenda 1993.
[116] Ministério da Fazenda 1993.
[117] de Souza 1999, p. 54.

the pension system and pointed out the social injustice of a system that allowed higher-income workers to retire at a young age with lavish pensions.[118] Cardoso also highlighted important institutional weaknesses that made the reform necessary, including fraud, under-reporting, waste, inefficacy, and inefficiencies.[119] These factors, the government insisted, made pension reform both necessary and fair. President Cardoso thus emphasized the themes of ending privileges and balancing the government accounts; he also maintained that reform was vital to preserving and strengthening the existing institution. "What is the administration seeking to obtain through the social security reform?" Cardoso said, "First, to correct unfairness and eliminate privileges. Second, to create the necessary conditions for preventing a public deficit. Third, to ensure that retired people continue to receive their pensions in the future and that these pensions continue to have the real value they do at least now."[120] The president also tied the success of his constitutional reforms to the maintenance of the newly won economic stability. Much as President Menem had done, Cardoso depicted the nation as standing at a critical juncture between the possibilities for prosperity and a return to the chaotic past. He argued, "We have two paths we can follow. One is to continue to administer the country without the reforms. This would mean going back to a past that we already know. It means going back to instability, to political patronage, to privileged corporations and to unbridled inflation rates. The other calls for the reforms in which I – as well as you – believe. This is a way of betting on our future, on democracy, on a strong currency, on increased earnings, on a better distribution of wealth and – in particular – on the end of privileges."[121] Cardoso thus tied his pension reform to the broad material gains that citizens had begun to reap from the stabilization of the economy and his early privatization efforts.

But these claims rang hollow, as did Cardoso's portrayal of his reform as fair. He argued, for instance, "What I seek through the social security reform is to eliminate cases of abuse, privileges. . . . Do you think it is fair that 4,800 public servants earn an average of R$21,000 per month, while the great majority earns very little and the government does not have the necessary funds to grant them an increase?"[122] These normative arguments were coupled with technical claims that few citizens could assess. For instance, Cardoso argued that "[i]n order to continue growing and to fight the injustices in our country, we need everyone's efforts and I am counting on your understanding. In particular, I need Congress to vote on the reforms that will allow us to speed up the growth, reducing the government's debt and, consequently, the interest rates."[123] And, he asserted, "The reforms are a precondition for the reduction of interest

[118] "Exposição de Motivos" 1995.
[119] "Exposição de Motivos" 1995; "Previdência/Reforma" 1997.
[120] "President Cardoso Appeals for Support for His Reform Programme" 1996.
[121] "President Cardoso Appeals for Support for His Reform Programme" 1996.
[122] "President Cardoso Addresses Nation on Anniversary of Real Plan" 1997.
[123] "President Cardoso Addresses Nation on Anniversary of Real Plan" 1997.

TABLE 6.3. *Attitudes toward President Cardoso's Pension Reform in Brazil Four-City Sample, 1999*

	Change to Time-of-Contribution Requirement	Reduction of Public Sector Pensions
Strongly oppose	40	48
Somewhat oppose	14	9
Somewhat favor	19	12
Strongly favor	27	31
N = 800	(646 valid responses)	(720 valid responses)

Source: Baker 2000, p. 6.

rates, the availability of more funds for investments, besides being a necessary condition to adjust the foreign accounts."[124] Most citizens experienced the costs of Brazil's high interest rates on an everyday basis, but the causal link to the pension reform was likely to be far from apparent. Cardoso thus had to ask citizens to delegate to him their judgment on the merits of the reform.

This proved to be something that few citizens were willing to do, however, and Cardoso's pension amendment was deeply unpopular.[125] As Table 6.3 reveals, a majority of Brazilian citizens opposed the two central provisions of Cardoso's pension amendment: the shift from a time-of-service to a time-of-contribution requirement and the creation of a ceiling on public sector pensions. The former was opposed somewhat or strongly by 54 percent of citizens surveyed, and the latter was disapproved by 58 percent of respondents. What is most striking about these results is that the losses imposed by those provisions incide fundamentally on public sector workers – a small fraction of the population, and typically high earners. Under the old rules of the pension system, public employees could count certain nonworking years, such as time spent in college, toward their time of service to qualify for retirement. For most citizens, this change had no material impact on old age pension benefits.[126] Nevertheless, the measure was greeted with broad public contempt. Widespread opposition to creating a ceiling on public sector pensions also cannot be explained strictly by self-interest. Cardoso's exhortations of the equity and necessity of his reform had quite clearly failed to persuade the majority of Brazilian citizens of the fairness of this change.

Why was the political backlash against Cardoso's pension reform so strong, even with regard to losses imposed on a small number of higher-income workers? As a starting point, the political challenge for any political leader to gain public consent to pension reform in Brazil is complicated by the institution's political legacy. In particular, the experience of arbitrary rule changes under the

[124] "Cardoso Again Criticizes Congress for Delay in Reforms" 1997.
[125] Fleischer 1998.
[126] Oliveira and Beltrão 2000, p. 4.

military regime led citizens to place a high value on the protections provided by the 1988 Constitution. By etching in stone the minutiae of government rights and responsibilities, Brazilian citizens could enforce state provision of the social benefits to which they had long been deprived under the authoritarian regime. Efforts to remove that institutional protection – which was a precondition for even the most modest institutional change – thus came to be seen as a request by the government for a blank check to erode citizens' hard-won benefits.[127] Quite apart from any specific loss-imposing provisions of the reform plan, therefore, deconstitutionalization represented a direct loss to most citizens, with largely uncertain benefits in return.

Citizens' street-level knowledge of the institution also complicated Cardoso's task of persuading citizens of the necessity of the reform. For when the amendment project was launched, the financial imbalances in the pension system were not yet apparent. And when they did emerge, financial deficits remained quite distant from the experience of most citizens as the government continued to pay pension benefits in full. What is more, pension reform came to the political agenda just as the real value of pension benefits was rising. Stabilization had allowed pension values to increase by 25 percent in real terms between 1993 and 2001.[128] Claims that the pension system was necessary, and much less that it was urgent, thus were directly contravened by citizens' everyday experience of an institution that was performing as well as ever.

Were any reforms necessary to rebalance the books, moreover, many citizens felt that they should be made not through benefit cuts but by combating fraud and cheating, which were considered widespread. Opponents of the reform seized upon this sentiment to undercut government claims that changes in the contribution and benefit rules of the pension system were necessary. For instance, the president of the Central Workers Union (Central Única dos Trabalhadores, CUT), Vicente Paulo da Silva, rebutted Cardoso's claims about the financial necessity of the reform, arguing, "The CUT never accepted that false argument. If the federal government had taken some essential decisions, the pension situation would be different; and we would not have to struggle in defense of the rights already assured through the historic battles of the workers. Three initiatives would significantly improve the social security coffers: combating under-reporting, incentivizing the formalization of labor, and combat against fraud."[129] Similar arguments were advanced by political party leaders on the left, who argued that the system could be fixed by combating fraud, rather than by "demolishing the public social security."[130]

For most citizens, it is likely that their ordinary knowledge of the pension institution proved little help in discerning whether the pension reform

---

[127] Bresser-Pereira 2003; Oliveira and Beltrão 2000.
[128] Data from *Anuário Estatístico da Previdência Social* and *Boletim Estatístico da Previdência Social*, cf. Afonso 2004.
[129] "Falso argumento" 1998.
[130] Quote from Miro Teixeira, "Quero reformas, sim" 1997.

proposed by Cardoso was in fact necessary, or whether management changes alone would correct any financial imbalances. When faced with such technical claims, therefore, citizens had to rely on credibility cues to discern which side to support. And on this level, the opponents of the reform held distinct advantages. For although President Cardoso's Social Democratic Party (Partido da Social Democracia Brasileira, PSDB) generally held a centrist position, he formed an alliance with the conservative Liberal Front Party (Partido da Frente Liberal, PFL, now the Partido Democrata). The center-right coalition was opposed by the left-wing Worker's Party (Partido dos Trabalhadores, PT), which was allied with one of Brazil's largest and most militant labor confederations, the CUT. The civil servants were one of the largest and most militant sectors in the CUT, representing approximately 40 percent of its membership. Having consistently promoted workers' rights and social justice causes since its creation in 1980, the PT could credibly portray itself as the proponent of the average citizens' interests on social welfare issues, even if it was in fact defending the privileges of the better-off minority of pension beneficiaries. The National Association for Social Security Auditors (Associação Nacional dos Fiscais de Contribuições Previdenciárias, ANFIP) also opposed the reform and could convincingly contradict the government's claim that the pension system was in crisis. ANFIP acted aggressively against pension reform, using television, radio, and newspaper media to publicize claims that reform would cut pension benefits and destroy the system.[131] Cardoso's adversaries thus took full advantage of their credibility as defenders of the welfare state to mobilize the public around opposition to his pension reform.[132]

Opponents gained further advantage in turning public opinion against the government by using ideological rhetoric to undercut Cardoso's reform. They did so most powerfully by labeling the pension amendment a "privatization." As we have already seen, the political legacy of Brazil's pension system imbued this term with a heavy stigma. Although privatization was not part of Cardoso's constitutional amendment project, unions charged that the reform would "strengthen the privatizing mode, [which is] morally unacceptable in the area of social welfare, where the financial contribution to insurance by the poorest workers to insure against the misfortunes of illness, disability and death should never be captured by the optic of insurance business, banks and profit-oriented insurance industries, nor social welfare by the mercantilist mold of the Chilean model."[133] Opponents derided Cardoso's pension reform as "a neoliberal package aimed at hurting workers and selling the country out

[131] "Fiscais da Previdência Social Provam que o Sistema é Viável" 1994; cf. ANFIP 1994; Melo and Silva 1999, p. 25.
[132] After the pension reform project was largely dismantled in the first round of voting in the Chamber of Deputies, critics cited the government's failure to provide "credible information" on the status of the pension system as a major reason for its ill fate. "Previdência/Reforma" 1997.
[133] DIAP 1998, p. 11.

to foreign capital."[134] Despite their falsehood, such claims held important sway due to the partisan structure of the political conflict. Cardoso's alliance with the promarket PFL lent credence to the idea that the government intended to privatize the pension system. Cardoso's extensive privatization of state-owned enterprises further reinforced this view, as twenty-four federal SOEs were sold with revenue of more than US$5 billion between 1995 and 1996.[135] Whereas the privatization of the state monopolies in telephone, mining, electricity, and shipping met with little public disapproval, the privatization of social security remained overwhelmingly unpopular.[136] As one Social Democratic Party Deputy explained, "The privatization of state monopolies was carried out relatively effectively without such a condemning stigma attached to that word. That was because the common people could associate those monopolies with government elitism and [the] rich, whereas in welfare, the term privatization strikes at something that is common to most people."[137] By labeling the pension reform a privatization, therefore, opponents could simplify the pension reform issue into a simple choice between the preservation or destruction of the state responsibility for social protection.

Cardoso's own words did not help allay fears that the government sought to impose losses on retirees. In one speech on the reform, Cardoso called those who retire before age 50 "vagabonds," or bums. This expression triggered broad indignation as opponents were quick to point out that Cardoso himself had taken a pension at age 37 when he left his position as university professor.[138] Public opinion polls recorded a sharp drop in Cardoso's approval ratings as citizens called the vagabond remark "unfair."[139] Cardoso's comments had run afoul of an important aspect of the political legacy of Brazil's pension system: that privileges were seen much less as an injustice than as a possibility. And as a politician who had enjoyed these advantages himself, Cardoso was in a poor position to argue that others should not claim the same benefit.

Although Cardoso continued to underscore the social justice implications of his reform, he made little impact on public opinion.[140] Perceptions that reform was necessary only shifted in his favor after the country suffered an international currency crisis in August 1998. In the wake of that crisis, Cardoso won the sanction of his pension reform amendment and was reelected to a second term in office with 53.4 percent of the vote. Cardoso's surge of public

---

[134] Pinhiero 2004, p. 127.
[135] By the end of 1998, Cardoso had privatized seventy-eight SOEs with proceeds topping US$37 billion. Castelar Pinheiro 2002, p. 25.
[136] Fleischer 1998, p. 124.
[137] Crusius 1999.
[138] "Falso argumento" 1998. Cardoso's social security minister until 1998, Reinhold Stephanes, also was the beneficiary of a civil service pension, which he allegedly took at age 42. Melo 2003.
[139] Polls by Vox Populi and Ibope reported in "Cardoso Government Loses Support in Opinion Polls" 1998.
[140] "FH/Ornélas/Defesa" 1998.

approval was short-lived, however. With the fading of the crisis, and as he continued his pension reform efforts, public opinion polls revealed that 66 percent of the population disapproved of his government by September 1999.[141] Taken together, Cardoso's pension reforms in 1998 and 1999 made significant changes in the public and private sector pension systems; they were projected to cut the long-run pension deficit of the private sector pension system from 12 to 6 percent of GDP by 2050.[142] Still, these measures fell short of Cardoso's objectives, leaving in place many privileges for the public sector workers. By the end of 2002, the deficit in the public sector pension scheme reached R$39.8 billion (about US$17 billion), or 3.1 percent of GDP.[143] The task of addressing the inequities and structural imbalances in the civil service pension system thus would fall to Cardoso's successor, President Luiz Inácio Lula da Silva.

Political Strategy of the 2003 Amendment

Shortly after taking office in 2003, President Lula da Silva ("Lula") began work on a constitutional amendment that would complete and extend the changes in the public sector pension system that Cardoso initiated. Many of the same motives – and even the language – that Cardoso had employed were used to justify Lula's reform project as well. Yet, Lula sidestepped the broad political backlash that Cardoso faced in his reform effort. Not only did Lula win the sanction of his pension reform amendment before the end of his first year in office, dramatically curtailing the previously untouchable privileges of civil servants in Brazil, but he also did so with broad public support.

The themes framing Lula's pension reform effort were much the same as Cardoso's, namely, social justice and financial viability.[144] In the "exposition of motives" for his amendment project, Lula justified the project as a means to correct actuarial distortions in the pension model while improving the equity between the public and private sector pension regimes.[145] Also like Cardoso, Lula tied his reform to the goal of promoting shared macroeconomic gains – in this case, economic growth. Like Presidents Menem and Cardoso, moreover, Lula argued that Brazil stood at a critical moment in its history where the conflicts between justice and inequity, poverty or prosperity would be decided. Describing his pension reform, for instance, Lula argued, "The moment has arrived in which we are going to have to decide if we want to continue with the Brazil where less than 50 million [of a population of 178 million] have access to the material goods that this country produces, or if we want a country where everyone has access to the material goods that we produce."[146] Lula also

---

[141] "Cardoso Government Is Approved by 58% of Population" 1998; Fleischer 1998, p. 3; "IBOPE: Cardoso's Disapproval Rating at 66 Percent in September" 1999.
[142] World Bank 2005, p. i.
[143] Ministério da Previdência Social 2003.
[144] "Previdência justa e sustentável" 2003.
[145] "Exposição de Motivos" 2003.
[146] "Lula a Congresso: Ou Reforma ou Desigualdade" 2003.

TABLE 6.4. *Attitudes toward President Lula's Pension Reform in Brazil*

	Agree	Disagree	Respondents	Date
Creation of a cap on public sector pensions	56	44	1431	July 14–21, 2003
Tightening eligibility to 100% replacement rate[a]	55	45	1204	July 21–28, 2003
Support for the pension reform as a whole[b]	60	40	1963	June 20–29, 2003
The reform is "good for the country"	57	43	703	August 11–18, 2003

[a] Previously civil servants could retire at age 48 with a 100 percent replacement rate. The reform proposed to concede this benefit only after reaching age 60/55 and 35/30 years of contribution for men/women.

[b] Respondents recorded only for the private sector. A "majority" of public sector workers were reported to oppose the reform.

Source: Agencia de Noticias da Previdência Social, available from http://www.previdenciasocial.gov.br.

highlighted the contrasts between the benefits lavished on the civil servants, and the penury of the masses, saying, "The privileged sector does not agree with the reform proposal. Because there are people, who in a country where some 40 million people are hungry, in a country where the minimum salary is R\$240 [US\$73 per month], there are people who think little if they retire on 17 thousand, 19 thousand, 20 thousand, 30 thousand reis [US\$5,200, 5,750, 6,100, 9,100 per month]."[147] He thus took a similar approach to that of Cardoso by juxtaposing the advantages of the public sector workers and the suffering of Brazil's poor. In Lula's case, however, claims that such benefits were unfair became persuasive. As Table 6.4 reveals, Lula consistently won broad public approval of his pension reform project in surveys taken by the social security ministry. Citizens expressed approval of reform provisions that they had previously objected to when advanced by President Cardoso.

Indeed, Lula enjoyed an important credibility advantage as leader of the Workers' Party and long-time advocate of social justice and rights of the poor.[148] In addition, the pension reform targeted one of his party's main constituents – the civil servants – who had recently mobilized powerfully in support of Lula's 2002 election. While facing howls of betrayal from this group, Lula could credibly argue that his reform was necessary to repair the hemorrhaging pension system. And in contrast to Cardoso, who had been a beneficiary of the civil service privileges, Lula had not enjoyed these benefits. He had, however, experienced poverty and want. Indeed, Lula's personal history lent further

[147] "Lula: Tem Gente que Acha Pouco se Aposentar com R\$17 mil" 2003.
[148] Public sector unions constitute nearly 40 percent of the CUT, which is allied with Lula's Workers' Party.

credibility to his claims that the reform would improve the social justice of the system. As a metal worker who had risen from poverty, Lula came to be known by Brazil's poor as "Our President" (*Nosso Presidente*).[149] From this position, Lula could more persuasively challenge the fairness of sharp inequalities in benefits provided by the state.

Lula's claims about the fairness and necessity of the pension reform did not go uncontested, however, as the president faced strong criticism both from civil servants and from parties to the left of the PT. The Brazilian Socialist Party (PSB), for instance, criticized Lula's pension reform as "neither democratic nor just."[150] Public sector unions also mobilized aggressively against the reform. Prior to one congressional vote, the CUT held a violent three-day strike in front of the National Congress. With such divisions in the left over the question of pension reform, there was not an unambiguous credibility advantage for one side in the conflict or the other. Given that most citizens reported being poorly informed on the specifics of Lula's pension reform, it is likely that significant confusion existed as to which side was correct in its assessment of the necessity and fairness of the reform.[151]

Lula's response to this opposition from unions and leftist parties, however, significantly aided his effort to win public support for his reform. For he responded by expanding public dialogue on the reform, presenting it in simple terms, and framing it through reference to shared norms. As one analysis observed, "The legitimacy of the proposal increased, and consequently of the existing system diminished as the government broadened the space for public debate on the [pension reform] question. Diverse meetings, seminars, public audiences, workshops and public consultations were held throughout the country, with the population and with local political actors like governors, mayors and state deputies."[152] Lula even employed a prominent public relations firm to help elucidate his message on the reform and used his weekly radio address to further disseminate his interpretation of the measure.[153] As one government ally explained, "the idea of the President is that we clarify to the maximum possible what is happening with the country."[154] Lula thus sought to broaden the scope of conflict, mobilizing the public behind his cause through simplifying, ideological rhetoric.

Throughout this process, Lula described the reform through reference to shared symbols and national values. For instance, in a speech on the anniversary of a national hero Tiradentes, who led an uprising against the Portuguese

---

[149] Green 2003.
[150] "Contribuição progressiva dos inativos" 2003.
[151] 76.5 percent of respondents to one survey reported being poorly informed about the pension reform. "Internautas se dizem mal informados sobre reforma" 2003.
[152] Gomes de Araújo 2003, p. 26.
[153] Duda Mendonça of Propeg was hired to lead the public relations campaign behind the pension reform.
[154] Jorge Viana, quoted in "Reformas: 'Nossas ideas são claras" 2003.

crown, Lula compared his pension reform struggle to that historical battle, saying, "211 years after the death of Tiradentes, the ideals that inspired it are ever more present and vigorous among us. It is fitting for us now to take new, steady and bold steps, and it is what we are doing and we are going to do."[155] Lula even drew upon Brazil's widespread religious beliefs to justify his call for sacrifice on his constitutional reforms. "Either we make changes in the Social Security system, or in a few years the states will not have money to pay either a little or a lot. Either we make the tax reform or the country will not be competitive. Will someone lose? Yes. Will someone pay more? Yes. But that is life. Jesus Christ needed to be crucified in order to save humanity, why cannot each one of us make a little sacrifice to save this immense Brazil?"[156] Lula thus justified the reform at once as a way to save the pension institution – and Brazil as a whole – and one that was fair. By using these symbols, Lula could cut through the murkiness of the complex pension issue, encouraging citizens to support the reform. Compared to Cardoso, moreover, Lula could more credibly advocate curtailing the privileges of public sector workers. And when faced with the opposition from other credible actors, Lula's embrace of ideological rhetoric simplified the reform issue and framed it as consistent with shared norms.

An alternative explanation for the divergent public responses to the two pension reform amendments advanced in Brazil would point to Lula's narrower targeting of the public sector in his reform. As we saw earlier, Cardoso's amendment combined revisions of the public and private sector pension systems, expanding the scope of potential losers from the reform. But this explanation is not fully satisfactory, for the logic of collective action strongly favored the civil servants, who stood to lose from both of the pension reform amendments. The country's poor, who stood to gain only diffusely from Lula's amendment, were largely unorganized and thus were not natural candidates for mobilization in favor of his reform. And as mentioned earlier, public opinion surveys found that provisions in Cardoso's reform that imposed losses directly on public sector workers, who represent less than 7 percent of the labor force, were opposed by a *majority* of survey respondents – far more than stood to lose in that reform. Even though Lula's amendment imposed its heaviest losses on civil servants, it was not costless for private sector workers. Indeed, Lula raised the ceiling on taxable wages for the private sector pension system as a way to raise revenue for the pension system, therein increasing the contribution rate for higher-income workers.[157] Thus despite imposing losses on the private as well as public sector, Lula's reform won broad support among a population that hitherto was largely opposed to any threat to hard-won pension benefits, even if they were concentrated on the higher-earning public sector workers.

[155] "Isenção com Limite Maior" 2003.
[156] "Lula Pede Sacrifícios e Recorre Até a Jesus" 2003.
[157] "A Reforma e o INSS" 2003.

Brazil Summary

Brazil provides an important within-country comparison of the role of partisan credibility in mediating the effectiveness of political strategies to win public approval of structural pension reforms. We have seen that the two presidents used similar claims and did so in the context of the same political legacy. However, President Cardoso faced broad public opposition to his pension reform amendment, while President Lula da Silva won broad public support for very similar provisions. What differed across these cases was the partisan structure of political conflict, and thus the credibility of the reform-seeking government. Whereas Cardoso's center-right coalition faced a credible left-labor opposition, Lula da Silva enjoyed considerable credibility in advancing his reform, despite civil servants' protests.

URUGUAY

Uruguay stands out in Latin America for its strong and enduring statist legacy and solidaristic ethos embodied in the nation's social institutions. Despite having followed a similar development strategy as Argentina and Brazil, and having endured the debt crisis and subsequent pressure for market-oriented reform, Uruguay maintained broad state interventions in social and economic relations. In the area of social protection, the clientele of Uruguay's state pension system is not only large, but social welfare spending also is very high. At 12 percent of GDP in 1995, Uruguay's pension spending was the highest (as a share of GDP) in Latin America, and even surpassed OECD countries (except Italy) in this proportion.[158] The clientele of the pension system in Uruguay is also one of the largest (relative to population) in Latin America. With 600,000 beneficiaries in a population of just 3 million, pension costs accounted for half of public outlays in the 1990s.[159] Retirees, moreover, represented 19.6 percent of the population in the 1990s and were a well-organized and influential political force.[160] According to the standard institutional legacy theory, pension privatization in Uruguay should have been impossible.

Uruguay's pension reform reveals the significant opportunities and limits created by the institution's political legacy. In an extremely inhospitable reform context, as defined by the structural inheritance, the Uruguayan government won public support for pension privatization by seizing upon perceptions that the institution's performance had fallen short of expectations and was unfair. Reformers also framed the proposed reform in terms consistent with the political legacy of solidarity, while raising the bar for performance expectations and touting the material benefits to be won through the new institution. After

[158] San Martino 2007, p. 6.
[159] Calvo 1998; MacCulloch 2003.
[160] See Kay 1998.

repeated failures of pension reform, the 1995 privatization was enacted with broad public support.

Long-Term Political Legacy

The Uruguayan pension system dates to 1829, placing it among the pioneers in the development of social security in Latin America.[161] Although pension provision in the nineteenth century was constituted as a series of disparate laws covering a limited range of social risks for military (and their widows and orphans) who had fought for the nation's independence, it was institutionalized as a coherent system in 1896 with the passage of the Ley Ciganda. The system was expanded broadly under the leadership of President José Batlle y Ordoñez (1903–7 and 1911–15).[162] Borrowing from European social welfare models, Batlle established an array of social services that formed the centerpiece of his project for social and political modernization in Uruguay.[163] What had begun as a privilege for a few occupational strata in the nineteenth century thus became a right of citizenship under Batlle, generating power for the poorer citizens while inculcating broad norms of solidarity and social justice.[164]

In addition to transforming the institutional landscape, Battle radically altered the political discourse, norms, and expectations in ways that continue to dominate public life in Uruguay. His ideological legacy, *"Batllismo,"* transcends any one political party and has come to signify the unique Uruguayan style of welfare state capitalism: a singular confidence in, and public preference for, a large state presence in society. More than that of any other political leader, Batlle's legacy captured the popular imagination of Uruguayan citizens. This legacy reinforced the maintenance of a broad state role in social policy and was a by-product of the effectiveness of that intervention. Indeed, Uruguay has long been distinguished in Latin America for its well-educated population, low levels of poverty, and relatively modest level of income inequality.[165] As an executive of the Social Welfare Bank (BPS) sums up the welfare legacy, "Uruguay is a country that had a long trajectory of strong social security with a very broad coverage – bigger than every other in the region. This is a vital starting point for understanding the reform. This cultivated in the citizens a very strong consciousness of the rights that they enjoyed."[166] The long-term political legacy of social security in Uruguay thus centers on a strong confidence in the role of the state as provider and shared beliefs in the principles of universality and solidarity, and of social security as a social *right*.

[161] Mesa-Lago 1978.
[162] Pensions accounted for 35.1 percent of the state expenditure as early as 1858. Papadópolous 1992.
[163] Finch 1981, p. 37.
[164] Colotuzzo 1998; Labadie 1998.
[165] Forteza et al. 2004, p. 5.
[166] Tebot 1998.

Confidence in the Uruguayan state was defined furthermore in contrast to the risks inhering in market systems. The state, and in particular, the social security system in Uruguay, thus came to be viewed as a source of security or "protection" against the vicissitudes of market forces.[167] For the general manager of the BPS, Myra Tebot, strong support for state provision of services such as banking, insurance, water, and electricity drew from "a lack of confidence in the private sector; the state was always relied on to save things in the end – it would pay if something went wrong. The credibility of purely private things was lower than the state."[168] She continued, "[T]he profitability of the [private pension] funds does not interest the people most. What they want is certainty, clarity, and they want to diminish risk."[169] Similarly, Finance Minister Ignacio de Posadas (1990–5) argued that Uruguay has a "culture of risk aversion," which leads citizens to turn to the state for income security. For him, "People [in Uruguay] are averse to markets and risk...when people get money, they put it in bricks...concrete is safe."[170] The terms on which public support could be won for pension privatization in Uruguay therefore would differ from those on which the measure was sold elsewhere in the world. The concepts of high rates of return, choice, and ownership would have to be supplanted with assurances of the security and guarantees provided by the state.

The implications of this shared confidence in the state and wariness of market risk can be observed further in the country's gradual and partial approach to market-oriented reform. Unlike many other Latin American governments, the Uruguayans did not pursue democratization and economic liberalization simultaneously in the 1980s. Instead, reinstating democracy became the first and most fundamental concern of the returning democratic government (1985–90). And when economic reforms were addressed, they entailed much less-radical departures from the state-led economic model than were embraced by Uruguay's neighbors. Indeed, public service provision was so highly valued that following the adoption of a 1991 state enterprise privatization law, public outrage at this measure forced a referendum that *returned* the provision of utilities and telephone service to the hands of the state.[171] Support for the state-centric economic paradigm thus remained quite strong.[172]

Short-Term Performance Legacy

The Uruguayan social security system enjoyed a long period of effective functioning evidenced in the high social achievements in the areas of education and poverty reduction. As we saw in Chapter 5, the booming livestock exports

[167] Calvo 1998; Colotuzzo 1998; Tebot 1998.
[168] Tebot 1998.
[169] Tebot 1998.
[170] de Posadas 1998.
[171] Filgueira et al. 1999, p. 15; Forteza et al. 2004, p. 9.
[172] Filgueira et al. 1999, p. 4, fn. 1.

in the early twentieth century – the era of the "fat cows" – underwrote the vast expansion of Uruguay's welfare state. With the decline in international commodity prices in the 1950s, however, state revenue fell sharply. Financial imbalances began to emerge as the BPS came under the authority of the political parties, rather than a professionalized bureaucracy. Instead of curtailing social policy spending in response to declining revenue, social benefits became the currency of patronage, resulting in the further expansion of social benefits.[173] Structural deficits in the state pension system yawned in the next decade. As inflation flared (by national standards) sharpening political conflict gave way to military rule in 1973. Changes in the inflation-indexation rules by the military regime resulted in a severe erosion of pension values relative to inflation, as benefits oscillated around 50 percent of the average wage.[174] Indeed, the 1979 decree AI-9 (Acto Institucional #9) created a series of "income bands" to replace the common indexation formula previously used to revalue old age benefits with changing prices. Although the band system was a progressive change that favored low-income workers, it spurred broad discontent by reducing the growth rate of old age pensions for most of the system's beneficiaries.[175] As in Brazil, discontent with the erosion of pension values under the military prompted a forceful movement to *expand* the state pension commitment after democratization.

With the return to democracy in 1985, the pension issue became a galvanizing force behind the formation of a powerful movement of retirees in Uruguay, the Organización Nacional de Jubilados y Pensionistas del Uruguay (ONJPU).[176] This organization sought to amend the nation's constitution through a plebiscite that would require the government to index pensions to changes in wages (index of average salaries) each time public sector salaries were adjusted (i.e., four times per year rather than once).[177] Most analysts warned that such a measure would create a fiscal crisis, as public sector salaries typically rise faster than inflation. The political incentives, however, favored the retirees, who made up 22 percent of the population and nearly one-third of the electorate. Despite technocrats' warnings, competition to win the support of the retirees in the 1989 election led *all* the political parties to support the pension referendum, which was approved by an overwhelming 82.5 percent of the vote.[178]

The 1989 plebiscite reveals both the Uruguayan citizens' broad confidence in the state as provider of social protection and the tremendous political obstacles to pension reform that lay before the new government in 1990.[179] For advisers to newly elected President Luis Alberto Lacalle de Herrera, the projected

[173] Colotuzzo 1998.
[174] Kay 1998; Papodópolous 1992.
[175] Filgueira et al. 1998; Labadie 1995, pp. 12–13; Papodópolous 1992, p. 69.
[176] Colotuzzo 1998.
[177] Saldaín 1996.
[178] Instituto Nacional de Estadísticas 2000.
[179] Filgueira et al. 1999, p. 13.

financial toll of the pension referendum left little choice but to initiate pension reform. Indeed, in response to the referendum, pension spending rose from 9 to 14 percent of GDP between 1989 and 1995. The impact of the measure was broadly felt. Old age poverty fell sharply; whereas 14.9 percent was below the poverty line in 1989, this rate fell to 5.1 percent in 1995.[180] Thus even though the need for reform was apparent to technocrats in 1990, few citizens saw the situation as one of crisis; to the contrary, citizens' street-level experience of the pension system suggested that it had finally begun to live up to long-adapted expectations.

Importantly, the 1989 pension referendum did not resolve all the performance problems associated with Uruguay's pension system; rather, it responded only to the grievances of the retirees. Surveys taken before the reform showed that 68 percent of the population believed that the existing institution did not provide sufficient protection and that 70 percent of respondents considered the system to be unfair.[181] There was a perception of widespread evasion that was encouraged by the pension rules allowing workers to retire on the basis of time of service, rather than any record of contributions.[182] Upon retirement, workers needed only a "testimony" to the length of their work history because pension benefits were gauged only on the basis of the last three years' wages. It thus became more common for workers and employers to collude in the under-reporting of income until the final three years before retirement. Dissatisfaction with such behavior led to a broadening sense that the existing bargain was unfair.[183] At the same time, the pension system allowed special privileges to be claimed by workers in critical sectors and parastatal industries, including the notaries, professors, and bankers. As the representative of the retirees on the BPS board explained, "the trust, moral integrity and basic incentives built into the old system were all off; it needed to be set right so that it would be participated in by all, and it would be financially sound."[184] For government actors, these responses signaled the opening of political space for reform advanced on the grounds of enhancing both the equity and efficiency of the existing pension system.[185] Even though there was little perception of support for a thorough dismantling of the pay-as-you-go model – as Uruguayans call it, the "system of intergenerational solidarity" – reformers perceived that they could gather public backing for a *repair* of the public PAYG system.[186] Support for the core principles of universalism and solidarity thus remained strong in Uruguay in the 1990s.[187] Citizens also were concerned with their material benefit. As one official explained, "[Uruguayans] wanted to know how the reform was going

[180] Instituto Nacional de Estadísticas 2001.
[181] Labadie 1995; Mila Belistri, p. 159; Saldaín 1995, pp. 30–1.
[182] Mitchell 1996, p. 5.
[183] Quisique 1998; Vera 1998.
[184] Colotuzzo 1998.
[185] Michelin 1998.
[186] Michelin 1998.
[187] Calvo 1998; Labadie 1995, p. 29; 1998.

to affect them. They all believe in solidarity, but on top of that, they wanted to make sure they, individually, came out well."[188] Thus for the new pension system in Uruguay to win broad and self-reinforcing support, it would have to ensure that the average worker perceived an advantage from the reform.

Political Strategy of Reform Failure, 1990–1994

Although many politicians in Uruguay believed that the national pension system was in urgent need of reform in the wake of the 1989 referendum, they disagreed over how exactly to do so.[189] Amidst this lack of consensus, President Lacalle sent his first pension reform proposal to the General Assembly in April 1992. He did so, however, without significant political or public support for the measure.[190] Rather, Lacalle sought to sidestep these conflicts – "depoliticizing" the reform – by restricting debate over the measure solely to the realm of technical commissions. This strategy, according to one member of that commission, was "a novelty in Uruguay."[191] And, it was one that did not succeed.

When Lacalle did justify this reform proposal, he relied heavily on technical arguments.[192] Such claims required citizens to delegate judgment on the issue to government experts. But Lacalle, of the center-right "Blanco" Party (Partido Nacional), lacked the partisan credibility to persuade citizens to do so. For he was opposed by a coalition of leftist parties, the Frente Amplio (Broad Front), unions, and retirees, who could more credibly claim to be protecting the interests of pensioners.[193] Lacalle's contention that pension reform would transform individual pension contributions into "motors of the economy," financing national projects from housing, to health, public safety and education, thus did little to persuade citizens of the fairness or necessity of such a reform.[194] The president also spoke openly of the losses imposed by the reform, arguing that "[n]obody is going to like these measures, but they have to be taken if we want to honor the reform in the social security system – with its new indexation criteria."[195] For most citizens in Uruguay, the financial imbalances caused by the 1989 plebiscite were far from apparent at the street level in 1992, and thus the technical justifications for reform based on a funding crisis fell flat.[196]

---

[188] Tebot 1998.
[189] Davrieux 1998.
[190] Davrieux 1998; Labadie 1998; Vera 1998.
[191] Labadie 1995, p. 10.
[192] Filgueira et al. 1999, p. 15.
[193] Although retirees were a significant political force in Uruguay's political system, the two major labor confederations in Uruguay, the CNT (Confederación Nacional de Trabajadores) and the PIT (Plenario Izquierda de Trabajadores) played a relatively minor role in the pension reform. Astori 1998; Colotuzzo 1998; Kay 1999, p. 411.
[194] Lazarov and Saldaín 1997, p. 3.
[195] Filgueira et al. 1999, p. 15.
[196] de Posadas 1998.

Moreover, opponents credibly inveighed against the "loss of solidarity" in the pension reform proposal.[197] Technocrats associated with the leftist coalition also contradicted the government's technical claims. They criticized the pension reform as "catastrophic" and called projections of fiscal imbalance "inaccurate."[198] In this way, Lacalle's partisan rivals "captured public opinion," turning it against Lacalle's pension reform.[199] Despite the Frente Amplio's minority position in the legislature in the early 1990s, it therefore held considerable sway in the conflict over pension reform as a result of its capacity to credibly depict the measure as unfair and unnecessary.

Lacalle's structural pension reform proposal met with firm resistance in the legislature and in society.[200] Not only did he fail to engage partisan allies or opponents on the question of reform, but he also did not present the reform in terms of citizens' widely held normative beliefs or expectations. As one government report concluded, "Technical rationality did not succeed in imposing itself on the political logic" of reform.[201] President Lacalle sent four subsequent pension reform proposals to the National Assembly before his five-year term in office ended; all ultimately failed. For one national deputy, President Lacalle's pension reform setbacks owed largely to a failure of political strategy: "Lacalle's initiatives were made with a thin political agreement that was hardly explained to the people. More than that, this is a people that form their own ideas, make up their own mind, and will not be convinced of what they do not want."[202] We will see next that despite the seemingly insurmountable political obstacles to pension reform in Uruguay, a partial privatization was adopted in 1995 that was nearly identical to one of Lacalle's failed proposals. It was the political strategy that differed most significantly across these reform efforts.

Political Strategy of the 1995 Pension Reform

The 1994 election in Uruguay brought a shift in power from Lacalle's Blanco Party to the centrist Colorado Party and President José Maria Sanguinetti (1985–9, 1995–9). In the transition period before Sanguinetti's inauguration, plans to launch a structural pension reform were put in motion.[203] The government's political strategy was informed by a survey of public attitudes toward the old age pension system that pointed to dissatisfaction with the performance of the existing system but continuing public support for a solidaristic public pension system.

---

[197] Colotuzzo 1998.
[198] Kay 1999, p. 411.
[199] Astori 1998; de Posadas 1998.
[200] Labadie 1995, p. 10.
[201] Labadie 1995, p. 10.
[202] Atchugarri 1998.
[203] Although representatives of the left parties were invited, they walked out early in the negotiations. The small center-left Nuevo Espacio party remained in the multiparty talks. Astori 1998; Michelini 1998.

One of the biggest complaints was that many citizens were under-reporting income, as mentioned earlier, which was considered unfair. Sanguinetti thus chose a slogan for his pension reform that defined it as "solidary, effective and just" (*solidário, eficaz y justo*).[204] The proposal called for a mixed public and private pension system with privately managed individual accounts on top of a large public and redistributive social insurance component. The government touted the system of individual accounts as an equity-enhancing move that would increase incentives for compliance by linking pension benefits more tightly to workers' lifetime contributions, making it costly for workers that under-report income.[205] Reformers also justified the reform as necessary to save the existing pension system. They pointed to a looming fiscal crisis, which by 1995 had become apparent in the ballooning government deficit and rising tax rates. The government dramatized this point by providing simulations of the level of payroll contributions – reaching over 40 percent of wages – that would be required to maintain the rapid rise in pension benefits if no reform were adopted.[206] Given that payroll contributions already were high in 1994 – at 27.5 percent of wages – the thought of further, and significant, increases was alarming to most citizens.[207] Thus the pension reform was touted as a way to "avoid crisis" and sidestep the need for an immense tax hike, while also improving the equity of the pension system. The reform was greeted with broad approval, and to date has maintained one of the highest contribution rates in the region.

Uruguay Summary

Reformers in Uruguay drew upon two critical elements of the pension system's political legacy: the long-term tightly held belief that the system should rest upon solidarity principles and the short-term perception that the institution had fallen short of performance and fairness standards. By framing the proposed reform as "solidary, effective, and just," Sanguinetti could neutralize considerable public opposition to an unlikely partial privatization of old age pensions. Indeed, after five failed reform attempts, the passage of the 1995 pension privatization in Uruguay is a striking defiance of most structurally bound conceptions of institutional legacy. In Uruguay, however, the frequent use of referenda to overturn unpopular legislation meant that sanctioning of the pension privatization by the National Assembly would not end political conflict over the pension reform. Thus immediately following the 1995 reform's adoption, government actors launched a substantial public information campaign to reinforce public confidence in the new pension institution. The campaign centered on the theme of security, to cultivate trust and confidence that the "state was still there

---

[204] See Lazarov and Saldaín 1997, p. 2.
[205] Lazarov and Saldaín 1997, p. 2.
[206] Vera 1998.
[207] Márquez Mosconi 1997, p. 4.

for them," and that the new social security institution would be, "sound, well-financed, and improved" as a result of the reform.[208] Indeed, when the law was passed a BPS poll found that 35 percent of respondents opposed the reform and 25 percent favored it; two years later, however, opinions had improved with 40 percent supporting the reform and 20 percent against.[209] The new pension system also won resounding public endorsement in a more apparent way: by citizens' pocketbook vote. More than 80 percent of workers who were given the option of joining the new mixed regime did so; this rate was well above that which the government had expected.[210]

CONCLUSION

This chapter has sought to explain how path-dependent institutions – those that long were stable and self-reinforcing – may be subject to path-departing change through mechanisms that once sustained and reinforced the institution. I have focused on one element of the institutional inheritance – its political legacy of shared norms and expectations. Although these may long uphold and stabilize an institution, they can under certain conditions permit or even promote its fundamental path-departing transformation. The causal role of this institutional legacy is mediated heavily by the nature of that legacy and on the terms and partisan structure of political conflict. Beliefs and expectations associated with old age pensions thus may be more pliant to challenge by parties of the left than of the right and may depend heavily on citizens' everyday experiences and expectations of the institution. Political legacies, however, are only one element of a complex process of institutional change. It is, nevertheless, an important one: Such a legacy may place firm limits on the extent of structural reform for which government leaders can win public consent. And where this legacy is overlooked, the long-term stability of the reformed institution may be in doubt. But governments can, in the short term, change a law without renegotiating the social bargain that it represents. As we will see in Chapter 7, reformers may do so within a set of legislative structures that previously upheld and stabilized state-run pension institutions. Alternatively, such a reform may be stalled despite the government's command of a large legislative majority. It is to this puzzle that the study next turns.

[208] Tebot 1998.
[209] Tebot 1998.
[210] Lazarov and Saldaín 1997, p. 3.

7

Legislative Conflict and Institutional Change

Building Majorities behind Loss-Imposing Reform

The legislature represents the final battlefield in formal political conflicts over institutional change. As such, it has been the focus of considerable attention by scholars seeking to explain how democratic governments legislate deep, loss-imposing reforms such as pension privatization. This dilemma arises from the fact that loss-imposing legislation such as pension privatization presents elected politicians with significant threats to their careers.[1] Scholars seeking to explain when career-minded legislators vote for such measures have commonly looked to the structure and distribution of legislative authority to explain when majorities form behind such an institutional reform. This research divides quite sharply over whether concentrated or dispersed political authority is more hospitable to the adoption of loss-imposing reform. Neither stream of research, however, has adequately explained how a given configuration of legislative authority could long uphold and stabilize a policy structure, but later permit its fundamental change. The central puzzle in the legislative process of institutional change thus is to explain how, within a given legislative system, political and institutional incentives that long upheld a given old age pension system can later give way to loss-imposing institutional restructuring.

The analysis in Chapter 2 challenged existing knowledge on this question. First, the statistical result showed that the effect of legislative institutions on pension privatization is conditional: As the size of the governing majority increases the likelihood of pension privatization diminishes, *except* when a left party is in power; in that case, privatization becomes *more* likely as left-party majorities increase. The cross-national analysis also showed, however, that left parties systematically adopt smaller movements toward market-based pension provision. The political conditions that make institutional change more likely thus also tend to curtail the extent of path departure that is achieved. Cross-national data in this way suggest that who governs is deeply consequential for understanding how and when formal institutional power translates into

---

[1] See Pierson 1994; 2001; Pierson and Weaver 1993; Weaver 1986.

effective power to legislate institutional change. These findings lend support to my alternative theoretical proposal: that the effects of political institutions on pension reform are conditioned by the way that political conflicts play out, with the partisan structure of legislative conflict being highly consequential for the unfolding of such political battles.

RECAPITULATION OF THE ARGUMENT

In Chapter 3, I argued that by contrast to retrenchment, or benefit cuts, pension privatization entails both the imposition of losses *and* the possibility for distributive gains through the creation of new private saving schemes. It is this second dimension, and the political opportunities to which it gives rise, that sets the politics of pension privatization apart from that of retrenchment alone.

Specifically, where reformers can organize legislative conflict over pension privatization around the measure's creative elements (i.e., the potential gains to be won through private savings systems), politicians may reduce, or even neutralize, the threat of electoral backlash associated with loss imposition. This entails what Weingast calls increasing the "distributive tendency" of proposed legislation.[2] Left-wing parties enjoy substantial credibility advantages in doing so for pension reform on account of their traditional association with the defense of the welfare state. As we saw in Chapter 6, left governments may be more persuasive in using distributive rhetoric to win popular support for reform. Such consent in turn may activate a distributive political logic in the legislative arena, facilitating the creation of large, if not oversized, majorities behind reform. However, efforts by left parties to win the support of its base, particularly organized labor, are likely to entail compromises that attenuate the degree of privatization enacted through the reform. Thus the left may be more likely to enact structural pension reform, but those measures will be less radical than reforms passed by the ideological right.

Strategies to organize political conflict around privatization's distributive elements are extremely fragile, however, and may not be available to all politicians. For such efforts may be undermined where the potential losers enjoy substantial credibility and can use that to bring attention to the loss-imposing elements of reform. When this occurs, the more familiar veto logic takes hold, raising the likely electoral costs for legislators that support the unpopular measure. A veto dynamic does not foreclose privatization. It does, however, raise the cost of building legislative majorities behind loss imposition. Whether the cost of majority-building involves compromise in the extent of institutional change depends on the resources available to political leaders and the unpopularity of the measure. Such resources include institutional authority – to enforce cooperation through the use of partisan sanctions and rewards – and the exchange of pork-barrel provisions for support of the legislation. Where these strategies fail, reform-seeking governments may be obliged to compromise the scope and

[2] Weingast 1994.

depth of institutional change in order to win majority support for reform, or forego revising the institution altogether.

EVIDENCE IN THE CHAPTER

I evaluate this causal argument through analysis of the legislative conflicts over pension reform in the four Latin American cases. In Argentina and Mexico, reformers from labor-backed parties commanded disciplined majorities in the national legislatures, while in Brazil and Uruguay, legislative power was more fragmented, and reform-seeking governments faced credible left-wing opposition. In Brazil, I also examine the partisan switch to a government led by the erstwhile opponents of pension reform, the Workers' Party.

Whereas structural conditions in the first two cases are said to favor the approval of structural pension reform,[3] in neither case did formal majority power translate frictionlessly into support for ambitious structural pension reforms. Despite vast institutional authority and ostensible partisan advantages, President Menem in Argentina and Presidents Salinas and Zedillo in Mexico faced resistance from their labor allies and were obliged to make significant compromises in the depth of institutional reform. The dynamics of political conflict thus interceded directly between the formal and effective legislative authority, lending confidence to my conditional hypothesis of the institutional and partisan foundations of welfare state reform.

The antecedent processes of economic liberalization influenced the legislative politics of pension reform in Argentina and Mexico in substantially different ways. Whereas President Menem's traditional labor ally, the General Labor Confederation (Confederación General de Trabajo, or CGT), was internally divided over its position toward market-oriented economic reform, it reunited in resistance to structural pension reform. Labor's opposition thus activated a veto dynamic in the Argentine legislative process. So even though labor ultimately negotiated support for the pension reform, it was able to exact a considerable price for its support of the Menem government, dramatically altering in turn the design and extent of pension privatization in Argentina. In Mexico, the PRI-linked labor confederation backed President Salinas' broad economic liberalization program in exchange for a veto over social policy reform. This prior bargain, along with the experience of economic and financial crises that were widely attributed to the economic liberalization, made the negotiation of labor support for structural pension reform much more difficult in Mexico, even though legislative power was tilted substantially in favor of ratification of the government's reform agenda. As in Argentina, Mexico's labor unions charged dearly for their support of Zedillo's pension privatization, winning significant compromises in the degree of institutional change in that case. Indeed, Mexico's pension privatization entailed considerably greater compromises – both to labor and to opposing parties – than the structure of

[3] Kay 1998; 1999; Madrid 2003, p. 89.

political authority would predict. These political conflicts and compromises shaped not only the terms on which legislative conflict was fought but also the viability and depth of structural reform itself.

The cases of Brazil and Uruguay reveal that the absence of a formal legislative majority does not foreclose institutional change if reformers succeed in activating a distributive logic in legislative conflicts. The pension reforms in Brazil and Uruguay thus defy the conventional wisdom about the structural conditions under which loss-imposing institutional change is likely to be approved. Given the high levels of legislative fragmentation and extensive veto points in these cases, conventional theories predict that very little, if any, movement toward the adoption of loss-imposing reform should be (or has been) feasible.[4] President Cardoso in Brazil and Presidents Lacalle and Sanguinetti in Uruguay also faced credible left-labor opponents that effectively raised the salience of the loss-imposing nature of pension reform. Yet in neither country were these factors deterministic of the possibilities for institutional change. The structural pension reforms that were approved in each case, moreover, were no less ambitious than previously defeated proposals.

Brazil and Uruguay also demonstrate how shifts in reformers' credibility due to external corroboration, along with bargains made to enhance the distributive tendency of pension reform helped to alter perceptions of the relative cost of maintaining the status quo versus reform. Broader public perceptions of pension reform as a loss-imposing, rather than loss-*avoiding,* measure thus were mediated by features of the broader context, rather than strictly by the partisan identification of government leaders. Rhetoric alone was not sufficient to secure legislative sanction of loss-imposing reforms in either case. In Brazil, Presidents Cardoso and Lula da Silva relied on the exchange of appropriations and jobs for support on the structural reform, while also compromising the depth of institutional change that they sought. In doing so, both Brazilian presidents turned the infamous vice of short-sighted and particularistic legislative tendencies into the virtue of instruments for gaining support for significant long-term institutional change. Particularistic and collective goods-oriented legislation thus proved not to be strictly exclusive features in Brazil, as the former became an instrument through which to achieve the latter.[5] Partisanship still mattered, however. Lacking credibility, Cardoso gave ground on many more provisions of his reform than Lula did; the latter also imposed considerable losses on his own constituency. In Uruguay, reformers enhanced the distributive character of Sanguinetti's pension reform by offering direct subsidies to participants in the private pension system. The reform still included a significant retrenchment and rationalization of the public, pay-as-you-go system, and thus imposed considerable losses on the beneficiaries of the old pension system. Although the bargains differed in nature, the attachment of distributive provisions to pension reforms in Uruguay and Brazil operated in similar ways to dampen the threat

---

[4] See, for example, Kay 1998; Madrid 2003. See however, Figuereido and Limongi 1998.
[5] Also see Alston and Mueller 2005.

of electoral punishment for legislators supporting the reform. Career concerns and electoral incentives that long held old age pension systems into place in these veto-laden political systems thus became consistent with support for loss imposition on account of efforts to increase the distributive perception – and reality – of structural pension reform.

ARGENTINA

When the structural pension reform was introduced into the Argentine National Congress in 1992, President Carlos Saúl Menem commanded a disciplined voting majority in both chambers. Nevertheless, Menem was forced to make deep concessions in his structural pension reform in order to win legislative approval: Participation in the private pension system was made optional in the course of legislative negotiations, and the government expanded the size of the basic public pension; it also limited the reach of market forces in the private pension market. This outcome resulted in considerable part from the activation of a veto logic by labor unions and retirees, who raised the salience of the loss-imposing nature of the reform, elevating the cost of building majority support behind its approval. In this context, the marginal size of Menem's majority left him vulnerable to internal defection, resulting in a bare-knuckled fight that obliged him to make deep concessions to win majority support for Argentina's 1993 pension reform law.

Institutional Authority

Political power in the Argentine National Congress is relatively concentrated in the hands of a few political party leaders. Not only do these leaders hold extensive power to discipline their rank and file members, but from the return to democracy in the mid-1980s until the mid-1990s, legislative politics in Argentina was organized around two-party competition pitting the center-left Peronist Party (Partido Justicialista, PJ) against the centrist Radical Party (Unión Cívica Radical, UCR).[6] Although it was infrequent that any single party held an absolute majority in the Chamber of Deputies in the late 1980s and early 1990s (see Table 7.1), Jones and Hwang point out that "throughout most of this period the majority party possessed a sufficient number of seats such that it was able to exercise majority control of the Chamber, either alone or through the tacit support of a subset of the numerous minor parties in the Chamber."[7] Although the PJ claimed just short of 50 percent of the seats in the lower chamber, Menem solidified his governing majority there by allying with the small ideologically conservative Unión del Centro Democrático (UCeDé) and with representatives of small provincial parties.[8] These alliances

---

[6] Jones 1997; Levitsky 2003, pp. 158, 159, 173; Stokes 2001a.
[7] Jones and Hwang 2003, pp. 11–12.
[8] Cetrángolo 1998; Rofman 1998.

TABLE 7.1. *Distribution of Seats in Argentine Chamber of Deputies*

Political Party	Percentage of Seats in Chamber of Deputies, 1991–1993
Partido Justicialista (Peronist Party)	50.2
Unión Cívica Radical (Radical Party)	33.1
Unión del Centro Democrático (UCeDé)	4.3
Center-right provincial parties	9.3
Center-left provincial parties	2.0
MODIN	1.2

Source: Jones 1997, p. 265.

gave Menem extensive institutional authority that should have easily cleared the way to approval of his legislative reform agenda.

For in addition to the command of a voting majority, Menem enjoyed a relatively high level of party discipline arising from Argentina's closed-list proportional representation system.[9] Although reelection rates were rather low in Argentina (around 20 percent in the early 1990s), PJ leaders used influence over their partisans' career paths outside of Congress as a way to discipline their rank and file.[10] Career-minded Peronist deputies thus enjoyed little autonomy to stake out independent positions on legislative issues.[11] As president of the nation and leader of the governing party, Menem also enjoyed significant influence over both the selection of candidates for national office and the appointment of party members to leadership positions. For Jones, such power means that "[i]f the president so desires, he or she can make life very difficult for rebellious party leaders/legislators via the mechanisms of either the party or the state."[12] And Menem did not hesitate to do so. Shortly after taking office, Menem undertook a "housecleaning" of his party's leadership, offering key posts in his cabinet to leaders of the Argentine business community, ideological conservatives, and orthodox economists.[13] Although most Peronist leaders fell in line behind Menem, such support rested on the use of selective incentives and punishments, rather than agreement on his reform goals.

Menem also did not face stringent programmatic or ideological constraints on his market-oriented reform agenda, despite the Peronist Party's long association with the promotion of state-run social and economic programs. In part, this flexibility owed to the popular association of state intervention with economic calamity in the 1980s that weakened longstanding attachments to statist economic policies.[14] Yet the weak internal organization of the Peronist Party also

[9] Jones 1997, pp. 277–8; Jones et al. 2002, p. 658.
[10] Carey and Shugart 1995; Jones 1997, pp. 276–7.
[11] Jones and Hwang 2003, p. 11–12.
[12] Jones 1997, p. 279. Also see Levitsky 2000; McGuire 1997, p. 62.
[13] Levitsky 2003, p. 159.
[14] Grüner 1991, p. 90.

broadened Menem's scope for ideological maneuver.[15] Not only was the Peronist Party base deeply splintered when Menem came to office, but the PJ's loose internal organization also allowed Menem to sidestep internal party opposition and launch a radical reversal of traditional Peronist doctrine.[16] Rather than engaging or persuading reluctant partisans of his position, therefore, Menem reached beyond them, forging alliances with big business and international market actors.[17] Menem also made direct appeals to the Argentine population and inveighed against traditional party politics (*partidocracia*).[18] Menem thus did not challenge or redefine Peronist doctrine; instead, he circumvented the party platform altogether.

Despite his programmatic flexibility and vast institutional authority, President Menem did not enjoy free rein to privatize Argentina's pension system. For his authority was abridged considerably when labor and retiree groups brought attention to the loss-imposing elements of the pension reform, activating a veto dynamic in the legislature. The result was to isolate the Peronists, rendering them vulnerable to internal defection by Menem's partisans who had not been persuaded of the legitimacy of his reform goals.

Activating a Veto Dynamic

The longstanding alliance between the Peronist Party and Argentina's dominant labor movement, the General Labor Confederation, offered Menem important advantages in bringing forward his structural pension reform. Labor's support for Menem's social policy reform agenda, however, was not automatic. Instead, unions conceded their support only in exchange for the concession of advantages to labor under the market system.[19] This bargaining power drew largely from the CGT's organizational and political autonomy from the Peronist Party. Labor also was recognized as a significant player in Argentine politics, particularly on social policy issues.[20] This influence allowed the CGT to exert its independence from the government early in the political conflict over pension reform and to negotiate its support for this program in exchange for extensive compromises in the social policy agenda.

The relative autonomy of the Argentine labor movement dates to the founding of its alliance with Peronism in the 1940s. When elected president in 1946, Juan Domingo Perón elevated workers to a position of respect in Argentine politics for their contribution to the nation's economic development.[21] Although many of the laws that Perón issued to enhance the strength and internal cohesion of the union confederation were also aimed at controlling and co-opting

[15] Levitsky 2003.
[16] Palermo and Novaro 1996, p. 23.
[17] Levitsky 2003. Also see Collier and Collier 1991, p. 346.
[18] McGuire 1997, p. 212; Roberts 1995; Weyland 1999.
[19] Murillo 2001.
[20] Lloyd-Sherlock 1997.
[21] Collier and Collier 1991, p. 338.

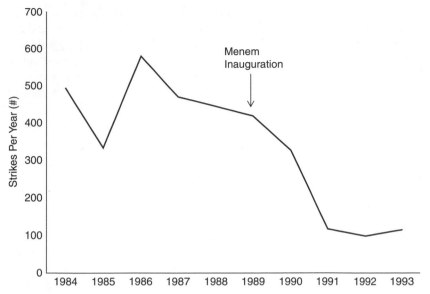

FIGURE 7.1. Strike Activity in Argentina, 1984–1993. *Source:* McGuire 1997, Table 8, p. 239.

labor, the CGT was not subordinate to the PJ. Rather, having mobilized prior to and independently of the Peronist alliance, the Argentine labor movement forced Perón to make "real concessions" in order to win labor's support from the beginning.[22] Thus labor provided the organizational base and was the strongest branch of Peronism, but its partisan support was not unconditional.

After years of repression by the military dictatorship, labor unions reemerged as a forceful political actor in Argentina with the transition to democracy in 1983. The CGT exercised considerable influence over the economic reform agenda, mobilizing broad demonstrations against the structural reforms attempted by the UCR President Raúl Alfonsín. Under Menem, however, labor leaders took a more moderate and conciliatory posture toward the much-deeper structural reforms proposed by their partisan ally. By contrast to the thirteen general strikes against the Alfonsín government, the CGT held only one general strike during Menem's first term in office.[23] Smaller-scale strike activity also fell considerably under Menem; whereas the CGT held 582 strikes in 1986, this number fell to 99 in 1992 (see Figure 7.1).[24]

Despite labor's relative quiescence during President Menem's first years in office, union support for the Peronist government was equivocal. Indeed, by the

[22] Collier and Collier 1991, pp. 92–3, 349.
[23] The average number of strikes per year under Alfonsín (1984–8) was 465; under Menem (1989–93), it was less than half of that, at 216. McGuire 1997, p. 239.
[24] McGuire 1997. Orlansky offers a higher figure, reporting the peak in labor conflict with 949 conflicts in 1988. Orlansky 1997, p. 629.

time the structural pension reform was proposed in 1992, the labor movement had endured bitter conflicts with Menem over his broader economic liberalization program, giving rise to a deep rupture in the movement.[25] The resolution of those divisions in the labor movement resulted in the declining influence of the sectors opposed to the market-oriented reform agenda, while supportive unions claimed influence over both the reform outcomes and distributive rewards.[26] The cleaving of the labor movement was attended also by a weakening of the ties between unions and the Peronist Party structure through which it had traditionally exercised legislative power.[27]

Although labor strikes had declined precipitously following the success of the inflation-ending Convertibility Plan in 1991, union mobilization began to rise again by mid-1992 as Menem prepared to send the pension reform to the National Congress. Economic growth and consumption remained strong, but labor protests shifted from their previous emphasis on wage and workplace grievances toward contestation over the structural reform agenda. High on the list of targets for labor opposition were the social policy reforms, which included labor market regulation, health insurance, and the old age pension system. Indeed, conflicts over state social policies rose from 8.9 percent of all labor conflicts between 1991 and 1992, to 13.8 percent between 1992 and 1993.[28] Having already sustained a considerable loss of material and institutional resources in the process of macroeconomic reform, Menem's social policy restructuring agenda acquired greater urgency. Since unions derived sizable institutional and financial benefits from management of health insurance programs (*Obras Sociales*), the defense of this program was of paramount importance. Leaders of the opposing factions of the CGT thus overcame their differences in 1992, calling a general strike to oppose Menem's social policy agenda, which included the pension reform.[29]

President Menem has been cited as an archetype of the Nixon-goes–to-China logic through which labor-based parties enjoy greater credibility and political leeway to win support for economic liberalization; however, this partisan advantage diminished by 1992 with the emergence of labor opposition to the reform.[30] Labor leaders were well aware of the losses they would bear as a result of the reform, and Menem could not point to a credible pro-market opposition party to portray his reform as a "lesser evil" compared to an ostensibly more painful alternative.[31] Indeed, it was Menem who launched the orthodox market-based structural reform of the macroeconomy. What is more, the centrist Radical Party, which was based in the middle class, took a firm position *against* the increasingly unpopular social security privatization.

---

[25] McGuire 1997, p. 233; Murillo 2001.
[26] Murillo 2001; Orlansky 1997.
[27] Orlansky 1997, p. 630.
[28] Gómez 1997, pp. 649–51.
[29] McGuire 1997, p. 234.
[30] See Cukierman and Tommasi 1998; Rodrik 1994.
[31] Kitschelt 2001.

Menem's partisan alliances likewise diminished his own partisan credibility, for when looking to broaden his legislative majority, Menem reached out to the ideologically conservative and promarket UCeDé, while also forming alliances with the business community. The ostensible credibility signaled by Menem's partisan label and the PJ's historic ties to labor thus was considerably dampened by the time the structural pension reform was proposed in 1992. Labor unions, in turn, were prepared for, and launched, forceful opposition to this reform.

Although the CGT leadership came under the control of more moderate unions when it reunited in 1992, union leaders immediately denounced the government's plan to privatize the state pension system. The opening salvo of this battle was issued at a seminar cosponsored by the CGT and International Labour Organization to discuss the proposed pension reform where the CGT leader Oscar Lescano announced, "We are not going to permit the liquidation of our pension system."[32] In taking this position, union leaders set in motion a powerful veto dynamic that would pull opposition parties in the legislature into a position of confrontation and render Menem vulnerable to defection from within his own party.

Labor unions were not alone in their opposition. Retiree associations joined in protest against the pension reform seeking to "win the street" – that is, to mobilize public opinion against the pension reform through vocal public mobilization.[33] Retirees and labor unions held weekly marches in front of the National Congress in 1992 and 1993, decrying the loss of social rights in the reform and the absence of solidarity in a privatized pension system.[34] In doing so, they brought attention to the loss-imposing elements of structural pension reform, countervailing Menem's emphasis on the material wealth to be gained through privatization that we saw in Chapter 6. Although they were not well organized, with only 10 percent of retirees being members of formal associations, many maintained informal ties to the unions with which they were affiliated during their working years.[35] This allowed retirees to participate as a forceful political actor. Through weekly protests in front of the National Congress, retirees elevated the question of pension reform in the public eye. Crucially, their longstanding association with the defense of the welfare state lent credibility to retirees' claims about the grave consequences of privatization for beneficiaries of the pension system.[36] Early protests by labor and pensioner groups thus cast a pall over Menem's proposed pension reform, fostering a "great lack of confidence" in the government's intentions vis-à-vis the reform

[32] Alonso 1998, p. 23.
[33] Alonso 1998, p. 20.
[34] Schulthess 1998.
[35] In particular, a large umbrella movement of retiree organizations, the Plenario Permanente de Organizaciones de Jubilados, was closely connected to the Central de los Trabajadores Argentinos (CTA), as well as to the Movimiento de Trabajadores Argentinos (MTA), which Alonso argues was the nucleus of dissidence within the CGT. Alonso 1998, p. 19.
[36] Alonso 1998, p. 20.

on the part of the public.[37] With the reform's public image tainted, politicians faced strong incentives to stake out positions against it.[38]

Indeed, when the reform was proposed, the opposition Radical Party and smaller provincial parties immediately announced their opposition to it.[39] With this veto dynamic established, the bargaining leverage wielded by labor unions increased dramatically, even as the number and visibility of protests declined. In part, this leverage owed to the narrow size of the Peronist majority. Having barely a majority in the Chamber of Deputies, Menem became highly vulnerable to defection from within. And it was from within his party ranks that the pressure to make the most extensive compromises in his proposal came.

Legislative Negotiation within a Veto Dynamic

The activation of a veto dynamic curbed dramatically the president's ability to use institutional authority to gather legislative support for the pension reform. In part, this dampening of Menem's authority was presaged by the quelling of the economic crisis, which reduced legislators' willingness to concede to Menem's pressure for unquestioned support. Instead, legislators sought to reclaim authority previously usurped by the executive, whose claims of "urgency" surrounding his reforms began to lose force in the context of the booming economy.[40] As the Secretary for Social Security recalled, "In the first hundred days of Cavallo, [President Menem] would go to the Congress with the Convertibility plan and tell the Deputies that they had to vote for this plan because otherwise, everything would explode; some deputies accepted it very well, and others not, but anyway all would commit to vote for it. But later, each time we would send them a law, they would contest more and more."[41]

For instance, when Menem pressured legislatures to commence hearings on his pension reform proposal, Peronist leaders responded by expressing misgivings about the measure.[42] This resistance forced Menem to strike a deal with Peronist congressional leaders that would enhance the distributive appearance of the pension reform. In exchange for initiating committee hearings on the pension reform, Menem agreed to dedicate a portion of revenue from the sale of stock in the state-owned petroleum enterprise, Yacimientos Petroliferos Fiscales (YPF), to the settlement of pension arrears owed to retirees from the temporary suspension of payments and indexation in the late 1980s.[43] The YPF deal was important for it created an opportunity for the government to associate the pension reform with the resolution of an important pension problem. And claiming credit for securing the payment of benefits to retirees was particularly important for Peronist deputies standing in the shadow of the

[37] Cetrángolo 1998; Etala 1998.
[38] Alonso 1997, p. 2; Isuani and San Martino 1995.
[39] Cetrángolo 1998; Gonzales Gaviola 1998.
[40] Torre and Gerchunoff 1998.
[41] Alonso 1997, p. 2.
[42] Alonso 1998; Santín 1998.
[43] Cetrángolo 1998; Díaz 1998; Torre and Gerchunoff 1998.

1993 midterm elections.[44] Early protests thus elevated the political costs of supporting the pension reform, which Peronist congressional leaders used as leverage in negotiations over the reform. The resulting bargains enhanced the distributive tendency of the pension reform, aiding its approval and the party's electoral prospects in the upcoming elections.

Labor unions also used the leverage created by the emergent veto dynamic to negotiate important compromises in the pension reform. After the CGT's reunification, its leadership was dominated by unions in sectors such as electricity and telephone services that took a pragmatic stance vis-à-vis market-oriented reform. Their approach was to support reform in exchange for new business opportunities in the market system – a strategy that drew criticism from the hard-line unions who derided this tactic as "business unionism."[45] The CGT took a similarly pragmatic stance with regard to the pension privatization. Following a general strike on November 9, 1992, PJ congressional leaders began to negotiate with the CGT leaders over the terms of labor's support for the pension reform. In exchange for their backing of the measure, CGT leaders demanded that unions be allowed to form private pension fund management firms (AFJPs) in the new private pension industry.[46] They also sought to retain power over health care funds. The Peronist Party leaders agreed, and the unions permitted their labor-based deputies in the PJ to endorse the reform proposal in the committee hearings – a critical veto opportunity. After considerable delay and compromise, therefore, the pension reform proposal was approved in committee and at the end of December 2002 was sent to the floor of the Chamber of Deputies for debate.

The bill was slated to begin floor debate after the summer break ended in February 1993. Given the executive's urgency to use the pension reform as a signal to international markets, as we saw in Chapter 5, Peronist leaders found themselves in a race against time to pass the reform before the congressional term ended on April 30. For any legislation that remained unfinished at the end of the term would be returned to the committees to restart the legislative process under the subsequent congressional session. The rising vulnerability of the Argentine economy at this time heightened the bargaining leverage of reform opponents who sought concessions in the reform in exchange for its sanction.

The principal negotiations over the reform were carried out between the representatives of the executive and a group of dissident Peronist deputies, most of whom were linked to the union movement. Although labor unions traditionally enjoyed the power to nominate one-third of the deputies on the PJ ballot, the number of labor-nominated deputies on the PJ list had declined from thirty-five in 1982 to just nineteen in the 1991–3 congressional term.[47] Despite their small numbers – approximately twenty in all – the dissident PJ deputies

[44] Diaz 1998; Rodriguez 1998; Torre and Gerchunoff 1998.
[45] Murillo 2001; Alonso 1998; McGuire 1997, pp. 236–7.
[46] Isuani and San Martino 1995.
[47] In the 1991–3 Congress, 7.39 percent of the Chamber of Deputies was labor-based PJ deputies, who represented 15.2 percent of the Peronist bloc. This share declined from 25.23 percent of the Peronist delegation in 1983–5. Alonso 1998, p. 25; McGuire 1997, p. 209.

TABLE 7.2. *Labor-Based Deputies within the Peronist Party Argentine Chamber of Deputies, 1983–1995*

Year	1983	1989	1991	1995
# Labor Deputies	35	23	18	10

Source: Etchemendy and Palermo 1997

exerted a level of influence over the pension reform that vastly exceeded their formal institutional authority in the Chamber of Deputies (see Table 7.2). They did so by joining with the Radical Party opposition to deny the government quorum to begin debate on the pension reform in the Chamber of Deputies.

On four successive attempts between March and April 1993, the government failed to achieve quorum to begin the pension reform debate.[48] As word of the fourth failure leaked into the streets on April 1, a celebration erupted among the approximately 3,000 people gathered outside the legislature to protest the anticipated vote.[49] Resistance to the pension reform remained firm within the legislature as well, leading Menem to step up his public rhetoric touting the potential growth-enhancing benefits of structural reform.[50] Technocrats also engaged in frantic back-room meetings with the dissident Peronist deputies. Although technocrats initially sought to persuade legislators on the merits of the reform by emphasizing its macroeconomic benefits, such arguments were unpersuasive.[51] The unpopularity of the pension reform meant that rhetoric alone would not dampen the political costs associated with the measure. Indeed, in response to Menem's threats to use his executive authority to nullify any changes that opponents demanded, dissident PJ deputies only hardened their positions. For even if their demands for revision were later reversed, opposing deputies could still claim political credit for having moderated the losses imposed by the reform.[52] If the distributive tendency was to be increased, the government would have to negotiate real compromises in the law.

As the end of the congressional term approached, Menem's urgent desire to pass the pension reform obliged him to make substantial compromises in the measure. The standoff ended on April 27, just three days before the end of the legislative session, when the executive reform team agreed to compromises that significantly curtailed the reach of market governance in the reformed pension system while creating new privileges for organized labor.[53] The first and most important revision demanded by union leaders was to make workers' participation in the new private pension system optional for all current and future members of the labor force. Although coverage by social security in Argentina is mandatory for all workers, participation in the private market would not be. Under the new terms of the reform, all workers in Argentina

[48] Mustapic 2002.
[49] "El festejo por el fracaso" 1993.
[50] Cetrángolo 1998.
[51] Cetrángolo 1998; Rondina 1998.
[52] "La mano de Cavallo en los nuevos cambios" 1993.
[53] "La CGT de Brunelli va con un rosario de quejas a su primera cita con el Gobierno" 1993.

would receive a basic pension from the public "solidarity" tier, which offered a flat-rate universal basic pension (prestación básica universal, PBU). And all workers could choose whether to participate in the private pension market and thus receive the ordinary retirement benefit (the jubilación ordinaria, or JO), or to stay in a reformed public, defined-benefit system and receive the additional permanence benefit (the prestación adicional por permanencia, PAP) for their second-tier pension.[54] The government initially proposed a very low PAP value but was obliged to raise this to win the support of the dissident PJ faction. This concession not only made the public pension system an attractive choice but elevated the fiscal cost of the new public pension system for the government as well. It also enhanced the distributive tendency of the pension reform.

Peronist deputies also negotiated state guarantees that limited even further the reach of market forces in the private pension market. The first was an agreement to create a state-run pension fund manager organized by the Argentine Central Bank (Banco de la Nación) that would compete in the private pension market. The state-run pension fund would offer affiliates a "double" guarantee: of the rate of return to invested pension funds and of the exchange rate. The latter was important because it meant a state guarantee of the dollar return to pension fund investments; no other Latin American government has offered such broad assurances.[55] Following the agreement on these revisions, the Argentine government succeeded in its fifth attempt to achieve quorum, beginning debate over the pension reform.[56] On May 6, the pension reform project was approved in the Chamber of Deputies and was sent to the National Senate. There, with a larger Peronist majority that was more supportive of the pension reform, Menem won the rapid sanction of his substantially modified pension privatization on September 23, 2003.

The effect of labor unions on the legislative conflict over Argentina's pension reform thus was quite mixed. On the one hand, labor protests, along with the retirees, activated the veto dynamic early in the negotiations over the pension reform, isolating Menem's narrow majority and rendering it vulnerable to defection. But union leaders also negotiated critical support for the reform, allowing the measure to advance, albeit in modified form, through the legislative process. Unions thus created the conditions under which they become a veto player, while also making it possible for the structural pension reform law ultimately to be approved.

Argentina Summary

The legislative dynamics of pension privatization in Argentina challenge existing accounts of the importance of institutional authority in pension reform,

---

[54] The executive initially proposed a formula for the PAP of 0.50 percent times the average salary in ten years prior to retirement per year of participation in the new system. This was later increased to 0.85 percent.

[55] Menem later issued a decree to eliminate Article 39 in response to financial sector opposition.

[56] "The CGT negotiated changes in exchange for attendance" 1993.

particularly the advantages of majority status.[57] For although President Menem commanded a disciplined legislative majority, he was forced to make deep concessions in the scope and market orientation of his reform. Menem's legislative authority was significantly curtailed when labor and retiree organizations activated a veto dynamic around the reform. The terms on which the political conflict over pension reform unfolded thus modified the formal institutional authority with which the government could legislate this institutional restructuring.

MEXICO

At the time of Mexico's pension reform, the Institutional Revolutionary Party controlled a disciplined majority in both legislative chambers. PRI presidents also could count on the support of organized labor due to a tightly controlled system of state corporatism.[58] This formal authority created what may be considered extremely hospitable conditions for the approval of far-reaching institutional reform. Thus it is not surprising that President Ernesto Zedillo won legislative approval for the extensive reform of Mexico's old age pension institution in 1995. What is striking, however, is that the magnitude of institutional change Zedillo achieved was *much less* than what the government originally sought. Despite the virtual absence of formal veto points in the legislative process, the Mexican government attenuated the market orientation in the pension reform at the behest of the labor unions and opposition parties. Labor's ability to heighten the salience of the losses imposed by the reform led government actors to make important compromises that enhanced the distributive content in the pension reform and abridged the role of market forces in the new system.

Institutional Authority in Mexico

In 1995, the Institutional Revolutionary Party controlled not only the presidency, as it had for the previous sixty-five years, but also 60 percent of the 500 seats in the Chamber of Deputies of the Mexican National Congress.[59] Although the Mexican presidency is not formally very strong, particularly vis-à-vis Congress, the executive nevertheless wielded extensive power over legislation through most of the second half of the twentieth century.[60] As leader of the longstanding hegemonic party, the PRI president enjoyed formal and informal powers including unified control of the executive and legislative branches of government (until 1997), which allowed him to exert nearly unconditional sway over the legislative process.[61] This authority was bolstered by high party discipline and recognition of the president as unquestioned party

[57] e.g., Madrid 2003.
[58] Burgess 1999.
[59] Nacif 1997, p. 2; Weldon 1997.
[60] Casar 2002.
[61] Arellano Gault and Guerrero Amparán 2003, p. 151–3. See also Casar 2002; Nacif 1997, p. 7.

leader.[62] Strong party discipline in Mexico is linked to the prohibition on reelection, which makes legislators heavily dependent upon party leaders for their careers after serving in the legislature.[63] Like the legislators in Argentina, career-minded PRI legislators enjoyed very little autonomy to stake out independent positions on legislative initiatives. The Mexican legislature thus has been considered the "unconditional servant" of the president – at least until the end of the PRI's hegemonic status.[64]

The PRI also held domination over the expression of societal interests in the political arena for most of the twentieth century. Having defined the relationship with civil society through tightly controlled corporatist institutions, the PRI could circumscribe interest group mobilization through the exchange of recognition and representation for political support. Groups representing organized labor, urban "popular" sectors, peasants, and bureaucrats were all given formal positions in the PRI structure.[65] The result was to narrow considerably the possibilities for members of civil society to articulate independent voices in the political process. The formal organization of political, social, and legislative authority in Mexico thus gave the president authority to legislate institutional change with little consultation or compromise with opposing interests.

Even in this semiauthoritarian context, the Mexican government appealed to its social and political base for support to legitimate its political initiatives. In this respect, the PRI enjoyed the additional advantage of a long-term relationship with Mexico's main labor confederation, the Confederation of Mexican Workers (Confederación de Trabajadores de México, or CTM). Although labor was largely subordinate to the PRI, this relationship was based fundamentally on the practice of exchange, albeit unequal, through which the PRI extended representation and privileges (both material and institutional) to "official" unions who in return offered political support in the form of quiescence and votes.[66] These ties date to the founding of the PRI in 1938 (as the Partido de la Revolución Mexicana) when organized labor became one of the three official "sectors" of the party, along with the popular sector and the peasants.[67] This three-pillar system was formalized in the apportioning of PRI-held seats in the legislature across these sectors, with 30 percent of the PRI deputies representing labor unions, 40 percent being tied to the urban "popular" sectors, and 30 percent supporting the peasantry.

The official labor movement was organized principally in the CTM. The specific terms of the PRI's corporatist bargain with labor were shaped by Fidel Velázquez, the pragmatic leader of the CTM for most periods since its founding in 1936. As principal interlocutor between the labor movement and government, Velázquez sought to negotiate *within* the established pattern of unequal exchange, embracing compromise with the hegemonic PRI rather

[62] Casar 2002, p. 9; Weldon 1997, p. 227.
[63] Casar 2002, p. 127; Nacif 1997, p. 4; 2002, p. 282; Weldon 1997, pp. 246–8.
[64] Arellano Gault and Guerrero Amparán 2003, p. 154.
[65] Centeno 1994, p. 36; Teichman 1995, p. 19.
[66] Collier 1992; Murillo 2001; Samstad 2002, p. 4; Zapata 1998.
[67] Collier 1992.

than challenge to the terms of this alliance. For some observers, the support
of Velázquez for President Salinas's economic liberalization appeared to be a
wholesale ratification of the neoliberal program and evidence of labor's declining political leverage. But such a view is incomplete, for it overlooks the critical
political bargain on which labor backing for economic liberalization was conditioned. For Trejo and Jones, the influence of PRI-linked unions advanced to
the point where unions had acquired a veto over social policy reform in the late
1980s.[68] This veto power was traded for consent to Salinas' deep macroeconomic liberalization program, and particularly the North American Free Trade
Agreement. Labor's support for economic restructuring thus was offered only
conditionally as it maintained the power to resist, or at least influence, market-
oriented reform in the social realm, including of the pension system.[69]

Labor's conditional support for the PRI's economic programs long defined
the terms of social protection development in Mexico. While bargains of political representation offered labor elites an important voice in policy making,
social protection benefits provided the currency through which the PRI could
claim the loyalty of the CTM's rank-and-file members.[70] The vast expansion
of health care, education, and social security programs thus coincided with the
extension of state control over industrial development in Mexico. In addition to
material benefits for its members, labor leaders acquired important institutional
privileges through the expansion of Mexico's social insurance system, including administration of the Mexican Social Security Institute (IMSS).[71] Social
insurance was one of the few protections that labor unions retained through
the process of economic liberalization, so the IMSS privatization represented
a considerable loss not just of institutional privilege for the CTM but also of
economic security for Mexican wage laborers.

The material basis of the PRI's corporatist exchange with labor was weakened steadily by the social costs imposed by Mexico's economic liberalization
program. Although many of the macroeconomic goals of economic restructuring were achieved over this period, including the control of inflation and
restoration of growth, economic restructuring failed to slow the real decline in
wages that began in the early 1980s.[72] Indeed, the removal of state protections
of domestic industry provoked a sharp rise in unemployment and a steady
decline in real wages, which by 1990 had fallen to just 71 percent of the 1980
level.[73] Although labor leaders periodically voiced concern over falling wages,
the CTM maintained consistent political support for the PRI's economic liberalization program through a series of economic and social "pacts."[74] For some
scholars, this support resulted from labor's incapacity for effective mobilization

[68] Trejo and Jones 1998, p. 75.
[69] Dion 2002; 2008.
[70] Dion 2002.
[71] Trejo and Jones 1998, p. 74.
[72] Middlebrook 1991, p. 2.
[73] Dussell Peters 1998, p. 45.
[74] Burgess 1999; Middlebrook 1991, p. 13.

against the PRI. For others, it was a condition that labor accepted for maintaining a critical voice on social policy issues.[75]

Democratization and Political Conflict

The role of labor in Mexico's pension reform was influenced powerfully by two attendant transformations in the 1990s: democratization and the weakening of the tightly controlled state corporatist system. The emergence of pluralism within the labor movement created broader opportunities for unions to oppose the government's pension reform without suffering political repression. Although labor elites could no longer block social sector reforms from within the executive branch, the increasingly democratic and competitive electoral processes allowed labor to threaten the PRI with unprecedented electoral costs by bringing attention to the loss-imposing aspects of the government's reform agenda.

Democratization in Mexico was unlike that in any other Latin American country due to its very gradual nature and the absence of a transfer from military to civilian rule. From the PRI's foundation in 1929 as the National Revolutionary Party, no other party won the presidency in Mexico until 1999, and no other party won a state governorship until 1989. The PRI also did not lose a Senate seat until 1988. Democratization thus involved a measured strengthening of electoral processes, such as through the reform of the Federal Electoral Institute (Instituto Federal Electoral) and the gradual curtailing of the PRI's legislative authority.[76] Although the PRI still retained 60 percent of the seats in the Chamber of Deputies in 1994, the ascent of the center-right PAN (Partido Acción Nacional) and leftist PRD (Partido de la Revolución Democrática) presented clear electoral threats to the PRI's dominance – underscored by its near loss of the presidency in 1988. Indeed, the rising electoral competition in the mid-1990s culminated in the rupture in the PRI's legislative majority in the 1997 midterm elections, which followed the implementation of the pension privatization.

Democratic political competition could only strengthen as state corporatism eroded. The corporatist arrangement in Mexico had developed hand in hand with the state-led industrialization strategy, and thus the first major fissures in that bargain emerged with the shift toward a liberal, market-oriented economic strategy in the 1980s.[77] Economic liberalization curtailed many of the state's allocative functions that long served as the currency of the state-corporatist (and clientelist) exchange. Critical divisions in the labor movement thus emerged during the sexenio, or six-year term, of President Salinas, who oversaw the deepening of Mexico's economic restructuring. The breakdown of the corporatist system was manifest in a variety of incremental changes in the system of

[75] Dion 2002; Trejo and Jones 1998.
[76] Dominguez and McCann 1995, p. 35; Klesner 1998, p. 482; Scherlen 1998, pp. 19–20.
[77] Samstad 2002, p. 5.

organized labor, including the creation in 1990 of a new federation of workers in the goods and services industries, called Fesebes (Federación de Sindicatos de Empresas de Bienes y Servicios), which became a political and economic counterweight to the CTM.[78] Salinas took advantage of this competition to reward compliant unions and punish dissenters with exclusion from political access.[79] The process thus did not translate directly into an enhancement of labor authority in the policy-making arena. It did, however, multiply the voices that were articulated in the political process, allowing opponents to bring public attention to the loss-imposing character of government policy initiatives. In some cases, such mobilization would block such reforms altogether.

By 1995, the labor movement in Mexico had become considerably fragmented relative to the previous half century. This fragmentation expanded the range of labor voices and divergent positions available to unions vis-à-vis the government, and diminished the ability of independent unions to organize a coherent position against the pension reform. Divisions within the labor movement were intensified by the creation of a new union organization, the Forum on Unionism Facing the Nation (Foro: El Sindicalismo ante la Nación, or Foro). Comprised of approximately two dozen official and independent unions – including the militant social security workers union (SNTSS) – the Foro sought to articulate an "alternative" voice for labor.[80] Although the Labor Congress (Congreso de Trabajo, CT – a multiconfederation PRI-linked umbrella group) had endorsed the pension privatization in Mexico, the Foro condemned it as a loss for Mexican workers.[81]

The increasingly bold articulation of opposition voices from labor acquired even greater force in the context of increasingly competitive elections. As labor's influence within the government declined, its strategy shifted from behind-the-scenes negotiation with the PRI, to active, albeit marginal, participation in open political competition. Increasing electoral competition meant that the PRI for the first time faced the prospect of being held accountable by voters for imposing losses through its reform agenda. To the extent that labor mobilization raised the specter of such unprecedented electoral losses, the PRI faced powerful incentives to negotiate concessions in their pension reform that would enhance its distributive nature. Despite the dearth of institutional vetoes, therefore, the legislative process of pension reform in Mexico would result in the concession of many more of the demands of labor and opposition parties than would be predicted by the government's tremendous legislative authority.

Negotiation within a Veto Dynamic

Upon his inauguration in December 1994, President Ernesto Zedillo Ponce de León was forced to confront a profound economic crisis emanating from the speculative attack on, and subsequent devaluation of, the national currency.

[78] Samstad 2002, p. 13.
[79] Murillo 2001, p. 43.
[80] Samstad 2002, p. 12.
[81] Samstad 2002, p. 13.

Although the pension reform had been high on the list of government priorities in January 1995, the depth of the economic crisis provoked a breakdown in the political cooperation of labor elites, forcing Zedillo to temporarily shelve the pension reform until political and economic conditions improved.[82] Unable to agree on how economic losses would be apportioned, negotiations over a new economic pact were suspended in early March 1995, and the government announced its economic plan without the support of either business or labor.[83]

Even though the public announcement of the pension privatization was delayed, a tightly knit and well-insulated technocratic reform team began negotiations with labor and business leaders over their proposal. The team was composed of technocrats representing the finance ministry (Secretaría de Hacienda y Crédito Público), CONSAR (Comisión Nacional del Sistema de Ahorro para el Retiro, which regulated the private pension system), IMSS, and the Mexican central bank (Banco de México). Over a period of three months, technocrats drafted the specific provisions of the pension reform law, sharing them with "interested parties," including labor leaders and representatives of the main institutions and bureaucracies involved in pension provision. This process was meant to gauge the political salability of the reform, allowing technocrats to "test the water" and plan a strategy to "convince" resistant groups to support the reform.

Before any formal legislative process began, therefore, the PRI government had engaged in protracted negotiations with representatives of its political base, including labor and business leaders. Only after securing the backing of these groups was the pension reform proposal introduced into the legislature. The director of IMSS headed the political negotiations over the reform as a way to enhance its credibility with labor.[84] Since IMSS directors had long defended labor's social policy interests in the executive branch, it was anticipated that the IMSS directors could more credibly persuade union leaders that the pension reform was in their interests.[85]

When the first draft of the structural pension reform was presented to labor leaders in early 1995, it called for the full replacement of the IMSS defined-benefit pension system with a privately managed defined-contribution program with no minimum pension guarantee or other unfunded state pension liabilities. Workers under that plan would retire only on the funds accumulated in their individual pension accounts. The reform also called for the workers' housing funds in the National Housing Fund (INFONAVIT) to be transferred from labor control to the private pension fund administrators.

The transfer of income and investment risks to workers could not have come at a worse time from the perspective of Mexican unions. In early 1995, Mexican workers were still suffering the deep social and economic costs of the peso crisis. Household consumption had declined sharply in the first half of 1995 with the severe economic recession. By the end of the year, inflation

---

[82] Noriega 1999.
[83] Springer and Molina 1995, p. 70.
[84] Cerda 1999; Martínez 1999; Noriega 1999; Solís 1999.
[85] Gonzalez Pier 1999; Saenz Garza 1999; Vaquera 1999.

was running at over 50 percent, and real wages had fallen by 13.5 percent from their already depressed level.[86] Over the course of 1995, Mexico's GDP would contract by 6 percent.[87] Since the mid-1980s, social protection benefits, including disability insurance, work accident, severance, and maternity and health care, had provided Mexican workers with an important buffer from the impact of economic liberalization.[88] With deep economic recession caused by the peso crisis, their importance was magnified even further.

The crisis prompted labor leaders to withdraw from the "stability and growth pact" that had previously upheld labor support for macroeconomic liberalization.[89] The crisis also raised the value that workers attached to the IMSS social insurance benefits, particularly the severance pay system. For Undersecretary of Finance Carlos Noriega, who oversaw negotiations with labor over the pension reform, the peso crisis hardened the bargaining position of labor. As he explained, "When many people found themselves without a job and only with IMSS, they began to value it highly and would not accept the possibility that the government would take it away or alter some of those benefits."[90] Facing stiff resistance from its labor base, the Mexican government temporarily set aside the pension privatization initiative in early 1995 until economic conditions improved. It did not, however, dispense with these plans altogether.

In addition to presenting the loss of material benefits, the pension privatization also jeopardized critical institutional resources controlled by CTM leaders. For one thing, the proposed termination of the IMSS pension functions threatened modest job losses for the employees of the institution who were organized in the National Union of Social Security Workers (SNTSS). More importantly, the privatization would increase the transparency and market governance of the housing fund INFONAVIT, to which Mexican workers contribute 5 percent of covered wages. INFONAVIT long served as a valuable patronage vehicle for union leaders, and thus its reform put at risk this source of considerable institutional and financial power for the CTM.

The most forceful resistance to Mexico's pension reform came from the SNTSS. Along with thirteen other official unions, the SNTSS broke with the CT and the CTM to launch highly visible marches and publicity campaigns against the pension reform.[91] The fragmentation of the private sector labor movement meant that there was little chance that opposing unions could single-handedly veto the 1995 pension reform. At best, labor leaders sought to secure critical institutional privileges and reduce the material and redistributive losses to labor implied by the reform. Although this resistance was isolated, it raised the visibility of the losses imposed by the pension reform, and thus threatened unprecedented losses for the PRI in the ever-more-competitive electoral arena.

---

[86] Lustig 2001, p. 89.

[87] Larre 1999, p. 14.

[88] Dion 2002.

[89] Springer and Molina 1995, p. 70.

[90] Noriega 1999.

[91] "Mexico Passes Social Security Reform Despite Massive Labor Union Protests" 1996. The SNTSS did mobilize, but it did not strike. Marier and Mayer 2007, p. 594.

To dampen labor opposition, the Mexican government agreed to significantly curtail the scope and depth of its structural pension reform. For all of its efforts, labor was unable to block the pension privatization. It did, however, win revision of the terms of the reform. The most significant of these came in response to labor's demand for a minimum pension guarantee. Because a principal objective of Mexico's pension reform was to eliminate the government's unfunded pension liabilities, the original privatization plan did not include a publicly provided safety net for workers whose incomes were too low to generate sufficient savings for retirement. The CTM leaders demanded the inclusion of such a guarantee as a condition for their endorsement of the reform. The Mexican government agreed to this stipulation and revised their proposal to allow new workers entering the workforce to be entitled to a minimum pension guarantee after twenty-five years of contributions. The new minimum pension would equal the nominal value of one minimum wage at the end of 1996 (indexed to price changes). This concession lessened the loss-imposing character of the structural reform and forced the government to relinquish one of its central institutional objectives, namely closing the long-term unfunded liabilities of the IMSS pension system.[92]

To further placate reluctant unions, Mexican government negotiators also agreed to allow IMSS to retain institutional authority over certain social protection functions. IMSS, rather than private firms, thus would provide disability pensions and work injury insurance under the reform plan. IMSS also retained authority over the choice of private sector health care insurance companies that could participate in a rebate program for health care premiums. Through this program, called the reversion of quotas, IMSS returns a portion of the employer and employee premiums to firms that contract health insurance for their employees with private firms.[93] IMSS directors had long retained discretionary power to select the businesses that could participate in this system. The original pension privatization plan sought to remove this discretionary power from IMSS in order to broaden access to the program. But in a last-minute deal to secure SNTSS support, the government removed this provision from the reform. After the SNTSS concessions were granted, it faced both minimal job losses and little threat to its own pensions or health care.[94] Its protests thus dissipated considerably.

In response to labor demands the government also created a "social quota" through which the state would contribute a peso per day to the private pension account of all workers. IMSS also would continue as the legal enforcer of all social security collections and provider of benefits to all existing pensioners and would retain responsibility for the minimum pension guarantee and for delivering benefits to transition workers who took the "lifetime switch" option at retirement. Finally, the government allowed the CTM to continue managing the Mexican housing credit fund, INFONAVIT, albeit under more transparent

---

[92] World Bank 1999, p. 197.
[93] González-Rosetti and Mogollon 2000, p. 46, fn. 64.
[94] Dion 2008.

principles. The goal of these concessions was to reduce the political costs of an otherwise potentially explosive reform, should it be seized upon by opposition parties in the next election. Critically, such costs were raised by the early defection of hitherto-loyal unions from support of the majority party. In response to these electoral threats, the Mexican government conceded significant revisions in the balance between public and private functions in the pension system.

The product of these extensive back-room negotiations between the government and labor was a draft pension reform proposal that was presented to President Zedillo by the Tripartite Commission for the Strengthening of IMSS (La Comisión Tripartita para le Fortalecimiento del IMSS) on November 1, 1995. Zedillo then sent the draft legislation to the National Congress, where it was subject to additional negotiation and compromise.

Compromise in the Legislature

The fulsome and disciplined majority held by the PRI in 1995 left few formal obstacles before the enactment of its structural pension reform. The early mobilization of labor against the reform, however, had raised the visibility of the pension privatization's loss-imposing character. The result was the activation of a veto logic in the legislature, where both the opposition PRD and PAN assumed vocally antagonistic positions vis-à-vis the reform. Faced with the specter of bearing sole responsibility for loss imposition, the PRI sought to negotiate the support of opposition parties for the pension reform by making further, albeit modest, compromises in the measure.

When it reached the legislature, Mexico's structural pension reform was divided into two laws. The first, the Social Insurance Law (Ley del Seguro Social) established the basic principles along which responsibility for old age pension provision would be divided between state and market institutions. The second, the Law of the Retirement Savings System (Ley de los Sistemas de Ahorro para el Retiro), regulated the new private pension management industry, and in particular the funds that would manage private savings, called AFOREs (Administradoras de Fondos para el Retiro). The first law was sanctioned by the Mexican Congress in a mere twenty-eight days from its introduction. This rapid enactment was made possible in part by the consent of the PRI's labor base following the compromises discussed earlier. Indeed, committee hearings on the reform would not begin until the CTM leadership signed off on the reform, bringing the labor-based deputies into line with party leaders.

The second law, however, was subject to more extensive contestation and protracted negotiation in the legislature. These concessions to legislative opponents further diluted the role of market forces in Mexico's private pension market such as through the creation of a public (IMSS-affiliated) and union-run AFOREs, stricter state regulation of pension fund managers, and the imposition of limits on the investment of pension funds. Partisan opposition to the structural pension reform drew from both the leftist PRD and the center-right

PAN, as well as from members of the (usually disciplined) PRI itself. One of the most vocal critics of the pension reform was PAN Senator José Angel Conchello, who decried the loss of solidarity in the pension system that would result from the privatization. As we saw in Chapter 6, the rhetoric of solidarity held powerful sway in social security politics in Mexico. Such criticisms rendered the PRI even more vulnerable to a broader political backlash because concepts of solidarity were intimately linked both to the public support for the IMSS system and the government's constitutional obligations in the social protection realm. The concession of a "social quota" thus was a direct response to the charge of betraying the founding principles of the Mexican social insurance system. Although modest, the state's contribution of one peso per day (approximately 5.5 percent of the minimum wage) to each worker's private pension account expanded the public role in the reformed pension system well beyond the government's original reform design. Indeed, the social quota would cost approximately 0.1 percent of GDP per year and would constitute a meaningful redistribution in favor of low-income workers.[95]

Legislative opponents also drew attention to the risks associated with private financial markets. These risks, as mentioned previously, had become highly salient in the wake of Mexico's banking system crisis in 1995. As we saw in Chapter 6, the banking sector came to be viewed with suspicion by most workers after its costly public bailout.[96] Opposition legislators demanded stricter limits on the magnitude of risk that pension fund managers could assume in the investment of pension funds. In making these claims, legislators cited "a very clear concern in the labor movement that workers' capital would not be drastically reduced by devaluation or inflation."[97] Labor mobilization against the reform thus directly influenced the terms of the legislative conflict, leading the Zedillo government to strengthen regulations on the pension fund investments and to create a state regulatory agency that would establish risk ratings for private sector firms. The government also agreed to prohibit the AFOREs from investing in foreign securities, while also requiring a portion of investments to be channeled to "national economic development." The latter provision was ostensibly to ensure the reinvestment of funds domestically and to contribute to the economic recovery from the peso crisis. More broadly, the concessions bridled the market governance of the private pension funds.

The left-leaning PRD, which opposed the privatization altogether, endorsed the concession of a public, IMSS-linked AFORE, as well as the possibility that labor unions could establish collectively owned funds.[98] Along with labor leaders, the PRD insisted that unions have an institutional role in the *regulation* of the private pension market. This demand was met with the creation of a tripartite governing counsel for the private pension regulator, CONSAR. The

[95] Corbacho and Schwartz 2002, p. 31.
[96] Latinobarómetro 2004.
[97] Suarez Dávila 1996, p. 727.
[98] Ramirez 1999; Saenz Garza 1999; Suarez Dávila 1996.

right-wing PAN was generally more favorable to the notion of privatization and demanded that the public AFORE compete on a level playing field with the private fund managers. The PAN thus won the assurance that, unlike the situation in Argentina, the IMSS-linked pension fund would not provide additional financial guarantees to its members.

The compromises made to win legislative support were not restricted solely to the opposition parties, however, but involved further limits on the market governance of the private pension system that were demanded by members of the PRI itself. Even before the pension reform measure came up for a vote, PRI legislators expressed a general wariness of the implications of Mexico's weakened financial sector, which endured a general banking crisis prior to the peso collapse. Fear of contagion from the banking crisis into the pension system led PRI legislators to demand that no private banks that were involved in financial sector collapse and subsequent government bailout could participate in the private pension fund industry.[99] PRI legislators likewise insisted on a limit of 17 percent of the market share that any single AFORE could claim (at least initially).[100] On the morning of the vote, the government conceded even further restrictions on the portfolio allocations of the private pension fund managers to assure that pension funds be invested "fundamentally" (i.e., at least 51 percent) in inflation-protected instruments.

The concession of significant revisions to reluctant legislators – both within the PRI and opposition parties – bears powerful evidence of the emergence of a veto dynamic, and thus of the conditioning effect of this logic on institutional power. For despite the PRI's fulsome majority in the National Congress, it made concessions to opponents in order to gain their support. Further evidence of the veto dynamic came in the last-minute decision of PAN legislators to vote against the pension privatization on December 8, 1995. Although the conservative PAN had a programmatic interest in the advance of the pension reform, the souring public sentiment toward the reform raised the prospects of an electoral backlash associated with the privatization. Even the PRI failed to bring all of its legislators in line with the vote. Of the 300 PRI deputies, only 289 were present in the Chamber at the time of the vote and voted in favor of the measure. Among the opposition, 66 deputies of the PRD, 10 of the PT, and 6 independent deputies voted against the measure, as did 54 PAN deputies, while only 18 deputies of the PAN voted in favor of the reform, and 19 abstained. Ultimately, the measure passed by a vote of 289 votes in favor and 160 against. This sanction marked the endpoint of six months of formal legislative deliberations over Mexico's structural pension reform. As we will see later, this was even longer than legislative deliberation over pension privatization in the much-more-competitive Uruguayan legislature. Including

---

[99] Suarez Dávila 1996, p. 728.
[100] The 1996 pension reform law (*Ley de los Sistemas de Ahorro para el Retiro*, Article 26, p. 17) established that this 17 percent limit would be raised to 20 percent in four years. Suarez Dávila 1996, p. 727.

informal negotiations with labor unions prior to the introduction of the pension reform law to the National Congress, Mexico's legislative process of pension reform extended more than a year.[101]

Mexico Summary

The privatization of the Mexican pension system brought a dramatic change in the way that the cost and risks of saving for retirement are apportioned in that country. But it did not remove the state from the pension system. Rather, the Mexican state continues to play important roles in the private pension market that were not anticipated in the government's original reform plan. These functions were expanded by concessions to labor unions and to opposition parties prior to and during the legislative process. To be sure, the Mexican structural pension reform was a deeply transformative project. The final legislation, however, was considerably less radical than it is often characterized to be, for it emerged from extensive negotiation. Indeed, the legislative process was considerably more difficult than we should expect on the basis of the government's formal legislative majority. Notably, the 1995 pension reform was one of only two reforms introduced by President Zedillo that was revised in the legislative process between 1994 and 1997.[102]

These concessions are significant not only for their political implications but also for their economic and material consequences. In an analysis of Mexico's pension reform, the U.S. Federal Reserve observed that the effect of the minimum pension guarantee and the lifetime switch option "casts doubt that substantial savings can be achieved in the short run."[103] That study also noted that for the transitional generation, the approximately 70 percent of workers covered by IMSS who earn at or below the minimum wage will be unlikely to retire under the rules of the private pension system.[104] Efforts to reduce the loss-imposing appearance of Mexico's pension reform thus involved both the curtailment of the role of market forces in the operation of the new pension system and the effective delay of the implementation of these rules for a generation.

These compromises cannot be understood solely through analysis of formal veto points because the PRI government confronted very few institutional roadblocks to the enactment of its reform agenda. In the context of increasing democratic competition, however, the mobilization of labor unions against the reform heightened the salience of the pension reform's retrenchment elements, raising the specter of significant electoral loss for the PRI. The threat of electoral punishment compelled the Zedillo government to make real concessions to its

---

[101] Suarez Dávila 1996.
[102] Casar 2002, pp. 128–9.
[103] Edmonds 1996, pp. 4–5.
[104] Edmonds 1996, p. 5.

base and (less so) to opposition parties both prior to and during the legislative process. Together, these changes limited the transfer of risk to individuals through the structural pension reform and increased the state's financial obligations within the reformed pension system. Such concessions were a logical consequence of the enactment of reform in a veto dynamic.

BRAZIL

The legislative conflicts over pension reform in Brazil are distinguished by the unique challenges created by the constitutional status of the pension system and by the government's decision not to privatize it. The latter meant that the option of organizing political conflict around the creative dimension of the pension reform – the establishment of new private savings options – was not available. Yet, significant reform was possible. Although the rules of the game were the same for both Presidents Cardoso and Lula da Silva, the former encountered a much greater challenge to building legislative support for pension reform than the latter; this difficulty also varied markedly over the course of Cardoso's two pension reform efforts. Cardoso's oversized governing coalition did not secure the passage of his pension reforms, but the notorious fragmentation and personalism of Brazil's legislature did not condemn these efforts to failure either. Rather, the ease of building legislative majorities behind pension reforms varied with the ability of the government to enhance the distributive appearance of the measure through political rhetoric, compensation, authority, and compromise.

Obstacles to Reform

The challenge of winning legislative sanction of loss-imposing institutional change in Brazil was considerably greater than in the other countries examined in this study. The first reason for this owes to the single-dimensional nature of Brazil's pension reform. Because neither the Cardoso nor Lula government sought to privatize, leaders could not use the potential individual gains to be won through private savings options to obfuscate the loss-imposing dimension of pension reforms. The constitutional status of Brazil's pension rules further complicated the task of legislating loss imposition. Before any structural reform could be enacted, the government had to deconstitutionalize the detailed minutiae of Brazil's pension system. Doing so, however, requires leaders to gain the cooperation of supermajorities, winning the votes of three-fifths of the legislators in two separate votes in each chamber of the National Congress.

The very notion of deconstitutionalizing pension rules in Brazil was fraught with political peril due to the high value that citizens attached to the system's constitutional protections. As we saw in Chapter 6, such reticence drew from the institution's political legacy of arbitrary benefit cuts under Brazil's military regime. Aside from any material losses imposed by the reforms, therefore, citizens viewed deconstitutionalization as a blank check to cut pension benefits.

For participants in this process, the challenge involved "asking politicians to make a lousy tradeoff. Vote against something that is a clear benefit to your constituency – and in return get an uncertain future."[105] Any measure of success at enhancing the distributive appearance of the pension reform thus would be partial at best, as reform could only be achieved through the removal of constitutional protections on the existing institution. The challenge for both the Cardoso and Lula da Silva governments thus was to persuade citizens – and thus legislators – that this tradeoff was worthwhile.

The design of Brazil's electoral and legislative institutions limits the authority of national party leaders and thus complicates the task of legislating loss imposition. Brazil's bicameral National Congress consists of a 513-seat Chamber of Deputies and an 81-member Senate and is often regarded as one of the most highly fragmented in Latin America.[106] Legislative power is apportioned among a high number of effective political parties, which averaged 6.3 between 1945 and 1995, qualifying the party system as "extremely pluralistic," bordering on "atomistic."[107] This level of fragmentation makes it unlikely that any single party can win a majority of seats, obliging presidents to form large multiparty governing coalitions.[108] Electoral rules in Brazil also are said to cultivate a high level of personalism that weakens the authority of national party leaders over their rank and file.[109] This is because voters in Brazil may cast their ballot directly for a party, a coalition, or a candidate, and most citizens choose to vote directly for the candidate. Votes are allocated first according to the total number received by each party, but within parties, seats are allocated to the candidates receiving the most personal votes. Brazilian legislators enjoy further autonomy from party leaders due to a system called *candidato nato*, or "candidate birthright," which allows federal and state deputies and town council representatives, once they are elected, to have automatic access to the ballot for the same position.

These electoral rules are said to create incentives for legislators to establish stronger ties to their constituents rather than to national party leaders, narrowing legislators' time horizons and shifting political concerns from the provision of collective goods toward particularistic ones.[110] Scholars also cite a strong centrifugal force in Brazilian politics created by the federal system that places the local and state-level party leaders, especially the governors, at the center of political authority.[111] The power of local political leaders is said to further undermine the ability of national party leaders to command the cooperation of federal deputies on difficult legislation.

---

[105] Oliveira 1999.
[106] Mainwaring 1997. Also see Ames 2001; Taagepera and Shugart 1993.
[107] Samuels 2000, p. 241.
[108] Ames 1995b, p. 407; Mainwaring 1997; Smith and Messari 1998, p. 12.
[109] Ames 1994; 1995a; Carey and Shugart 1995; Jones 1993; Mainwaring 1997.
[110] Ames 1995a; 1995b; 2001, p. 7; Kingstone 2000; Mainwaring 1997, p. 55; Mainwaring and Scully 1995; Mainwaring and Shugart 1997; Power 1998; Weyland 1996b.
[111] Abrucio and Samuels 1997, p. 141; Ames 1994; Samuels 2000; 2003.

For some scholars, these institutional features have stymied pension reform in Brazil.[112] Other scholars, however, challenge this view.[113] For Figuereido and Limongi, party leaders and executives possess institutional resources that allow them to command partisan cooperation on important reform issues.[114] Melo has argued, moreover, that the challenges to reform depend more on the interests and popularity of different issues than on Brazil's legislative and electoral institutions.[115] In the case of the pension reforms, as we will see, however, the obstacles to reform also vary *within* a given issue area, depending heavily on the perceptibility of the losses imposed by the reform.

The design of electoral and legislative rules in Brazil certainly narrows the reach of institutional authority that national political leaders may use to command legislators to support loss-imposing reform. They do not, however, condemn such reforms to failure. Rather, such possibilities have varied with the ability of political leaders to enhance the distributive appeal of the reform – through the use of rhetoric and compensation. The deep unpopularity of pension reform in Brazil, however, put firm limits on both strategies. Even though Lula enjoyed critical partisan advantages over Cardoso to enhance the distributive appearance of his pension reform amendment, both presidents had to employ costly pork-barrel compensation and compromise in order to build legislative supermajorities behind loss-imposing constitutional amendments.

The 1998 Pension Reform Amendment

When President Fernando Henrique Cardoso took office in January 1995, his Social Democratic Party (Partido da Social Democracia Brasiliera, PSDB) held just 12 percent of the seats in the Chamber of Deputies and 14 percent of the seats in the Senate. The Social Democrats allied with the conservative Liberal Front Party (Partido da Frente Liberal, PFL), and with the center-right Brazilian Labor Party (Partido Trabalhista Brasileiro, PTB.) Because this coalition held only 183 of the 513 seats in the Chamber of Deputies, far short of the 308 votes (three-fifths majority) needed to pass a constitutional amendment, Cardoso reached out to the "catch-all" Democratic Movement Party (Partido do Movimento Democrático Brasileiro, PMDB) and the Progressive Party (Partido Progressista Brasileiro, PPB) to expand the size of his governing coalition to 377 seats, or 73 percent of the Chamber of Deputies. This majority grew further in the 1996 midterm elections to 77 percent of the Chamber seats. Although Cardoso controlled a large majority of seats in the lower house, this majority power did not assure passage of his pension reform amendment.

In March 1995, President Cardoso sent to the National Congress his ambitious pension reform amendment project (PEC-33). As we have seen, the biggest

---

[112] Kay 1999; Madrid 2003.
[113] Meneguello 1998; Pereira and Mueller 2000; Weyland 1996b, p. 61.
[114] Figueiredo and Limongi 1998; Limongi and Figueiredo 1995.
[115] Melo 1997; 2004a. Also see Bresser Pereira 2003, p. 99.

potential losers from Cardoso's pension reform amendment were the public sector workers, who were also among the most well-organized and powerful interest groups in the nation. Civil servants enjoy a high level of unionization and are centrally organized under Brazil's largest and most militant labor confederation, the CUT. Civil servant unions also benefit from ample funding and direct access to legislators, which greatly enhance their capacity to exert pressure on the government in support of their cause.[116] Although the main pensioners organization (Confederação Brasileira de Aposentados e Pensionistas, COBAP) also opposed the pension reform, it was poorly funded and weakly organized, and thus was not a dominant actor in the pension reform process in Brazil.

Intense mobilization by the CUT and partisan adversaries of the reform, especially the Workers' Party (PT), nourished broad societal opposition to the pension reform and activated a veto dynamic within the legislature.[117] President Cardoso sought to neutralize early opposition to the reform by reaching out to the leaders of the main labor confederations. The Cardoso government signed an accord with leaders of the three labor confederations (CUT, Confederação Geral dos Trabalhadores, and Força Sindical) in 1995 endorsing the broad principles and objectives of the reform.[118] However, the civil servant unions, as the largest sector of the CUT, rejected the accord and launched a massive campaign opposing the pension reform, placing strong pressure on the CUT leadership to back out. By the end of 1995, the CUT president Vicente Paulo da Silva relented to this pressure and withdrew his support for the pension reform. The civil servants thus activated a veto logic even outside of the legislative chambers.

Public sector opposition to Cardoso's pension reform was also felt within the National Congress. As the proposed amendment came before the Chamber of Deputies in early 1996, the CUT led demonstrations against the reform that were cited as the "decisive element in the government's defeat."[119] With local elections on the horizon that year, union mobilization cast a pall over the pension reform debate by bringing widespread attention to the loss-imposing nature of the reform. The Força Sindical, which represented private sector workers, also withdrew support for Cardoso's pension reform and joined the CUT in protests against the reform as the disfigured proposal moved to the National Senate in early 1997. Unions kept up the pressure as metallurgists staged protests in their home states and organized caravans to protest the pension reform in Brasília.[120]

Opponents of the pension reform further elevated its political cost by naming the legislators who voted for the measure on billboards and in other media,

---

[116] The unions enjoyed financing from automatic deductions from worker payroll. NEPP 1998.
[117] "Previdência, misério para deputados" 1998.
[118] "O acordo da previdência" 1996.
[119] "Brazil: Congress Double Whammy Knocks Government for Six" 1996.
[120] "CUT e Força Sindical se unem contra reforma" 1995.

and labeling them "traitors" to the nation.[121] As Cardoso faced a series of defeats in the early votes on the pension reform, political columnists noted the force of these opposition strategies. One editorial observed, "In politics, they can ask for anything, except to work against your electoral survival. The social security reform, intensely opposed by the corporative interests, interferes with this fundamental rule. It touches on the most delicate themes that threaten a large portion of the population.... The politicians refuse to vote for it and have their name exposed on the billboards and streets in the coming electoral campaign."[122] Given the partisan structure of the political conflict – a center-right government opposed by a left-labor alliance – it became extremely difficult for Cardoso to credibly use political rhetoric to redefine the pension reform as a distributive reform, rather than a loss-imposing measure.

While organized labor took to the streets to protest the reform, Cardoso's partisan adversaries, led by the Workers' Party, or PT, activated a veto dynamic in the legislature by forcing roll-call votes on the most controversial, loss-imposing provisions of the pension reform. They did so through the use of a legislative procedure that separates individual provisions of the constitutional amendment for roll-call votes called a *Destaque para Votação em Separado*, or DVS. Using this technique, the PT exploited the reliance of individual legislators on their name recognition by making visible the position of each deputy on the most contentious provisions of the amendment.[123] And given the unpopularity of the pension reform, the DVS became a powerful weapon through which Cardoso's partisan rivals, especially the PT, could threaten immense political costs for legislators who supported the pension reform.

Legislating Retrenchment within a Veto Dynamic

Cardoso's pension reform amendment suffered a significant setback in the constitutional review committee (CCJ), its first stopping point in the Chamber of Deputies, where it was cleaved into four parts and laden with more than 400 amendments.[124] Even Cardoso's party leaders were reluctant to express support for the reform. The amendment's rapporteur distanced himself from the government by publicly charging Cardoso with asking for a blank check from Congress. For Bresser Pereira, the rapporteur's response was predictable, given the unpopularity of the reform, for the legislator had "decided to do what was obvious to him and to most of his colleagues in Parliament: he 'signed' the check, that is, he disfigured the reform, reintroducing into the Constitutional text all the privileges that the reform had intended to eliminate."[125] When the basic text of the project was approved by the Chamber of Deputies in late

[121] Crusius 1999; Madeira 1999.
[122] "Erro de cálculo" 1998.
[123] The defeat of the DVS would allow the detached provision to remain in the text of the bill.
[124] NEPP 1998, pp. 141–2.
[125] Bresser Pereira 2003. Also see Madeira 1999; NEPP 1998, p. 143; Oliveira 1999.

1996, it bore little resemblance to the government's original proposal; it not only failed to remove most of the benefit rules from the Constitution, but it also *added* new guarantees and privileges.[126]

In early 1997, the amendment was taken up by the National Senate where Cardoso enjoyed a larger legislative coalition and stronger support for the reform. Indeed, with eight-year terms, senators in Brazil enjoy greater latitude from public opinion, and thus faced a lower electoral cost for supporting the pension legislation.[127] The Senate restored many of Cardoso's original proposals to the amendment, which was returned for approval by the Chamber of Deputies in the end of 1997 and was to be taken up in early 1998. Once again, upon arriving in the Chamber of Deputies, the most controversial provisions were detached in committee for separate roll-call votes using the DVS procedure.[128] Because 1998 was again an election year, this tactic proved highly effective in raising the political cost of voting for the reform.

Despite this electoral pressure, intense lobbying and sometimes-violent demonstrations by public sector workers, President Cardoso secured important victories on key provisions of the amendment. These victories allowed the Chamber of Deputies to approve the basic text of the pension reform amendment before the end of the congressional session and before their states' party conventions in mid-1998. However, these votes came at a high price. Without the advantages of partisan credibility or the levers of institutional authority with which to command the cooperation party allies, Cardoso was obliged to exchange costly pork-barrel provisions for votes on the reform.

Nevertheless, through such exchanges Cardoso built oversized majorities behind the establishment of a minimum retirement age for civil servants and the change from time-of-service to a time–of-contribution rule, which required workers to contribute for thirty-five years (thirty years for women) in order to claim a retirement pension. Even before the most controversial votes were taken, the government was estimated to have spent between US$16 million and 32 million to gain the support of resistant deputies *within* the governing bloc.[129] For some votes, resources were allocated to the leaders of the allied parties who would apportion them within their party blocs to reward the more loyal members. In other cases, legislators negotiated in multiparty blocs organized by state or sector. The price demanded by legislators for their support, and the effectiveness of such compensatory exchanges, however, depended on the unpopularity of the issue at hand.

For the most controversial votes, pork-barrel compensation proved insufficient to neutralize the political costs of support for the reform. On one particularly contentious vote to remove the constitutional guarantee for civil servants

---

[126] Fleischer 1998, pp. 128–9; Kliass 1999.
[127] NEPP 1998, p. 148; Veras 1999.
[128] These included a tax on high-income public sector pensions, the creation of a cap on public sector benefits, the establishment of minimum retirement ages for public and private sector pensions, and the elimination of privileged pension regimes for specific occupations.
[129] "Meia-sola" 1998, p. 23.

of a pension equal to 100 percent of their gross final salaries, President Cardoso sent a team from the finance ministry along with the President of the Federal Savings Bank (Caixa Econômica Federal) to the Chamber of Deputies to negotiate with party leaders in the governing bloc. The government offered to release US$117 million in appropriations from the Federal Savings Bank, and US$96 million from the finance ministry secretary of regional policy to fund municipal improvement projects that had been negotiated in accords over earlier votes in exchange for the promise of support on this provision. The negotiations among executive-branch reformers, party leaders, and state delegations lasted the entire day prior to the vote, as did forceful lobbying efforts by the opposition judicial magistrates, who, as the most highly paid civil servants, stood to lose the most in this provision. Ultimately, the face-to-face lobbying by the judges, who promised to "create chaos in the next election" if the provision were passed, proved sufficient to defeat the measure in the Chamber of Deputies.[130]

A provision to tax high-income public sector pensions also was taken up by the Chamber of Deputies in 1998. Again, however, this measure proved so unpopular that pork-barrel exchanges could not compensate legislators for the electoral risks associated with support for the reform. Indeed, the tax provision had been defeated during the amendment's first turn through the Chamber of Deputies but was restored in the Senate the previous year. President Cardoso saw the pension tax as a vital means to reduce the yawning pension system deficit. Although just a fraction of retired civil servants would be affected by the measure, it was deeply unpopular, as opponents seized upon it as a symbol of the government's effort to abolish workers' pension rights. As Social Security Minister Waldek Ornélas explained in an interview, "For society, they never understood the issues because these were never separated and made clear. They thought of the public sector tax for retirees as if this meant the private sector would have to pay as well."[131] This negative public sentiment translated directly into broad legislative hostility toward the tax. In a survey of legislators' attitudes toward the pension reform, for instance, nearly 87 percent of deputies expressed opposition to the tax.[132] Responses to this survey in Table 7.3 lay bare the depth of legislators' antagonism toward the amendment. Not surprisingly, the tax was resoundingly defeated on the DVS vote.

With neither the partisan credibility to redefine the pension reform's distributive nature nor the institutional authority to command the cooperation of his allies, Cardoso was forced to use distributive exchange to build legislative support for his reform. For very unpopular measures, however, even pork-barrel politics could not overcome the veto logic activated by the reform's opponents. Cardoso was thus obliged to compromise the most unpopular

[130] "Câmara derruba redutor para pensão de servidores" 1998.
[131] Interview with Waldek Ornélas.
[132] DIAP 1998, p. 8.

TABLE 7.3. *DIAP Survey on Pension Reform Amendment in the Brazilian Chamber of Deputies, January 20–February 5, 1998*

View that Legislators Have of the Pension Reform	Total	Government Coalition (%)						Opposition (%)					
		PSDB	PMDB	PFL	PTB	PPB	PT	PDT	PCdoB	PPS	PSB	PL
(1) Urgent	29.2	50.9	28.9	55.6	37.5	15.4	–	–	–	–	–	40
(2) Best reform possible	11.2	12.7	8.9	19	12.5	23.1	–	5.6	–	–	–	20
(3) Unnecessary and merely a fiscal adjustment	17.9	1.8	13.3	–	6.3	10.3	51.2	41.2	87.5	–	60	20
(4) Needing further discussion; should delay for next Congress	36.2	27.3	40	23.8	43.8	43.6	46.5	47.1	12.5	85.7	20	40
Number of deputies interviewed	312	55	45	63	16	39	43	17	8	7	10	5

[a] Excludes PSD, PTSU, PRONA, and PMN of which only one legislator each was interviewed.

provisions of his pension reform while postponing other critical votes until after the October 1998 election.

Shifting the Legislative Dynamic: External Corroboration

In late 1998, the political dynamic in Brazil shifted in such a way that enhanced the resources available to President Cardoso to increase the distributive tendency of his pension reform and claim critical victories. This change resulted first from the outcome of the October election, which offered Cardoso new compensatory resources with which to bargain legislative support. It also dampened electoral pressures on legislators. The political dynamic also shifted as a result of intensifying international economic pressure, which corroborated Cardoso's claims of the urgency of reform. Even with the enhanced credibility and compensatory resources, however, important provisions in Cardoso's pension amendment fell to defeat.

Compensatory Resources

In the October 1998 general election, President Cardoso won a clear first-round victory over his rival, Luiz Inácio Lula da Silva, with 53.4 percent of the vote. His reelection brought an important, but temporary, shift in power from the legislative to the executive branch following the election. Having received a strong popular endorsement of his mandate, Cardoso faced a lame-duck congress that included a substantial number of legislators who had recently lost their own bids for reelection. The consequence was to make compensatory exchange an effective means of gaining cooperation on the final votes on the pension reform.

The completion of the electoral cycle also dampened the political threats to legislators for supporting the pension reform, making it once again possible for Cardoso to use pork-barrel exchange to build voting majorities behind key provisions of his amendment. Legislators did not hesitate to demand these resources. In one instance, a bloc of 178 deputies representing rural states threatened to deny quorum unless the government conceded an array of lucrative appropriations for their constituents.[133] In negotiations with the rural bloc deputies, the Cardoso government promised more than US\$580 million in benefits for these legislators in return for quorum and for support on key provisions of the amendment.

In addition to pork-barrel appropriations, a prevalent currency of political negotiation throughout the reform process in Brazil had been the exchange of votes for jobs and other political favors.[134] This type of wheeling and dealing

---

[133] "Deputados da base aliada cobram caro para ajudar a dar quorum ao Governo" 1998; "Planalto negocia favores e derruba destaque" 1998.
[134] Executives in Brazil have the power to make broad political appointments. Fleischer 1995, p. 12.

(*troca-troca*), while costly, allowed the government to turn what is often considered a pathology of the Brazilian legislature – the narrow time horizons and
concern for securing particularistic legislation – into an opportunity to build
legislative majorities behind meaningful institutional reform.[135] With nearly
half (45 percent) of the legislators in the Chamber of Deputies having lost their
seats in the 1998 election, the exchange of jobs for votes – the "jobs game"
(*jogo do cargo*) – became an effective bargaining tool in the final votes on
the amendment. A newspaper, for instance, described the importance of jobs
as the currency of cooperation on one vote in November 1998, reporting that
"the release of budget funds, used as a bargaining tool in most other votes on
the social security reform, was not the most valued currency of trade yester-
day."[136] In one vote that was marked by a rare show of allied cooperation, 127
of the 157 allied deputies who did not win reelection voted with the government
to maintain the provision establishing a minimum retirement age (53 for men
and 48 for women) and time of contribution (35 years for men and 30 years
for women) for civil servants, which had been challenged through DVS.[137] The
personalism that once seemed to present insuperable obstacles to institutional
change thus receded dramatically in importance following the 1998 election.

Enhanced Credibility

Cardoso's efforts to redefine his pension amendment as a loss-avoiding measure
also became more effective in late 1998 following an international economic
crisis. The crisis was sparked by Russia's sovereign default in August 1998.
Investors who had thought that Russia was "too big to fail" began to fear that
Brazil was next and withdrew more than US$25 billion from the country in
the end of August. The crisis had a profound effect on politicians in Brazil,
who suddenly began to perceive that the risk of hyperinflation was real if the
country failed to stem the crisis by approving Cardoso's reforms.[138]

Cardoso took advantage of this context to rhetorically link the approval
of his pension reform to the avoidance of major crisis – and thus a benefit
for the nation. He called on legislators to "think in the national interest"
and pass the pension reform.[139] Cardoso spoke of the country as being at
an historic moment of opportunity, between solidifying stability and risking a
return to chaos. "Without the reforms," he argued, "Congress will be impeding
the future of the Brazilian people"[140] Cardoso's cabinet ministers also linked
the pension reform and the crisis to galvanize support for the reform. As
Social Security Minister Ornélas explained, it was not the accord with the

[135] Ames 2002, p. 209. See also Cox and McCubbins 1993.
[136] "Aliados comemoram baixos indices de dissidencia na votação das mudancas" 1998.
[137] "Governo planeja 2a etapa da reforma" 1998, p. 9.
[138] Interview with José Cechín.
[139] "FH usa crise nas bolsas para cobrar reformas" 1997.
[140] "Cardoso Again Criticizes Congress for Delay in Reforms" 1997.

International Monetary Fund that provided leverage for the government to gather support for the reform, "[b]ut we did use the context of the crisis itself; the vulnerability of the country, the vulnerability of the economy, and showing that this was brought on by the pension system."[141] Similarly, the leader of the Social Democratic Party (PSDB) in the Chamber of Deputies described the pension reform vote as "a signal to international markets that measures are being taken to prevent a currency crisis."[142]

Cardoso's rhetoric about the necessity of the reform thus only gained force when it was corroborated by the emergence of the currency crisis. Indeed, the pension reform figured prominently in negotiations with the IMF, with which the Brazilian government signed a US $41.5 billion emergency loan agreement in October 1998. The loan was intended to regain market confidence and stem capital flight. In it, the Brazilian government committed to achieving a primary fiscal surplus by the end of 1999. And since the pension system was the largest contributor to the fiscal deficit, the passage of the pension reform amendment came to be viewed by market actors as a portent of the government's ability to achieve its fiscal targets. Indeed, the social security deficit was mentioned in almost all of the press coverage of the economic crisis. With this international pressure came a marked shift in the tone of the legislative conflict over the pension reform. Whereas the term "traitor" had previously been applied to legislators who had voted *for* the pension reform, the crisis brought a reversal: Those who voted against the pension reform became traitors of the nation.[143] The importance of the pension reform to the country's economic stability was further endorsed by the gyrations of the São Paulo stock exchange that accompanied the fate of the pension reform; the market rallied after successful votes and plunged in the wake of government defeats.

Despite the victories achieved with Cardoso's enhanced bargaining leverage, the deep unpopularity of the reform meant that rhetoric and compensatory exchange were insufficient to win over the most truculent opponents on key provisions of the pension reform. The civil service pension tax, for instance, fell to defeat for the fourth time in November 1998, as did a provision to cap public sector pensions at the same level as private sector (approximately US$600). Without these provisions, Cardoso's pension reform amendment was promulgated on December 15, 1998, as Constitutional Amendment 20. Even though it fell short of the government's ambitious goals, the 1998 constitutional amendment brought significant changes in the terms on which citizens could gain access to old age pensions and projected financial savings of US$3.85 billion over the next year alone.[144] Nevertheless, considerable privileges remained in place, perpetuating several highly regressive and deficitary features of the pension institution.

[141] Ornélas 1999.
[142] Quote by Aécio Neves (PSDB), in "Brazil: Austerity Package Faces Tough Passage" 1998.
[143] Melo 2003, p. 224.
[144] Ministério da Previdência Social 1999, p. 4.

Resurgent Crisis

International economic pressure did not recede following the approval of the pension reform amendment, prompting President Cardoso to convene a special session of the National Congress in January 1999. The Congress was to consider again the most controversial provisions of the reform, which were also those that were expected to have the greatest impact on the pension system deficit. Chief among these was the tax on high-income civil service pensions. Before the special session began in January, market pressures came to a head when the governor of the state of Minas Gerais declared a moratorium on state debts owed to the national government. The moratorium set off a speculative attack on the currency that forced the government to allow the real – long managed in a tight link to the dollar – to float freely on global currency markets. The result was a sharp devaluation of the real as capital was flowing out of Brazil at a rate of about US$1 billion per day in the final two weeks of January.[145]

The devaluation rattled the Brazilian politicians, offering greater leverage to President Cardoso in his negotiations with the Congress. This is because the devaluation affected *all* of society by vastly raising import prices and sparking a generalized inflation that immediately reduced living standards. Devaluation became the most credible indication yet that a return to the inflationary past was possible, and that it could result from failure to act on the pension reform. Whereas previously most citizens shared the common prospect of losses *imposed* by the reform, the renewed threat of inflation became the common enemy; its circumvention through pension reform would hold the prospect of *avoiding* more significant costs of a return to hyperinflation. The devaluation was also politically consequential because the strong currency had become a symbol of the country's economic stability. Investor confidence in the real had rested heavily on the government's commitment to keeping the currency closely linked to the dollar. As one newspaper reported, "More important than any savings, however, was the message that the [pension reform] bill's approval would send to international investors."[146]

The Cardoso government did not miss the opportunity to use the crisis to demand legislative cooperation on the final pension reform provisions.[147] The President of the Chamber of Deputies, Michel Temer (PSDB), put the pension reform's importance in the starkest of terms, "We are talking about the future of the country here."[148] Other deputies emphasized the symbolic importance of the measure: "This shows the Brazilian government's absolute commitment to cutting the budget deficit. It sends the clearest sign we can to the international community about how serious Brazil is about taking the necessary steps

---

[145] Barclays Bank 1999, p. 37.
[146] "Brazil's Congress to Vote on Key Economic Reform Measure" 1999.
[147] "Fernando Henrique vai dizer que a superação da crise depende da votação dessa proposta" 1999; Ornélas 1999.
[148] "Brazil Appears Headed toward Some Stability" 1999, p. B11.

to get out of this crisis."[149] The crisis also provided critics of the government with an opportunity to shift blame for voting for the reform. As the prominent PPD deputy and former finance minister Antônio Delfim Netto argued, "Now I have to vote in favor because of that irresponsible commitment that the government signed with the IMF. It's a brutality to have to vote this way. But it is a question of a greater force. We have no other alternative. The consequences of a defeat would be even worse."[150] Despite a forceful lobbying effort by high-income civil servants, the pension tax was approved on January 20, providing an estimated US$ 2.6 billion in additional revenue for the state pension system and sending the São Paulo stock market's Bovespa index up nearly 4 percent.[151]

The vote on the pension tax was significant not only because this provision had been defeated four previous times, but also because the version that was approved in January 1999 was *even more restrictive* than the earlier versions. It was won in large measure because the shift in economic conditions allowed the government to neutralize the veto dynamic around the pension reform. Evidence of this shift toward a distributive logic is apparent from the fact that Cardoso secured an oversized majority to support this loss-imposing bill, winning 334 votes where only 308 were needed to pass the bill in the Chamber of Deputies. The political obstacles to reform that repeatedly proved insuperable thus gave way to an oversized vote in favor of a highly visible loss-imposing measure of the reform.

Restructuring the Private Sector Pension Regime

With the approval of the 1998 constitutional amendment, President Cardoso moved immediately to the second stage of his pension reform: redesigning the private sector pension system through ordinary law. As we saw in Chapter 5, Cardoso's technocratic reform team drew up a proposal to restructure the private sector pension system while legislative conflict over the constitutional amendment was still in progress. Given the force of public sector opposition to that amendment, Cardoso chose to focus the second stage of reform only on the private sector pension system in order to assure its rapid sanction. The proposed reform, which was sent to the National Congress in mid-1999, would create a pension system based on notional individual accounts that linked old age benefits closely to each worker's lifetime contributions and life expectancy. It did so, as we saw in Chapter 5, by means of a new benefit formula called the "social security factor" (*fator previdenciário*). Although the notional account scheme mimicked many features of pension privatization, such as the transfer of important demographic and income risks and costs to individuals, it did not

---

[149] Quote by Fabio Feldmann in "Brazilian House Adopts Reform Bill; Pension Measure Seen as Crucial to Stabilizing Nation's Economy" 1999.
[150] Quote by Antônio Delfim Netto in "Inativos: a hora da decisão" 1999.
[151] "Brazil's Chamber of Deputies Approves Highly Unpopular Key Tax" 1999.

privatize.[152] Rather, it sought to restore financial and actuarial balance to the pension system while maintaining public management of old age pension funds and financing benefits on a pay-as-you-go basis.

The absence of a privatization element in Cardoso's 1999 pension reform meant that like the 1998 amendment, this measure also had only one relevant political dimension: that of loss imposition. However, unlike the 1998 amendment, the private sector reform had the advantage that its loss-imposing nature was relatively opaque. Indeed, the vague concept of a social security factor offered little in the way of straightforward interpretation as a gain or loss. In the face of such lack of clarity, however, it was the reform's opponents that held the credibility advantage in interpreting the measure as a loss-imposing one.

Indeed, any credibility that Cardoso gained during the January currency crisis had largely dissipated by August of 1999 when he sent the pension reform proposal to the National Congress. The easing of economic pressures also brought the resurgence of deep schisms within the governing coalition, expanding the range of distinct actors with whom Cardoso would have to negotiate to pass his reform even by a simple majority. Allied party leaders who had expended tremendous political capital to support the constitutional amendment were reluctant to countenance further political costs and thus gave the proposal a cool reception.

The government sought to counter this political wariness by defining the reform in distributive terms – as a new benefit for workers. Social Security Minister Ornélas argued, for instance, that by tying benefits to life expectancy at retirement, the measure represented a "bonus" for workers who delayed retirement. Opponents countered that the reform would cut benefits for most workers. Two of the major union confederations in Brazil, the CUT and Força Sindical, denounced the reform as an unjust bow to the IMF.[153] The Workers' Party (PT), for its part, issued a study projecting that the government's pension reform proposal would cut pension benefits up to 55 percent.[154] Because these opponents enjoyed important credibility advantages vis-à-vis Cardoso on the issue of social security, their condemnation provoked many legislators to take defensive postures against the reform. As one newspaper reported, "Although [allied party leaders] agree with the concession of a bonus for workers that continue in the labor market beyond the normal time to gain a pension, legislators caution that they are not going to support any measure that causes further losses to retirees."[155] As media reports increasingly labeled the government's pension reform proposal as a "reduction" in benefits, a veto dynamic was activated around the reform. The task of building even a simple majority behind the reform thus was greatly complicated.

---

[152] Melo 2004a; Pinhiero and Vieira 2000.
[153] "CUT quer derrotar proposta no plenário" 1999.
[154] "Projeto pode ser alterado para evitar nova derrota" 1999.
[155] "Redutor sem chance de passar" 1999.

A critical sticking point for legislators was the immediate implementation of benefit cuts, which the government needed to achieve its end-of-year fiscal targets. Immediate implementation made the reform much more politically costly, however, because benefit cuts were more perceptible and direct. Given the shadow of municipal elections in late 1999, legislators in the National Congress felt strong pressure from local political leaders to avoid imposing losses on their constituents.[156] Undaunted, the government worked strenuously to combat the image of the reform as a loss-imposing measure. "No one loses," Social Security Minister Ornélas argued in an interview with the prominent newspaper *O Estado de São Paulo*.[157] The new benefit rule, Ornélas asserted, would advantage all workers by offering a greater pension to those who contribute for a longer period of time.

Despite the optimistic framing, the government's rhetoric failed to gain traction. Indeed, a national public opinion survey found that the pension reform proposal was opposed by 58 percent of the population, who most strongly disapproved of the tight link between pension benefits and retirement age.[158] With the failure of efforts to dampen the perception of losses, Cardoso was forced to make compromises to mitigate the reform's true redistributive impact. He did so first by delaying the implementation of the new pension rules. He also allowed workers who retire under the age pension (who are typically lower-income) to choose the better of the rules under the new regime – the social security factor – or the benefit rules of the 1998 constitutional amendment.[159] Despite these compromises, the unpopularity of the measure left government allies wary of supporting the reform.[160]

The Specter of Crisis, Again
Just as the prospects for winning support for the divisive pension reform became bleak, the political tide shifted in favor of the government. In late September, Brazil's Supreme Court (Supremo Tribunal Federal) struck down the tax on civil service pensions that had been approved earlier that year, calling it unconstitutional. The defeat of the tax meant that the government would have to make up approximately US\$1.3 billion to 2.3 billion in revenue from other sources to meet its fiscal targets. And with the deficit in the public sector pension system already projected to reach US\$11.1 billion in 1999, news of the court decision sent stock markets in Brazil tumbling while the real fell sharply against the dollar.[161]

In the context of the economic panic, Cardoso and his social security minister invoked the urgency and necessity of their pension reform to spare Brazil

---

[156] "Redutor sem chance de passar" 1999.
[157] "Para Ornélas, novas regras vão beneficiar maioria" 1999.
[158] "Pension Law Change Rejected by 58%, According to CNT/Vox Populi Survey" 1999.
[159] "Planalto faz concessão no cálculo de benefício para aprovar Previdência" 1999.
[160] "Manobra de aliados abre caminho para mudança na aposentadoria" 1999.
[161] "Mercado financeiro – Bovespa tem perda de 4,9% na semana" 1999; "Nova lei da Previdência Social não resolve déficit" 1999.

from a return to economic chaos. Social Security Minister Ornélas, for instance, launched a media campaign portraying the pension system as a "time-bomb" that needed to be defused before causing terrible destruction.[162] He warned that the private sector pension system (INSS) deficit, which was on track to reach 1.1 percent of GDP by the end of 1999, would balloon to 2.4 percent of GDP by 2020 without reform.[163] This time, the government admonitions of the loss-avoiding nature of the reform were persuasive, and even the forceful mobilization by the PT and labor unions failed to undermine the government's claims.[164] When the pension reform came to a vote, it passed with an over-whelming 66 percent of the vote in the Chamber of Deputies and 68 percent of the votes in the Senate – well above 51 percent of the votes required to enact the 1999 legislation.[165] With the news of the reform's impending passage the São Paulo stock index jumped nearly 4 percent.[166] The 1999 pension reform law was expected to have a significant effect on the pension system deficit, reducing it by 2 percent of GDP (from 5 to 3 percent).[167]

The oversized majority that Cardoso gathered behind the reform, moreover, provides important evidence of the highly conditional ability of the government to induce a distributive logic around loss-imposing reform. Again, putatively immovable obstacles gave way to reform as the perception of the measure as one that imposed losses shifted toward one that could *avoid* loss, therein offering legislators something for which to claim credit. Nevertheless, the political conflict to win the two pension reforms exacted a heavy political cost of President Cardoso in terms of public opinion. Having exhausted his political capital advancing his 1998 and 1999 reforms, Cardoso was unable to move forward any further reform of the nation's financially hemorrhaging pension system. The task of reforming the regressive and costly public sector pension system thus would fall to Cardoso's successor and longtime political adversary, Luiz Inácio Lula da Silva.

Lula's Constitutional Amendment

In his inaugural address on January 2, 2003, President Lula da Silva of the PT issued a broad call for structural transformation in Brazil. "The people of Brazil deeply desire change," he argued, laying out his plans to forge a new path toward social justice, growth and economic independence.[168] By the end of his first year in office, Lula would make good on a key component of this

---

[162] Quote from Dacísio Perondi (PMDD-RS) in "A nova matemática do INSS" 1999.
[163] "Nova lei da Previdência Social não resolve déficit" 1999.
[164] "Dentro de alguns dias quando o Governo enviar ao Congresso as medidas compensatórias vamos reconquistar a credibilidade diz Amadeo" 1999; "Previdência – Ornélas panfleta contra CUT para aprovar projeto" 1999.
[165] "A nova matemática do INSS" 1999; "Senado aprova novo cálculo da Previdência" 1999.
[166] "Brazil, Oct '99: Economic/Financial Update" 1999.
[167] Melo 2003, p. 22.
[168] "Carta ao Povo Brasileiro" 2003.

platform by signing into law a constitutional amendment that curtailed important privileges in Brazil's public sector pension system. Although most of the
revisions would come into effect only for new entrants into the public sector,
the amendment brought a profound change in the structure of that regime by
establishing a ceiling on defined-benefit pension benefits equal to that of the private sector pensions and establishing a defined-contribution "complementary"
pension plan for savings above that level. The amendment also reinstated the
tax on higher-income civil servant pensions and delinked pension benefits for
active and retired civil servants. In short, the 2003 reform dramatically revised
the deeply entrenched and seemingly untouchable public sector pension system in Brazil. By maintaining the basic risk-pooling design of the institution,
however, Lula's reform did not constitute a path departure for that system.

This reform was striking nevertheless for the magnitude of losses it imposed
as much as for the swiftness of its approval: Lula won the sanction of this
constitutional amendment in just eight months – a sharp contrast to the nearly
four years that Cardoso fought to enact his amendment. Critically, both reforms
were advanced under the same rules of the game – Brazil's notoriously fractured
and personalistic legislature. Although Lula enjoyed the support of the singular
highly institutionalized and disciplined party in Brazil, his PT held just 18
percent of the seats in the Chamber of Deputies and 17 percent of the seats in
the Senate. The disciplined characteristic of the PT thus cannot account for the
success of Lula's pension reform amendment. Indeed, the cooperation of the
other 40 percent of the National Congress was far from assured.

Lula's partisan orientation proved to be an advantage in his efforts to
define the 2003 pension amendment in distributive terms; nevertheless, he faced
the strong resistance and counterframing by civil servant unions. To build the
requisite supermajorities to sanction his amendment, Lula made extensive use
of institutional authority – not that of national congressional leaders, but rather
of Brazil's governors – as well as pork-barrel exchange and programmatic
compromise. These strategies of enhancing the distributive tendency of the
reform thus were strikingly similar to those employed by Cardoso. With a
more favorable partisan structure of political conflict, however, Lula could
enact his constitutional amendment at a much lower political and financial
price than Cardoso could.

As a long-time union leader and champion of social justice issues, Lula
enjoyed substantial credibility to frame his pension reform amendment in distributive terms, and to portray it as necessary, rather than ideologically motivated.[169] In the legislature, moreover, the governing PT faced two center-right
opposition parties (PSDB and PFL) that had spent the better part of the previous decade advancing the reform that now rested in Lula's hands. The PT's
alliance with the CUT, which included civil servants, also lent credibility to
Lula's claims about the necessity of reform, as losses imposed by the measure
fell directly on the party's core constituency.

---

[169] Alston et al. 2004, p. 99.

Despite the CUT's alliance with the PT, the labor confederation maintained full organizational autonomy from its partisan ally. The relationship came under great strain on account of the pension reform, however, and labor leaders sought to mediate these tensions by articulating their support for the PT *government* while maintaining firm opposition to Lula's pension reform. Even though the CUT led strikes and marches in Brasília against the amendment, union leaders accepted Lula's invitation to negotiate the terms of the reform. This decision evoked bitter criticism from the public sector unions who condemned the "business unionism" of the CUT leadership. As in Argentina, union leaders extracted important compromises in the terms of the reform. They did so, moreover, after staking out an early position against the reform, raising the cost of building legislative majorities behind it.

Institutional Authority

Lula enjoyed the support of the highly disciplined Workers' Party, whose leaders command "near total tutelage" over its legislative delegation – a stark anomaly in Brazil's notoriously inchoate party system.[170] Once a position is reached through internal party vote and the question is "closed," the PT's congressional delegation is obliged to follow the position selected in that vote.[171] With less than a fifth of the seats in the Congress, however, PT leaders could not deliver alone the three-fifths majority required to sanction the amendment. To expand his authority, Lula called upon state governors to support his pension reform. State governors are critical actors in Brazil's political party system.[172] Nominations for all offices (except the president and local government) are decided in state-level conventions, giving national legislators strong incentives to ally with state-level gubernatorial candidates who typically control much stronger and broader clientelistic networks than even the president.[173] With the support of the governors, Lula could vastly expand the scope of legislative cooperation that could be won through the exercise of authority, rather than compromise or exchange.

Fortunately for Lula, Brazil's governors had a strong material interest in seeing the approval of the 2003 pension reform, for they would also benefit financially from provisions such as the tax on public sector pensions.[174] Lula thus was able to sign an accord with all twenty-seven state governors, who pledged support for the amendment.[175] Nevertheless, the measure remained unpopular, leading governors to demand some compensation in exchange for

---

[170] Quote from Fleischer 1995, p. 14; also see Ames 2002, p. 200; Keck 1992; Mainwaring 1992, p. 690.

[171] Although the PT has divergent currents *(tendências)* that often clash forcefully in these internal deliberations, the party almost always votes in unity. Nylen 2000, p. 139; Keck 1992, pp. 110–20.

[172] Ames 1994; Samuels 2000; 2003.

[173] Abrucio and Samuels 1997, p. 141; Samuels 2000, pp. 241–3.

[174] "O Poder dos Governos" 2003.

[175] "PT bancará Lula, diz Genoino sobre inativos" 2003.

their support. Lula offered in return to include favorable provisions for the states in a second amendment, on tax reform, that was being considered alongside the pension amendment.[176] The multiparty nature of the governors' accord was significant, for it spread responsibility for the pension reform across a range of parties. It also offered Lula an important source of institutional leverage with which to enforce the cooperation of reluctant legislators. For instance, when a deputy from the PFL, José Carlos Aleluia, challenged the tax on civil servant pensions, the PT president José Genoino responded by reminding him of the multiparty nature of the governors' accord, which included powerful PFL governors. "There are just four PT governors. All twenty-seven signed a pact on the points [of the reform], in other words, it is a combined game, and we are not going to be put on the defensive on this question." Genoino continued, "I said to Aleluia, 'How are you going to vote against [the tax on civil service pensions] if governor Paulo Souto [PFL, of Bahia] was there and signed the accord?'"[177] By leveraging the institutional power of the governors, Lula thus extended his authority in the legislature and effectively broadened his ability to build voting coalitions behind his reform agenda.

Lula also sought to broaden the social foundations of his coalition prior to sending his pension reform amendment to the National Congress by courting major interest groups that would be affected by his reform agenda. He did so by creating a Council on Social and Economic Development (Conselho de Desenvolvimento Econômico e Social, CDES), which included representatives of business, labor, and other organized interests – particularly civil servants. The CDES produced statements of principle offering broad guidelines for the pension reform. It did not, however, gain the support of the most important group affected by the reform: the civil servants. Public sector unions launched a vigorous countermobilization through direct lobbying, marches, and extensive media campaigns aimed at undermining Lula's pension reform. In early July 2003, a general strike in Brasília brought more than 400,000 civil servants together in a march on the National Congress.[178] Civil servants also attended committee hearings, objecting, waiving banners and calling the politicians "traitors" who spoke in favor of the measure.[179] As the labor mobilization increased, the threat of electoral costs for politicians supporting the measure increased, activating a veto dynamic in the legislature.

In this context the PT came under attack not only from labor but also from partisan allies on the left, revealing deep fissures in the governing coalition. As a result, the opposition PSDB – Cardoso's party, which had led the pension reform effort over the previous decade – signaled that it would not offer unqualified support for the amendment unless the *entire* governing coalition

[176] "Reforma Emperrada" 2003.
[177] José Carlos Aleluia (BA) was the leader of the PFL in the Chamber of Deputies. "PT vai usar acordo para pressionar a oposição" 2003.
[178] "Brazil Strikes Win Rethink on Pensions" 2003.
[179] "Gritos e tumulto na votação" 2003.

supported it. For if there were defections from the governing coalition on the question of pension reform, then PSDB legislators supporting the amendment would be vulnerable to electoral attacks from the left in the next election. Such costs would be mitigated, however, if Lula held together his ever more fragile left-wing coalition. Accordingly, as the first votes on the controversial pension tax came to the floor, the PSDB leader in the Chamber of Deputies warned Lula, "We are not going to be the mortar for the cracks in their coalition by supplying the votes they lack on the tax on the pensions. If they think that they are going to liberate part of the PT [and its allies on the left], to preserve their discourse and later count on us to fill the hole, they are quite mistaken."[180] With Lula's ability to gather a supermajority in the balance, the PSDB became a critical veto player on the pension amendment, conditioning its support on Lula's ability to provide political cover by delivering the cooperation of his large left-wing coalition on the reform.

Strikes against the amendment continued throughout July 2003, which deepened the veto dynamic, spurring government and opposition parties alike to stake out public positions against the reform. As one opposition (PFL) deputy observed, "Everyone thinks that the financial result of the tax on civil servants will not compensate for the political costs."[181] Notably, the PFL (now, Democratas) had advocated strongly for the civil service pension reform during the Cardoso government. Now, with electoral costs rising, Lula was obliged to offer compensatory resources to dampen political costs for legislators of the government and opposition alike that supported his amendment. In exchange for moving the amendment out of committee and to the floor of the Chamber of Deputies, for instance, legislators demanded an array of pork-barrel appropriations, including federal funds to support infrastructure and basic sanitation projects in their states.[182] Even though union mobilization had raised the cost of building a legislative coalition behind the pension reform, it had not made it so costly that pork-barrel compensation could not purchase votes on the reform. This marked a significant contrast from Cardoso's pension reform conflict.

The day on which Lula's pension reform amendment came to a vote in the Chamber of Deputies was marked by dramatic scenes of violence. Civil servants stormed the Congress, breaking more than fifty large-paned glass windows and burning PT flags. Protestors even stormed the Congress to challenge the leaders of the governing coalition. For many of the estimated 50,000 to 60,000 protestors, the pension reform represented a betrayal of the country and embrace of the IMF and bankers. Protestors yelled "Out 'Mister' Silva, come back Lula!" ("*Fora Mister Silva, Volta Lula!*").[183] After fourteen hours of intense negotiations between PT leaders, allies, and opposition legislators,

[180] Quote from Deputy Jutahy Júnior (PSDB) in "Oposição diz não" 2003.
[181] "Falei do assunto durante toda a campanha eleitoral" 2003.
[182] "Estratégia do governo é votar reforma da Previdência nesta terça-feira" 2003; "PMDB e governo negociam cargos no dia da votação" 2003.
[183] "A maior manifestação contra Lula" 2003; "Servidores chegaram a agredir deputado" 2003.

the government won the first vote of approval for the amendment with an over-sized majority of 358 in favor (and 126 against) – fully 50 votes more than were required to pass the amendment. The amendment, critically, retained impor-tant loss-imposing provisions such as a ceiling on civil service pensions equal to that of private sector pensions. The amendment also laid the groundwork for the creation of complementary defined-contribution pension funds for civil ser-vants who wished to save above the new benefit ceiling. The amendment was approved, moreover, with the infamous tax on civil service pensions intact, albeit with a slightly higher ceiling on exempt income than the government originally proposed.

Lula's pension reform amendment passed in the Chamber of Deputies with significant support from the opposition PSDB and PFL parties; however, the governing coalition suffered notable defections, including from the Labor and Communist Parties (PDT and PC do B). Most strikingly, the PT itself sustained an unprecedented eleven defections (eight deputies abstained and three voted against the measure).[184] Those PT defections marked a breach of party rules, obliging PT leaders to initiate disciplinary action. The defections also prompted Lula to take steps to secure a wider margin of victory in the second-round vote in the Chamber of Deputies. To do so, he sought commitments from 380 to 420 legislators to vote in favor of the reform, which was well over the 308 needed to pass the amendment. Much of this support came from a bargain with leaders of the catch-all Party of the Brazilian Democratic Movement (Partido do Movimento Democrático Brasileiro, or PMDB), whose seventy deputies and twenty-two senators could provide Lula with the wide margin of victory he sought. In return for their support, Lula offered leaders of the notoriously incohesive PMDB monetary rewards and secondary administrative positions such as nominations to federal government positions; this was much less than the high-ranking cabinet positions its leaders demanded.[185] Lula also made clear that favors and appropriations were closely tied to legislators' votes, despite the fact that such exchanges had long been strictly condemned by the PT.[186] The task of legislating loss imposition in the context of a veto dynamic thus overwhelmed Lula's capacity to keep his party above "politics as usual" in Brazil.

In addition to the exchange of pork and appointments for votes, Lula com-promised certain loss-imposing provisions of the pension reform in order to quell civil servants' dissent and hold together his fragile coalition. The amend-ment passed in the second round of votes in the Chamber of Deputies by a narrower margin, 346 to 92, albeit still well above the minimum threshold of 308 votes. Although the PSDB supported the reform, the conservative PFL took

---

[184] "Genoino diz que Babá, Luciana Genro e João Fontes estão praticamenta fora do PT" 2003.
[185] "Governo é pressionado a liberar cargos federais para aliados fiéis" 2003.
[186] For instance, Lula was reported to have fired the husband of one PT deputy who abstained from the pension reform vote. "Suplicy critica loteamento de cargos e atuação de Dirceu" 2003; See also Alston et al. 2004, p. 100.

advantage of the souring public opinion to vote against the amendment.[187] The pension reform moved in the end of September 2003 to the National Senate, where it was taken up immediately by the constitutional oversight committee. Although Lula's governing coalition held a fulsome majority in the Senate, the amendment faced strong internal resistance from PT senators.[188] Opposition senators also moved against the amendment, initiating more than 200 DVS in an effort to remove its most contentious provisions. The reading of these DVS provisions alone forced the committee into a sixteen-hour overnight hearing.[189] Had any of the DVS votes been approved, the resulting modification of the amendment would have obliged the government to return it again to the Chamber of Deputies to restart the process. The risk of such a delay was too great for Lula to accept, given the rising specter of local elections in the following year.

Although the amendment was ultimately moved to the floor of the Senate with the support of the PSDB, defections in the committee left Lula two votes short of the forty-nine votes required to sanction the amendment by the full Senate.[190] The impasse threatened Lula's goal of sanctioning the constitutional amendment by the end of 2003. Delay also was financially costly, since the forgone revenue from the tax on civil service pensions was estimated at more than $US90 million per month.[191] And given that Lula had staked his reputation on achieving a fiscal surplus that was greater than the IMF target, his credibility vis-à-vis international market actors was also on the line. This urgency allowed opposition senators, particularly in the PSDB, to extract significant compromises in exchange for support on the pension reform. With their eleven senators, the Social Democrats became pivotal: They could make or break the pension amendment. Well aware of this fact, one PSDB senator observed that "[w]e ran the numbers and without the PSDB there is no reform."[192] In return for their support, PSDB leaders demanded revisions in the amendment for which they could later claim political credit, including revisions that dampened the magnitude of losses on civil servants such as less-harsh transitional rules and delayed implementation of the reform.[193] These compromises cost the government approximately US$ 2.3 billion in 2003, but they secured critical votes on the pension reform. On November 26, the combination of compromise and compensation allowed Lula to gather opposition party votes and

[187] Quote by Roberto Brandt in "Câmara aprova reforma em 2° turno" 2003.
[188] "Aliados, mas nunca se sabe" 2003.
[189] "Após 16 horas, CCJ do Senado aprova reforma da Previdência" 2003.
[190] "PSDB decide apoiar a emenda da Previdência" 2003.
[191] "Atraso na reforma custa R$ 270 milhões" 2003.
[192] Quote by Aécio Neves in "PMDB se rebela e Previdência não vai a votação" 2003.
[193] These were placed in a parallel amendment, which created different pension ceilings for federal, state, and local pension systems, broader exemptions from the pension tax, conditions for maintaining parity in the adjustment of active and retired civil service pensions, higher pension ceilings, and more lenient transitional rules for civil servants nearing retirement. "Mercadante quer decidir no voto impasse com oposição" 2003.

hold together his increasingly fractious coalition. Brazil's Senate approved the 2003 pension reform amendment by a 55 to 25 margin – six votes above the three-fifths threshold required to enact the measure.[194]

Lula's constitutional amendment to restructure the public sector pension system was promulgated on December 19, 2003, just seven months after President Lula sent the measure to the Congress. The amendment represented a significant milestone in Brazil's struggle to reform its old age pension institutions. Whereas civil servants had previously enjoyed high pensions without an upper benefit limit, the amendment created a ceiling on state-provided benefits that was equal to that of the private sector, while creating a second tier of individual, defined-contribution pension funds to which civil servants could contribute if they wished a higher pension above the new ceiling. The reform also added to the system important parametric changes that narrowed the financial gap in Brazil's old age pension institution, including the tax on civil service pensions and an increase in the minimum retirement age. More importantly, Lula's amendment, which was regulated in 2004, replaced the old salary reference for public servants from the last wage to the average contribution-salary over a worker's career. In the future, public sector pensions would be determined by the same formula used to calculate private sector pensions; this rule marked a significant curtailing of one of the most regressive policies in Brazil, and one that in the long term would improve the financial balance of the state pension system.[195]

In the short term, however, the costs of negotiation and the compromises made in the pension reform bill dampened the immediate financial impact of the institutional reform. Nevertheless, the Brazilian government estimated that Lula's 2003 pension amendment would yield a cost-savings of US$17 billion over eighteen years.[196] Indeed, following the measure's approval in the Senate, Standard & Poor's raised its risk rating for Brazil to "positive" from "stable."[197] Lula's amendment neither closed the financial gap in the pension system nor brought to an end the reform process that President Cardoso initiated nearly nine years earlier. It did, however, mark a significant transformation in an institution whose reform has been widely dismissed as unfeasible, abandoned, or doomed to failure.

Despite the contrasts in the outcome and ease with which changes to the nation's pension system were achieved in the 1998 and 2003 constitutional amendments, the goals and justifications for these reforms were nearly identical. For Brazilian technocrats, the close similarity between the two reforms was not surprising, given the technical consensus behind the problems in the system. As one technocrat put it, "What is surprising is not the continuity [between the two

---

[194] The second-round Senate vote on December 11, 2003, passed by 51 to 24.
[195] Ministério da Previdência Social 2004, p. 1.
[196] "Brazil's Senate Passes Pension Bill in Final Vote" 2003.
[197] "Senate Approves Pension Reform" 2003.

amendments], but the effort to disguise that continuity."[198] Even under Lula, rhetoric could only partially mitigate the veto dynamic that emerged around the reform. Although he made recourse to compensation and compromise, as Cardoso had, to build the supermajorities required to sanction his amendment, Lula did so at a considerably lower price, while achieving more extensive institutional change than was secured in the previous amendment.

Brazil Summary

The three pension reforms in Brazil present striking contrasts and continuities in process and outcome. Although all three measures were advanced within the same institutional milieu of a highly fragmented and notoriously personalistic legislature, the reforms met with markedly different political fortunes. The partisan structure of political conflict powerfully shaped the ability of these governments to use political rhetoric, compensation, and compromise to enhance the distributive tendency of these reforms. Facing the opposition alliance of the Workers' Party and CUT labor confederation, President Cardoso's amendment was subject to a durable veto dynamic, which was mitigated only in the context of an international economic crisis. External pressure also helped to dampen a veto dynamic that emerged around Cardoso's 1999 private sector pension reform. Although Lula enjoyed considerable partisan advantages in advancing his 2003 constitutional pension reform amendment, he also faced vehement mobilization by public sector unions who activated a veto dynamic around that reform. Lula resorted to playing by the rules of the game that his party had long reproved, including exchanging distributive appropriations and career favors for votes. He also made compromises in the text of his amendment in order to win the supermajorities required for its sanction. Despite the many differences characterizing the pension reform initiatives undertaken by Presidents Cardoso and Lula, both presidents gathered *oversized* legislative majorities to sanction loss-imposing institutional changes in legislative arenas that had long proved inhospitable to such reforms. The legislative fragmentation and pork-driven personalism that are said by many to be antithetical to cooperation behind the provision of unpopular collective goods legislation ultimately provided a mortar that bound large legislative coalitions behind these reforms.

URUGUAY

The Uruguayan pension privatization was sanctioned in September 1995, just six months after the inauguration of President Julio María Sanguinetti of the Colorado Party. The mixed pension system allows most workers the option of splitting their payroll contributions between the reformed public (DB) social

---

[198] Quote from Marcelo Estevão de Moraes, the former Secretário Nacional de Previdência Social in "Reforma segue obra de FHC, diz PSDB" 2003.

insurance system and an individual, privately managed DC retirement savings account. After the five failed pension reform attempts between 1990 and 1994 under President Luis Alberto Lacalle, the approval of the 1995 structural reform is significant. That these measures all were advanced within the same institutional context, moreover, lends confidence to the expectation that legislative structures are far from deterministic of reform outcomes. Unlike in Brazil, however, there was not a significant reversal in the partisan structure of political competition across the Sanguinetti and Lacalle governments. Both presidents came from traditional centrist parties and both faced opposition from the ascendant left-wing Broad Front (Frente Amplio), as well as from organized labor and retirees. Moreover, the share of seats held by the governing party *diminished* in the second instance, when the reform was passed. Nevertheless, President Sanguinetti gathered an oversized majority to enact a significant structural pension reform that was even *deeper* than several of the earlier, ill-fated proposals. President Sanguinetti's capacity to induce a distributive logic around the 1995 structural pension reform was enhanced by external corroboration of his claims that pension reform would avert a financial crisis. Sanguinetti also used an array of compensatory measures to enhance the distributive tendency of his pension reform, including generous subsidies and new benefits in the pension legislation. The government thus cultivated the perception that "no one loses – and many benefit" from pension reform, helping to sustain the reform against the threat of referendum.

Obstacles to Reform

Political institutions in Uruguay present considerable political obstacles to deep reform such as pension privatization.[199] Indeed, Uruguayan political institutions require a high degree of consensus in order to sanction – and sustain – new legislation. The bicameral legislature in Uruguay, the General Assembly (Asamblea General), consists of a ninety-nine-member Chamber of Deputies and a thirty-one-member Senate. Deputies and senators in the General Assembly are elected for five-year terms in simultaneous elections with that of the presidency.[200] Although the Uruguayan party system was long dominated by the two centrist, catch-all parties, the Colorado Party (Partido Colorado, PC) and the National, or "Blanco" Party (Partido Nacional, PN), the 1990s witnessed the rapid ascent of the left-wing Frente Amplio and the end of the two-party dominance.

Political authority in the Uruguayan legislature is much more broadly shared than the three major party labels would suggest. This is because the double-simultaneous vote system cleaves political parties into a series of autonomous

[199] Kay 1998; 1999.
[200] The 1994 election utilized the double simultaneous vote system to elect the president. This was changed in 1996 to a two-round absolute majority requirement for the president. Buquet et al. 1998, p. 40.

TABLE 7.4. *Distribution of Seats across Parties and Major Factions in Uruguay, 1995–1999 Chamber of Deputies*

Political Party	Faction	Faction Share of Party Votes	Party Share of National Votes	Number of Seats
Partido Nacional (Blanco)			31.4	32
	Herrerismo	45		14
	Volonte	48		15
	MNR	6		2
Partido Colorado[a]			32.5	31
	Foro Batllista	75		24
	Lista 15	6		2
	Cruzada 94	9		3
	PGB	3		1
	UCB	3		1
	Vaillant	3		1
Frente Amplio Encuentro Progresista			30.8	31
Nuevo Espacio			5.1	5

[a] In alliance with the Partido por el Gobierno del Pueblo.

factions that operate independently during elections and in government. The result is to proliferate the number of potential veto players in the legislature by organizing power around *sub*party factions while creating obstacles to cooperation among factions of the same party, much less among rival parties.[201] Factions, rather than parties, thus serve as the building blocks of legislative authority in the General Assembly.[202] Faction leaders organize separate closed-list electoral ballots and may enter or exit governing political coalitions independently. Because votes are pooled at the faction – rather than party – level, legislative authority in Uruguay is shared among a much wider range of actors than the relatively small number of "effective" political parties – which was 3.35 in 1995 – would suggest. Indeed, as Table 7.4 illustrates, when taking into account the factional structure of Uruguayan parties, the distribution of power in the Chamber of Deputies in 1995 was quite broad.

Beyond the greater dispersion of power within parties, Morgenstern has found that Uruguay's electoral rules create powerful incentives for intraparty competition "that pulls copartisan factions in opposite directions."[203] Indeed, the executive, even though he or she is the head of government, is only the leader of one faction, and not of the entire party, and thus cannot mandate

[201] González 1993, p. 241; Kay 1999, p. 414.
[202] Morgenstern 2001.
[203] Morgenstern 2001.

the cooperation of the rest of the party beyond his or her particular faction.[204] The ability of faction leaders to move independently of their copartisans, and the electoral *incentives* to do so, expands considerably the range of potential veto players with whom the executive must negotiate to build a legislative majority. Cooperation within or across political parties in Uruguay thus is far from assured. Nor, however, is it inevitable, despite broad fragmentation of power and competitive pressures.

The frequent use of the plebiscite to overturn legislation creates an additional barrier to unpopular reform; indeed, it is considered one of the most significant potential veto points in Uruguay.[205] To preempt the repeal of new legislation, government actors in Uruguay are obliged to anticipate the interests of potential opponents to their policy initiatives – and of the median voter. Often, this means shying away from unpopular, loss-imposing change altogether.[206] The task of making the 1995 pension reform in Uruguay "referendum-proof" – by assuring that it would be desirable to the median voter – entailed efforts to enhance the distributive nature and appearance of the reform. By doing so, Sanguinetti cleared the way for the rapid sanction of a modest, but stable, institutional path change.

Because faction leaders, who are the principal interlocutors in the formation of legislative decision making, compete in national elections, cooperation across factions – even within the same political party – varies over the electoral cycle.[207] Whereas higher levels of cooperation are observed in the first two years of a political term, rates of defection increase in the run-up to an election as competition among factions intensifies.[208] The rapid sanction of Uruguay's 1995 pension reform in the first six months of the Sanguinetti government may seem to offer prima facie support for the view that it was timing in the electoral cycle – in the "honeymoon" period – that explains the cooperation behind the 1995 reform.[209] Yet, earlier pension reforms also failed in the first half of the electoral calendar; indeed, President Lacalle's first pension reform proposal was issued within a month of his inauguration. That proposal was defeated and was followed by two more reform failures in the first two years of his term. The impact of the electoral cycle on pension reform outcomes in Uruguay thus cannot be discerned strictly from these cases.

Political Conflict in a Veto Dynamic

As we have seen in previous chapters, a 1989 referendum marked a critical turning point in the development of Uruguay's pension system by sharply

---

[204] Buquet et al. 1998, p. 47.
[205] Kay 1999, p. 415.
[206] Kay 1998; 1999.
[207] Buquet et al. 1998, p. 42.
[208] Moraes and Morgenstern 1995; Buquet et al. 1998, pp. 49–50.
[209] Calvo 1998; Davrieux 1998; Michelín 1998; Vera 1998. See also Kay 1998.

increasing old age pension costs.[210] The referendum was organized by the ONJPU, an umbrella organization of approximately 120 retiree associations. Despite warnings of the negative fiscal consequences of the referendum, its distributive implications created a formidable collective action problem among major candidates, all of whom endorsed the measure. Indeed, the referendum was held in conjunction with the national election, generating strong incentives for politicians to seek the support of retirees (who in Uruguay were not committed to a particular party). The result was a broad endorsement of the referendum across the political spectrum and passage of the measure with 82.5 percent of the vote.[211]

Along with a sharp increase in the value of state pensions the 1989 referendum brought new limitations on the discretion of the executive to revise pension benefits. President Luis Alberto Lacalle thus was forced to act quickly to revise the rules of this institution. Shortly after his inauguration in March 1990, Lacalle sent a packet of five reform measures to the General Assembly, including a social security reform that would slow the rise in pension costs. He also proposed a fiscal reform to create new sources of revenue to finance these benefits – largely through the value-added tax. Despite the warnings of an impending fiscal crisis, Lacalle's coalition partners – the so-called National Coincidence – would not countenance a reversal of the immensely popular referendum. The governing coalition was riven with internal conflicts, as was Lacalle's own Blanco Party.[212] Indeed, the National Coincidence proved to be little more than that: Three barely-coinciding factions of the Blanco Party and three factions of the Colorado Party that shared little common ground on the question of pension reform, among other issues.[213] One governing faction (Batllismo Radical, led by Jorge Batlle) endorsed a proposal for a radical Chilean-style complete privatization, while others took a firm position against *any* pension reform. The "winset" of issues that were preferred by a majority of legislators to the status quo thus was vanishingly small.

Lacalle's first pension reform proposal was governed by the classic political logic of retrenchment, where the direct imposition of losses threatened a strong electoral backlash by the institution's well-organized constituency. The benefit cuts that Lacalle proposed, moreover, were significant: He sought to retroactively modify the indexation rules to return them to the pre-1989 regulations.[214] The president also made little effort to obscure the loss-imposing nature of the reform. In one public address, Lacalle stated, "The message of the

---

[210] The referendum required that old age pensions be revalued along with public sector salaries according to the average wage index in Uruguay four times per year, rather than once, as before. Saldaín 1996.

[211] Colotuzzo 1998; Filgueira et al. 1998; Papadópolus 1992, p. 121.

[212] Filgueira et al. 1998.

[213] Factions of President Lacalle's own Blanco Party (Renova, Herrerismo [his faction], and MNR), as well as three factions from the Colorado Party (UCB, Batllismo Radical, and Foro Batllista).

[214] Filgueira et al. 1998.

Executive is very clear. The Social Security system, like many things in the country, requires rectification. It was conceived in the past, when life expectancy and the active-passive ratios were different.... If we do not act now, the political system will have to face two options, either pay with inflation and lie to retirees about their possibilities for the future, or raise the VAT tax before the end of this governing period to 30 to 40 percent, for example."[215] The salience of the loss-imposing nature of the retrenchment activated a forceful veto logic in the legislature, resulting in the defeat of this measure in early 1991.

President Lacalle issued another pension reform proposal after little delay. This time, the technical consensus behind the need to reform was forged by swelling pension costs and the result of studies undertaken by the Inter-American Development Bank (IDB). The IDB consultants drafted four pension reform options that were presented to the Uruguayan government in early 1992. Lacalle chose a proposal that would create a notional defined contribution pension system, which would establish individual accounts for recording each worker's contributions and benefits but would maintain pay-as-you-go financing and public management of pension funds. The NDC proposal would lower pension replacement rates from the average of 75 percent to 50 percent, depending on the length of time a worker stayed in the labor force.[216] That proposal was introduced to the General Assembly by Lacalle's legislative delegation in 1992.

If Lacalle's first reform proposal attenuated the (already-thin) political ties holding together his governing alliance, this proposal ruptured those bonds altogether. By designating the reform for "Urgent Consideration," Lacalle limited the possibility of bargaining support from allied – let alone opposition – factions. Once again, a veto logic prevailed, resulting in the departure of two of the Colorado Party factions (Foro Batllista and Batllismo Radical) from the governing coalition. Although the support from these factions was more apparent than real even before the pension reform conflict, the diminishing size of Lacalle's governing coalition further diminished the chances of building a majority behind structural pension reform.

In the next two years, two additional factions from the President's Blanco Party also broke from the governing coalition (Movimiento Nacional de La Rocha and Renovación y Victoria), leaving just two factions in support of the government: Lacalle's own Herrerismo and the Colorado Unión Colorada y Batllista (UCB). In the meantime, pension spending rose steadily, amounting to a 300 percent increase from the 1984 level. Despite the mounting political obstacles, Lacalle pressed forward with efforts to control the escalating pension costs.

A third pension reform proposal – this time calling only for parametric changes in the existing system – was included in the annual budget resolution bill (Rendición de Cuentas) in 1992. Although there was a legal precedent for including new policy provisions in such resolutions, the use of this

[215] Filgueira et al. 1998.
[216] Filgueira et al. 1998, p. 11.

tactic to reform the pension system provoked an immediate and forceful backlash against the government.[217] The public outcry against the pension reform, which was approved in the budget resolution bill that year, led to the calling of a referendum to overturn that measure. The referendum, which was held in conjunction with the 1994 presidential and legislative elections, not only repealed the 1992 Rendición de Cuentas pension reform, but it also prohibited Uruguayan presidents henceforth from legislating pension reform through the budget resolution bills.

Before the end of his term, President Lacalle drafted a fourth pension reform proposal that called for a *structural* pension reform. This measure enjoyed so little political support that it was not even taken up for discussion by Senate committees.[218] Unrelenting, Lacalle sent a fifth pension reform proposal to the General Assembly in February 1994, eight months before the end of his term. Once again, he designated the measure "Urgent," and once again the proposal was firmly rejected by legislative actors. As one legislator explained, "this project does not constitute a reform of the [pension] system, but merely an adjustment of ciphers and percentages, inspired by benefit cuts with the goal of obtaining mere financial balance. This is not the spirit with which we should approach . . . these matters with the clearest of social implications."[219] With the approach of the 1994 election adding force to what had become a seemingly intractable veto dynamic, this fifth pension reform proposal fell to defeat.

Lacalle's repeated failure to build legislative support for pension reform between 1990 and 1994 may seem to provide evidence of the inherent obstacles to institutional restructuring in this veto-laden context. But for some Uruguayan scholars, these defeats were instead the result of "poor political engineering" on the part of the president.[220] This is partially correct. Clearly, the embrace of technical justifications and labels of urgency hindered the possibility of building consensus on the reform. Yet, the same technical arguments used to establish the necessity and importance of the reform later would not stand in the way of an oversized majority that supported the partial privatization advanced by Lacalle's successor. Neither Uruguay's political institutions, nor the partisan structure of legislative competition changed significantly over these instances. Rather, the credibility of the president's contentions about the reform experienced the greatest change in impact, while efforts to enhance the distributive nature of the reform also facilitated structural reform in the second instance.

Inducing a Distributive Logic

A growing perception that Uruguay's pension system was heading toward crisis brought a decisive shift in the political logic of that country's institutional

---

[217] The reform called for parametric revisions that were similar to the first retrenchment bill that was rejected in 1990. Moraes and Morgenstern 1995.
[218] Filgueira et al. 1998, p. 10
[219] Filgueira et al. 1998, p. 23.
[220] Davrieux 1998; Filgueira et al. 1998, p. 7; Vera 1998.

reform. Technocrats, along with President Lacalle, had warned of such a crisis since 1990, but their projections lacked credibility. Not only was the crisis not evident early in the 1990s, but the rapid rise in consumption and the decline in poverty among the elderly were heralded as successful achievements of the referendum; claims that the system was flawed thus rang hollow, particularly when they were countered by the retiree organization. This context changed dramatically by 1995, however, when the geometric rise in pension costs left little room for doubt of the necessity of *some* kind of reform. For leaders of the Colorado and Blanco Parties, the political costs of failing to prevent a crisis suddenly outweighed the potential liability of supporting a reform. The possibilities for claiming credit for providing a "solution" to the pension crisis thus helped to spur cooperation around the 1995 pension system restructuring.

By late 1994, the signals coming from expert projections and observable trends in government spending led politicians to conclude that "things were going to blow up" if reform were not undertaken soon.[221] The sharp rise in pension costs was driven both by the indexation rules created by the 1989 referendum and by Uruguay's rapidly aging demographic profile. Indeed, Uruguay's old age dependency ratio (1.4:1) was even lower than that of the mature industrial democracies (2.6:1) and much lower than other Latin American countries (5:1).[222] Government economists projected that without reform, payroll contributions to finance the state pension system would have to rise to 54.6 percent by 2045.[223] The sharp rise in pension spending between 1990 and 1994 – from 9 to 14 percent of GDP – lent plausibility to these claims, subordinating rivalries among parties of the governing coalition that hitherto seemed intractable.[224] Even leaders within the opposition leftist coalition, the Frente Amplio, came to see pension reform as necessary by 1995.[225] Divisions remained, however, over the kind and extent of reform that was justifiable to correct structural imbalances in the existing system.

A common electoral threat from the left also prompted politicians from the two main parties – the Colorados and Blancos – to overcome differences on the question of pension reform. The 1994 national election had split the popular vote nearly evenly across the three major political party labels. The Blancos won 31 percent of the popular vote, the Colorados received 32 percent, and the leftist Frente Amplio, running as the 'Broad Front–Progressive Encounter' coalition (Frente Amplio–Encuentro Progresista) claimed its largest vote share ever, with 31 percent of the popular vote. The smaller center-left Nuevo Espacio Party (NE) won 5 percent of the vote. The rise of the leftist coalition threatened the duopoly of power that was long held by Blancos and Colorados, providing

---

[221] de Posadas 1998.
[222] Márquez Mosconi 1997, p. 3.
[223] Saldáin 1995, p. 280.
[224] Labadie 1998; Saldáin 1998.
[225] Astori 1998; Vásquez 1998.

strong incentives for competing factions of those parties to cooperate around the shared goal of staving off the external threat. As the pension "problem" grew, the goal of averting a crisis came to be seen as an important way to stem the growing electoral threat from the Frente Amplio.[226]

Multiparty Negotiation

President-elect Sanguinetti lost little time in addressing the pension issue. Shortly after the October 1994 election, Sanguinetti created a multiparty commission to draw up principles that would guide the pension reform. The committee was composed of all major factions in the Blanco and Colorado Parties, representatives of the state social insurance bureaucracy (the BPS), financiers in the ministry of labor and social security, and even rival parties of the left. Although representatives of the Frente Amplio–Encuentro Progresista were invited to join the multiparty committee, they withdrew their representatives early in the process when it became clear that they were outvoted by the Blanco and Colorado factions. The moderate left Nuevo Espacio, however, remained an important party to the negotiations.

The multiparty accord laid out the general principles that would guide the pension reform. These included correcting actuarial imbalances in the pension system and protecting acquired rights, while also guaranteeing that the process of reform would involve negotiation between the executive and legislative branches. Social actors – namely, employers, workers, and retirees – were treated as "valid interlocutors" in the reform process. The committee also agreed that the reform would maintain a pay-as-you-go component in the pension system and that it would be revised again in twenty-five years according to demographic necessity. Well before President Júlio Sanguinetti was inaugurated in March 1995, therefore, technocrats began to design the pension reform.

Technocrats sought to ensure that the new pension system would not only maintain workers' acquired pension rights but also strengthen the pension system. The former, they expected, would diminish the appearance of loss even if benefits were cut substantially. The proposed reform also created the possibility for new benefits so that the average citizen would perceive a *gain* from participating in the new mixed pension regime. The 1995 pension reform in Uruguay was thus designed to cultivate the perception that "no one lost." Most workers (fully 82 percent of the workforce) had the option of joining the partially private pension system.[227] The distributive appeal of the new pension system was further enhanced by offering a bonus to qualified workers who chose to split their payroll contributions between the public and private pension systems. Such workers would receive a subsidy in their private account equivalent to half of the contribution (or 25 percent of the total payroll contribution). Although this provision would be costly to the government, it was considered

[226] Berchese 1998; Davrieux 1998; de Posadas 1998; Vera 1998.
[227] Davrieux 1998; Vera 1998.

an essential condition for the political palatability of the measure.[228] Indeed, it was one that enhanced the distributive tendency of the reform.

Faction leaders enjoy considerable autonomy to form (and break) political alliances, and thus the cooperation of any more than President Sanguinetti's own faction of the Colorado Party was not assured. Yet, Uruguay's 1995 pension reform won the support of all the Blanco and Colorado factions and of the center-left Nuevo Espacio. The support of the latter, although not necessary to enact the reform (given that Sanguinetti already counted upon more than 60 percent of the votes in the General Assembly), was negotiated in exchange for important compromises in the measure. These concessions expanded even further the measure's political backing by increasing the distributive appearance of the reform. The endorsement of this leftist party also enhanced the partisan credibility of the pension reform.[229] In exchange for his support, the NE's leader, Rafael Michelini, added important provisions to the pension reform that enhanced its distributive nature. These included the creation of a "social quota," which would finance a modest health insurance benefit for low-income retirees.[230] This new health benefit improved the material rewards associated with the reformed pension system, and thus helped to obscure its loss-imposing dimensions. The reform thus won the backing of a credible political actor while also including substantial distributive provisions that obfuscated the costs and risks that it imposed on individuals.

The final details of Sanguinetti's pension reform proposal were drafted following his inauguration in March 1995. The law was promptly sent to the General Assembly in June of that year, where legislators made only modest changes to the bill. These included revisions to the timing and manner of implementation, the nature and investments of the private pension fund managers, and changes to the rules governing survivor benefits. The technical details of most legislation in Uruguay are typically worked out in the committees of the Chamber of Deputies, whereas the Senate committees are usually the location of the political negotiations over legislation. It was in the Senate, therefore, that representatives of the labor unions and the Frente Amplio expressed their opposition to the reform.[231] This time, however, the government's political strategy had won not only broad public support, but the backing of all other political parties and of the major social interests such as retirees. The Frente Amplio thus was unable to mobilize public support against the reform. In August 1995, just over two months after being sent to the General Assembly, the structural pension reform was approved with more than two-thirds of the votes in the legislature – well beyond the minimum threshold necessary to enact the law.

---

[228] Labadie 1998.

[229] Davrieux 1998; Michelini 1998.

[230] Article 186, Ley N° 16.713; Michelini 1998.

[231] Certain factions within the FA, such as Asamblea Uruguaya (AU), led by Danilo Astori, were open to negotiation on the pension reform. But when FA representatives left the multiparty commission, the AU went along "because of party discipline" and voted against the reform. Astori 1998.

This oversized majority provides dramatic evidence of a distributive logic that had been forged in 1995 around the legislative process of pension reform in Uruguay.

Uruguay Summary

Politicians seeking to restructure Uruguay's national pension system faced an array of institutional and political obstacles. The factionalized structure of political parties, along with the credible threat of a plebiscite, creates ample opportunities for opponents to impede institutional change and impose electoral costs on party factions that supported reform. Even though this institutional landscape remained constant over the Lacalle and Sanguinetti governments, pension reforms failed repeatedly in the first, but not in the second. This divergence owes to a shift in credibility across the two governments, which emerged in the second from external corroboration, and to efforts to enhance the distributive appearance of the 1995 reform. The distributive logic that governed the legislative process of pension reform under Sanguinetti allowed an important, loss-imposing structural reform to be sanctioned by an oversized legislative majority. This approach not only felled the seemingly immovable barriers to reform in Uruguay's factionalized party system, but also has held off so far the ultimate veto gate: the threat of a popular referendum to overturn unpopular laws.

CONCLUSION

The legislative conflicts over pension reform in these four countries show that the possibility of gathering support for loss-imposing reform is not given ex ante by the degree of losses imposed or by the structure of institutional authority in the political process. Rather, the cases have shown how the multidimensional nature of institutional restructuring, which involves potentially significant losses *and* gains, distinguishes the legislative politics of pension privatization from that of retrenchment alone. But the ability of reform-seeking leaders to heighten the salience of pension privatization's distributive elements is far from assured; similarly, a (putatively) disciplined legislative majority offers little guarantee of cooperation around structural reform where a veto logic takes hold. Institutional structures matter greatly for the enactment of structural pension reform; however, the cases reveal most clearly that institutions' effects are conditioned powerfully by the political logic that unfolds during legislative conflict rather than by their design or distribution of seat shares alone.

Even though the legislation of institutional change is a necessary element of institutional path departure, a theory of the legislative politics of structural reform cannot alone predict when such a law will result in a new and self-reinforcing institutional path. For it is possible to change a law, I have argued, without renegotiating the underlying social bargain that it implies. So although the legislative politics of pension reform have been examined separately from the broader social conflicts over institutional change, the implications of the former are deeply consequential for the latter. Indeed, the implications of legislative conflicts for the long-term stability of institutional path departure cannot be understood independently of the broader social milieu within which those conflicts occurred. Whether the so-called pension revolution will be sustained, or whether majorities once again will be constituted to revise the terms of old age income protection, will only be known in the medium to long term. Once again, however, the terms on which those majorities were formed – whether through persuasion or purchase – and the balance of distributive and redistributive effects of the pension reform are likely to bear powerfully on the stability of legislated path-departing pension reforms.

PART IV

CONCLUSIONS AND IMPLICATIONS

8

A New Social Contract?

Old age pension reform ascended to the top of political agendas around the world in the final quarter of the twentieth century. In some cases, attention to pension reform was impelled by the haunting specter of deep financial short-falls attending the retirement of large baby-boom generations; in other cases, governments contended that economic openness had made state-run social insurance programs unviable. In few cases, however, did the nature and depth of subsequent structural pension reforms actually correspond to underlying actuarial imbalances in state pension systems: While some reforms fell short of needed corrections, others went far beyond the functional realignment of pension system revenue and liabilities. Rather, a common theme uniting the diverse changes to old age pension systems in the last quarter century has been the heavy imprint of politics – of the diverse goals of state leaders and compro-mises with domestic political forces whose consent made way for institutional change.

As such, these reforms present scholars with important puzzles about the effects of both globalization and partisanship. In contrast to the accepted wis-dom of early globalization research, pension reforms have been *less* extensive in the more open and capital-scarce economies, despite their heightened vul-nerability to international pressures. And in many cases, left-wing governments not only have failed to resist such measures but they have increasingly taken the lead in privatizing state-sponsored social insurance programs. The conse-quences are profound: By transforming institutions that once pooled risk and reapportioned income into systems of individual savings and self-insurance, pension privatization has fundamentally rewritten the basic social contract underlying old age income protection and, with it, the very ends of this signifi-cant part of the welfare state.

The task of this study has been to explain how, when, and to what degree such transformations of old age pension institutions occur. The overwhelming stickiness of those systems provides the point of departure for the theoretical analysis: Given powerful mechanisms of institutional self-reinforcement, when and how do the forces that once held an institution into place later permit, or even promote, path-departing change? Answering this question necessitated a reexamination of key tenets of the received wisdom in welfare state research. The first was the widely accepted link between economic integration and social welfare reform. Even though many scholars anticipated that globalization would place downward pressure on the scope of the welfare state, I found instead that economic openness has created both incentives *and* constraints on structural pension reform, resulting in more of a double bind than a "race to the bottom." Second, even though theories of path dependence hold that a self-reinforcing path may change when positive feedbacks are simply overwhelmed by (typically enormous) exogenous pressures, I found that feedbacks to existing social insurance programs may themselves shift from being mechanisms of institutional reinforcement, to forces that permit, if not even promote, deep institutional reform. In this sense, I account for endogenous forces of institutional change, even in a path-dependent context. And finally, scholars are divided over whether the fragmentation of political authority or the possession of a legislative majority better accommodates institutional reform; however, neither literature has explained how a constant set of legislative institutions can long uphold a social policy design but later permit the formation of majorities behind its radical transformation. Reexamining this process, I found that the partisan structure of political conflict can mediate the challenge of forming legislative majorities behind loss-imposing pension reform, given the multidimensional nature of institutional restructuring.

Why is social security privatization so important? Indeed, understanding the causes and consequences of structural pension reform is crucial in substantive and theoretical terms. By shifting significant income, market, and demographic risks from society as a whole to individuals, pension privatization will have profound material and distributional implications. For privatization threatens to cleave societies along new lines of distributive advantage because those with the skill, income, and assets to more easily go it alone in the face of economic and demographic risks are privileged – economically and politically – relative to those on whom such risks incide negatively and who can less easily bear the cost of self-insurance. From a theoretical standpoint, the shift to private forms of self-insurance challenges our understanding of the very nature of path-dependent institutional change. It represents a critical departure from the once-stable and self-reinforcing path of state-run social insurance provision, but without the exogenous shock to drive it. One of the central achievements of institutional research in the postwar era has been to explain the remarkable persistence of social and political institutions despite the buffeting by demographic, economic, and ideological pressures. A central task of this study thus has been to understand how such long-standing institutions may be fundamentally transformed through processes that are not fully exogenous. To do so, I looked within the once-reinforcing feedback processes to understand how these may be transformed in their implications in systematic ways that make institutional reform possible.

EXPLAINING PATH DEPARTURE

I developed this analysis in Chapter 2 first by modeling the structural shift from social protection to market-based pension systems in a global data set. Using simulations of structural reform on two dimensions – the retrenchment of risk-pooling designs and the creation of private retirement savings – I modeled structural reform across nations as a two-step process. This controlled for the selection process through which governments initially decide to privatize while examining the causes of differing degrees of privatization. The quantitative cross-national analysis revealed systematic patterns of variation in the movement toward pension privatization. It also exposed important conditions in the effect of institutional legacies and partisan features of legislative conflict on the likelihood and degree to which governments privatize. The analysis revealed most paradoxically that neither globalization nor fiscal crisis explains reform. Instead, the more heavily indebted countries are systematically *less* likely to privatize old age pensions than other governments, all else being equal. Demographic pressures have lent strong impetus to the movement toward pension privatization, but the consequent rising social insurance liabilities have not translated into a firm embrace of privatization in any direct fashion. The effect, instead, is conditional. Greater implicit pension liabilities increase the likelihood of privatization in less generous welfare states, and rising pension costs reduce the tendency to privatize the more mature and affluent social insurance systems. Beyond structural characteristics, the actual performance of old age pension institutions also matters in predicting their resilience. Not everywhere does social insurance legislation effectively translate into compliance and active contribution by the bulk of the labor force. And where compliance is low, the analysis provided evidence, albeit modest, that privatization is more likely. Finally, the cross-national analysis indicated that by contrast to previous research, the command of a legislative majority does *not* itself make privatization more likely. Rather, unless a left-wing party dominates the legislature, increasing the size of the governing majority actually *diminishes* the likelihood of pension privatization. More favorable legislative conditions for structural pension reform thus may be found where the government is of the left, and claims broad authority.

Overall, the quantitative cross-national analysis lent significant support to my expectations that we must pursue a more contingent approach to understanding institutional change. In Chapter 3, I developed these causal arguments at the level of midrange theoretical propositions that break formal processes of institutional change into three analytically distinct but interrelated processes. These examine how structural pension reform is (1) launched in the technocracy, (2) justified or sold to society, and (3) enacted by democratic legislatures. The analysis of technocratic processes focused on how government actors decide whether and to what extent to privatize, for it is here that financial and macroeconomic concerns often weigh most heavily, and globalization's impact may be most directly assessed. In the second step, as reformers make the case for institutional change to society, we observe how strategic actors confront, and are often bound by, the political legacies of existing institutional designs. I take a view of such legacies that goes beyond their structural features (benefit levels, coverage) to include institutional performance, and the associated political feedbacks, namely, citizens' everyday beliefs and expectations about the institution, and the attendant satisfaction or dissatisfaction with it. These beliefs and attitudes may long uphold and reinforce social security institutions, but they may also open the door to structural change. Finally, the most explicit conflicts over institutional change occur in the legislative process through which democratic majorities must be forged behind loss-imposing structural reforms. I examined how efforts to enhance the distributive appearance of pension reform are shaped by the partisan hue of government and, where such efforts fail, how majorities may be built in the context of a veto logic. My arguments on each of these three dimensions are summarized next.

Setting the Agenda

To understand whether or how globalization has influenced the structural reform of old age pensions, I examined the initial drafting of these reforms in technocratic processes. Scholarship on social policy change has long upheld the view that insulated decision makers in the executive branch design structural reforms largely in response to long-term policy challenges (*viz.*, capital scarcity, demographic change) or are guided by neoliberal ideas and "good policy" concerns such as efficiency and solvency. But such a view does not comport well with the empirical record, even – or especially – in open economies where the putative "discipline" of market actors weighs heavily on policy design. Critically, although the threat of exit by owners of mobile financial assets has long been assumed to promote *greater* market-oriented social welfare reforms, I argue that financial globalization may instead oblige technocrats to *curtail* their proposed shift toward pension privatization. This is possible even while globalization creates incentives for governments to privatize as a way to reduce labor costs, deepen capital markets, and signal the government's commitment to market-oriented policy.

These contradictory tensions arise in part from the high fiscal toll that pension privatization exacts of governments during the transition to a private pension system. As workers begin to divert payroll contributions to privately managed pension funds, governments relinquish a major source of revenue with which to finance ongoing pension costs. Rather than immediately improving the reforming government's financial position, a more common near-term consequence of pension privatization is the creation of a yawning fiscal deficit and rising government indebtedness. Critically, such infelicitous short-term effects may be punished by international market actors through capital flight – even if they occur in the service of market-friendly reform for which governments would be rewarded in the long term. This paradoxical outcome arises in part from the short time horizons of highly liquid capital owners. Where international portfolios are well diversified, those investors must rely on information shortcuts such as policy signals and risk ratings to weigh investment decisions. When pension privatization results in the erosion of government performance on key indicators of sovereign default or inflation risk, reformers may well face market punishment – a rational response to short-term signals – rather than reward for the long-term goals associated with the privatizing reform.

When is this likely? Governments in the most dire financial straits (i.e., those whose fiscal deficits and sovereign debt burdens are high prior to reform and that lack access to discretionary revenue) enjoy narrower leeway to assume the costs of privatization without risking market punishment. This expectation challenges the conventional view that capital scarcity and financial deficits make privatization more likely by pointing to ways in which a country's vulnerability to capital flight may systematically constrain movements toward market-oriented reform. International market conditions also mediate this effect. In the context of high international liquidity, investors' greater tolerance for risk slackens the threat of capital flight in response to rising government debt or deficit ratios. Conversely, low international liquidity may oblige technocrats to guard more vigilantly the government's performance on short-term sovereign creditworthiness indicators as investors become more discriminating with regard to risk. Given the overwhelming costs of capital flight, technocrats may reasonably discount the long-term consequences of pension reform in order to avoid the near-term risk of punishment. Where this is likely (i.e., privatization is expected to push government risk indicators beyond the level tolerable to international market actors), technocrats in cash-strapped governments may curtail pension privatization or forego this reform altogether in order to maintain access to international credit. Rather than conducing strictly toward deeper privatization, therefore, globalization may powerfully bridle this reform, especially for governments in open, capital-importing nations.

Contesting Legacies in Society

Although social contracts need not be explicitly renegotiated in order for juridical institutional change to occur, in most democratic contexts reformers expend considerable time and energy in precisely such efforts. Quite often, however, they are thwarted by what scholars consider a fundamental political feedback loop: the attachment of an institution's beneficiaries to the existing design. Yet, in an increasing number of cases, reformers have sought *and won* public backing for welfare state reforms that not only amend the social bargain underlying old age income protection but also impose considerable losses on program beneficiaries in the process.

To explain when and how this may happen, I look beyond the structural features of the institutional inheritance to examine its *political legacy*. The latter entails locally shared beliefs (about what is fair, what the state should do) and performance expectations that establish a bar against which individuals assess the institution's ongoing performance. Where the program is perceived to fall short of these inherited standards, then public dissatisfaction may open the door to institutional reform. Mandates for reform – whether simply to repair or to fully transform an institution – thus need not arise fully exogenously. For they also may be induced by strategic reform-seeking actors who provide new information about the system's fairness or viability, or who challenge citizens' perceptions of what they are due by introducing new ideologies and evaluative standards. Legacies thus include more than just the structural features of the institution; they also incorporate the system's performance and may either reinforce or undermine the existing structural form. Support for deep institutional change thus may be won where institutional performance falls short of expectations – whether in reality or perception – and where the very beliefs and expectations that define this political legacy are transformed. The latter, while rare, implies a new social bargain and a wholly distinct institutional path.

Whether political strategies to induce discontent with the status quo are successful depends first on the nature of the institution's political legacy: the everyday knowledge that citizens hold tightly about the old age pension system and attitudes of satisfaction or dissatisfaction that are associated with these experiences. Where dissatisfaction is pervasive, reformers can more easily claim a mandate for reform. But if the institution is broadly perceived as fair and functioning, this task is far more difficult. For citizens' beliefs and attitudes about an institution may to some degree inoculate them from politicians' claims of crisis or unfairness in the institution. Political claims thus may ring hollow where they are contravened by citizens' everyday knowledge and beliefs, or where they are unwilling to delegate judgment on the institution to politicians who lack credibility on the issue of social protection. Issue-based credibility, such as that claimed by left or labor-based parties on social welfare concerns, may provide reformers with considerable leverage to shape public attitudes about facts that lie beyond everyday knowledge (e.g., whether the pension reform is necessary or beneficial) or are simply unknowable (e.g., the future viability of the existing institutional design). Reformers lacking such credibility – particularly those who are opposed by a coalition of the left, labor, or retirees – still may become persuasive if their claims are corroborated independently, such as by a manifest crisis or by endorsement of a credible actor. Thus where governments provide new information bringing attention to real or purported failures of the institution to meet longstanding expectations of performance or fairness, or where patent shortcomings on these dimensions corroborate political claims that the system is broken, broad public backing for institutional change may be won. Whether a new and self-reinforcing institutional path will be established in such contests, however, is far from assured.

Loss Imposition in the Legislature

The electoral hazards of loss imposition have long been said to encumber the goal of legislating welfare state retrenchment. In the case of pension privatization, legislators are asked to vote for a reform that is highly visible and that imposes losses on what is often a substantial and well-organized portion of the electorate. When and how is this likely? My argument on this dimension emphasized that, by contrast to the politics of retrenchment alone, pension system restructuring entails *two* critical dimensions: The imposition of losses through the shift away from risk-pooling and a creative dimension, which holds the possibility for distributive gain from new private savings schemes. It is the second dimension that distinguishes the politics of pension restructuring from that of retrenchment alone. For the high visibility of pension privatization's creative elements opens the possibility for reformers to organize political conflict around the potential gains to be won through new private savings accounts while dampening the salience of the losses imposed. The legislative politics of pension privatization thus may be characterized by multiple equilibria rather than by either a strictly credit-claiming or a blame-avoiding dynamic.

Where reformers can organize legislative conflicts around privatization's distributive elements, large, if not oversize legislative majorities may be formed around this loss-imposing reform. This is possible where reformers can enhance the distributive appearance – or reality – of the measure. The activation of such a distributive logic may be undermined, however, where credible opponents (e.g., labor unions or retiree associations) bring attention to privatization's retrenching elements; support for the reform in this case becomes electorally hazardous. In such cases, a veto logic obtains, raising the cost that reformers must pay to bring legislators' career interests in line with a vote for reform. Where reform is exceedingly unpopular, however, legislators may be unwilling to vote for reform at any price, obliging government leaders to compromise the depth of institutional change. The emergence of a veto logic thus does not necessarily foreclose privatization. Rather, it directs attention to the scope of bargaining and compromise required to form legislative majorities behind structural pension reform, and to the institutional and material resources available to leaders to compensate legislators and citizens for the losses associated with the reform.

EVIDENCE FROM THE CASES

The third part of the book gathered evidence to evaluate these arguments from structured comparisons of pension reform in four Latin American countries. Pension privatization entered the political agenda in that region as part of a general upsurge in confidence in the principles and promises of markets that in many instances followed in the wake of profound failures in the performance of traditional state-run institutions. Market-oriented reforms were buoyed by potent visions of a promised land in which free markets would deliver citizens from the pervasive want and insecurity of the past, and where competition and entrepreneurship would underwrite sustained economic growth and prosperity. In the realm of old age pensions, privatization was deemed a gateway to high savings and sustained macroeconomic growth, as well as to stronger compliance with broadening coverage of the pension system itself.

In the quarter century after the iconic Chilean pension privatization in 1981, nine other Latin American countries established individual, privately managed defined-contribution pension schemes within statutory old age pension systems. Indeed, Latin America has led the world in the adoption of structural pension reform. Within this region, however, pension reforms have varied considerably in their depth and performance. In the first instance, legislated privatizations range from radically private designs in which the average wage earner is expected to retire with a pension based fully on his or her own private savings (as in Chile, Peru, the Dominican Republic, and El Salvador), to more modest shifts toward market-based provision, as in Costa Rica where just 20 percent of the average wage earner's pension is expected to derive from his or her private savings. The track record of these institutions, as the data in Chapter 4 revealed, has been quite deficient relative to reformers' promises. Here too, however, considerable variation is evident. Private pension funds across the region have invested heavily (and in some cases almost exclusively) in government bonds, while charging steep commissions and exhibiting nearly identical investment decisions (i.e., herd behavior).[1] Although the relaxation of certain regulations (e.g., prohibitions on the purchase of stock or international assets) in recent years has allowed greater diversification of pension fund investments in some countries, commissions and fees continue to consume more than a third of payroll contributions in many cases. In none of the privatizing countries, moreover, has effective coverage increased relative to that of the old state system.[2] Even though strong enrollment rates have been driven by the programs' broad legal mandates, active contribution rates lag sharply; only in Chile is more than half of the labor market actively contributing to their private pension accounts.[3]

I assess my causal expectations about why and how privatization occurred through evidence from four diverse countries in this region. These nations – Argentina, Brazil, Mexico and Uruguay – vary widely in the nature and depth of institutional reform. Mexico enacted a deep (approximately 90 percent) private pension reform, and Brazil enacted three pension reform laws, none of which created a privatized system. Argentina and Uruguay undertook modest structural pension reforms in which most or all (in the Argentine case) workers could opt to join a partially private pension system or remain within the fully public defined-benefit program. For workers choosing to participate in the private pension market in Argentina, the 1993 law established an approximately 54 percent private system for the average wage earner, whereas a more modest 37 percent of old age benefits would derive from the private account of an average wage worker in Uruguay.

EVIDENCE: STRUCTURED COMPARISON OF FOUR
LATIN AMERICAN COUNTRIES

The case studies in Part III were organized around three analytical dimensions: the initiation of reform processes in the technocracy (Chapter 5), broader

---

[1] Gill et al. 2005.
[2] Mesa-Lago 2005.
[3] AIOS 2006.

social conflicts over pension reform (Chapter 6), and legislative contestation over pension reform laws (Chapter 7).

Chapter 5 examined the initial technocratic processes where pension reform efforts were launched in Argentina, Brazil, Mexico, and Uruguay. I evaluated evidence of globalization's contradictory incentives and constraints on structural pension reform, for which the four cases offer broad variation. Argentina privatized in the context of high international liquidity and enjoyed broad (but temporary) financial leeway to undertake the costs of transition, and Brazilian government actors developed structural pension reform plans in the context of tight international constraints and an exceedingly narrow scope for financial maneuver. Mexico and Uruguay occupy intermediate positions in terms of financial leeway and international market constraints.

In the Argentine case, strong capital inflows in the early 1990s slackened the government's domestic financing constraints and dampened investors' sensitivity to risk. With a yawning current account deficit, however, strong capital inflows left Argentina increasingly vulnerable to capital flight, lending urgency to technocrats' desire to enact *some* degree of pension privatization as a signal of credibility to market actors. The overwhelming near-term risk of capital flight led reformers to discount the medium- and longer-term costs associated with pension privatization. This was evident in costly compromises that reformers accepted in order to lower political obstacles to reform – costs that could be financed in the short term due to the government's broad financial leeway and slackened credit constraints. The exceedingly short-term considerations governing the reform design became apparent in the years following the reform as slowing economic growth and tightening international liquidity made these costs more difficult to bear. Argentina's pension reform thus bears out quite well the expectations of my argument about globalization's double bind.

Brazil represents the antipodal case to Argentina in terms of international market strictures and domestic financial leeway. Brazilian technocrats developed a structural pension reform proposal in 1997, but the following year external conditions became highly unfavorable. In the wake of the 1997 Asian financial crisis, investors' tolerance for emerging market risk was sharply on the wane. Brazil at the same time carried a heavy government debt burden and struggled to curtail its fiscal deficit. When technocrats proposed a structural pension reform that would have imposed a medium-term financial cost on the government, financiers in the central bank and finance ministry rejected the plan on the argument that international investors would not tolerate any reform that would raise the government's debt-to-GDP ratio. Thus even though Brazil might have been rewarded in the long term for its structural reform, the short-term intolerance for any additional government debt in the late 1990s led technocrats to forego structural pension reform plans, embracing instead a notional-account model for the reform of Brazil's private sector pension regime. By maintaining the pay-as-you go financing and state management of pension funds, Brazil's 1999 pension reform did not impose a transitional cost on the government, allowing it to escape market punishment.

The Mexican government had a moderate debt ratio and low fiscal deficit at the time of its reform, whereas Uruguay recorded a large fiscal deficit but a modest sovereign debt ratio when its structural pension reform was designed. Both countries faced tighter international liquidity conditions than Argentina did, narrowing reformers' scope to finance privatization through the issuance of new government bonds. As in Brazil, the years prior to structural reform in Mexico and Uruguay were characterized by deep vulnerability to capital flight, with wide current account deficits and declining foreign currency reserves. Government actors thus had to be sensitive to the risk signals transmitted to international markets in order to avoid a loss of investor confidence. Consistent with expectations, both countries developed pension reforms that were shaped by the desire to avoid the issuance of new government debt.

In Uruguay, reformers maintained the ceiling on the public pension tier and did not compensate workers who divided their contributions between the public and private systems, therein reducing their public benefit. This decision obviated the need for recognition bonds, which would have increased Uruguay's debt-to-GDP ratio. The lower potential transitional cost of privatization in Mexico permitted the government to adopt a deeper pension privatization. Nevertheless, Mexican technocrats took measures to avoid any short-term increase in sovereign debt by retaining considerable unfunded public pension liabilities to workers in the transitional generation. There, too, the use of explicit debt to finance the transition was avoided. Instead, the "lifetime switch" option allowed current workers to choose at the time of retirement the better of the balance in their individual pension account or the benefits owed to them under the rules of the old pension system. This decision revealed a direct tradeoff of the medium-term goal of closing the unfunded state pension liabilities for the more pressing short-term objective of avoiding a significant increase in sovereign debt. In Mexico and Uruguay, therefore, technocrats designed their structural pension reforms in ways that curtailed the medium- and long-term role of market forces in reformed pension systems in order to avoid the near-term risk of market punishment.

Chapter 6 turned attention to the ways in which institutional legacies – in particular, their political legacies – shape contestation over structural pension reform in society. I expected the efficacy of efforts to gain public support for pension reform to be mediated first by the credibility of reform-seeking leaders, where left or labor-based parties should enjoy distinctive advantages, and by citizens' everyday knowledge of the institution. The chapter began by examining the diverse portraits of the four nations' pension institutions generated by public opinion surveys at middecade. The surveys, while at best a rough proxy for the political inheritance, revealed broad support across these nations for state-run pension provision. Variations in these views, moreover, corresponded approximately to differences in movements toward privatization. Mexico, the more radical reformer of the four cases, exhibited the lowest support for a primarily state-run pension system, while Uruguay recorded the highest confidence in the state. The principal evidence in the chapter, however, drew from the comparative studies of the four countries.

In Argentina, the political legacy of the pension institution revolved around expectations of a robust and solidaristic state pension system. Even though such beliefs placed firm limits on the government's privatizing ambitions – obliging the government to maintain a universal state pension – the institution's conspicuous performance failures in the 1980s nurtured widespread dissatisfaction with it, opening the door to some kind of reform. President Menem won support for partial privatization on claims that such a reform would significantly improve pension benefits and provide great material rewards. As the leader of the Peronist Party, traditionally labor's representative, Menem could credibly assert that such reform would be in the interest of workers. His assertions were also lent credibility by the real material rewards resulting from Argentina's market-oriented economic reforms in the early 1990s. Public acquiescence to pension privatization thus rested heavily on instrumental expectations of material gain, as attachments to the state-run system had been dislodged by earlier poor performance. But the promised material gains of market-oriented reform in Argentina began to erode by the end of the decade, and with it, support for the private pension system frayed as well. Sharp declines in compliance with Argentina's pension system and public acquiescence to state incursions in and curtailment of the private pension system reveal the fragility of the reformed institution's social foundations, and the merely instrumental commitments to it.

In Mexico, the modest benefits and limited coverage of the nation's relatively young pension institution would predict weak obstacles to deep structural reform. But privatization of Mexico's IMSS pension system proved much more difficult than the structural legacy would envisage. Not only did the state inherit a constitutional duty to finance old age pensions, but Mexican citizens held strong expectations of the inviolability of acquired rights (*conquistas históricas*). What is more, the pension system's performance had not fallen short of expectations; to the contrary, benefits were increased significantly in the years prior to reform, and the economic fallout from the 1995 peso crisis only strengthened workers' attachment to their social insurance benefits as one of the few reliable sources of income. Winning labor unions' consent to the pension reform thus obliged the Mexican government to make significant compromises in the scope of market forces in the reformed pension system. Not only did the government concede a minimum-pension guarantee, but it also established an ongoing public financial contribution to each worker's private pension fund, the social quota. Reformers also delayed full implementation of the new system for a generation to protect the acquired rights of current workers. Far from closing pension liabilities as the government expected, reformers were obliged to retain significant unfunded state liabilities even in the reformed pension institution.

In Brazil, strong support for the notion of a fundamental public responsibility for social security placed immense obstacles before the reform of the nation's old age pension institution. Although the center-right Cardoso government pointed to stark regressivities in the benefit structure, such wide disparities had come to be expected of the system and thus did not provoke a loss of confidence in it. Because the institution's financial deficits were not perceptible to most citizens, moreover, government claims of an institutional crisis rang hollow. Opposition to President Cardoso's reform was reinforced further by its denunciation as unjust and unnecessary by the left-wing Workers' Party. Thus it was only when Cardoso's claims of necessity were corroborated by an international currency crisis that support for modest institutional change was won; reform nevertheless remained deeply unpopular.

A few years later, ironically, leftist President Luiz Inácio Lula da Silva of the Workers' Party used much of the same rhetoric to advance his reform of the public sector pension system. By contrast to President Cardoso's protracted and hard-fought battle over pension reform, Lula's partisan credibility on the pension issue enabled him to win rapid sanction and broad public support for a 2003 constitutional amendment to significantly restructure the nation's civil service pension system despite its similarities to earlier and more unpopular Cardoso proposals.

In Uruguay, the broad coverage and generous benefits provided by the long-established state pension system should have made privatization nearly impossible. But high expectations of a fair and effective pension system would trigger broad public dissatisfaction in the 1990s when citizens came to perceive the institution as having fallen short of these standards. Nevertheless, even the modest privatization enacted in 1995 was not easily won. After repeated failures at reform under President Lacalle, centrist President Julio Sanguinetti won support for structural pension reform on the basis of the system's patent financial crisis and widespread perceptions of fraud. Sanguinetti defended this measure as being consistent with widely shared norms, labeling it "solidary, effective and just." Despite being led by a centrist government with left-wing opposition, Sanguinetti gathered an oversize legislative majority to back his structural pension reform, revealing the emergence of a distributive, credit-claiming logic around his reform. He did so by adding important subsidies and benefits to the measure, touting its material reward and finally, by gaining the endorsement in the legislature of the small, center-left Nuevo Espacio party, which lent partisan credibility to the reform. The reform's social foundations thus appear to be strong: Of the three pension privatizations examined here, Uruguay's has recorded the highest level of active compliance following the reform.

Chapter 7 examined legislative conflicts over pension reform in the four Latin American cases. In Argentina and Mexico, reformers from labor-backed parties held disciplined majorities in the national legislatures; however, such power was more fragmented in Brazil and Uruguay, and reform-seeking governments faced a credible left-wing opposition. Although the distribution of legislative authority in the first two cases strongly favored the approval of structural pension reform, formal majority power did not assure legislative sanction of those reforms. Rather, reluctant labor unions in Argentina and Mexico activated a veto logic in legislative conflicts, isolating the majority party and obliging government leaders to make significant compromises in their proposed reform in order to win the backing of labor and hence of legislative majorities.

In Brazil and Uruguay, by contrast, significant loss-imposing reforms were sanctioned by oversized coalitions despite the fact that no governing party commanded a legislative majority – much less a disciplined one. This was possible only when reformers induced a distributive logic in legislative conflict over pension reform. These outcomes stand in sharp contrast to the conflicts over pension reform in Argentina and Mexico, where only threadbare majorities were formed behind structural reform. Nevertheless, pension reform in Brazil and Uruguay was hard-fought and won only after repeated defeats. In both countries, however, the final pension reforms enacted were no less ambitious than previously defeated proposals. This was possible when reformers' efforts to enhance the distributive tendency of reform gained external corroboration, allowing reformers to bargain the support of erstwhile veto players. Even though such bargains in Uruguay entailed measures to enhance the actual distributive nature of the pension reform, pork-barrel compensation provided the cement for voting coalitions in Brazil.

Ultimately, the task of this analysis has been to explain how, when, and to what degree formal institutions undergo fundamental change, where such change implies a departure from what was long a stable social bargain. The argument and evidence examined in this study thus hew closely to the process of formal, legal institutional change associated with pension reform. Two elements emerge from this analysis as necessary for juridical change to occur in the near term: that proposals for privatization reach the political agenda and that they achieve legislative enactment. Although democratic governments expend considerable time, energy, and effort seeking public support for institutional change, we have seen that reforms can be won in the short term even where they receive only lukewarm public backing, or where citizens lack a clear understanding of the nature and implications of the reform altogether. Indeed, it is possible to change a law without changing its underlying social bargain. But where reform proceeds without societal consent, what happens after it is enacted? Can the new institution be *sustained,* and even be self-sustaining, where its basic social underpinnings have not changed? Or will such reform be merely a temporary disturbance in the long-run path, with the old equilibrium ultimately reasserting itself?

FROM JURIDICAL CHANGE TO LONG-TERM CONSOLIDATION

The theoretical and empirical analyses in this book have focused on the formal, juridical process of institutional change; questions of implementation and long-term consolidation – and thus the change of *informal* institutions and social foundations on which the formal institutions rest – provide an ample agenda for future research. Although we may begin to develop hypotheses about these long-term processes, evidence to bear them out will emerge only over the medium to long term. Several important questions define this agenda. First, will the new social bargains implied by the formal transformation of old age pensions consolidate around a new, stable, and self-reinforcing institutional path? Or, will tightly held principles of solidarity and expectations of a dominant state in social protection prove inhospitable to the reproduction of positive attitudes and behaviors associated with these systems, leading to their ultimate demise?

If we take seriously the view that institutions such as old age pensions entail much more than formal rules and legal provisions but also are constituted by a set of normative principles and expectations that emerge over the long term, then we must view the formal process of institutional change as just one step – albeit an important one – in the broader process of institutional change. Indeed, a rich body of research has located belief systems at the center of processes of institutional reproduction and change. This study has drawn upon that literature to examine how the political, social, and institutional forces that long reinforced a given institution may later accommodate or become the very mechanisms of fundamental institutional change. The view that a new institution is legitimate, and that it will make good on its benefit promises, is an important part of that feedback process. One implication of that argument thus is that a new institutional path is more likely to become stable and self-reinforcing where it rests upon a *social* foundation of beliefs that the new bargain is fair and effective. To the extent that such beliefs are subject to contestation in the formal political processes, we may observe through such contests the establishment of its social foundations – the beliefs and attitudes – that underpin the new design.

Analysis of these foundations may yield insight into whether the new institutions will be stable and self-reinforcing, or weak and ultimately self-undermining. In formal conflicts over institutional change, therefore, we may observe more than simply the mechanisms of formal institutional change, but also the laying of the groundwork for a new social bargain. While their full implications will only be apparent in the medium to long term, emergent compliance data offer preliminary evidence of the solidity of the new paths in social risk protection in Latin America. Indeed, in order to operate, the new private pension institutions require that individuals are willing to forego consumption during working life by contributing regularly to their individual pension account. Without the confidence that the institution will return a decent or fair pension benefit at a much later time, citizens may face powerful incentives to evade such contributions, particularly where incomes are quite low and state enforcement mechanisms are weak, as in many parts of the developing world. In such cases where compliance with the new private pension institutions is quasi-voluntary, active contribution rates may be taken as a powerful signal that positive and reinforcing beliefs about their justice and efficacy have emerged, and a fertile social foundation for their consolidation has been established.

When is this likely? I have argued that citizens' beliefs and attitudes associated with an institution – its political legacy – are shaped by socially transmitted knowledge and information provided by the political process. If this is correct, then privately managed defined-contribution pension systems will face much steeper challenges to consolidation than the traditional public social insurance pension systems did. This is because public pay-as-you-go pension systems began to offer pensions to a generation of elderly citizens immediately upon their creation, therein establishing highly visible "evidence" of their effectiveness. By contrast, private pension schemes will take three to four *decades* to yield broad material evidence of their effectiveness. If confidence in the efficacy of these institutions is not established along the way, then negative expectations may become self-fulfilling, and pessimism may undermine compliance, and possibly the institution itself.

The agenda for research that lies ahead is thus to understand when a step off the path will establish a new road, and when it will become just a temporary diversion from the previous institutional equilibrium. Although we will only have evidence of the solidity of these new paths in Latin America over the medium to long term, we may begin to consider hypotheses that emerge from this study about the mechanisms and prospects for the consolidation of the new social contracts in income protection. The question is already in the offing: The recent partial rollback of the Argentine pension system offers an ominous portent for what was once upheld as a model among Latin America's private pension systems. So too is the movement in Chile to expand the state role in pensions an unpromising sign for the institution once upheld as the poster child of privatization around the world.

Inquiry into the prospects for consolidation of the new institutional bargains in old age income protection may include, inter alia, analysis of the way in which political conflicts over institutional change were fought, and thus the political foundations of public consent to this reform. Was privatization embraced as a way to save the existing pension system from impending bankruptcy? Or, were underlying norms of fairness and expectations of what people are due from the state and each other challenged and transformed? Further yet, did support for reform rest largely on instrumental expectations of greater wealth? By reexamining the terms on which institutional change was fought, we may find important evidence of the new program's social bases, and thus of its likely long-term stability. Depending upon the correspondence between the program's functioning and the promises on which consent to institutional change was won, scholars may draw expectations regarding whether those new designs will prove stable, or whether they will prove to be mere disturbances that unvaryingly return to the long-established institutional path.

The premise of this line of inquiry is that the long-term possibilities for new social institutions to consolidate may rest to an important degree, but not exclusively, in the hands of political actors. This does not diminish the importance of establishing a sound technical and financial foundation for the institution. For good design and sound institutional functioning are critical to sustaining any institution like old age pensions that involves significant financial commitments. But technical criteria alone may not be *sufficient* for institutions such as old age pensions to become stable and self-reinforcing in the long term, given the importance of citizens' perceptions of the existing program in the processes of institutional change. The implication of this view is that the *terms* on which conflicts over the new institution are fought may influence not only the prospects for reform to occur, as evidenced in this study, but those political conflicts may also have longer-lasting effects on the durability of the new designs.

A NEW PATH IN SOCIAL PROVISION?

José Piñera, the architect of Chile's pension privatization, was known to have said, "Good policy is good politics."[4] That is, with the proper technical foundations, political support for a reform policy will eventually fall into place. If this view is correct, then well-designed private pension models should, in time, be consolidated; a liberal social order will eventually emerge from the effective operation of technically sound institutional reforms. Proponents have upheld Chile's free-market turn as evidence for this view.[5] Despite having been enacted by decree under the military dictatorship of Augusto Pinochet, the cross-party endorsement of Chile's pension privatization after the transition to democracy in 1989 and the nation's strong macroeconomic performance in subsequent years are taken as hallmarks of the reform's success.

But in Chile, as elsewhere in Latin America, the prospects for private pension institutions to create their own social foundations looks ever more remote. Not only have the market-based institutions in the region failed to live up to promises of the market-oriented paradigm, but citizens are displaying little of the confidence in the new programs that reformers anticipated, as evidenced by anemic compliance rates. This disenchantment may not owe exclusively to wariness of expanded market-based governance. For in many cases, technical and administrative incompetence corroded public faith in traditional state institutions as well. Ongoing state regulation, the imprint of which permeates nearly every aspect of privatized pension institutions, offers little advantage to private pension funds seeking to win citizens' confidence in their efficacy. Even where the market-based pension systems rest upon sound technical foundations, if perceptions of legitimacy *and* efficacy prove elusive, then these institutions may stand little chance of replacing wholesale the social and intergenerational bargains that long underpinned the risk-pooling social insurance models.

But change is possible; history provides strong evidence of departures from long-stable paths of social organization that arise from the suspension of long-held beliefs and expectations of what the state can and should do. The emergence of the welfare state in the twentieth century is one such example. Such "great" transformations may be difficult to repeat as long as political beliefs and material expectations remain powerful constraints on institutional change. Given the tremendous economic forces militating against pension privatization – including globalization itself – the prospect for liberal reform models to fully displace the social-insurance pension systems is in serious doubt,

---

[4] Piñera 1994, p. 231; cf. Rodrik 1996, p. 10.
[5] Rodrik 1996, p. 10.

though it remains an open question for future research. Yet even in Chile, where attention to good policy over politics seemed to have been borne out, deep fissures in the groundwork of the market archetype have begun to emerge. Under the leadership of President Michelle Bachelet, a significant reform to expand the state role in pension provision has been launched. Most threatening to the private pension industry, moreover, is that the shift back toward state responsibility has been impelled by challenges *not* to the technical design of the institution, but rather by the potentially more damning charge that the once-lauded private pension system is "unfair."[6]

[6] "Chile's Candidates Agree to Agree on Pension Woes" 2006.

References

ABRAPP. 1999. *Consolidado Estatístico* VIII, 11.

Abrucio, Fernando, and David Samuels. 1997. "A 'Nova' Política dos Governadores." *Lua Nova* 40, 41: 137–66.

"O acordo da prevideîncia." 16 January 1996. *Jornal do Brasil.*

Achen, Christopher H. 1986. *The Statistical Analysis of Quasi-experiments.* Berkeley: University of California Press.

Afonso, José Roberto. 2004. "Previdência Social e Combate à Pobreza." Available at http://www.e-agora.org.br/.

AIOS (Asociación Internacional de Organismos de Supervisión de Fondos de Pensiones). 2004, 2006, 2007. *Boletín Estadístico AIOS.* Available at http://www.aiosfp.org/estadisticas/estadisticas_boletin_estadistico.shtml.

Alarcón, Diana, and Eduardo Zepeda. 2004. "Economic Reform or Social Development? The Challenges of a Period of Reform in Latin America: Case Study of Mexico." *Oxford Development Studies* 32, 1: 59–86.

Aldrich, John. 1995. *Why Parties? The Origin and Transformation of Political Parties in America.* Chicago: University of Chicago Press.

Aldrich, John H. and David W. Rohde. 1997–8. "The Transition to Republican Rule in the House: Implications for Theories of Congressional Politics." *Political Science Quarterly* 112, 4: 541–67.

"Aliados comemoram baixos indices de dissidência na votação das mudanças." 5 November 1998. *Estado de São Paulo.*

"Aliados, mas nunca se sabe." 15 October 2003. *O Globo*: 3.

Allan, James P. and Lyle Scruggs. 2004. "Political Partisanship and Welfare State Reform in Advanced Industrial Societies." *American Journal of Political Science* 48, 3: 496–512.

Alonso, Guillermo V. 1997. "Democracia y Reformas: Las Tensiones entre Decretismo y Participación: El Caso de la Reforma Previsional Argentina." Paper delivered at the III Congreso Nacional de Ciencia Política, Mar de Plata, Argentina.

———. 1998. "Democracia y Reformas: Las Tensions Entre Descretiso y Deliberación. El Caso de la Reforma Previsional Argentina." *Desarrollo Económico* 38, 150: 595–626.

Alston, Lee and Bernardo Mueller. 2005. "Pork for Policy: Executive and Legislative Exchange in Brazil." *Journal of Law Economics and Organization* 22, 1: 87–114.

Alston, Lee, Marcus André Melo, Bernardo Mueller, and Carlos Pereira. 2004. "Political Institutions, Policymaking Processes and Policy Outcomes in Brazil." Research Network Working Papers # R-509, 30 April. Inter-American Development Bank, Washington, DC.

Alvarez, R. Michael and John Brehm. 1995. "American Ambivalence Towards Abortion Policy: Development of a Heteroskedastic Probit Model of Competing Values." *American Journal of Political Science* 39, 4: 1055–82.

Ames, Barry. 1994. "The Reverse Coattails Effect: Local Party Organization in the 1989 Brazilian Presidential Election." *American Political Science Review* 88, 1: 95–111.

———. 1995a. "Electoral Rules, Constituency Pressures, and Pork Barrel: Bases of Voting in the Brazilian Congress." *The Journal of Politics* 57, 2: 324–43.

———. 1995b. "Electoral Strategy under Open-List Proportional Representation." *American Journal of Political Science* 39, 2: 406–33.

———. 2001. *The Deadlock of Democracy in Brazil.* Ann Arbor: University of Michigan Press.

———. 2002. "Party Discipline in the Chamber of Deputies." In Scott Morgenstern and Benito Nacif, eds., *Legislative Politics in Latin America.* Cambridge: Cambridge University Press: 185–221.

Anderson, Karen M. 2001. "The Politics of Retrenchment in a Social Democratic Welfare State: Reform of Swedish Pensions and Unemployment Insurance." *Comparative Political Studies* 34, 9: 1063–91.

Anderson, Karen M. and Traute Meyer. 2003. "Social Democracy, Unions, and Pension Politics in Germany and Sweden." *Journal of Public Policy* 23, 1: 23–54.

Andrews, David M. 1994. "Capital Mobility and State Autonomy: Toward a Structural Theory of International Monetary Relations." *International Studies Quarterly* 38, 2: 193–218.

ANFIP (Asociação Nacional dos Auditores Fiscais da Receta Federal do Brasil). 1994. *ANFIP Na Revisão Constitucional.* Brasília: Fundação ANFIP.

Antokoletz, Daniel. 1941. *Tratado de Legislación del Trabajo y Previsión Social, con Referencias Especiales al Derecho Argentino y de las Demás Repúblicas Americanas.* Tomo II, Buenos Aires, Argentina: Kraft ltda.

"Após 16 horas, CCJ do Senado aprova reforma da Previdência." 26 September 2003. *O Globo*: 2.

Arellano Gault, David, and Juan Pablo Guerrero Amparán. 2003. "Stalled Administrative Reforms of the Mexican State." In Ben Ross Schneider and Blanca Heredia, eds., *Reinventing Leviathan: The Politics of Administrative Reform in Developing Countries.* Boulder, CO: Lynne Rienner.

Armijo, Leslie Elliott. 1999. *Financial Globalization and Democracy in Emerging Markets,* New York: Palgrave/St. Martin's Press.

Arnold, R. Douglas. 1979. *Congress and the Bureaucracy: A Theory of Influence.* New Haven, CT: Yale University Press.

———. 1998. "The Politics of Reforming Social Security." *Political Science Quarterly* 113, 2: 213–40.

Arrau, Patricio. 1990. "Social Security Reform: The Capital Accumulation and Intergenerational Distribution Effect." Policy Research Working Paper #512. The World Bank, Washington, DC.

Arrau, Patricio and Klaus Schmidt-Hebbel. 1993. "Macroeconomic and Intergenerational Welfare Effects of Transition from Pay-as-you-go to Fully-Funded Pension Systems." Unpublished Manuscript. June. The World Bank, Washington, DC.

Aspe, Pedro. 1993. *Economic Transformation the Mexican Way.* Cambridge, MA: Massachusetts Institute of Technology Press.

Astori, Danilo. October 29, 1998. Senator, National Assembly. Asamblea Uruguaya, Frente Amplio. Personal interview, Montevideo, Uruguay.

Atchugarri, Alejandro. October 21, 1998. Representative to National Assembly, Chamber of Deputies. Personal interview, Montevideo, Uruguay.

"Atraso na reforma custa R$ 270 milhões." 18 November 2003, *O Estado de São Paulo.*

Auerbach, Alan and Laurence Kotlikoff. 1987. *Dynamic Fiscal Policy.* New York: Cambridge University Press.

Austen-Smith, David. 1990. "Credible Debate Equilibria." *Social Choice and Welfare* 7, 1: 75–93.

———. 1992. "Strategic Models of Talk in Political Decision Making." *International Political Science Review* 13, 1: 45–58.

Austen-Smith, David and Timothy J. Feddersen. 2006. "Deliberation, Preference Uncertainty and Voting Rules." *American Political Science Review* 100, 2: 209–18.

Axelrod, Robert. 1970. *Conflict of Interest: A Theory of Divergent Goals with Applications to Politics.* Chicago: Markham.

Azuara, Oliver. 2003. "The Mexican Defined Contribution Pension System: Perspective for Low Income Workers." Background Paper for Regional Study on Social Security Reform. The World Bank, Washington, DC.

Babb, Sarah. 2001. *Managing Mexico: Economists from Nationalism to Neoliberalism.* Princeton, NJ: Princeton University Press.

Baker, Andy. 2000. "Mass Support for Free Market Reforms: Self-Interest and Elite Influence in Brazil." Paper presented at the Annual Meeting of the American Political Science Association, Washington, DC, August 31–September 3.

Baker, Dean and Mark Weisbrot. 1999. *Social Security: The Phony Crisis.* Chicago: University of Chicago Press.

Baldwin, Peter. 1990. *The Politics of Social Solidarity: Class Bases of the European Welfare State, 1875–1975.* New York: Cambridge University Press.

Ball, Robert. 2000. *Insuring the Essentials.* New York: Century Foundation.

Banco Central do Brasil. "Gross and Net General Government Debt (% GDP)." Time Series Statistics. Available at http://www.bcb.gov.br/?NPDDEBTN.

Barclays Bank. 1999. *International Financial Outlook: Brazil.* February. London: Barclays Bank.

Barr, Nicholas. 2002. "The Pensions Puzzle: Prerequisites and Policy Choices in Pension Design." *Economic Issues,* 29. International Monetary Fund, Washington, DC. Available at www.imf.org/external/pubs/ft/issues/issues29/index.htm.

Bartolini, Leonardo and Allan Drazen. 1997. "Capital-Account Liberalization as a Signal." *American Economic Review* 87, 1: 138–54.

Bates, Robert. 1994. "Comment on John Williamson's 'In Search of a Manual for Technopols'" In John Williamson, ed., *The Political Economy of Economic Policy Reform.* Washington, DC: Institute for International Economics: 29–34.

Bates, Robert and Anne Krueger, eds. 1993. *Political and Economic Interactions in Policy Reforms.* Cambridge, MA: Basil Blackwell.

Beck, Thorsten, George Clarke, Alberto Groff, Philip Keefer, and Patrick Walsh. 2001. "New Tools in Comparative Political Economy: The Database of Political Institutions." *World Bank Economic Review* 15, 1: 165–76. 2005 Edition. Available at http://go.worldbank.org/2EAGGLRZ40.

Becker, Gary S. 1996. "A Social Security Lesson from Argentina." *Business Week*, 21 October: 9.

Bejar, Alejandro Alvarez, Gabriel Mendoza Pichardo, and John F. Uggen. 1993. "Mexico 1988–1991: A Successful Economic Adjustment Program?" *Latin American Perspectives* 20, 3: 32–45.

Béland, Daniel. 2001. "Does Labor Matter? Institutions, Labor Unions and Pension Reform in France and the United States." *Journal of Public Policy* 21, 2: 153–72.

———. 2005. "Ideas and Social Policy: An Institutionalist Perspective." *Social Policy and Administration* 39, 1: 1–18.

Beltrão, Kaizô. 1994. "Viabilidad de la Seguridad Social." *Diagnóstico y Perspectivas de la Seguridad Social en Uruguay*. Programa de Cooperación Técnica Banco Inter-Americano de Desarollo. 704-OC. Montevideo, Uruguay.

———. June 23, 1999. Pension expert and Superintendent, Escola Nacional de Ciências Estatísticas, Instituto Brasileiro de Geografia e Estatística (IBGE). Personal interview, Rio de Janeiro, Brazil.

Berchese, Juan. October 19, 1998. Former President, Banco de Previsión Social. Personal interview, Montevideo, Uruguay.

Berelson, Bernard R., Paul F. Lazarsfeld, and William N. McPhee. 1954. *Voting: A Study of Opinion Formation in a Presidential Campaign*. Chicago: University of Chicago Press.

Bergmark, Åke, Mats Thorslund, and Elisabet Lindberg. 2000. "Beyond Benevolence-Solidarity and Welfare State Transition in Sweden." *International Journal of Social Welfare* 9, 4: 238–49.

Bergquist, Charles. 1986. *Labor in Latin America: Comparative Essays on Chile, Argentina, Venezuela, and Colombia*. Stanford, CA: Stanford University Press.

Berinsky, Adam J. 2002. "Silent Voices: Social Welfare Policy Opinion and Political Equality in America." *American Journal of Political Science* 46, 1: 276–87.

———. 2004. *Silent Voices: Public Opinion and Political Participation in America*. Princeton, NJ: Princeton University Press.

Bernhard, William and David Leblang. 2006. *Democratic Processes and Financial Markets: Pricing Politics*. New York: Cambridge University Press.

Bertranou, Fabio M., Rafael Rofman, and Carlos O. Grushka. 2003. "From Reform to Crisis: Argentina's Pension System." *International Social Security Review* 56, 2: 103–14.

Bevilaqua, Afonso Sant'anna, Dionísio Dias Carneiro, Márcio Gomes Pinto Garcia, Rogéro Furquim Laderia Werneck, Fernando Blanco, Patrica Pierotti, Marcelo Rezende, and Tatiana Didier. 2001. "The Structure of Public Sector Debt in Brazil." Research Network Working Paper #R-424. Inter-American Development Bank, Washington, DC.

Bier, Amaury. June 9, 1999. Executive-Secretary, Ministério da Fazenda. Personal interview, Brasília, Brazil.

Blyth, Mark M. 2002. *Great Transformations: Economic Ideas and Institutional Change in the Twentieth Century*. New York: Cambridge University Press.

Bodie, Zvi, Alan J. Marcus, and Robert C. Merton. 1988. "Defined Benefit versus Defined Contribution Pension Plans: What Are the Real Trade-offs?" In Zvi Bodie, John Boden, and David Wise, eds., *Pensions in the U.S. Economy.* Chicago: University of Chicago Press: 139–62.

Bonoli, Giuliano. 1997. "Classifying Welfare States: a Two-dimension Approach." *Journal of Social Policy* 26, 3: 351–72.

———. 2000. *The Politics of Pension Reform: Institutions and Policy Change in Western Europe.* New York: Cambridge University Press.

———. 2001. "Political Institutions, Veto Points, and the Process of Welfare State Adaptation." In Paul Pierson, ed., *The New Politics of the Welfare State.* Oxford: Oxford University Press: 314–37.

Börsch-Supan, Axel and Christina Wilke. 2003. "The German Social Security System: How It Was and How It Will Be." MEA-Discussion Paper 43–2003, MEA, Universität Mannheim and MRRC-Discussion Paper, University of Michigan, Ann Arbor.

Borzutzky, Silvia. 2002. *Vital Connections: Politics, Social Security, and Inequality in Chile.* Notre Dame: University of Notre Dame Press.

"Brazil Appears Headed toward Some Stability." 21 January 1999. *The Wall Street Journal*: B11.

"Brazil: Austerity Package Faces Tough Passage." 6 November 1998. Geoff Dyer. *Financial Times.*

"Brazil Comes of Age on the Global Stage." 14 September 2004. Raymond Colitt and Richard Lapper. *Financial Times,* Comment and Analysis: Ft.com.

"Brazil: Congress Double Whammy Knocks Government for Six." 7 March 1996. *IPS-Inter Press Service.*

"Brazilian House Adopts Reform Bill; Pension Measure Seen as Crucial to Stabilizing Nation's Economy." 21 January 1999. Anthony Faiola. *Washington Post*: A19.

"Brazil, Oct '99: Economic/Financial Update." 8 October 1999. *Financial Times.*

"Brazil's Chamber of Deputies Approves Highly Unpopular Key Tax." 21 January 1999. *Agence France Presse.*

"Brazil's Congress to Vote on Key Economic Reform Measure." 20 January 1999. *The Associated Press.*

"Brazil's Senate Passes Pension Bill in Final Vote." 11 December 2003. Bloomberg.com.

"Brazil Strikes Win Rethink on Pensions." 10 July 2003. Raymond Colitt. *Financial Times.*

Brehm, John. 1993. *The Phantom Respondents: Opinion Surveys and Political Representation.* Ann Arbor: University of Michigan Press.

Bresser-Pereira and Luiz Carlos. 2003. "The 1995 Public Management Reform in Brazil: Reflections of a Reformer." In Ben Ross Schneider and Blanca Heredia, eds., *Reinventing Leviathan: The Politics of Administrative Reform in Developing Countries.* Boulder, CO: Lynne Rienner: 89–109.

Brodkin, Evelyn Z. and Dennis Young. 1989. "Making Sense of Privatization: What Can We Learn from Economic and Political Analysis?" In Sheila B. Kamerman and Alfred J. Kahn, eds., *Privatization and the Welfare State.* Princeton, NJ: Princeton University Press.

Brooks, Sarah. 2002. "Social Protection and Economic Integration: The Politics of Pension Reform in an Era of Capital Mobility." *Comparative Political Studies* 35, 5: 491–525.

————. 2005. "Interdependent and Domestic Foundations of Policy Change: The Diffusion of Pension Privatization Around the World." *International Studies Quarterly* 49, 2: 273–94.

————. 2007. "When Does Diffusion Matter? Explaining the Spread of Structural Pension Reforms Across Nations." *The Journal of Politics* 69, 3: 701–15.

Brooks, Sarah and R. Kent Weaver. 2006. "Lashed to the Mast: The Political Economy of National Defined Contribution Pensions." In Robert Holzmann and Edward Palmer, eds. *Pension Reform: Issues and Prospects for Non-Financial Defined Contribution (NDC) Schemes*, Washington, DC: The World Bank: 345–85.

Bruno, Michael and William Easterly. 1996. "Inflation's Children: Tales of Crises that Beget Reforms." *American Economic Review* 86, 1: 213–17.

Bucheli, Marisa, Alvaro Forteza, and Ianina Rossi. 2006. "Seguridad Social y Género en Uruguay: Un Análisis de las Diferencias de Acceso a la Jubilación." Documento de Trabajo # 0406. Department of Economics (dECON), Universidad de la República, Montevideo, Uruguay.

Buquet, Daniel, Daniel Chasquetti, and Juan Andrés Moraes. 1998. "Fragmentación Política y Gobierno en el Uruguay: ¿Un Enfermo Imaginario?" Unpublished Manuscript. Facultad de Ciencias Sociales, Universidad de la República, Montevideo, Uruguay.

Burgess, Katrina. 1999. "Loyalty Dilemmas and Market Reform: Party-Union Alliances under Stress in Mexico, Spain, and Venezuela." *World Politics* 52, 1, October: 105–34.

Burgoon, Brian. 2001. "Globalization and Welfare Compensation: Disentangling the Ties that Bind." *International Organization* 55, 3: 509–51.

Bustos, Pablo. 1995. "Argentina: Un Capitalismo Emergente?" *Más Allá de la Estabilidad: Argentina en la época de Globalización y la Regionalización*. Buenos Aires, Argentina: Fundación Friedrich Ebert.

————. July 26, 1998. Economist, Fundación Ebert. Personal interview, Buenos Aires, Argentina.

Cailloux, Jacques and Stephany Griffith-Jones. 2003. "Global Capital Flows to East Asia: Surges and Reversals." In Stephany Griffith-Jones, Ricardo Gottschalk, and Jacques Cailloux, eds. *International Capital Flows in Calm and Turbulent Times: The Need for New International Architecture*. Ann Arbor: University of Michigan Press.

Calvo, Carlos. October 14, 1998. Manager of Administration, Banco de Previsión Social. Personal interview, Montevideo, Uruguay.

Calvo, Guillermo and Jacob Frenkel. 1991. "Credit Markets, Credibility, and Economic Transformation." *Journal of Economic Perspectives* 5, 4: 139–48.

Calvo, Guillermo, Leonardo Leiderman, and Carmen M. Reinhart. 1993. "Capital Inflows to Latin America: The Role of External Factors." IMF Staff Papers: 108–51.

————. 1996. "Inflows of Capital to Developing Countries in the 1990s." *The Journal of Economic Perspectives* 10, 2: 123–39.

Calvo, Guillermo and Enrique Mendoza. 2000. "Contagion, Globalization and the Volatility of Capital Flows." In Sebastian Edwards, ed., *Capital Flows and the Emerging Economies*. Chicago: University of Chicago Press.

"Câmara aprova em primeiro turno." 6 August 2003. *Jornal do Brasil*.

"Câmara aprova reforma em 2° turno." 25 September 2003. *Folha de São Paulo.*

"Câmara derruba redutor para pensão de servidores." 18 June 1998. *O Globo*: 5.

Cameron, David. 1978. "The Expansion of the Public Economy: A Comparative Analysis." *The American Political Science Review* 72, 4: 1243–61.

Campbell, John L. 1998. "Institutional Analysis and the Role of Ideas in Political Economy." *Theory and Society* 27, 1: 377–409.

Cantor, Richard and Frank Packer. 1996. "Determinants and Impacts of Sovereign Credit Ratings." Federal Reserve Bank of New York Research Paper No. 9608.

Cardinale, Mirko. 2002. "A Model of the UK Equity Premium." Watson Wyatt Technical Paper #2002-RU12. London.

"Cardoso Again Criticizes Congress for Delay in Reforms." 7 August 1997, *Gazeta Mercantil Invest News.*

"Cardoso Government Is Approved by 58% of Population." 10 December 1998, *Gazeta Mercantil Invest News.*

"Cardoso Government Loses Support in Opinion Polls." 25 May 1998, *Gazeta Mercantil Invest News.*

Carey, John M. and Matthew Soberg Shugart. 1995. "Incentives to Cultivate a Personal Vote: A Rank Ordering of Electoral Formulas." *Electoral Studies* 14, 1: 417–39.

Caro Figueroa, Armando. July 27, 1998. Former Minister of Labor and Social Security. Personal interview, Buenos Aires, Argentina.

Carroll, Barry J. 1987. "Business Goals and Social Goals." In Barry J. Carroll, Ralph W. Conant, and Thomas A. Easton, eds., *Private Means – Public Ends: Private Business in Social Service Delivery*. New York: Praeger Publishers.

"Carta ao Povo Brasileiro." 2003. Luiz Inácio Lula da Silva. Available at http://www.pt.gov.br.

Casar, María Amparo. 2002. "Executive-Legislative Relations: The Case of Mexico." In Scott Morgenstern and Benito Nacif, eds., *Legislative Politics in Latin America*. Cambridge: Cambridge University Press: 114–46.

Castelar Pinheiro, Armando. 2002. "The Brazilian Privatization Experience: What's Next?" Working Paper CBS 30-02. University of Oxford Centre for Brazilian Studies, Oxford.

Castiglioni, Rossana. 2001. "The Politics of Retrenchment: The Quandaries of Social Protection under Military Rule in Chile, 1973–1990." *Latin American Politics and Society* 43, 4: 37–66.

Castillo Marin, Luis. June 11, 1998. Ministry of Labor and Social Security. Personal interview, Buenos Aires, Argentina.

Castles, Francis. 1998. *Comparative Public Policy: Patterns of Post-War Transformation*. Northampton, MA: Edward Elgar Publishers.

———. 2002. "Developing new measures of welfare state change and reform." *European Journal of Political Research* 41, 5: 613–41.

Cechín, José. May 18, 1999. Executive Secretary, Ministério da Previdência e Assistência Social, Personal interview, Brasília, Brazil.

Centeno, Miguel Angel. 1993. "The New Leviathan: The Dynamics and Limits of Technocracy." *Theory and Society* 22, 3: 307–35.

———. 1997. *Democracy within Reason: Technocratic Revolution in Mexico*. University Park: Penn State Press.

Cerda, Luis. 1999. February 15, 1999. Economist, Ministry of Finance. Personal interview, Mexico City, Mexico.

Cetrángolo, Oscar. 1994. "El Nuevo Sistema Previsional: Una Reforma Definitica?" *Serie Notas*. October. Centro de Estudios Para el Cambio Estructural, Buenos Aires, Argentina.

──────. June 9, 1998. Economist, Centro de Estudios para el Cambio Estructural. Personal interview, Buenos Aires, Argentina.

Cetrángolo, Oscar and Carlos Grushka. 2004. "Sistema Previsional Argentino: Crisis, Reforma y Crisis de la Reforma." Santiago, Chile: Comisión Económica para América Latina (CEPAL). *Serie Financiamiento del Desarrollo #151*.

Cetrángolo, Oscar and Juan Pablo Jiménez. 2003. "Política fiscal en Argentina durante el régimen de convertibilidad." Santiago, Chile: Comisión Económica para América Latina (CEPAL). *Serie Gestión Pública # 35*.

"La CGT de Brunelli va con un rosario de quejas a su primera cita con el Gobierno." 15 April 1993. *Clarín*: 8–9.

"The CGT negotiated changes in exchange for attendance." 29 April 1993. *Clarín*: 22.

"Chile's Candidates Agree to Agree on Pension Woes." 10 January 2006. Larry Rohter. *New York Times*.

Clayton, Richard and Jonas Pontusson. 1998. "Welfare-State Retrenchment Revisited: Entitlement Cuts, Public Sector Restructuring, and Inegalitarian Trends in Advanced Capitalist Societies." *World Politics* 51, 1: 67–98.

Cobb, Roger W. and Charles D. Elder. 1983. *Participation in American Politics: The Dynamics of Agenda-building*, 2nd ed. Baltimore: Johns Hopkins University Press.

Collie, Melissa P. 1988. "The Rise of Coalition Politics: Voting in the U. S. House, 1933–1980." *Legislative Studies Quarterly* 3, August 13: 321–42.

Collier, Ruth Berins. 1992. *The Contradictory Alliance: State-Labor Relations and Regime Change in Mexico*. Berkeley: University of California.

Collier, Ruth Berins and David Collier. 1991. *Shaping the Political Arena: Critical Junctures, the Labor Movement, and Regime Dynamics in Latin America*. Princeton, NJ: Princeton University Press.

Colotuzzo, Luis Alberto. October 16, 1998. Director representing retirees, Banco de Previsión Social. Personal interview, Montevideo, Uruguay.

Comité de Evaluación y Seguimiento. 1998. "Informe Sobre la Implantación y Avances del Nuevo Sistema Previsional." 23 de Diciembre 1998, Available at http://www.opp.gub.uy/documentos.php.

Congressional Budget Office. 1999. "Social Security Privatization: Experiences Abroad." CBO Paper, January. Congressional Budget Office, Washington, DC. Available at http://www.cbo.gov/ftpdocs/10xx/doc1065/ssabroad.pdf.

CONSAR (Comisión Nacional del Sistema de Ahorro para el Retiro). 2005, 2007. *Boletín Estadístico: Estadísticas del SAR*. Available at http://www.consar.gob.mx/boletin_estadistico/afiliados.asp.

"Contribuição progressiva dos inativos." 20 April 2003. *O Globo*.

Corbacho, Ana and Gerd Schwartz. 2002. "Income Distribution and Social Expenditure Policies in Mexico: What Can We Learn from the Data?" *Lateinamerika Analysen* 1: 5–64.

Corrales, Javier. 1997. "Do Economic Crises Contribute to Economic Reform? Argentina and Venezuela in the 1990s." *Political Science Quarterly* 112, 1: 617–44.

──────. 2002. *Presidents Without Parties: The Politics of Economic Reform in Argentina and Venezuela in the 1990s*. University Park: Penn State University Press.

Corsetti, Giancarlo and Klaus Schmidt-Hebbel. 1997. "Pension Reform and Growth." In Salvador Valdés-Prieto, ed., *The Economics of Pensions: Principles, Policies, and International Experience*. Cambridge: Cambridge University Press: 127–59.

Cortés, Rosalía and Adriana Marshall. 1998. "Growth Strategy Requirements and Institutional Barriers in the Restructuring of Social Policy – The Case of Argentina." Paper prepared for delivery at the 1998 meeting of the Latin American Studies Association, Chicago, 24–26 September.

———. 1999. "Estrategia Económica, Instituciones y Negociación Política en la Reforma Social de los Noventa." *Desarrollo Económico* 39, 154: 195–212.

Cox, Gary W. and Mathew McCubbins. 1993. *Legislative Leviathan: Party Government in the House*. Berkeley: University of California Press.

Crabbe, Carolin A., ed. 2005. *A Quarter Century of Pension Reform in Latin America and the Caribbean: Lessons Learned and the Next Steps*. Washington, DC: Inter-American Development Bank.

Crabbe, Carolin A. and Juan Giral. 2004. "Transition Issues and Deepening Pension Reforms: Cases in Four Countries." SDS Working Paper. Inter-American Development Bank, Washington, DC.

Creedy, John and Richard Disney. 1985. *Social Insurance in Transition: An Economic Analysis*. Oxford: Oxford University Press.

Crepaz, Markus. 2001. "Veto Players, Globalization and the Redistributive Capacity of the State: A Panel Study of 15 OECD Countries." *Journal of Public Policy* 21, 1: 1–22.

Crusius, Yeda. May 20, 1999. Deputy, Partido da Social Democracia Brasileira (PSDB), National Congress. Personal interview, Brasília, Brazil.

Cruz-Saco, María Amparo and Carmelo Mesa-Lago, eds. 1998. *Do Options Exist? The Reform of Pension and Health Care Systems in Latin America*. Pittsburgh: Pittsburgh University Press.

Cukierman, Alex and Mariano Tommasi. 1998. "When Does It Take a Nixon to Go to China?" *The American Economic Review* 88, 1: 180–97.

"CUT e Força Sindical se unem contra reforma." 13 December 1985. *O Estado de São Paulo*: A-5.

"CUT quer derrotar proposta no plenário." 30 September 1999. Fred Ferreira. *O Estado de São Paulo*.

Dalton, Russell, Scott Flanagan and Paul Beck, eds. 1984. *Electoral Change in Advanced Industrial Democracies: Realignment or Dealignment?* Princeton, NJ: Princeton University Press.

Davrieux, Ariel. October 27, 1998. Director, Oficina de Planeamiento y Presupuesto. Personal interview, Montevideo, Uruguay.

Deacon, Bob, and Michelle Hulse. 1997. "The Making of Post-Communist Social Policy: The Role of International Agencies." *Journal of Social Policy* 26, 1: 43–62.

De Biase, Marcelo and Carlos Grushka. 2003. "Historias previsionales y la regularidad de los afiliados al SIJP." Buenos Aires: Superintendencia de Administradoras de Fondos de Pensiones. Serie Historias laborales en la seguridad social.

Demarco, Gustavo. June 16, July 18, 1998. General Manager, Superintendencia de Administradoras de Fondos de Jubilaciones y Pensiones (SAFJP). Personal interview, Buenos Aires, Argentina.

———. 2004. "The Argentine Pension System Reform and International Lessons." In Kurt Weyland, ed., *Learning from Foreign Models in Latin American Policy Reform*. Baltimore: Johns Hopkins University Press.

"Dentro de alguns dias quando o Governo enviar ao Congresso as medidas compensatórias vamos reconquistar a credibilidade diz Amadeo." 6 October 1999. *O Globo*: 22.

Denzau, Arthur and Douglass North. 2000. "Shared Mental Models: Ideologies and Institutions." In Arthur Lupia, Mathew McCubbins, and Samuel Popkin, eds., *Elements of Reason: Cognition, Choice and the Bounds of Rationality.* Cambridge: Cambridge University Press.

"Deputados da base aliada cobram caro para ajudar a dar quorum ao Governo." 5 November 1998. *O Globo*.

"Desempenho dos índices de preços." Ministério da Fazenda, *Balanço dos 24 meses do Real*. Available at http://www.fazenda.gov.br/portugues/real/real24.asp.

Diamond, Peter. 1997. "The Insulation of Pensions from Political Risk." In Salvador Valdés-Prieto, ed., *The Economics of Pensions*. Cambridge: Cambridge University Press.

———. 1999. *Issues in Privatizing Social Security: Report of an Expert Panel of the National Academy of Social Insurance.* Cambridge, MA: MIT Press.

DIAP (Departamento Intersindical de Assessoría Parlamentar). 1998. "Relatório de Pesquisa Sobre a Reforma da Previdência." Brasília, Brazil: Departamento Intersindical de Assessoría Parlamentar.

"Diario de sesiones de la Cámara de Representatives." 23 February 1997. Tomo 687 Miércoles. Uruguay: Asamblea Nacional.

Díaz, Rodolfo. June 25, 1998. Former Minister of Labor and Social Security. Personal interview, Buenos Aires, Argentina.

Díaz de León Carrillo, Alejandro. April 14, 1999. Manager of Microfinancial Analysis, Banco de México. Personal interview, Mexico City, Mexico.

Diéguez, Héctor and Alberto Petrecolla. 1975. *Estudio Estadístico del Sistema Previsional Argentino en el Período 1950–1972.* Buenos Aires: Instituto Torcuato Di Tella, Centro de Investigaciones Económicas.

Dion, Michelle. 2002. *The Progress of Revolution? Mexico's Welfare Regime in Comparative and Historical Perspective.* Ph.D. Dissertation, University of North Carolina at Chapel Hill.

———. 2006. "Globalización, democratización, y reforma del sistema de seguridad social en México, 1988–2005." *Foro Internacional* 183, XLVI, 1: 51–80.

———. 2008. "Workers and Welfare in Latin America: Mexico in Comparative and Historical Perspectivē." Unpublished Book Manuscript. Georgia Institute of Technology.

Dominguez, Jorge I. and James A. McCann. 1995. "Shaping Mexico's Electoral Arena: The Construction of Partisan Cleavages in the 1988 and 1991 National Elections." *American Political Science Review* 89, 1: 34–48.

Dornbusch, Rudiger and Alejandro Reynoso. 1989. "Financial Factors in Economic Development." *American Economic Review* 79, 2: 204–9.

Dowers, Kenroy, Stefano Fassina, and Stefano Pettinato. 2001. "Pension Reform in Small Emerging Economies." Sustainable Development Department Technical Papers Series. Inter-American Development Bank, Washington, DC.

Downs, Anthony. 1957. *An Economic Theory of Democracy.* New York: Harper.

Draibe, Sônia M., Maria Helena Guimarães de Castro, and Beatriz Azeredo. 1995. "The System of Social Protection in Brazil." Working Paper No. 3 Democracy and Social Policy Series. Kellogg Institute for International Studies, University of Notre Dame.

Drazen, Allan. 1996. "Policy Signaling and Open Economy." Working Paper 19. University of Maryland.

Drazen, Allan and Vittorio Grilli. 1993. "The Benefit of Crises for Economic Reform." *American Economic Review* 83, 3: 598–607.

Drazen, Allan and Paul Masson. 1994. "Credibility of Policies Versus Credibility of Policymakers." *Quarterly Journal of Economics* 109, 1: 335–54.

Druckman, James. 2001a. "The Implications of Framing Effects for Citizen Competence." *Political Behavior* 23, 3: 225–56.

———. 2001b. "On the Limits of Framing Effects: Who Can Frame?" *The Journal of Politics* 63, 4: 1041–66.

Dussell Peters, Enrique. 1998. "Social Implications of Mexico's 1994–1995 Crisis." In United Nations Development Programme & Korea Development Institute, *Social Implications of the Asian Financial Crisis*. EDAP Joint Policy Studies 9: 43–63.

Eaton, Kent. 2001. "Decentralisation, Democratisation and Liberalisation: The History of Revenue Sharing in Argentina, 1934–1999." *Journal of Latin American Studies* 33, 1, February: 1–28.

———. 2002. *Politicians and Economic Reform in New Democracies: Argentina and the Philippines in the 1990s*. University Park: Pennsylvania State University Press.

Eatwell, John. 1996. "International Financial Liberalization: The Impact on World Development." Official Documents System (ODS) Discussion Paper Series, no. 12. United Nations Development Program, New York.

Ebbinghaus, Bernhard. 2005. "Can Path Dependence Explain Institutional Change? Two Approaches to Welfare State Reform." MPIfG Discussion Paper/ No. 05/2. Max Planck Institute for the Study of Societies, Cologne.

Edelman, Murray. 1964. *The Symbolic Uses of Politics*. Urbana: University of Illinois Press.

Edmonds, Howard. 1996. "Pension Reform in Mexico." *Financial Industry Issues*. Federal Reserve Bank of Dallas, Third/Fourth Quarters: 1–7.

Edwards, Sebastian. 1995. *Crisis and Reform in Latin America: From Despair to Hope*. New York: Oxford University Press.

Eichengreen, Barry and Ashoka Mody. 2000. "What Explains Changing Spreads on Emerging Market Debt?" In Sebastian Edwards, ed., *Capital Flows and the Emerging Economies: Theory, Evidence, and Controversies*. Chicago: University of Chicago Press: 107–36.

"El festejo por el fracaso." 1 April 1993. *Clarín*: 3.

"Empezaron los traspasos a la jubilación estatal." 13 April 2007. *El Día*.

"Erro de cálculo." 9 May 1998. Ruy Fabiano. *Corrêio Brasilense*.

Ervasti, Heikki J. 1998. "Civil Criticism and the Welfare State." *Scandinavian Journal of Social Welfare* 7, 4, October: 288–99.

Esping-Andersen, Gøsta. 1978. "Social Class, Social Democracy, and the State: Party Policy and Party Decomposition in Denmark and Sweden." *Comparative Politics* 11, 1 October: 42–58.

———. 1990. *The Three Worlds of Welfare Capitalism*. Princeton, NJ: Princeton University Press.

———. 1996. "Welfare States Without Work." In Gøsta Esping-Andersen, ed., *Welfare States in Transition: National Adaptations in Global Economies*. Thousand Oaks, CA: Sage: 66–87.

———. 1999. *Social Foundations of Postindustrial Economies*. Oxford: Oxford University Press.

"Estratégia do governo é votar reforma da Previdência nesta terça-feira." 4 August 2003. Catia Seabra. *O Globo.*

Etala, Carlos. July 20, 1998. Lawyer and analyst, Yomho, Antúnez & Etala. Personal interview, Buenos Aires, Argentina.

Etchemendy, Sebastián and Vicente Palermo. 1991. "Conflicto y concertación: Gobierno, congreso y organizaciones de interés en la reforma laboral del primer gobierno de Menem." Working Paper # 41, Buenos Aires, Argentina: Universidad Torcuato Di Tella.

Euzéby, Alain. 2002. "The Financing of Social Protection and Employment in the Context of Economic Globalization." In Roland Sigg and Christina Behrendt, eds., *Social Security in the Global Village.* New York: Oxford University Press: 33.

Evans, Peter B. 1995. *Embedded Autonomy: States and Industrial Transformation.* Princeton, NJ: Princeton University Press.

Exposição de Motivos do Projeto de Reforma da Previdência Social. 10 March 1995. Brasília, Brazil: Ministério da Previdência e Asistência Social. MPAS-EMI 12 #306.

Exposição de Motivos do Projeto de Reforma Previdenciária. 29 April 2003. Brasília, Brazil: Ministério da Previdência Social. MPS/CCIVIL-PR # 29.

"Exposición de Motivos enviada por el C. Presidente Constitucional de los Estados Unidos Mexicanos a la H. Cámara de Diputados del 8 de noviembre de 1995." *Ley del Seguro Social,* DF. México, December 1995.

Facal, Carlos. July 6, 1998. Pension Analyst and President, Berkley International ART. Personal interview, Buenos Aires, Argentina.

"Falei do assunto durante toda a campanha eleitoral." 7 June 2003. João Domingos. *O Estado de São Paulo.*

"Falso Argumento." 11 February 1998. *O Globo.*

Fearon, James. 1997. "Signaling Foreign Policy Interests: Tying Hands versus Sinking Costs." *Journal of Conflict Resolution* 41: 68–90.

Feldstein, Martin. 1995. "Would Privatizing Social Security Raise Economic Welfare?" NBER Working Papers 5281. Cambridge: National Bureau of Economic Research.

Feng, Yi. 2001. "Political Freedom, Political Instability, and Policy Uncertainty: A Study of Political Institutions and Private Investment in Developing Countries." *International Studies Quarterly* 45, 2: 271–294.

Ferejohn, John A. 1974. *Pork Barrel Politics: Rivers and Harbors Legislation, 1947–1968.* Stanford, CA: Stanford University Press.

Ferejohn, John, Morris Fiorina, and Richard D. McKelvey. 1987. "Sophisticated voting and agenda independence in the distributive politics setting." *American Journal of Political Science* 31, 1: 169–94.

"Fernando Henrique vai dizer que a superação da crise depende da votação dessa proposta." 18 January 1999. *O Globo.*

Ferrera, Maurizio and Matteo Jessoula. 2005. "Reconfiguring Italian Pensions: From Policy Stalemate to Comprehensive Reforms." In Giuliano Bonoli and Toshimitsu Shinkawa, eds., *Ageing and Pension Reform around The World: Evidence from Eleven Countries.* Cheltenham, UK, Northampton, MA: Edward Elgar.

"FH/Ornélas/Defesa." 11 August 1998. *Jornal do Brasil.*

"FH usa crise nas bolsas para cobrar reformas." 30 October 1997. *O Estado de São Paulo.*

FIAP (Federación Internacional de Administradoras de Fondos de Pensiones). 2003. *Series Históricas: Cartera de Inversiones.* Available at http://www.fiap.org.cl.

――――. 2006. *Series Históricas: Rentabilidad Real Anual.* Available at http://www.fiap.org.cl.

Figueiredo, Argelina and Fernando Limongi. 1998. "Reforma da previdência e instituições políticas." *Novos Estudos* 51, July: 63–91.

———. 2000. "Presidential Power, Legislative Organization and Party Behavior in the Legislature." *Comparative Politics* 32, 1: 151–70.

Filgueira, Fernando, Juan Andrés Moraes, and Constanza Moreira. 1998. "INFORME: Efectos políticos y econômicos de la Reforma de la Seguridad Social." Presented at the Political Economy of Institutional Reform in Latin America, Washington, DC: Inter-American Development Bank.

———. 1999. "Political Environments, Sector Specific Configurations, and Strategic Devices: Understanding Institutional Reform in Uruguay." Documento de Trabajo #R-351. Inter-American Development Bank, Washington, DC.

Finch, Henry. 1981. *A Political Economy of Uruguay Since 1870.* New York: St. Martin's Press.

"Fiscais da Previdência Social Provam que o Sistema é Viável." 21 November 1993–5 January 1994. *Folha do Aposentado.*

Fleck, Robert. 2001. "Inter-Party Competition, Intra-Party Competition, and Distributive Policy: A Model and Test Using New Deal Data." *Public Choice* 108, 1–2: 77–100.

Fleischer, David. 1995. "Brazilian Politics: Structures, Process, Elections, Parties, and Political Groups." Working Paper 95-2. George Washington University, Washington, DC.

———. 1998. "The Cardoso Government's Reform Agenda: A View from the National Congress, 1995–1998." Special issue: Brazil: The Challenge of Constitutional Reform, *Journal of Interamerican Studies and World Affairs* 40, 4: 119–36.

Forteza, Alvaro, Daniel Buquet, Mario Ibarburu, Jorge Lanzaro, Andrés Peryra, Eduardo Siandra, and Marcel Vaillant. 2004. "Understanding Reform, The Uruguayan Case." Documentos de Trabajo # 603. Department of Economics (dECON), Montevideo, Uruguay.

Forteza, Alvaro, Anna Caristo, Natalia Ferreira-Coimbra, and Ianina Rossi. 2004. "Pay-Roll Contribution Financed Social Protection Programs in Uruguay." Documentos de Trabajo # 0305. Department of Economics (dECON), Montevideo, Uruguay.

Freedom House. "Freedom in the World" Country Ratings 1972–2004. Available at http://www.freedomhouse.org.

Frieden, Jeffry. 2006. *Global Capitalism: Its Fall and Rise in the Twentieth Century.* New York: W. W. Norton and Company.

Gamboa, Rafael. April 14, 1999. Manager of Microfinancial Analysis, Banco de México. Personal interview, Mexico City, Mexico.

Gardner, Jonathan and Michael Orszag. 2007. "How Have Workers Responded to Scary Markets?" In Hazel Bateman, ed., *Retirement Provision in Scary Markets.* Cheltenham, UK; Northampton, MA: Edward Elgar: 100–22.

Garrett, Geoffrey. 1998. *Partisan Politics in the Global Economy.* New York: Cambridge University Press.

———. 2000. "The Causes of Globalization." *Comparative Political Studies* 33, 6 August: 941–91.

Garrett, Geoffrey and Peter Lange. 1995. "Internationalization, Institutions, and Political Change." *International Organization* 49, 4: 627–55.

Garrett, Geoffrey and Deborah Mitchell. 2001. "Globalization, Government Spending and Taxation in the OECD." *European Journal of Political Research* 39, 2: 145.

Geddes, Barbara. 1994. *Politician's Dilemma: Building State Capacity in Latin America.* Berkeley: University of California Press.

"Genoino diz que Babá, Luciana Genro e João Fontes estão praticamenta for do PT." 6 August 2003. *O Globo.*

Gerchunoff, Pablo and José Luis Machinea. 1995. "Un Ensayo Sobre la Política Económica Después de la Estabilización." In Pablo Bustos, ed., *Más Allá de la Estabilidad: Argentina en la Época de la Globalización y la Regionalización.* Buenos Aires: Fundación Friedrich Ebert: 39–92.

Giambiagi, Fabio and Luiz de Mello. 2006. "Social Security Reform in Brazil: Achievements and Remaining Challenges." OECD Economics Department Working Papers, No. 534. Organization for Economic Cooperation and Development, Paris.

Gilbert, Neil. 1983. *Capitalism and the Welfare State: Dilemmas of Social Benevolence.* New Haven, CT: Yale University Press.

Gill, Indermit, Truman Packard, and Juan Yermo. 2005. *Keeping the Promise of Social Security in Latin America.* Palo Alto, CA: Stanford University Press.

Goldfajn, Ilan. 2000. "The Swings in Capital Flows and the Brazilian Crisis." Texto para Discussão #422. Department of Economics PUC-Rio, Rio de Janeiro, Brazil.

Gomes de Araújo, Wagner Frederico. 2003. "A reforma da previdência social no Brasil enquanto mudança institucional." Paper presented at the XVII Concurso del CLAD Sobre Reforma del Estado y Modernización de la Administración Pública, Caracas, Venezuela.

Gómez, Marcelo. 1997. "Conflictividad laboral durante el Plan de Convertibilidad en Argentina (1991–1995): Las prácticas de lucha sindical en una etapa de restructuración económica y desregulación del mercado de trabajo." *Estudios Sociológicos* XV, 45: 649–51.

Gonzáles Gaviola, Juan. June 17, 1998. Deputy to the Argentine National Congress, Partido Justicialista. Personal interview, Buenos Aires, Argentina.

Gonzáles Pier, Eduardo. April 19, 1999. Coordinator of Planning, IMSS. Personal interview, Mexico City, Mexico.

González, Luis Eduardo. 1993. *Estructuras Políticas y Democracia en Uruguay.* Montevideo: Fundación de Cultura Universitaria.

González-Rosetti, Alejandra, and Olivia Mogollon. 2000. "Enhancing the Political Feasibility of Health Reform: The Case of Mexico." Working Paper #41. Harvard School of Public Health, Cambridge, MA.

Gough, Ian. 2002. "Globalization and National Welfare Regimes: The East Asian Case." In Roland Sigg and Christina Behrendt, eds., *Social Security in the Global Village,* International Social Security Series No. 8. London: Transaction Publishers.

Gourevitch, Peter. 1986. *Politics in Hard Times: Comparative Responses to International Economic Crises.* Ithaca, NY: Cornell University Press.

"Governo é pressionado a liberar cargos federais para aliados fiéis." 12 August 2003. *O Globo.*

"Governo planeja 2ª etapa da reforma." 6 November 1998. *Folha de São Paulo.*

Grandolini, Gloria, and Luis Cerda. 1997. "The 1997 Pension Reform in Mexico." Policy Research Working Paper #1933. The World Bank, Washington, DC.

Green, Duncan. 2003 "Lula Plus One: Brazil after One Year of PT Government." CAFOD Policy Papers: International Finance. December. Catholic Agency for Overseas Development, London.

Green-Pedersen, Christoffer. 2001. "Welfare-state Retrenchment in Denmark and the Netherlands, 1982–1998: The Role of Party Competition and Party Consensus." *Comparative Political Studies* 34, 9: 963–85.

———. 2002. "The Dependent Variable Problem within the Study of Welfare-State Retrenchment: Defining the Problem and Looking for Solutions." Working Paper 26/2002. University of Aalborg, Centre for Comparative Welfare Studies.

Greif, Avner and David D. Laitin. 2004. "A Theory of Endogenous Institutional Change." *American Political Science Review* 98, 1: 633–52.

Griffith-Jones, Stephany. 1998. *Global Capital Flows: Should They Be Regulated?* New York: St. Martin's Press.

Grindle, Merilee S. 2000. "The Social Agenda and the Politics of Reform in Latin America." In Joseph Tulchin and Allison M. Garland, eds., *Social Development in Latin America*. Boulder, CO: Lynne Rienner: 17–52.

"Gritos e tumulto na votação." 6 June 2003. Adriana Vasconcelos. *O Globo*.

Groseclose, Tim and James M. Snyder, Jr. 1996. "Buying Supermajorities." *The American Political Science Review* 90, 2, June: 303–15.

Grüner, Eduardo. 1991. "Las fronteras del (des)orden: Apuntes sobre el estado de la sociedad civil bajo el menemato." In Atilio Borón et al., eds., *El menemato. Radiografía de dos años de gobierno de Carlos Menem*. Buenos Aires: Ediciones Letra Buena.

Guidotti, Pablo E. 2006. "Argentina's Fiscal Policy in the 1990s: A Tale of Skeletons and Sudden Stops." In Luiz de Mello, ed., *Challenges to Fiscal Adjustment in Latin America: The Cases of Argentina, Brazil, Chile and Mexico*. Paris: Organization for Economic Cooperation and Development: 69–92.

Guillén, Ana M. and Santiago Álvarez. 2002. "Southern European Welfare States Facing Globalization: Is There Social Dumping?" In Roland Sigg and Christina Behrendt, eds., *Social Security in the Global Village*. International Social Security Series No. 8. London: Transaction Publishers.

Guillermo, Calvo and Enrique Mendoza. 2000. "Capital-Markets Crises and Economic Collapse in Emerging Markets: An Informational-Frictions Approach." *American Economic Review*. Papers and Proceedings, 90, 2 May: 59–64.

Guitián, Manuel. 1997. "Reality and the Logic of Capital Flow Liberalization." In Christine Ries and Richard Sweeny, eds., *Capital Controls in Emerging Economies*. Boulder, CO: Westview Press: 189–244.

Gunther, Richard. 1989. "Electoral Laws, Party Systems, and Elites: The Case of Spain." *The American Political Science Review* 83, 3, September: 835–58.

Hacker, Jacob S. 2002. *The Divided Welfare State: The Battle over Public and Private Social Benefits in the United States*. Cambridge: Cambridge University Press.

———. 2004. "Privatizing Risk without Privatizing the Welfare State: The Hidden Politics of Social Policy Retrenchment in the United States." *American Political Science Review* 98, 2: 243–60.

Haggard, Stephan. 2000. "Interests, Institutions and Policy Reform." In Anne Krueger, ed., *Economic Policy Reform: The Second Stage*. Chicago: University of Chicago Press.

Haggard, Stephan and Robert Kaufman. 1995. *The Political Economy of Democratic Transitions*. Princeton, NJ: Princeton University Press.

———. 2008. *Development, Democracy, and Welfare States: Latin America, East Asia, and Eastern Europe*. Princeton, NJ: Princeton University Press.

Haggard, Stephan and Robert Kaufman, eds. 1992. *The Politics of Economic Adjustment: International Constraints, Distributive Politics, and the State*. Princeton, NJ: Princeton University Press.

Haggard, Stephan and Sylvia Maxfield. 1996. "The Political Economy of Financial Internationalization and the Developing World." *International Organization* 50, 1, Winter: 35–68.

Haggard, Stephan and Stephen B. Webb. 1994. *Voting for Reform: Democracy, Political Liberalization and Economic Adjustment.* New York: Oxford University Press.

Hall, Peter A. 1993. "Policy Paradigms, Social Learning and the State: The Case of Economic Policymaking in Britain." *Comparative Politics* 28, 1: 275–96.

———. 2005. "Public Policy-Making as Social Resource Creation." *APSA-CP Newsletter* 16, 2: 1–5.

Hall, Peter A. and David Soskice, eds. 2001. *Varieties of Capitalism: The Institutional Foundations of Comparative Advantage.* New York: Oxford University Press.

Hardin, Russell. 2002. "Street-Level Epistemology and Democratic Participation." *Journal of Political Philosophy* 10, 2 June: 212–29.

Heckman, James. 1979. "Sample Selection Bias as a Specification Error." *Econometrica* 47: 153–61.

Heclo, Hugh. 1974. *Modern Social Politics in Britain and Sweden: From Relief to Income Maintenance.* New Haven, CT: Yale University Press.

Hering, Martin. 2003. "Institutional Interference in the European Union: The Stability Pact and the Reform of Public Pensions in Germany." Paper prepared for presentation at the European Union Studies Association 8th Biennial International Conference, Nashville, 27–29 March.

———. 2004. "Rough Transition: Institutional Change in Germany's 'Frozen' Welfare State." Ph.D. Dissertation, Johns Hopkins University.

Hicks, Alexander M. 1999. *Social Democracy and Welfare Capitalism: A Century of Income Security Politics.* Ithaca, NY: Cornell University Press.

Hicks, Alexander M. and Duane H. Swank. 1992. "Politics, Institutions, and Welfare Spending in Industrialized Democracies, 1960–82." *The American Political Science Review* 86, 3: 658–74.

Hicks, Alexander and Christopher Zorn. 2005. "Economic Globalization, the Macro Economy, and Reversals of Welfare: Expansion in Affluent Democracies, 1978–94." *International Organization* 59, 3: 631–62.

Hinich, Melvin and Michael Munger. 1994. *Ideology and the Theory of Political Choice.* Ann Arbor: University of Michigan.

Hinrichs, Karl and Olli Kangas. 2003. "When Is a Change Big Enough to Be a System Shift? Small System-shifting Changes in German and Finnish Pension Policies." *Social Policy and Administration* 37, 6: 573–91.

Hirschman, Albert O. 1970. *Exit, Voice, and Loyalty: Responses to Decline in Firms, Organizations, and States.* Cambridge, MA: Harvard University Press.

———. 1987. "The Political Economy of Latin American Development: Seven Exercises in Retrospection." *Latin American Research Review* 22, 3: 7–36.

Holzmann, Robert and Richard Hinz. 2005. *Old Age Income Support in the 21st Century.* Washington, DC: The World Bank.

Holzmann, Robert, Robert Palacios, and Asta Zviniene. 2004. "Implicit Pension Debt: Issues, Measurement and Scope in International Perspective." Social Protection Discussion Paper Series, No. 403, March 2004. The World Bank, Washington, DC.

Huber, Evelyne and John D. Stephens. 2000. "The Political Economy of Pension Reform: Latin America in Comparative Perspective." United Nations Research Institute for Social Development Occasional Paper 7, May, Geneva.

———. 2001a. "Welfare State and Production Regimes in the Era of Retrenchment." In Paul Pierson, ed., *The New Politics of the Welfare State*. Oxford: Oxford University Press: 107–45.

———. 2001b. *Development and Crisis of the Welfare State: Parties and Policies in Global Markets*. Chicago: University of Chicago Press.

"IBOPE: Cardoso's Disapproval Rating at 66 Percent in September." 30 September 1999. *Brazilian Financial Wire*.

Immergut, Ellen. 1992a. "The Rules of the Game: The Logic of Health Policy-Making in France, Switzerland and Sweden." In Kathleen Thelen and Sven Steinmo, eds., *Structuring Politics: Historical Institutionalism in Comparative Perspective*. New York: Cambridge University Press: 57–89.

———. 1992b. *Health Care Politics: Ideas and Institutions in Western Europe*. Cambridge: Cambridge University Press.

———. 1998. "The Theoretical Core of the New Institutionalism." *Politics and Society* 26, 1: 5–34.

"Inativos: a hora da decisão." 20 January 1999. Catia Seabra, Isabel de Paula, and Monica Gugliano. *O Globo*.

"ING: Higher contributions to compensate affiliate flight – Argentina." 20 November 2007. *Business News Americas*.

Instituto Mexicano de Seguridad Social (IMSS). 1995. *Diagnóstico IMSS*. Presentación, Marzo.

Instituto Nacional de Estadísticas. 2000. *Encuesta Continua de Hogares*. Montevideo, Uruguay: Instituto Nacional de Estadísticas.

———. 2001. "Evolución de la Pobreza por el Método del Ingreso: Uruguay 1986-2001." Available at http://www.ine.gub.uy.

Inter-American Development Bank (IDB). 1997. "IDB Invests $770 Million in Social Security and Pension Reform." Press Release. 4 March 1997. NR-053/97. Available at http://www.iadb.org.

International Monetary Fund (IMF). 1999. *International Capital Markets Developments, Prospects, and Key Policy Issues*. World Economic & Financial Surveys. September. International Monetary Fund, Washington, DC. Available at http://www.imf.org/external/pubs/ft/icm/1999/index.htm.

———. 2000. *International Financial Statistics*. Washington, DC: International Monetary Fund.

———. 2004a. "Debt-Related Vulnerabilities and Financial Crises: An Application of the Balance Sheet Approach to Emerging Market Countries." Policy Development and Review Departments, International Monetary Fund, Washington, DC.

———. 2004b. "A Retrospective on Argentina's Fiscal Policy, 1991–2001." Appendix 3 in Evaluation Report: The IMF and Argentina, 1991–2001. Independent Evaluation Office, Washington DC: International Monetary Fund.

"Internautas se dizem mal informados sobre reforma." 11 August 2003. Agência de Notícias da Previdência Social. Brasília: Ministério da Previdência Social. Available at http://www.previdenciasocial.gov.br/reforma/noticias/noticias.asp.

"Isenção com Limite Maior." 22 April 2003. *O Globo*.

Isocrates. 1968. *Works*. George Norlin and La Rue Van Hook, eds. Cambridge, MA: Harvard University Press.

Isuani, Ernesto A. and Jorge San Martino. 1995. "El nuevo sistema previsional argentino ¿Punto final a una larga crisis?" *Boletín Informativo Techint* April–June 282: 281–2.

Isuani, Ernesto A., Rafael Rofman, and Jorge San Martino. 1996. "Las Jubilaciones del Siglo XXI, Podemos Gastar la Cuenta?" *Boletín Informativo Techint* April–June, 286: 79–104.

Iversen, Torben. 2001. "The Dynamics of Welfare State Expansion: Trade Openness, De-industrialization, and Partisan Politics." In Paul Pierson, ed., *The New Politics of the Welfare State*. Oxford: Oxford University Press: 45–79.

Iversen, Torben and Thomas R. Cusack. 2001. "The Causes of Welfare State Expansion: Deindustrialization or Globalization?" In Paul Pierson, ed., *The New Politics of the Welfare State*. New York: Oxford University Press: 305–33.

Iversen, Torben and Anne Wren. 1998. "Equality, Employment, and Budgetary Restraint: The Trilemma of the Service Economy." *World Politics* 50, 1: 507–46.

Jackson, Patrick and Ronald R. Krebs. 2003. "Twisting Tongues and Twisting Arms: The Power of Political Rhetoric." Paper Presented at the Annual Meeting of the American Political Science Association, Philadelphia, 3–5 September.

James, Estelle. 1995. "Averting the Old-Age Crisis." *Finance and Development* June: 4–15.

————. 1998. "The Political Economy of Social Security Reform: A Cross-Country Review." *Annals of Public and Cooperative Economics* 69, 4: 451–82.

James, Estelle and Sarah Brooks. 2001. "The Political Economy of Pension Reform." In Robert Holzmann and Joseph Stiglitz, eds., *New Ideas about Old Age Security: Toward Sustainable Pension Systems in the 21st Century*. Washington, DC: The World Bank: 133–70.

James, Estelle, Alejandra Cox Edwards, and Rebeca Wong. 2003. "The Gender Impact of Pension Reform." *Journal of Pension Economics and Finance* 2, 2: 181–219.

Jensen, Nathan. 2003. "Democratic Governance and Multinational Corporations: Political Regimes and Inflows of Foreign Direct Investment." *International Organization* 57, 3: 587–616.

Johnson, Gregg B. and Brian F. Crisp. 2003. "Mandates, Powers, and Policies." *The American Journal of Political Science* 47, 1 January: 128–42.

Jones, Mark P. 1993. "The Political Consequences of Electoral Laws in Latin America and the Caribbean." *Electoral Studies* 12, 1: 59–75.

————. 1997. "Evaluating Argentina's Presidential Democracy: 1983–1995." In Scott Mainwaring and Matthew Soberg Shugart, eds., *Presidentialism and Democracy in Latin America*. New York: Cambridge University Press: 259–99.

Jones, Mark P. and Wonjae Hwang. 2003. "Majority Cartels, Distributive Politics and Inter-party Relations in a Unidimensional Legislature: The Argentine Chamber of Deputies." Paper Delivered at the Meeting of the Latin American Studies Association, Dallas, 27–29 March.

Jones, Mark P., Sebastian Saiegh, Pablo T. Spiller, and Mariano Tommasi. 2002. "Amateur Legislators-Professional Politicians: The Consequences of Party-Centered Electoral Rules in a Federal System." *American Journal of Political Science* 46, 3, July: 656–69.

Kahler, Miles. 1992. "External Influence, Conditionality, and the Politics of Adjustment." In Stephan Haggard and Robert Kaufman, eds., *The Politics of Economic Adjustment: International Constraints, Distributive Politics, and the State*. Princeton, NJ: Princeton University Press: 89–136.

Kahneman, Daniel and Amos Tversky. 1984. "Choices, Values and Frames." *American Psychologist* 39, 1: 341–50.

Kaminsky, Graciela and Sergio L. Schmukler. 2002. "Emerging Markets Instability: Do Sovereign Ratings Affect Country Risk and Stock Returns?" *The World Bank Economic Review* 16, 2: 171–95.

Kane, Cheikh. 1995. "Uruguay: Options for Pension Reform." Working Paper 68. The World Bank, Washington, DC.

Kane, Cheikh and Robert Palacios, 1996. "The Implicit Pension Debt." *Finance & Development* 33, 2: 36–38.

Kata, Hugo. 2001. "Privatizing pensions in the context of stabilization and structural adjustment." Paper delivered at the meeting of the Latin American Studies Association (LASA), Washington, DC, 6–8 September.

Katzenstein, Peter J. 1985. *Small States in World Markets: Industrial Policy in Europe.* Ithaca, NY: Cornell University Press.

Kaufman, Robert and Alex Segura-Ubiergo. 2001 "Globalization, Domestic Politics and Social Spending in Latin America: A Time-Series Cross-Section Analysis, 1973–1997." *World Politics* 53, 4: 553–87.

Kay, Stephen. 1998. *Politics and Social Security Reform in the Southern Cone and Brazil.* Ph.D. Dissertation. Department of Political Science, University of California, Los Angeles.

———. 1999. "Unexpected Privatizations: Politics and Social Security Reform in the Southern Cone." *Comparative Politics* 31, 1: 403–22.

———. 2000. "Privatizing Pensions: Prospects for the Latin American Reforms." *Journal of Interamerican Studies and World Affairs* 42, 1: 133–42.

———. 2001. "Politics, Economics and Pension Reform in the Southern Cone." Paper presented at the Social Security and Pension Reform Conference, ITAM, Mexico City, 2 March.

———. 2003. "State Capacity and Pensions." Prepared for the LASA XXIV International Congress, Dallas, 27–29 March.

Keck, Margaret E. 1992. *The Workers' Party and Democratization in Brazil.* New Haven, CT: Yale University Press.

Keefer, Philip and David Stasavage. 2003. "The Limits of Delegation: Veto Players, Central Bank Independence, and the Credibility of Monetary Policy." *American Political Science Review* 97, 3: 407–23.

Keohane, Nannerl O. 1976. "Philosophy, Theory, Ideology: An Attempt at Clarification." *Political Theory* 4, 1: 80–100.

Keohane, Robert O. 2001. "Governance in a Partially Globalized World." *American Political Science Review* 95, 1: 1–13.

Keohane, Robert O. and Joseph Nye. 1998. "Power and Interdependence in the Information Age." *Foreign Affairs* 77, 5: 81–95.

Kingstone, Peter. 2000. "Muddling through Gridlock: Economic Policy Performance, Business Responses and Democratic Stability." In Peter R. Kingstone and Timothy J. Power, eds., *Democratic Brazil: Actors, Institutions, and Processes.* Pittsburgh: University of Pittsburgh Press: 185–203.

Kitschelt, Herbert. 2001. "Partisan Competition and Welfare State Retrenchment: When Do Politicians Choose Unpopular Policies?" In Paul Pierson, ed., *The New Politics of the Welfare State.* New York: Oxford University Press: 265–304.

Kitschelt, Herbert, Peter Lange, Gary Marks, and John D. Stephens, eds. 1998. *Continuity and Change in Contemporary Capitalism.* New York: Cambridge University Press.

Klesner, Joseph L. 1998. "An Electoral Route to Democracy? Mexico's Transition in Comparative Perspective." *Comparative Politics* 30, 4: 477–97.

Kliass, Paulo. May 26, 1999. Secretary of Complementary Social Security, Ministério da Previdência e Assistência Social. Personal interview, Brasília, Brazil.

Korpi, Walter and Joakim Palme. 2003. "New Politics and Class Politics in the Context of Austerity and Globalization: Welfare State Regress in 18 Countries, 1975–95." *American Political Science Review* 97, 3: 425–46.

Krueger, Anne. 2002. "Crisis Prevention and Resolution: Lessons from Argentina." Paper presented at the conference "The Argentina Crisis," National Bureau of Economic Research, July 17, Cambridge, MA.

Krugman, Paul. 1998. *The Return of Depression Economics*. New York: W. W. Norton.

Kuklinski, James H. and Paul Quirk. 2000. "Reconsidering the Rational Public: Cognition, Heuristics, and Mass Opinion." In Arthur Lupia, Mathew D. McCubbins, and Samuel Popkin, eds., *Elements of Reason: Cognition, Choice, and the Bounds of Rationality*. New York: Cambridge University Press: 153–82.

Kuklinski, James H., Paul J. Quirk, Jennifer Jerit, David Schwieder, and Robert F. Rich. 2000. "Misinformation and the Currency of Democratic Citizenship." *Journal of Politics* 62, 1: 791–816.

Kumlin, Staffan. 2002. "Institutions-Experiences-Preferences: How Welfare State Design Affects Trust and Ideology." In Bo Rothstein and Sven Steinmo, eds., *Restructuring the Welfare State: Political Institutions and Policy Change*. New York: Palgrave: 20–50.

_____. 2004. *The Personal and the Political: How Personal Welfare State Experiences Affect Political Trust and Ideology*. New York: Palgrave Macmillan.

Kurtz, Marcus. 1999. "Chile's Neo-Liberal Revolution: Incremental Decisions and Structural Transformation, 1973–89." *Journal of Latin American Studies* 31 May: 399–427.

_____. 2004. *Free Market Democracy and the Chilean and Mexican Countryside*. New York: Cambridge University Press.

Kurzer, Paulette. 1993. *Business and Banking: Political Change and Economic Integration in Western Europe*. Ithaca, NY: Cornell University Press.

Labadie, Gastón. 1995. "Aspectos Políticos y Sociales de la Reforma de la Seguridad Social." Unpublished Manuscript. Universidad ORT, Montevideo, Uruguay.

_____. October 27, 1998. Analyst of pension reform project, Director, Universidad ORT. Personal interview, Montevideo, Uruguay.

Larre, Bénédicte. 1999. "Mexico: Looking Forward with Caution." *OECD Observer* October: 14.

Latinobarómetro. 1995, 1998, 2004, 2005. Santiago, Chile: Corporación Latinobarómetro. Includes both Spanish- and English-language datasets and questionnaires.

Laurell, Asa Christina. 2000. "Structural Adjustment and the Globalization of Social Policy in Latin America." *International Sociology* 15, 2, June: 306–25.

Lazarov, Luis and Rodolfo Saldaín. 1997. "Perspectivas de la Reforma de la Seguridad Social en el Uruguay: Evaluación del Primer Año de Vigencia de la Nueva Ley." Montevideo: Centro Latinoamericano de Economía Humana (CLAEH), Documento Base de Evaluación.

Leblang, David. 1999. "Domestic Political Institutions and Exchange Rate Commitments in the Developing World." *International Studies Quarterly* 43, 4: 599–620.

Leon, Samuel. March 15, 1999. Director, Instituto Mexicano del Seguro Social (IMSS). Personal interview, Mexico City, Mexico.

Levi, Margaret. 1990. "A Logic of Institutional Change." In Karen Schweers Cook and Margaret Levi, eds., *The Limits of Rationality*. Chicago: University of Chicago Press: 402–19.

———. 1997. *Consent, Dissent and Patriotism*. Cambridge: Cambridge University Press.

Levitsky, Steven. 2000. "The 'Normalization' of Argentine Politics." *Journal of Democracy* 11, 2: 56–69.

———. 2003. *Transforming Labor-Based Parties in Latin America: Argentine Peronism in Comparative Perspective*. New York: Cambridge University Press.

Levy, Jonah. 1999. "Vice into Virtue? Progressive Politics and Welfare Reform in Continental Europe." *Politics and Society* 27, 2: 239–73.

Limongi, Fernando and Angelina Cheibub Figueiredo. 1995. "Partidos políticos na Câmara dos Deputados, 1989–1994." *Dados* 38, 3: 497–525.

Lindblom, Charles. 2001. *The Market System: What It Is, How It Works, and What to Make of It*. New Haven, CT: Yale University Press.

Lipset, Seymour M. and Stein Rokkan. 1967. *Party Systems and Voter Alignments: Cross-National Perspectives*. New York: Free Press.

Lipsmeyer, Christine. 2002. "Parties and Policy: Evaluating Economic and Partisan Influences on Welfare Policy Spending during the European Post-Communist Transition." *British Journal of Political Science* 32, 4: 641–61.

Lizzeri, Alessandro and Nicola Persico. 2001. "The Provision of Public Goods under Alternative Electoral Incentives." *The American Economic Review* 91, 1 March: 225–39.

Lloyd-Sherlock, Peter. 1997. "Models of Public Sector Intervention: Providing for the Elderly in Argentina (c. 1890–1994)." *Journal of Latin American Studies* 29, 1: 1–21.

Lodge, Milton, Kathleen McGraw, and Patrick Stroh. 1989. "An Impression-Driven Model of Candidate Evaluation." *American Political Science Review* 83, 1: 399–419.

Loureiro, André Soares, and Fernando de Holanda Barbosa. 2003. "Public Debt and Risk Premium of Public Securities in Brazil." Technical Notes Number 42. Banco Central do Brasil.

Lo Vuolo, Rubén M. 1991. "INFORME Sobre el Resultado Uno." CIEPP, Buenos Aires.

———. 1996. "Reformas previsionales en América Latina: El caso argentino." *Comercio Exterior* 46, 1: 692–702.

"Lula a Congresso: Ou Reforma ou Desigualdade." 24 April 2003. *O Globo*.

"Lula Pede Sacrifícios e Recorre Até a Jesus." 23 April 2003. *O Globo*.

"Lula: Tem Gente que Acha Pouco se Aposentar com R$17 mil." 27 July 2003. *O Globo*.

Lupia, Arthur, Mathew D. McCubbins, and Samuel L. Popkin, eds. 2000. *Elements of Reason: Cognition, Choice, and the Bounds of Rationality*. New York: Cambridge University Press.

Lustig, Nora. 1995. "Introduction." In Nora Lustig, ed., *Coping with Austerity: Poverty and Inequality in Latin America*. Washington, DC: Brookings Institution: 1–42.

———. 2001. "Life Is Not Easy: Mexico's Quest for Stability and Growth." *Journal of Economic Perspectives* 15, 1: 85–106.

MacCulloch, Christina. 2003. "La madre de las reformas: Cómo Uruguay enfrentó la complicada tarea de reestructurar su sistema de seguridad social." *BIDAmérica: Revista del Banco Interamericano de Desarrollo*. April. Available at http://www.iadb.org.

Madeira, Arnaldo. May 27, 1999. Deputy, Partido da Social Democracia Brasileira (PSDB), National Congress of Brazil. Personal interview, Brasília, Brazil.

Madrid, Raúl. 2002. "The Politics and Economics of Pension Privatization in Latin America." *Latin American Research Review* 37, 2: 159–82.

———. 2003. *Retiring the State: The Politics of Pension Privatization in Latin America and Beyond*. Stanford, CA: Stanford University Press.

———. 2005. "Ideas, Economic Pressures, and Pension Privatization." *Latin American Politics and Society* 47, 1: 2.

Mahoney, James, 2000. "Path Dependence in Historical Sociology." *Theory and Society* 29, 4: 507–48.

Mainwaring, Scott. 1992. "Brazilian Party Underdevelopment in Comparative Perspective." *Political Science Quarterly* 107, 4: 677–707.

———. 1997. "Multipartism, Robust Federalism, and Presidentialism in Brazil." In Scott Mainwaring, and Matthew Soberg Shugart, eds., *Presidentialism and Democracy in Latin America*. Cambridge: Cambridge University Press: 55–109.

Mainwaring, Scott and Timothy R. Scully. 1995. "Introduction: Party Systems in Latin America." In Scott Mainwaring and Timothy Scully, eds., *Building Democratic Institutions: Party Systems in Latin America*. Stanford, CA: Stanford University Press: 1–34.

Mainwaring, Scott and Matthew Soberg Shugart, eds. 1997. *Presidentialism and Democracy in Latin America*. Cambridge: Cambridge University Press.

"A maior manifestação contra Lula." 7 August 2003. *O Globo*.

"La mano de Cavallo en los nuevos cambios." 29 April 1993. *Clarín*: 22.

"Manobra de aliados abre caminho para mudança na aposentadoria." 1 October 1999. Sônia Cristina Silva, Sílvia Faria, and Vânia Cristino. *O Estado de São Paulo*.

Manow, Philip. 2001. "Comparative Institutional Advantages of Welfare State Regimes and New Coalitions in Welfare State Reforms." In Paul Pierson, ed., *The New Politics of the Welfare State*. Oxford: Oxford University Press: 146–65.

Mares, Isabela. 2003. *The Politics of Social Risk: Business and Welfare State Development*. Cambridge: Cambridge University Press.

Margheritis, Ana. 2002. "Policy Innovation and Leaders' Perceptions: Building a Reformist Consensus in Argentina." *Journal of Latin American Studies* 34, 4: 881–914.

Marier, Patrik and Jean F. Mayer. 2007. "Welfare Retrenchment as Social Justice: Pension Reform in Mexico." *Journal of Social Policy* 36, 4: 585–604.

Marques, Rosa Maria, Mariana Batich, and Áquilas Mendes. 2003. "Previdência Social Brasileira: Um Balanço da Reforma." *São Paulo em Perspectiva* 17, 1: 111–21.

Márquez Mosconi, Gustavo. 1997. "An Assessment of Pension System Reform in Uruguay in 1995." Working Paper #XN° SOC97–105. Inter-American Development Bank, Washington, DC.

Marshall, Thomas Humphrey. 1964. *Class, Citizenship, and Social Development*. Garden City, NY: Doubleday.

Martin, Lisa L. 1993. "Credibility, Costs, and Institutions: Cooperation on Economic Sanctions." *World Politics* 45: 406–32.

Martinez, Gabriel. March 5, 1999. Director of Systems and Finance, Instituto Mexicano del Seguro Social (IMSS). Personal interview, Mexico City, Mexico.

Maxfield, Sylvia. 1997. *Gatekeepers of Growth: Central Banking in Developing Countries*. Princeton, NJ: Princeton University Press.

———. 1998. "Understanding the Political Implications of Financial Internationalization in Emerging Market Countries." *World Development* 26, 7: 1201–19.

McGuire, James W. 1997. *Peronism without Perón: Unions, Parties, and Democracy in Argentina*. Stanford, CA: Stanford University Press.

McKelvey, Richard D. and Richard Niemi. 1978. "A Multistage Game Representation of Sophisticated Voting for Binary Procedures." *Journal of Economic Theory* 18, 1: 1–22.

Medici, André. 2004. "The Political Economy of Reform in Brazil's Civil Servant Pension Scheme." Technical Paper Series #002. Inter-American Development Bank, Sustainable Development Department, Washington, DC.

"Meia-sola: O Congresso aprova a reforma da Previdência, mas outras mudanças terão de vir em breve." 20 May 1998. Leonel Rocha, *Veja*: 23.

Melo, Marcus André. 1997. "O Jogo das Regras: A Política da Reforma Constitucional, 1993–1996." *Revista Brasileira de Ciencias Sociais* 12, 33: 63–87.

———. 2002. *As Reformas Constitucionais no Brasil: Instituições Políticas e Processo Decisório*. Rio de Janeiro, Brazil: Editora Revan.

———. 2003. "When Institutions Matter: A Comparison of the Politics of Administrative, Social Security, and Tax Reforms in Brazil." In Ben Ross Schneider and Blanca Heredia, eds., *Reinventing Leviathan: The Politics of Administrative Reform in Developing Countries*. Coral Gables, FL: North-South Center Press: 211–49.

———. 2004a. "Institutional Choice and the Diffusion of Policy Paradigms: Brazil and the Second Wave of Pension Reform." *International Political Science Review* 25, 3: 320–41.

———. 2004b. "Escolha Institucional e a Difusão dos Paradigmas de Política: O Brasil e a Segunda Onda de Reformas Previdenciárias." *DADOS – Revista de Ciências Sociais* 47, 1: 169–206.

Melo, Marcus André and Pedro Luiz Barros Silva. 1999. "Reforma da Seguridade Social no Brasil." NEPP Caderno #39. Universidade Estadual de Campinas – Núcleo de Estudos de Políticas Públicas. Campinas, Brazil.

"Memorando de Política Econômica." 1998. *Ajuste Fiscal* 13 November.

Meneguello, Rachel. 1998. *Partidos e Governo No Brasil Contemporâneo (1985–1997)*. São Paulo: Paz e Terra.

"Mercadante quer decidir no voto impasse com oposição." 17 November 2003. *Gazeta Mercantil*.

"Mercado financeiro – Bovespa tem perda de 4,9% na semana." 2 October 1999. *Folha de São Paulo*.

Mesa-Lago, Carmelo. 1978. *Social Security in Latin America: Pressure Groups, Stratification, and Inequality*. Pittsburgh: University of Pittsburgh Press.

———. 1989. *Ascent to Bankruptcy: Financing Social Security in Latin America*. Pittsburg: University of Pittsburgh Press.

———. 1994. *Changing Social Security in Latin America*. Boulder, CO: Lynne Reinner.

———. 1997. "Social Welfare Reform in the Context of Economic – Political Liberalization: Latin American Cases." *World Development* 25, 1: 497–517.

———. 2002. "Myth and Reality of Pension Reform: The Latin American Evidence." *World Development* 30, 8: 1309–21.

———. 2005. "Evaluation of a Quarter Century of Structural Pension Reforms in Latin America." In Carolin A. Crabbe, ed., *A Quarter Century of Pension Reform in Latin America and the Caribbean: Lessons Learned and the Next Steps.* Washington, DC: Inter-American Development Bank: 43–82.

Mesa-Lago, Carmelo and Fabio Bertranou. 1998. *Manual de Economía de la Seguridad Social.* Montevideo: CLAEH.

Mesa-Lago, Carmelo and Katharina Müller. 2002. "The Politics of Pension Reform in Latin America." *Journal of Latin American Studies* 34, 1: 687–715.

"Mexico Passes Social Security Reform Despite Massive Labor Union Protests." January 1996. Dan La Botz. *Mexican Labor News and Analysis*: 1.

Michelín, Gustavo. October 13, 1998. Economist, Ministerio de Economía y Finanzas. Personal interview, Montevideo, Uruguay.

Michelini, Rafael. November 3, 1998. Senator, National Assembly. Nuevo Espacio Party. Personal interview, Montevideo, Uruguay.

Middlebrook, Kevin J., ed. 1991. *Unions, Workers, and the State in Mexico.* San Diego: Center for U.S. –Mexican Studies, University of California.

Mila Belistri, Ofelia. 1997. "El Sistema de Pensiones en Uruguay: Reflexiones Sobre las Reformas en la Seguridad Social." Serie Estudios # 34. Centro de Desarrollo Estratégico para la Seguridad Social (CEDESS), Mexico City, Mexico.

Ministério da Fazenda. 1993. *Programa de Ação Imediata.* Available at http://www.fazenda.gov.br/portugues/documentos/publica.asp#Plano%20Real.

Ministério da Previdência e Assistência Social. 1997. "A Reforma da Previdência." *Informe de Previdência Social* 9, 12: 1–3.

Ministério da Previdência Social. 1999. "Balanço das Principais Medidas Adotadas para o Aperfeiçoamento do Sistema Previdenciário Brasileiro." *Informe de Previdência Social* 11, 2: 1–4.

———. 2003. "A Previdência Social em 2002." *Informe de Previdência Social* 15, 1: 1–19.

———. 2004. "Regulamentação da Reforma da Previdência: A Nova Formula de Calculo das Aposentadorias dos Servidores Públicos." *Informe de Previdência Social* 16, 7: 1–15.

Mitchell, Olivia S. 1996. "Social Security Reform in Uruguay: An Economic Assessment." Pension Research Council Working Papers 96-20. Wharton School Pension Research Council, University of Pennsylvania.

Mody, Ashoka and Mark P. Taylor. 2002. "International Capital Crunches: The Time-Varying Role of Informational Asymmetries." Working Paper # 02/43. International Monetary Fund, Washington, DC.

Moon, J. Donald. 1988. "The Moral Basis of the Democratic Welfare State." In Amy Gutman, ed., *Democracy and the Welfare State.* Princeton, NJ: Princeton University Press: 27–52.

Moraes, Juan Andrés and Scott Morgenstern. 1995. "Los Vetos del Poder Ejecutivo en el Proceso Político Uruguayo (1985–1995)." Unpublished Manuscript. Departamento de Ciencia Política, Universidad de la República. Montevideo, Uruguay.

Morgenstern, Scott. 2001. "Organized Factions and Disorganized Parties: Electoral Incentives in Uruguay." *Party Politics* 7, 2: 235–56.

———. 2002. "Towards a Model of Latin American Legislators." In Scott Morgenstern and Benito Nacif, eds., *Legislative Politics in Latin America.* New York: Cambridge University Press: 1–22.

Mosley, Layna. 2000. "Room to Move: International Financial Markets and National Welfare States." *International Organization* 54, 4: 737–73.

————. 2003. *Global Capital and National Governments*. Cambridge: Cambridge University Press.

Müller, Katharina. 1999. *The Political Economy of Pension Reform in Central-Eastern Europe*. Cheltenham: Edward Elgar.

————. 2001. "The Political Economy of Pension Reform in Central-Eastern Europe." *Journal of Comparative Economics* 29, 1: 579–80.

————. 2003. *Privatising Old-age Security: Latin America and Eastern Europe Compared*. Cheltenham: Edward Elgar.

Munnell, Alicia and Annika Sundén. 2004. *Coming Up Short: The Challenge of 401(k) Plans*. Washington, DC: The Brookings Institution Press.

Murillo, María Victoria. 2000. "From Populism to Neoliberalism: Labor Unions and Market Reforms in Latin America." *World Politics* 52, 2: 135–74.

————. 2001. *Labor Unions, Partisan Coalitions, and Market Reforms in Latin America*. Cambridge: Cambridge University Press.

————. 2002. "Political Bias in Policy Convergence: Privatization Choices in Latin America." *World Politics* 54, 4: 462–93.

————. 2005. "Partisanship amidst Convergence: The Politics of Labor Reform in Latin America." *Comparative Politics* 37, 4: 441–58.

Murillo, María Victoria and Andrew Schrank. 2005. "With a Little Help from My Friends: Partisan Politics, Transnational Alliances, and Labor Rights in Latin America." *Comparative Political Studies* 38, 8: 971–99.

Mustapic, Ana María. 2002. "Oscillating Relations: President and Congress in Argentina." In Scott Morgenstern and Benito Nacif, eds., *Legislative Politics in Latin America*. Cambridge: Cambridge University Press: 185–221.

Myles, John, and Paul Pierson. 2001. "The Comparative Political Economy of Pension Reform." In Paul Pierson, ed., *The New Politics of the Welfare State*. New York: Oxford University Press: 305–33.

Nacif, Benito. 1997. "Legislative Parties in the Mexican Chamber of Deputies." Documento de Trabajo # 93. Centro de Investigación y Docencia Económicas, Mexico City, Mexico.

————. 2002. "Understanding Party Discipline in The Mexican Chamber of Deputies: The Centralized Model." In Scott Morgenstern and Benito Nacif, eds., *Legislative Politics in Latin America*. Cambridge: Cambridge University Press: 254–86.

Najberg, Sheila. December 13, 1998, June 24, 1999. Special Advisor to the President, Banco Nacional de Desenvolvimento Econômico e Social. Personal interview, Rio de Janeiro, Brazil.

Nelson, Joan. 1996. "Promoting Policy Reforms: The Twilight of Conditionality." *World Development* 24, 9: 1551–9.

————. 1999. *Reforming Health and Education: The World Bank, the IDB, and Complex Institutional Change*. Washington, DC: Overseas Development Council.

————. 2004. "External Models, International Influence, and the Politics of Social Sector Reforms." In Kurt Weyland, ed., *Learning from Foreign Models in Latin American Policy Reform*. Baltimore: Johns Hopkins University Press: 273–94.

Nelson, Thomas and Zoë M. Oxley. 1999. "Framing Effects on Belief Importance and Opinion." *Journal of Politics* 61, 4: 1040–67.

Nelson, Thomas, Zoë M. Oxley, and Rosalie A. Clawson. 1997. "Toward a Psychology of Framing Effects." *Political Behavior* 19, 1: 221–46.

NEPP (Nucleo de Estudos de Políticas Públicas). 1998. *Reforma da Seguridade Social no Brasil*. December. UNICAMP.

Ness, Walter, Elizabeth Guedes, and Roberto Marcos Montezano. 1992. "Previdência Social no Brasil: Evolução Recente, Perspectivas e Princípios para Reformulação." *Revista Brasileira de Mercado de Capitais* 17, 45: 55–156.

Nielsen, Guillermo. 2003. Speech of the Secretary of Finance Guillermo Nielsen at EMTA (Emerging Markets Traders Association), 4 December. Available at http://www.argentinedebtinfo.gov.ar/ documentos/emta-gn-4-12-2003-english.pdf.

Niggle, Christopher J. 2003. "Globalization, Neoliberalism and the Attack on Social Security." *Review of Social Economy* 61, 1: 51–71.

Niou, Emerson and Peter C. Ordeshook. 1985. "Universalism in Congress." *American Journal of Political Science* 29, 1: 246–58.

Nobre, Freitas. 1974. *Debate Sobre Problemas Brasileiros*. Brasília: Coordenada, Editora de Brasília.

Noriega Curtis, Carlos. March 26, 1999. General Coordinator, Subsecretario de Hacienda y Crédito Público and Coordinador de Asesores para Asunto de Políticas Económicas y Social del Presidente Ministerio de Hacienda. Personal interview, Mexico City, Mexico.

North, Douglass C. 1990. *Institutions, Institutional Change, and Economic Performance*. New York: Cambridge University Press.

North, Douglass and Barry Weingast. 1989. "Constitutions and Commitment: The Evolution of Institutions Governing Public Choice in 17th Century England." *Journal of Economic History* 49, 4: 803–32.

"Nova lei da Previdência Social não resolve déficit." 3 October 1999. *O Estado de São Paulo*.

"A nova matemática do INSS." 7 October 1999. *O Globo*: 3.

Noya, Nelson and Silvia Laens. 2000. "Efectos fiscales de la reforma de la seguridad social en Uruguay." *Serie Financiamiento del Desarollo*. 101. July. Santiago de Chile: CEPAL.

Noya, Nelson, Silvia Laens, and Adrián Fernández. 1999. "Efectos económicos de la reforma de la seguridad social en Uruguay." Montevideo: Centro de Investigaciones Económicas (CINVE).

Nylen, William R. 2000. "The Making of a Loyal Opposition: The Workers' Party (PT) and the Consolidation of Democracy in Brazil." In Peter R Kingstone and Timothy J. Power, eds., *Democratic Brazil: Actors, Institutions, and Processes*. Pittsburgh: University of Pittsburgh Press: 126–43.

OECD (Organization for Economic Co-operation and Development). 1996. "Mexico: Economic Aspects." In *OECD Economic Outlook: Development in Individual OECD Countries*. Paris: Organization for Economic Co-operation and Development. June.

Offe, Claus. 1984. *Contradictions of the Welfare State*. Cambridge, MA: MIT Press.

———. 1996. *Modernity and the State: East, West*. Cambridge, MA: MIT Press.

Oficina de Planeamiento y Presupuesto (OPP). 1996. "Programa de Reforma de la Seguridad Social." Resumen Ejecutivo (UR-0108). Available from http://www. iadb.org.

Olave, Patricia. 1999. "Privatización, Bienestar y Equidad: El Caso de la Reforma de salud en Chile." In Bernice Ramirez López, ed., *La Seguridad Social: Reformas y Retos*. Mexico City: Instituto de Investigaciones Económicas, UNAM.

Oldersma, Jantine. 1997. "The Corporatist Channel and Civil Society in the Netherlands." In Jan W. van Deth, ed., *Private Groups and Public Life: Social Participation, Voluntary Associations and Political Involvement in Representative Democracies.* New York: Routledge: 144–62.

de Oliveira, Francisco Eduardo Barreto. June 25, 1999. Economist, Instituto de Pesquisa Econômica Aplicada. Personal interview, Rio de Janeiro, Brazil.

de Oliveira, Francisco Eduardo Barreto and Kaizô Iwakami Beltrão. 2000. "The Brazilian Social Security System." Texto para Discussão # 775. Instituto de Pesquisa Econômica Aplicada (IPEA), Rio de Janeiro, Brazil.

de Oliveira, Francisco Eduardo Barreto, Kaizô Iwakami Beltrão, and Mônica Guerra Ferreira. 1997. "Reforma da Previdência." Rio de Janeiro, Brazil: Instituto de Pesquisa Econômica Aplicada (IPEA)." Texto para Discussão #508.

de Oliveira, Francisco Eduardo Barreto, Kaizô Iwakami Beltrão, and Maria Tereza de Marsillac Pasinato. 1999. "Reforma estrutural da Previdência: Uma proposta para assegurar proteção social e eqüidade." Texto para Discussão # 690. Instituto de Pesquisa Econômica Aplicada (IPEA), Rio de Janeiro, Brazil.

"Oposição diz não." 23 April 2003. Jutahy Júnior. *O Globo.*

Organización Internacional del Trabajo (OIT). 2002. "Diagnóstico Institucional del Sistema Previsional Argentino y Pautas para Enfrentar la Crisis." Julio. Available at http://www.seguridadsocial.gov.ar/institucional/archivos/INFORMEOIT.pdf.

Orlansky, Dora. 1997. "Reforma del Estado, restructuración laboral y reconversión sindical: Argentina 1989–1995." *Estudios Sociológicos* XV: 45.

Orloff, Ann Shola. 1993. *The Politics of Pensions: A Comparative Analysis of Britain, Canada, and the United States, 1880–1940.* Madison: University of Wisconsin Press.

Orloff, Ann Shola and Theda Skocpol. 1984. "Why Not Equal Protection? Explaining the Politics of Public Social Spending in Britain 1900–1911 and the United States, 1880s–1920." *American Sociological Review* 49, 1: 726–50.

Ornélas, Waldek. June 9, 1999. Social Security Minister, Ministério da Previdência e Assistência Social. Personal interview, Brasília, Brazil.

Ornélas, Waldek and Solange Vieira. 1999. "Novo Rumo da Previdência Brasileira." *Revista do BNDES* 6: 31–48.

Orszag, Peter and Joseph Stiglitz. 1999. "Rethinking Pension Reform: Ten Myths about Social Security Systems." Paper presented at the World Bank Conference on New Ideas about Old Age Security, Washington, DC, 14–15 September.

Ostrom, Elinor. 1990. *Governing the Commons: The Evolution of Institutions for Collective Action.* New York: Cambridge University Press.

———. 1998. "A Behavioral Approach to the Rational Choice Theory of Collective Action." *American Political Science Review* 92, 1: 1–22.

O'Toole, Gavin. 2003. "A New Nationalism for a New Era: The Political Ideology of Mexican Neoliberalism." *Bulletin of Latin American Research* 22, 1: 269–90.

Pal, Leslie A. and R. Kent Weaver. 2003. *The Government Taketh Away: The Politics of Pain in the United States and Canada.* Washington, DC: Georgetown University Press.

Palacios, Robert and Montserrat, Pallarés-Miralles. 2000. "International Patterns of Pension Provision." Social Protection Discussion Paper # 0009. The World Bank, Washington, DC.

Palacios, Robert and Edward Whitehouse. 1998. "The role of choice in the transition to a funded pension system." Social Protection Discussion Paper 9812. World Bank, Washington, DC.

Palermo, Vicente and John Collins. 1998. "Moderate Populism: A Political Approach to Argentina's 1991 Convertibility Plan." *Latin American Perspectives* 25, 1: 36–62.

Palermo, Vicente and Marcos Novaro. 1996. *Política y Poder en el Gobierno de Menem.* Buenos Aires: Grupo Editorial Norma S.A.

Palier, Bruno. 2001. "Beyond Retrenchment: Four Problems in Current Welfare State Research and One Suggestion on How to Overcome Them." In Jochen Clasen, ed., *What Future for Social Security? Debates and Reforms in National and Cross-National Perspective.* The Hague: Kluwer Law International: 93–106.

Palmer, Edward and Marek Góra. 2004. "Shifting Perspectives in Pensions." Discussion Paper #1369. Institute for Labor Studies, Bonn.

Papadópulos, Jorge. 1992. *Seguridad Social y Política en el Uruguay.* Montevideo: CIESU.

"Para Ornélas, novas regras vão beneficiar maioria." 18 August 1999. *O Estado de São Paulo.*

Parmentier Vandenhende, Pierre. March 17, 1999. Director General, PROCESAR. Personal interview, Mexico City, Mexico.

Parmigiani, Carlos. October 9, 1998. Banco Central de Uruguay, Manager of Division of Control over Private Pension Fund Administrators. Personal interview, Montevideo, Uruguay.

Pastor, Manuel, Jr. and Carol Wise. 1999. "The Politics of Second-Generation Reform." *Journal of Democracy* 10, 3: 34–48.

"Pension Law Change Rejected by 58%, According to CNT/Vox Populi Survey." 13 September 1999. *Gazeta Mercantil Invest News.*

Pereira, Carlos and Bernardo Mueller. 2000. "Uma Teoria da Preponderância do Executivo: O Sistema de Comissões no Legislativo Brasileiro." *Revista Brasileira de Ciências Sociais* 15, 43: 45–67.

Pierson, Paul. 1994. *Dismantling the Welfare State: Reagan, Thatcher and the Politics of Retrenchment.* New York: Cambridge University Press.

———. 1996. "The New Politics of the Welfare State." *World Politics* 48, 1: 143–79.

———. 1998. "Irresistible Forces, Immovable Objects: Post-Industrial Welfare States Confront Permanent Austerity." *Journal of European Public Policy* 5, 4 December: 539–60.

———. 2000a. "Increasing Returns, Path Dependence, and the Study of Politics." *American Political Science Review* 94, 1: 251–67.

———. 2000b. "The Limits of Design: Explaining Institutional Origins and Change." *Governance* 13, 1: 475–99.

———. 2001. "Coping with Permanent Austerity: Welfare State Restructuring in Affluent Democracies." In Paul Pierson, ed., *The New Politics of the Welfare State.* New York: Oxford University Press: 410–56.

———. 2004. *Politics in Time: History, Institutions, and Social Analysis.* Princeton, NJ: Princeton University Press.

Piñera, José. 1994. "Chile." In John Williamson, ed., *Political Economy of Policy Reform.* Washington, DC: Institute for International Economics: 225–31.

———. 1996. "Empowering Workers: The Privatization of Social Security in Chile." *The Cato Journal* 14: 2–3.

_____. 2001. "Liberating Workers: The World Pension Revolution." Cato's Letter #15, Cato Institute.

Pinheiro, Vinícius Carvalho. 1998. "Instituições Previdenciárias e Modelos de Desenvolvimento no Brasil e Argentina." M.A. Thesis, Universidade de Brasília.

_____. 2004. "The Politics of Social Security Reform in Brazil." In Kurt Weyland, ed., *Learning from Foreign Models in Latin American Policy Reform*. Washington, DC: Woodrow Wilson Center Press: 110–38.

Pinheiro, Vinícius and Solange Vieira. 2000. "Reforma previsional en Brasil: La nueva regla para el cálculo de los beneficios." Serie Financiamiento del Desarrollo # 97. CEPAL, Santiago de Chile.

"Planalto faz concessão no cálculo de benefício para aprovar Previdência." 29 September 1999. Vânia Cristino and Liège Albuquerque. *O Estado de São Paulo*.

"Planalto negocia favores e derruba destaque." 5 November 1998. *O Estado de São Paulo*.

"Plan Nacional de Desarollo." 1995. Presidencia de la República de los Estados Unidos Mexicanos.

"PMDB e governo negociam cargos no dia da votação." 6 August 2003. Valderez Caetano. *O Globo*.

"PMDB se rebela e Previdência não vai a votação." 26 November 2003. Eugênia Lopes. *O Estado de São Paulo*.

"O Poder dos Governos." 9 February 2003. *O Globo*.

Polanyi, Karl. 1957. *The Great Transformation: The Political and Economic Origins of Our Time*. Boston: Beacon Press.

Pontusson, Jonas and Hyeok Yong Kwon. 2003. "Welfare Spending, Government Partisanship, and Varieties of Capitalism." Paper presented at the 2003 Annual Meeting of the American Political Science Association, Philadelphia, 28–31 August.

Popkin, Samuel. 1991. *The Reasoning Voter: Communication and Persuasion in Presidential Campaigns*. Chicago: University of Chicago Press.

Popkin, Samuel L. and Michael A. Dimock. 2000. "Knowledge, Trust, and International Reasoning." In Arthur Lupia, Mathew McCubbins, and Samuel L. Popkin, eds., *Elements of Reason: Cognition, Choice, and the Bounds of Rationality*. New York: Cambridge University Press: 214–38.

de Posadas, Ignacio. October 14, 1998. Former Minister of Finance. Personal interview, Montevideo, Uruguay.

"Poupar com a Previdência." 20 September 1999. Suely Caldas. *Estado de São Paulo*.

Power, Timothy. 1998. "Brazilian Politicians and Neoliberalism: Mapping Support for the Cardoso Reforms, 1995–1997." *Journal of Interamerican Studies and World Affairs* 40, 4: 51–72.

"President Cardoso Addresses Nation on Anniversary of Real Plan." 2 July 1997. *BBC Summary of World Broadcasts*, Globo TV, Rio de Janeiro, 30 June 1997.

"President Cardoso Appeals for Support for His Reform Programme." 25 March 1996. *BBC Summary of World Broadcasts*, Globo TV, Rio de Janeiro, 19 March 1996.

"Previdência justa e sustentável." 24 January 2003. *Folha de São Paulo*.

"Previdência, misério para deputados." 1998. *Gazeta Mercantil*.

"Previdência-Ornélas panfleta contra CUT para aprovar projeto." 7 October 1999. Denise Madueño. *Folha de São Paulo*.

"Previdência/Reforma." 3 February 1997. *Jornal do Brasil*: jbonline.terra.com.br.

"Privatização adiada." Ricardo Leopoldo. 11 October 1998. *Correio Brazilense.*
"Projeto pode ser alterado para evitar nova derrota." 2 October 1999. Liege Albuquerque. *O Estado de São Paulo.*
Przeworski, Adam. 1991. *Democracy and the Market: Economic Reforms in Eastern Europe and Latin America.* New York: Cambridge University Press.
———. 2001. "Public Support for Economic Reforms in Poland." In Susan Stokes, ed., *Public Support for Market Reforms in New Democracies.* New York: Cambridge University Press.
"PSDB decide apoiar a emenda da Previdência." 12 November 2003. *Folha de São Paulo.*
"PT bancará Lula, diz Genoino sobre inativos." 10 May 2003. *Folha de São Paulo.*
"PT vai usar acordo para pressionar a oposição." 24 April 2003. Ranier Bragon. *Folha de São Paulo.*
Putnam, Robert. 1977. "Elite Transformation in Advanced Industrial Societies." *Comparative Political Studies* 10, 3: 383–412.
Quadagno, Jill. 1987. "Theories of the Welfare State." *Annual Review of Sociology* 13, 1: 109–28.
Queisser, Monika. 1998. *The Second Generation Pension Reforms in Latin America.* Paris: OECD.
———. 2000. "Pension Reform and International Organizations: From Conflict to Convergence." *International Social Security Review* 53, 2: 31–46.
"Quero reformas, sim." 3 November 1997. *O Globo.*
Quisique, Armando. October 15, 1998. Vice-president, Banco de Previsión Social. Personal interview, Montevideo, Uruguay.
Ramírez, Berenice López. March 19, 1999. Researcher, Universidad Nacional Autónomo de México. Personal interview, Mexico City, Mexico.
Ramírez, Berenice López and Juan Arancibia Córdova. 1999. "Introducción." In Bernice López Ramírez, ed., *La Seguridad Social: Reformas y Retos.* UNAM: Grupo Editorial Miguel Angel Porrua: 11–18.
"Redutor sem chance de passar." 17 August 1999. *O Globo.*
"Reforma Emperrada." 16 July 2003. *O Globo.*
"A Reforma e o INSS." 14 July 2003. Ricardo Berzoini. *Correio Brazilense:* Opinião.
"Reforma Segue obra de FHC, diz PSDB." 26 November 2003. *Folha de São Paulo.*
"Reformas: 'Nossas ideas são claras.'" 18 April 2003. *O Globo.*
Reinhart, Carmen, Kenneth Rogoff, and Miguel Savastano. 2003. "Debt Intolerance." NBER Working Paper # W9908. National Bureau for Economic Research (NBER), Cambridge, MA.
"Relatório de pesquisa sobre a reforma da Previdência." 1998. *DIAP: Departamento Intersindical de Assessoria Parlamentar.* Brasilia: Associação Nacional dos Funcionários do Banco do Brasil. February.
Remmer, Karen L. 1991. "The Political Impact of Economic Crisis in Latin America in the 1980s." *American Political Science Review* 85, 3: 777–800.
———. 2002. "The Politics of Economic Policy and Performance in Latin America." *Journal of Public Policy* 22, 1: 29–59.
Remorino, Jerónimo. 1953. *La Nueva Legislación Social Argentina.* Buenos Aires: Ministerio de Relaciones Exteriores y Culto.
República AFAP. 2007. "Principales Indicadores Previsionales." Available at http://www.rafap.com.uy/mvdcms/noticia_84_1.html.

Resende-Santos, João. 2001. "Democracy, Equity, and Governance in Brazil." *Latin American Research Review* 36, 1: 207–37.

Reynoso del Valle, Alejandro. March 15, 1999. Director of Financial Systems, Banco de México. Personal interview, Mexico City, Mexico.

Riker, William. 1962. *The Theory of Political Coalitions*. New Haven, CT: Yale University Press.

Rinne, Jeffrey. 2003. "The Politics of Administrative Reform in Menem's Argentina: The Illusion of Isolation." In Ben Ross Schneider and Blanca Heredia, eds., *Reinventing Leviathan: The Politics of Administrative Reform in Developing Countries*. Boulder, CO: Lynne Rienner Publishers: 33–57.

Roberts, Andrew. 2003. *Social Policy Reform in Eastern Europe*. Dissertation, Princeton University, Department of Politics.

Roberts, Kenneth M. 1995. "Neoliberalism and the Transformation of Populism in Latin America: The Peruvian Case." *World Politics* 48, 1: 82–126.

Roca, Emília. June 11, 1998. Economist, Ministerio de Trabajo y Seguridad Social. Personal interview, Buenos Aires, Argentina.

Rodriguez, Enrique. July 29, 1998. Former Minister of Labor and Social Security. Personal interview, Buenos Aires, Argentina.

Rodrik, Dani. 1989. "Promises, Promises: Credible Policy Reform via Signalling." *Economic Journal* 99, 397: 756–72.

———. 1994. "The Rush to Free Trade in the Developing World: Why so Late? Why Now? Will it Last?" In Stephan Haggard and Stephen Webb, eds., *Voting for Reform: Democracy, Political Liberalization and Economic Adjustment*. New York: Oxford University Press: 61–87.

———. 1996. "Understanding Economic Policy Reform." *Journal of Economic Literature* 34, 1: 9–41.

———. 1997. *Has Globalization Gone Too Far?* Washington, DC: Institute for International Economics.

———. 2000. "Participatory Politics, Social Cooperation, and Economic Stability." *The American Economic Review* 90, 2: 140–4.

Rodrik, Dani and Andrés Velasco. 1999. "Short-Term Capital Flows." Working Paper # W7364. National Bureau of Economic Research, Cambridge, MA.

Rofman, Rafael. 1996. "Crisis de la Seguridad Social y Reforma Previsional en Argentina. Un análisis de sus causas y consecuencias." Unpublished Manuscript. SAFJP and Universidad de Buenos Aires, Buenos Aires, Argentina.

———. 1997. "Pension Reform in Argentina: The Political Process and Transition Costs." Typescript. SAFJP, Buenos Aires, Argentina.

———. June 10, 1998. Buenos Aires. Pension Analyst, AFJP La Nación. Personal interview, Buenos Aires, Argentina.

———. 2000. "The pension system in Argentina Six Years after the reform." Social Protection Discussion Paper #15. The World Bank, Washington, DC.

———. 2003. "El sistema previsional y la crisis de la Argentina." Buenos Aires, Argentina: Banco Mundial. *Documento de Trabajo* N.7/o3, Julio.

———. 2004. "The Economic Crisis in Argentina and Its Impacts on the Pension System." Social Protection Working Paper, October. The World Bank, Washington, DC.

Rofman, Rafael and Hugo Bertín. 1996. "Lessons from Pension Reform: The Argentine Case." Paper Presented at the Conference on Pension Systems: From Crisis to Reform, Washington DC, 21–22 November.

Rondina, Eduardo. June 12, 1998. Economist, Ministry of Labor and Social Security. Personal interview, Buenos Aires, Argentina.

Rosendo Gurierrez, Luis. March 11, 1999. Coordinator of Advisers, Instituto Mexicano del Seguro Social (IMSS). Personal interview, Mexico City, Mexico.

Ross, Fiona. 1997. "Cutting Public Expenditures in Advanced Industrial Democracies: The Importance of Avoiding Blame." *Governance* 10, 2: 175–200.

———. 2000a. "Framing Welfare Reform in Affluent Societies: Rendering Restructuring More Palatable?" *Journal of Public Policy* 20, 1: 169–93.

———. 2000b. "Beyond Left and Right: The New Partisan Politics of Welfare." *Governance* 13, 1: 155–83.

Rothstein, Bo. 1998. *Just Institutions Matter: The Moral and Political Logic of the Universal Welfare State*. New York: Cambridge University Press.

———. 2002. "The Universal Welfare State as Social Dilemma." In Bo Rothstein and Sven Steinmo, eds., *Restructuring the Welfare State: Political Institutions and Policy Change*. New York: Palgrave Macmillan: 206–22.

Rozenwurcel, Guillermo. 1994. "Fiscal Reform and Macroeconomic Stabilization in Argentina." *Serie Economía* #103. CEDES, Buenos Aires, Argentina.

Rubinow, Isaac M. 1913. *Social Insurance*. New York: Williams and Norgate.

Rudra, Nita. 2002. "Globalization and the Decline of the Welfare State in Less-Developed Countries." *International Organization* 56, 1: 411–45.

Sáenz Garza, Miguel Angel. April 14, 1999. Adviser, Social Security Committee, National Congress. Personal interview, Mexico City, Mexico.

"SAFJP (Superintendencia de Administradoras de Fondos de Jubilaciones y Pensiones). 1998. *El Sistema Previsional Argentino*. Buenos Aires: Superintendencia de Administradoras de Fondos de Jubilaciones y Pensiones.

———. 2002. *Boletín Estadístico Mensual*, Marzo. Available at http://www.safjp.gov.ar.

———. 2003a. *El Regimen de Capitalización a 9 años de la Reforma Previsional*. Available at http://www.safjp.gov.ar.

———. 2003b. *Boletín Estadístico Mensual*. Marzo. Available at http://www.safjp.gov.ar.

———. 2007. *Boletín Estadístico Mensual*. Junio. Available at http://www.safjp.gov.ar.

Salazar, Hector and Luis Sanchez. 1997. "Uruguay: Proposed Adjustments to the Current Reform." EDI-HIID Workshop on Pension Reform. Available at http://www.worldbank.org.

Saldáin, Rodolfo. 1995. *Reforma Jubilatoria. El Nuevo Modelo Previsional*. Montevideo: Fundacion de Cultura Universitaria.

———. 1996. "La 'Segunda' Transición en el Uruguay: Modos de Gobierno y Reforma del Estado en una Década de Democracia." Montevideo: Transcript of Presentation at the Conference.

———. October 26, 1998. Former President, Banco de Previsión Social. Personal interview, Montevideo, Uruguay.

Sales-Sarrapy, Carlos, Fernando Solís Soberón, and Alejandro Villagómez. 1996. "Pension System Reform: The Mexican Case." Working Paper #W5780. NBER, Cambridge, MA.

———. 1998. "Pension System Reform: The Mexican Case." In Martin Feldstein, ed., *Privatizing Social Security*. Chicago: University of Chicago Press: 135–76.

Samstad, James G. 2002. "Corporatism and Democratic Transition: State and Labor during the Salinas and Zedillo Administrations." *Latin American Politics and Society* 44, 2: 1–28.

Samuels, David J. 2000. "The Gubernatorial Coattails Effect: Federalism and Congressional Elections in Brazil." *The Journal of Politics* 62, 1: 240–53.

———. 2003. *Ambition, Federalism, and Legislative Politics in Brazil.* Cambridge: Cambridge University Press.

San Martino, Jorge. June 17, 1998. Manager, Administración Nacional de la Seguridad Social (ANSeS). Personal interview, Buenos Aires, Argentina.

———. 2007. "Pension Reform and the Development of Pension Systems: An Evaluation of World Bank Assistance." Background Paper – Uruguay Country Study. The World Bank, Independent Evaluation Group, Washington, DC.

Santín, Eduardo. June 15, 1998. Diputado de la Nación, Union Cívica Radical. Personal interview, Buenos Aires, Argentina.

Santiso, Javier. 1999. "Wall Street and the Mexican Crisis: A Temporal Analysis of Emerging Markets." *International Political Science Review* 20, 1: 49–73.

———. 2003. *The Political Economy of Emerging Markets: Actors, Institutions, and Financial Crises in Latin America.* London: Palgrave Macmillan.

Sartori, Giovanni. 1976. *Parties and Party Systems.* Cambridge: Cambridge University Press.

"Save, Amigo, Save." 9 December 1995. *The Economist*: S15.

Savitsky, Joseph and Shavid Burki. 2003. "Capital Flows to Emerging Markets and Policy Implications: The Experience of Latin America and the Caribbean." The Japan Program's Working Paper Series on Globalization, No. 5. Inter-American Development Bank, Washington, DC.

Scarbrough, Elinor. 2000. "West European Welfare States: The Old Politics of Retrenchment." *European Journal of Political Research* 38, 2: 225–59.

Scharpf, Fritz W. 2002. "Globalization and the Welfare State: Constraints, Challenges, and Vulnerabilities." In Roland Sigg and Christina Behrendt, eds., *Social Security in the Global Village.* London: Transaction Publishers.

Scharpf, Fritz W. and Vivien A. Schmidt, eds. 2000. *Welfare and Work in the Open Economy.* New York: Oxford University Press.

Schattschneider, E. E. 1960. *The Semisovereign People: A Realist's View of Democracy in America.* New York: Holt, Rinehart and Winston.

Schelling, Thomas C. 1966. *Arms and Influence.* New Haven, CT: Yale University Press.

Scheper-Hughes, Nancy. 1992. *Death Without Weeping: The Violence of Everyday Life in Brazil.* Berkeley: University of California Press.

Scherlen, Renee. 1998. "Lessons to Build On: The 1994 Mexican Presidential Election." *Journal of Inter-American Studies and World Affairs* 40, 1: 19–38.

Schludi, Martin. 2005. *The Reform of Bismarckian Pension Systems: A Comparison of Pension Politics.* Amsterdam: Amsterdam University Press.

Schmidt, Vivian A. 2002. "Does Discourse Matter in the Politics of Welfare State Adjustment?" *Comparative Political Studies* 35, 2: 168–93.

Schneider, Ben Ross. 1998. "The Material Bases for Technocracy: Investor Confidence and Neoliberalism in Latin America." In Miguel Angel Centeno and Patricio Silva, eds., *The Politics of Expertise.* London: St. Martin's Press: 77–96.

Schram, Sanford F. and Joe Soss. 2001. "Success Stories: Welfare Reform, Policy Discourse, and the Politics of Research." *Annals, American Academy of Political and Social Science* 577, 1: 49–65.

Schulthess, Walter. June 11, 1998. Former Secretary of Social Security, Personal interview, Buenos Aires, Argentina.

Schulthess, Walter and Gustavo Demarco. 1994. *Reforma Previsional en Argentina.* Buenos Aires: Editoriales Abeledo-Perrot.

———. 1996. "El Sistema de Jubilaciones y Pensiones de Argentina a Dos Años de la Reforma." Serie Estudios Especiales #5. SAFJP, Buenos Aires.

Schwartz, Herman. 2001. "Round Up the Usual Suspects! Globalization, Domestic Politics, and Welfare State Change." In Paul Pierson, ed., *The New Politics of the Welfare State.* Oxford: Oxford University Press: 17–44.

Schwartz, Thomas. 1994. "Representation as Agency and the Pork Barrel Paradox." *Public Choice* 78, 1: 3–21.

"Senado aprova novo cálculo da Previdência." 18 November 1999. César Felício. *O Estado de São Paulo.*

"Senate Approves Pension Reform." 12 December 2003. *Latinnews Daily.*

"Servidores chegaram a agredir deputado." 6 August 2003. Doca de Oliveira. *Jornal do Brasil.*

Shadlen, Kenneth. 2004. *Democratization without Representation.* Philadelphia: Penn State University Press.

Shepsle, Kenneth A. and Barry R. Weingast. 1981. "Political Preferences for the Pork Barrel: A Generalization." *American Journal of Political Science* 25, 1: 96–111.

———. 1987. "The Institutional Foundations of Committee Power." *The American Political Science Review* 81, 1: 85–104.

Sigg, Roland and Christina Behrendt. 2002. "Introduction: Mapping the Issues." In Roland, Sigg and Christina Behrendt, eds., *Social Security in the Global Village.* London: Transaction Publishers.

Silva, Patricio. 1991. "Technocrats and Politics in Chile: From the Chicago Boys to the CIEPLAN Monks." *Journal of Latin American Studies* 23, 2: 385–410.

Singh, Ajit. 1996. "Pension reform, the Stock Market, Capital Formation and Economic Growth: A Critical Commentary on the World Bank's Proposals." *International Social Security Review* 49, 1: 21.

Sinha, Tapen. 2000. *Pension Reform in Latin America and Its Lessons for International Policymakers.* Boston: Kluwer Academic Publishers.

———. 2002. *Retrospective and Prospective Analysis of the Privatized Mandatory Pension System in Mexico.* Chicago: Society of Actuaries.

Skocpol, Theda. 1985. "Bringing the State Back In: Strategies of Analysis in Current Research." In *Bringing the State Back In.* Cambridge: Cambridge University Press.

———. 1992. *Protecting Soldiers and Mothers: The Political Origins of Social Policy in the United States.* Cambridge, MA: Belknap Press of Harvard University Press.

———. 1995. *Social Policy in the United States: Future Possibilities in Historical Perspective.* Princeton, NJ: Princeton University Press.

Skocpol, Theda and Edwin Amenta. 1986. "States and Social Policies." *Annual Review of Sociology* 12: 131–57.

Skowronski, John and Donal Carlston. 1989. "Negativity and Extremity Biases in Impression Formation: A Review of Explanations." *Psychological Bulletin* 105, 1: 131–42.

Smetters, Kent. 2005. "Social Security Privatization with Elastic Labor Supply and Second-Best Taxes." NBER Working Paper No. 11101. National Bureau of Economic Research, Cambridge, MA.

"The Smile of a Real Winner." 29 December 1997. *Newsweek.*

Smith, William and Nizar Messari. 1998 "Democracy and Reform in Cardoso's Brazil: Caught Between Clientelism and Global Markets?" *The North-South Agenda Papers* 33, 1: 12.

Sobel, Andrew. 1999. *State Institutions, Private Incentives, Global Capital.* Ann Arbor: University of Michigan Press.

Social Security Administration (SSA). 2005. *International Update: Recent Development in Foreign Public and Private Relations.* Available at http://www.ssa.gov/policy/docs/progdesc/intl_update/2005-02/2005-02.html.

Sociedad de Estudios Laborales (SEL). 2000. "Evaluación del régimen de capitalización: Análisis cuantitativo." Buenos Aires: Sociedad de Estudios Laborales (SEL).

Solís Soberón, Fernando. April 15, 1999. President, Comisión Nacional del Sistema de Ahorro para el Retiro (CONSAR). Personal interview, Mexico City, Mexico.

Solís Soberón, Fernando and Alejandro Villagómez. 1997. "Domestic Savings in Mexico and Pension Reform." Monica Serrano, ed. *Mexico: Assessing Neo-Liberal Reform.* London: Institute of Latin American Studies.

———. 1999. "Las Pensiones." In Fernando Solís Soberón and Alejandro Villagómez eds., *La Seguridad Social en México.* Lecturas 88. Mexico City, México: El Trimestre Económico: 103–59.

Soss, Joe. 1999. "Lessons of Welfare: Policy Design, Political Learning, and Political Action." *American Political Science Review* 93, 1: 363–80.

de Souza, Amaury. 1999. "Cardoso and the Struggle for Reform in Brazil." *Journal of Democracy* 10, 3: 49–63.

"Speech of the Secretary of Finance Mr. Nielsen at EMTA (Emerging Markets Traders Association)." December 4, 2003. Available at http://www.argentinedebtinfo.gov.ar/documentos/emta-gn-4-12-2003-english.pdf.

Springer Gary L. and Jorge L. Molina. 1995. "The Mexican Financial Crisis: Genesis, Impact, and Implications." *Journal of Interamerican Studies and World Affairs* 37: 57–81.

Srinivas, Pulle Subrahmanya and Juan Yermo. 1999. *Do Investment Regulations Compromise Pension Fund Performance? Evidence from Latin America.* Washington, DC: The World Bank.

Starr, Paul. 1989. "The Meaning of Privatization." In Alfred Kahn and Sheila Kamerman, eds., *Privatization and the Welfare State.* Princeton, NJ: Princeton University Press.

Steinmo, Sven, Kathleen Thelen, and Frank Longstreth. 1992. *Structuring Politics: Historical Institutionalism in Comparative Analysis.* New York: Cambridge University Press.

Stiglitz, Joseph. 1998. "Distinguished Lecture on Economics in Government: The Private Uses of Public Interests: Incentives and Institutions." *The Journal of Economic Perspectives* 12, 2: 3–22.

Stockman, David A. 1975. "The Social Pork Barrel." *Public Interest* 39: 3–30.

Stokes, Susan. 2001a. *Mandates and Democracy: Neoliberalism by Surprise in Latin America.* New York: Cambridge University Press.

———. 2001b. "Introduction: Economic Voting and Pro-market Reforms in New Democracies." In Susan Stokes, ed., *Public Support for Market Reforms in New Democracies.* New York: Cambridge University Press.

Stone, Deborah. 1984. *The Disabled State.* Philadelphia: Temple University Press.

Strange, Susan. 1996. *The Retreat of the State: The Diffusion of Power in the World Economy.* New York: Cambridge University Press.

Suarez Dávila, Francisco. 1996. "La Reforma Mexicana a los Sistemas de Ahorro para el retiro. Perspectiva de un Legislador." *Comercio Exterior.* September: 725–9.

"Suplicy critica loteamento de cargos e atuação de Dirceu." 2 September 2003. *O Globo.*

Svallfors, Stefan. 2002. "Political Trust and Support for the Welfare State: Unpacking a Supposed Relationship." In Bo Rothstein and Sven Steinmo, eds., *Restructuring the Welfare State: Political Institutions and Policy Change.* New York: Palgrave: 184–205.

Swank, Duane. 2001. "Political Institutions and Welfare State Restructuring: The Impact of Institutions on Social Policy Change in Developed Democracies." In Paul Pierson, ed., *The New Politics of the Welfare State.* Oxford: Oxford University Press: 197–237.

Taagepera, Rein and Matthew S. Shugart. 1993. "Predicting the Number of Parties: A Quantitative Model of Duverger's Mechanical Effect." *American Political Science Review* 87, 1: 455–64.

Tanzi, Vito. 2002. "Globalization and the Future of Social Protection." *Scottish Journal of Political Economy* 49, 1: 116–27.

Taylor-Gooby, Peter. 2002. "The Silver Age of the Welfare State: Perspectives on Resilience." *Journal of Social Policy* 31, 4: 597–621.

Taylor-Gooby, Peter, et al., eds. 2004. *New Risks, New Welfare: the Transformation of the European Welfare State.* Oxford: Oxford University Press.

Tebot, Myra. October 20, 1998. General Manager, Banco de Previsión Social. Personal interview, Montevideo, Uruguay.

Teichman, Judith A. 1995. *Privatization and Political Change in Mexico.* Pittsburgh: University of Pittsburgh Press.

———. 2001. *The Politics of Freeing Markets in Latin America: Chile, Argentina, and Mexico.* Chapel Hill: University of North Carolina Press.

Thelen, Kathleen. 1999. "Historical Institutionalism in Comparative Politics." *Annual Review of Political Science* 2, 1: 369–404.

———. 2004. *How Institutions Evolve: The Political Economy of Skills in Germany, Britain, the United States, and Japan.* New York: Cambridge University Press.

Thesing, Josef. 1995. "Seguridad Social y Estabilidad Democrática." *Seguridad Social en la Economia Social del Mercado.*

Torre, Juan Carlos. 1997. "El lanzamiento político de las reformas estructurales en America Latina." *Política y Gobierno* 4, 2: 471–98.

———. June 20, 1998. Professor, Universidad Torcuato di Tella. Personal interview. Buenos Aires, Argentina.

Torre, Juan Carlos and Pablo Gerchunoff. 1998. "La Economía Política de las Reformas Institucionales en Argentina. Los Casos de la Política de Privatización de Entel, la Reforma de la Seguridad Social y la Reforma Laboral." Unpublished Manuscript. Instituto Torcuato di Tella, Buenos Aires, Argentina.

Trejo, Guillermo and Claudio Jones. 1998. "Political Dilemmas of Welfare Reform: Poverty and Inequality in Mexico." In Susan Kaufman Purcell and Luis Rubio, eds., *Mexico under Zedillo.* Boulder, CO: Lynne Rienner.

Tsebelis, George. 1995. "Decision Making in Political Systems: Veto Players in Presidentialism, Parliamentarism, Multicameralism and Multipartyism." *British Journal of Political Science* 25, 1: 289–326.

———. 1999. "Veto Players and Law Production in Parliamentary Democracies: An Empirical Analysis." *American Political Science Review* 93, 1: 591–608.

————. 2002. *Veto Players: How Political Institutions Work.* Princeton, NJ: Princeton University Press.

UAFJP (Unión de Administradoras de Fondos de Jubilaciones y Pensiones). 2002. "Comparación de los Beneficios Capitalización-Reparto." Available at www.uafjp. org.ar/docs/UAFJP_Comparacion.pdf.

United Nations. 2004. "The 2004 Revision of World Population Prospects." Population Division, Department of Economic and Social Affairs. New York: The United Nations.

Urbiztondo, Santiago. July 20, 1998. Associate economist, Fundación de Investigaciones Economicas Latinoamericanas. Personal interview, Buenos Aires, Argentina.

Uthoff, Andras. 2002. 1994. "Some Features of Current Pension System Reform in Latin America." *Revista de Análisis Económico* 9, 1: 211–35.

Vail, Mark. 2003. "Rethinking Corporatism and Consensus: The Dilemmas of German Social-Protection Reform." *West European Politics* 26, 3: 41–66.

Valdés-Prieto, Salvador. 1998. "The Private Sector in Social Security: Latin American Lessons for APEC." APEC Regional Forum on Pension Reform, Cancún, Mexico, 4–6 February.

Valdes-Prieto, Salvador and Ricardo Cifuentes. 1993. "Credit Constraints and Pensions." Unpublished Manuscript.

Valencia Armas, Alberto. 2005. "Social Security and Population Ageing in Mexico: Analysis of the Individual Account Retirement Pension System." Paper prepared for the United Nations Expert Group Meeting on Social and Economic Implications of Changing Population Age Structures. Population Division Department of Economic and Social Affairs, United Nations Secretariat, Mexico City, 31 August–2 September 2005.

Van den Noord, Paul and Richard Herd. 1993. *Pension Liabilities in the Seven Major Economies.* Paris: OECD.

Vaquera García, Arturo. March 15, 1999. Asesor del Director General, Instituto Mexicano del Seguro Social (IMSS). Personal interview, Mexico City, Mexico.

Vásquez, Tabaré. October 28, 1998. Party leader, Frente Ámplio. Personal interview, Montevideo, Uruguay.

Vera, Tabaré. October 19, 27, 1998. General coordinator, Oficina de Planeamiento y Presupuesto. Personal interview, Montevideo, Uruguay.

Veras, Beni. June 30, 1999. Former Senator (Partido da Frente Liberal) and Rapporteur of Constitutional Amendment Project. Personal interview, Fortaleza, Brazil.

Vittas, Dimitri and Max Alier. 1999. "Personal Pension Plans and Stock Market Volatility." Policy Research Working Paper #2463. The World Bank, Washington, DC.

Vreeland, James. 2003. "Why Do Governments and the IMF Enter into Agreements? Statistically Selected Cases." *International Political Science Review* 24, 3: 159–83.

Weaver, R. Kent. 1986. "The Politics of Blame Avoidance." *Journal of Public Policy* 6, 1: 371–98.

————. 1988. *Automatic Government: The Politics of Indexation.* Washington, DC: The Brookings Institute.

————. 1998. "The Politics of Pensions: Lessons from Abroad." In R. Douglas Arnold, Michael Graetz, and Alicia Munnell, eds., *Framing the Social Security Debate: Values, Politics, and Economics.* Washington, DC: National Academy of Social Insurance: 183–228.

References

————. 2000. *Ending Welfare as We Know It.* Washington, DC: The Brookings Institution.

————. 2003. "The Politics of Public Pension Reform." CRR Working Paper. 6 May. Center for Retirement Research, Boston College, Boston.

————. 2005. "Public Pension Reform in the United States." In Giuliano Bonoli and Toshimitsu Shinkawa, eds., *Ageing and Pension Reform Around the World: Evidence from Eleven Countries,* Cheltenham: Edward Elgar Publishing.

Weingast, Barry. 1979. "A Rational Choice Perspective on Congressional Norms." *American Journal of Political Science* 23, 1: 245–61.

————. 1994. "Reflections on Distributive Politics and Universalism." *Political Research Quarterly* 47, 2: 319–27.

Weingast, Barry R., Kenneth A. Shepsle, and Christopher Johnsen. 1981. "The Political Economy of Benefits and Costs: A Neoclassical Approach to Distributive Politics." *The Journal of Political Economy* 89, 4: 642–64.

Weir, Margaret. 1992. *Politics and Jobs: The Boundaries of Employment Policy in the United States.* Princeton, NJ: Princeton University Press.

Weldon, Jeffrey A. 1997. "The Political Sources of Presidencialismo in Mexico." In Scott Mainwaring and Matthew Soberg Shugart, eds., *Presidentialism and Democracy in Latin America.* Cambridge: Cambridge University Press: 225–58.

Weyland, Kurt. 1996a. "How Much Political Power Do Economic Forces Have? Conflicts over Social Insurance Reform in Brazil." *Journal of Public Policy* 16, 1: 59–84.

————. 1996b. *Democracy without Equity: The Failure of Reform in Brazil.* Pittsburgh: University of Pittsburgh Press.

————. 1998. "Swallowing the Bitter Pill: Sources of Popular Support for Neoliberal Reform in Latin America." *Comparative Political Studies* 31, 5: 539–68.

————. 1999. "Neoliberal Populism in Latin America and Eastern Europe." *Comparative Politics* 31, 1: 379–401.

————. 2000. "A Paradox of Success? Determinants of Political Support for President Fujimori." *International Studies Quarterly* 44, 1: 481–502.

————. 2004. *Learning from Foreign Models: Latin American Policy Reform.* Baltimore: Johns Hopkins University Press.

————. 2005a. "The Diffusion of Innovations: How Cognitive Heuristics Shaped Bolivia's Pension Reform." *Comparative Politics* 38, 1: 21–42.

————. 2005b. "Theories of Policy Diffusion: Lessons from Latin American Pension Reform." *World Politics* 57, 2: 262–95.

————. 2007. *Bounded Rationality and Policy Diffusion: Social Sector Reform in Latin America.* Princeton, NJ: Princeton University Press.

Whitt, Joseph A., Jr. 1996. "The Mexican Peso Crisis." *Economic Review* January–February. Atlanta: Federal Reserve Bank of Atlanta.

Wibbels, Erik. "Dependency Revisited: International Markets, Business Cycles, and Social Spending in the Developing World." *International Organization* 60, 2: 433–68.

Wilensky, Harold L. 1975. *The Welfare State and Equality: Structural and Ideological Roots of Public Expenditures.* Berkeley: University of California Press.

Williams, Mark E. 2002. "Market Reforms, Technocrats, and Institutional Innovation." *World Development* 30, 3: 395–412.

Williamson, John, ed. 1990. *Latin American Adjustment: How Much Has Happened?* Washington, DC: Institute for International Economics.

_____. 1994. "In Search of a Manual for Technopols." In John Williamson, ed., *The Political Economy of Policy Reform*. Washington, DC: Institute for International Economics: 9–28.

Wilson, Berry, Anthony Saunders, and Gerard Caprio. 2000. "Mexico's Financial Sector Crisis: Propagative Linkages to Devaluation." *The Economic Journal* 110, 460: 292–308.

World Bank. 1994. *Averting the Old Age Crisis: Policies to Protect the Old and Promote Growth*. Washington, DC: The World Bank.

_____. 1999. *World Development Report 1998–99*. Washington, DC: The World Bank.

_____. 2002, 2005, 2007. *World Development Indicators*. Washington, DC: The World Bank. CD-ROM.

_____. 2005. "Program Document for a Proposed Programmatic Fiscal Reform Loan – Social Security Reform in the Amount Equivalent to US$658.3 Million to the Federative Republic of Brazil." 6 May. Report No. 32226-Br. Available at http://worldbank.org.

"World Financial Markets." 27 March 1997. *J.P. Morgan*.

Xing, Xuejing. 2004. "Why Does Stock Market Volatility Differ across Countries? Evidence from Thirty-Seven International Markets." *International Journal of Business* 9, 1: 84–102.

Zapata, Francisco. 1998. "Trade Unions and the Corporatist System in Mexico." In Philip Oxhorn and Graciela Ducatenzeiler, eds., *What Kind of Democracy? What Kind of Market?: Latin America in the Age of Neoliberalism*. University Park: Pennsylvania State University Press: 151–68.

Index